NATURAL LANGUAGE PARSING AND LINGUISTIC THEORIES

STUDIES IN LINGUISTICS AND PHILOSOPHY

formerly *Synthese Language Library*

Managing Editors:
ROBIN COOPER, *University of Wisconsin*
ELISABET ENGDAHL, *University of Wisconsin*
RICHARD GRANDY, *Rice University*

Editorial Board:
EMMON BACH, *University of Massachusetts at Amherst*
JON BARWISE, *CSLI, Stanford*
JOHAN VAN BENTHEM, *Mathematics Institute,
University of Amsterdam*
DAVID DOWTY, *Ohio State University, Columbus*
GERALD GAZDAR, *University of Sussex, Brighton*
EWAN KLEIN, *University of Edinburgh*
BILL LADUSAW, *University of California at Santa Cruz*
SCOTT SOAMES, *Princeton University*
HENRY THOMPSON, *University of Edinburgh*

VOLUME 35

NATURAL LANGUAGE PARSING AND LINGUISTIC THEORIES

Edited by

U. REYLE

and

C. ROHRER

*Institute for Computational Linguistics,
University of Stuttgart, F.R.G.*

D. REIDEL PUBLISHING COMPANY

A MEMBER OF THE KLUWER ACADEMIC PUBLISHERS GROUP

DORDRECHT / BOSTON / LANCASTER / TOKYO

Library of Congress Cataloging in Publication Data

Natural language parsing and linguistic theories / edited by U. Reyle and C. Rohrer.
    p.   cm. — (Studies in linguistics and philosophy; vol. 35)
    Includes index.
    ISBN 1-55608-055-7.
    1. Parsing (Computer grammar)   2.   Grammar, Comparative and general.
3. German language—Syntax.   4.   Machine translating.   I.   Reyle, U., 1955–
II. Rohrer, Christian, 1938–   .III.   Series: Studies in linguistic and philosophy; v. 35.
P98.5.P38N3   1987
415′.028′5—dc 19   87-35440
                                                                                                                                                                        CIP

Published by D. Reidel Publishing Company,
P.O. Box 17, 3300 AA Dordrecht, Holland.

Sold and distributed in the U.S.A. and Canada
by Kluwer Academic Publishers,
101 Philip Drive, Norwell, MA 02061, U.S.A.

In all other countries, sold and distributed
by Kluwer Academic Publishers Group,
P.O. Box 322, 3300 AH Dordrecht, Holland.

All Rights Reserved
© 1988 by D. Reidel Publishing Company, Dordrecht, Holland
No part of the material protected by this copyright notice may be reproduced or
utilized in any form or by any means, electronic or mechanical
including photocopying, recording or by any information storage and
retrieval system, without written permission from the copyright owner

Printed in The Netherlands

CONTENTS

UWE REYLE / CHRISTIAN ROHRER
    Introduction   1

STUART M. SHIEBER
    Seperating Linguistic Analyses from
    Linguistic Theories   33

GERALD GAZDAR
    Applicability of Indexed Grammars to
    Natural Languages   69

BRANIMIR BOGURAEV
    A Natural Language Toolkit: Reconciling
    Theory with Practice   95

JÖRG KINDERMANN / JUSTUS MEIER
    An Extension of LR-Parsing for Lexical
    Functional Grammar   131

HANS-ULRICH BLOCK / HANS HAUGENEDER
    An Efficiency-Oriented LFG Parser   149

ERIC WEHRLI
    Parsing with a GB-Grammar   177

HENK ZEEVAT
    Combining Categorial Grammar and Unification   202

PETE J. WHITELOCK
    A Feature-Based Categorial Morpho-Syntax for Japanese   230

CHRISTOPH SCHWARZE
    The Treatment of the French adjectif détaché
    in Lexical Functional Grammar   262

DIETER WUNDERLICH
    Some Problems of Coordination in German   289

GISBERT FANSELOW
    German Word Order and Universal Grammar   317
KLAUS NETTER
    Nonlocal-Dependencies and Infinitival
    Constructions in German   356
CHRISTA HAUENSCHILD
    GPSG and German Word Order   411
WILLIAM R. KELLER
    Nested Cooper Storage: The Proper Treatment
    of Quantification in Ordinary Noun Phrases   432
UWE REYLE
    Compositional Semantics for LFG   448

UWE REYLE, CHRISTIAN ROHRER
INSTITUT FÜR MASCHINELLE SPRACHVERARBEITUNG
UNIVERSITÄT STUTTGART

INTRODUCTION

This volume consists of a collection of the papers presented at the interdisciplinary workshop 'Word-order and Parsing in Unification Grammars' that took place in Friedenweiler (Schwarzwald) in April 1986. Two additional papers (Reyle, Wehrli) have been included that were not presented at the workshop. All the papers have been refereed and revised for publication. The workshop was organized by the members of the research project 'EUROTRA-D Begleitforschung (EUROTRA Germany accompanying research) which is sponsored by the BMFT (Secretary of Research and Technology). The aim of this research project is to investigate to what extent recent linguistic theories (especially Unification Grammars (UG) such as Lexical Functional Grammar (LFG) and Generalized Phrase Structure Grammar (GPSG)) can serve as a basis for machine translation. The results of this investigation, which is more oriented towards research than towards application, will be made available to EUROTRA, the Machine Translation Project of the EEC. At the workshop the problem was phrased in more general terms:

> What can recent linguistic theories contribute to natural language processing?[1]

Shieber's paper is an attempt to answer this question.

In the actual discussion during the workshop and the ensuing rewriting of the papers the participants also attacked the other direction: what can

---

[1] This question presupposes, of course, that it is desirable to make computational use of insights from linguistics as an aid to NLP. The participants at the workshop seemed to share this presupposition.

NLP contribute to recent linguistic theories? Within the theoretical framework of GPSG, for example, the difficulties one encounters in the implementation of a declaratively described theory are described by the Boguraev's paper. Within the framework of the Alvey programme in Great Britain a coordinated effort is under way to build a natural language parsing toolkit. The paper discusses the conflict between computational tractability and declarativeness in great detail.

Compared with LFG and GPSG, there has been little work published on implementations of Government and Binding Theory (GB). One of the first researchers to develop parsers for GB is Eric Wehrli, and we have included a paper by him, written especially for this volume. Undoubtedly, as more GB parsers become available, these may have implications on the theory as well.[2] We believe that certain analyses formulated within the framework of GB can be fruitfully incorporated into unification-based grammars.

In the BMFT project mentioned above, the source language for MT is, of course, German. Therefore problems of German syntax were a major topic at the workshop (Fanselow, Hauenschild, Netter). Problems in German syntax are adressed by the following contributors working in different frameworks: Fanselow (GB), Hauenschild (GPSG), Netter (LFG), Wunderlich (GB and GPSG).

There has been a tendency, recently, to introduce notions from Categorial Grammar into UG. This trend can be observed in the papers by Whitelock and Zeevat. They present analyses where UG has been enriched with ideas from Categorial Grammar.

Since MT also requires some semantic information, we include two papers that describe the mapping from syntax to semantics. Both are in the tradition of Montague/Frege. The first (Keller) extends Cooper's Storage Mechanism to complex NP's within the framework of GPSG. The second (Reyle) extends the traditional lambda-calculus such that it makes the formulation possible of a compositional semantics for LFG. Questions of implementation are addressed by both authors.

The papers gathered together in this volume presuppose familiarity with unification-based formalisms. In order to help the reader, where this

---

[2] See for instance Abney and Cole (1985).

presupposition fails, we now give a short introduction into Unification Grammar. Since all implementations discussed in this volume use PROLOG (with the exception of Block/Haugeneder), we felt that it would also be useful to explain the difference between unification in PROLOG and in UG.

After the introduction to UG we briefly summarize the main arguments for using linguistic theories in natural language processing.

We conclude with a short summary of the contributions to this volume.

UNIFICATION GRAMMAR

Feature Structures or Complex Categories.[3]

Unification Grammar was developed by Martin Kay (Kay 1979). Martin Kay wanted to give a precise definition (and implementation) of the notion of 'feature'. Linguists use features at nearly all levels of linguistic description. In phonetics, for instance, the phoneme b is usually described with the features 'bilabial', 'voiced' and 'nasal'. In the case of b the first two features get the value +, the third (nasal) gets the value -. Feature-value pairs in phonology are normally represented as a matrix.

$$\begin{vmatrix} \text{bilabial:} & + \\ \text{voiced:} & + \\ \text{nasal:} & - \end{vmatrix}$$

[Feature matrix for b.]

In syntax features are used, for example, to distinguish different noun classes. The Latin noun 'murus' would be characterized by the following feature-value pairs: gender: masculin, number: singular, case: nominative, pred: murus. Besides a matrix representation one frequently finds a graph representation for feature value pairs. The edges of the graph are labelled by features. The leaves denote the value of a feature.

---

[3] We follow Pereira (1987).

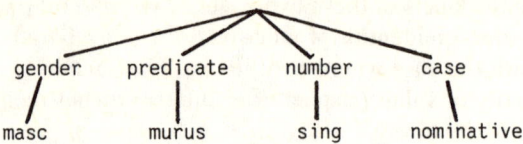

Martin Kay, however, was not only interested in feature-value pairs of this trivial form. He wanted to combine such pairs into complex linguistic categories (we use 'complex category' and 'feature structure' synonymously). Grammars for formal languages usually contain only atomic categories. But, the use of atomic categories for natural language sentences is a gross simplification. For the description of natural languages one needs a much richer classification. For instance, in English we have to express agreement between subject and verb in person and number. In German, article and noun agree in gender, number and case. In the area of verb classification linguists use features to define notions like transitive, intransitive, bitransitive, etc.

In the examples given so far, features have only atomic values. This need not be the case. All unification-based formalisms allow complex values for features. For instance, all the features that play a role in subject-verb agreement may be combined into one feature labelled 'agreement'.

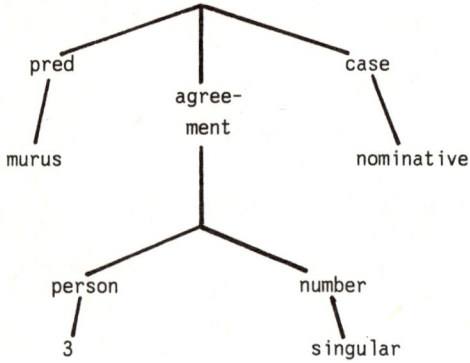

The last important property of feature graphs is reentrancy. Two edges may point to the same vertex in a graph. If two edges point to the same vertex, then the labels of these two edges have the same value. This notion of shared value or identity of value plays a crucial role. It must not be confused with the case where two features have two different but similar values. Identity of value (shared value) is like <u>token</u> identity (*eq* in Lisp) whereas similarity of value is like <u>type</u> identity (*equal* in Lisp).

In an infinitival construction like 'Hans will leave', 'Hans' is the subject of 'will' and of 'leave'. In other words, the subject of 'will' and the subject of 'leave' have the same value.

Mathematical properties of complex categories

A short remark about the mathematical properties of complex categories: complex categories form a lattice based on subsumption (notated as $\subseteq$). Subsumption is a partial order on feature structures which, roughly speaking, expresses whether two structures are consistent and whether one structure contains more specific information than the other.[4]

Two feature structures F_1 and F_2 are consistent if and only if there exists a structure FS such that

$$FS_1 \subseteq FS \quad \text{and} \quad FS_2 \subseteq FS.$$

Information from two feature structures may be combined into one. This combining of information is the most important operation in unification-based formalisms. It gave its name to all these formalisms: *unification*. The unification of two feature structures FS_1 and FS_2 is the most general feature structure FS, such that $FS_1 \subseteq FS$ and $FS_2 \subseteq FS$. More technically, FS is the *least upper bound* of FS_1 and FS_2.

From this abstract definition of unification there is a long way to an algorithm. Kaplan&Bresnan (1982) give an algorithm for unification in Lexical Functional Grammar. They use two main operations, 'locate' and 'merge'. The connection between their algorithm and our lattice theoretic definition may not be immediately obvious. A clear and simple PROLOG implementation of the merge operation can be found in Dörre and Eisele (1986). Block and Haugeneder (this volume) discuss the Kaplan-Bresnan algorithm and propose an implementation based on structure sharing.

---

[4] GKPS use the term 'extension' instead of 'subsumption'. Their definition (p. 27) is equivalent to Shieber's definition of subsumption in Shieber (1984).

The implementation is written in Interlisp-D.

This notion of unification differs from unification in PROLOG in two important respects:

The information contained in feature graphs could also be expressed as PROLOG terms. The graph for 'murus', without the 'pred' feature, corresponds to the following PROLOG term:

n (gender = masculin, number = singular, case = nominative)

In order to express agreement between adjective and noun, one could write the following term for the Latin adjective 'altus' (high):

adj (gender = X, number = Y, case = Z)

where X, Y and Z are variables. PROLOG unification would instantiate X to masculine, Y to singular and Z to nominative. Since for Latin nouns and adjectives gender, number and case must always be specified, there would be no argument for graph unification and against PROLOG.

However, if we think of the category assigned to the German noun phrase 'die kahle Sängerin' (the bald singer) it would probably look like follows [5]:

$$\begin{bmatrix} \text{cat} & : & \text{np} \\ \text{definite} & : & + \\ \text{attribute}: & \begin{bmatrix} \text{pred} & : & \text{'kahl'} \\ \text{agr} & : & [1] \begin{bmatrix} \text{gender:} & \text{fem} \\ \text{number:} & \text{sing} \end{bmatrix} \end{bmatrix} \\ \text{pred} & : & \text{'sängerin'} \\ \text{agr} & : & [1] \end{bmatrix}$$

The noun phrase 'die Sängerin' would have no feature 'attribute', and in the structure assigned to a noun phrase which consists only of a proper noun like 'Gretchen', both the features 'definite' and 'attribute' would be missing. It is impossible to give a PROLOG term which subsumes the noun phrases 'die Sängerin', 'die kahle Sängerin' and 'Gretchen'. In a PROLOG term the number of arguments is fixed, whereas in a feature graph we may add features as long as they do not lead to a contradiction.

---

[5] We notate a shared value by coindexed boxes on the values. In LFG shared values are indicated by a line.

Graph unification gives freedom to linguists. The grammar writer doesn't have to specify in advance how many features can show up in a graph and in which order they appear.

Syntactic rules with complex categories.

Having defined complex categories, we now have to show how complex categories can be built into syntactic rules. We use the PATR formalism because it is the simplest of the unification-based formalisms. Furthermore, Shieber (this volume) presupposes some familiarity with PATR. Differences between PATR, LFG and GPSG will be explained, as far as possible, in the course of our introduction. A syntactic rule in a unification grammar consists of a context-free part and a set of equations. In the following rule, written in the PATR-II notation,

$$S \rightarrow NP \quad VP$$
$$<NP\ agr> = <VP\ agr>^6$$

the equation expresses that NP and VP have the same value for the agreement feature.

The context-free phrase structure rules describe how new constituents are built up from the old constituents. The equations (or unifications) which are associated with the constituents specify constraints that must hold between daughter nodes, or between mother nodes and daughter nodes. The next rule specifies a constraint between the mother node and the daughter node.

It states that the agreement feature of the VP is equal to the agreement feature of the verb.

$$VP \rightarrow V \quad NP$$
$$<V\ agr> = <VP\ agr>$$

Speaking informally, the equations provide the possibility to transport information along the branches of a syntactic tree. A comparison with attribute grammars may be in order here. In attribute grammars features may percolate up the tree (synthesized attributes) or flow down the tree

---

[6] In the equation $<NP\ agr> = <VP\ agr>$, NP denotes the root node of the graph corresponding to the subject NP in the following figure. Please notice that here "=" means token identity, i.e., that the paths on the left and on the right share a common value.

(inherited attributes). The information that moves along the branches of the syntactic tree in our example comes from the lexicon. An entry in the lexicon associates a complex category with a word (word form). For our little grammar the relevant entries might look as follows:

Maria:

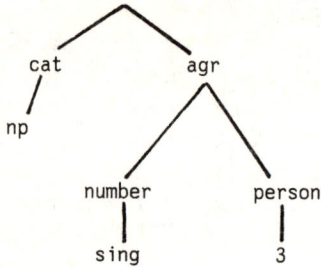

Hans:

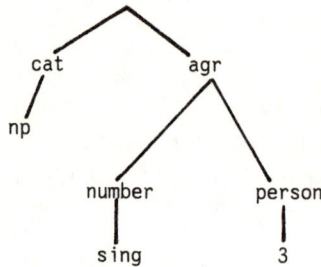

liebt:

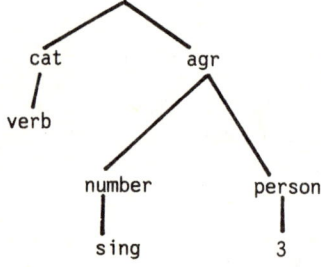

Our grammar accepts two sentences: 'Hans liebt Maria' and 'Maria liebt Hans'. A look at the syntactic tree shows which information moves along the tree and where feature structures are unified. There is, however, no inherent direction. Unification is order-free. One gets the same results regardless of whether one solves the equations top-down or bottom-up.

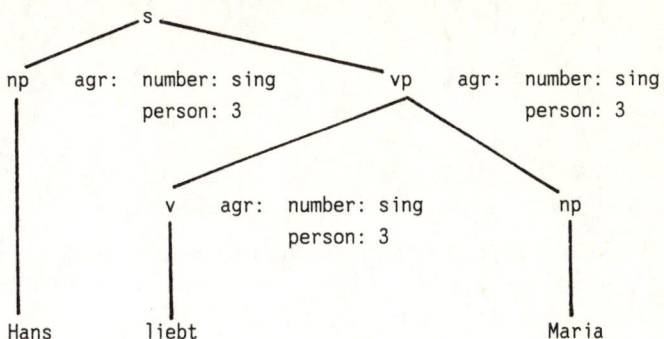

So far we have seen only morphological features like 'case', 'number', 'gender', etc. We have used these features for expository purposes. In practice much richer feature structures are used. Bresnan and Kaplan use functional features like 'subject', 'object', 'adjunct', 'xcomp', 'comp', etc. In a configurational language like English, these features are introduced in connection with phrase structure rules. The next rule, for instance, expresses the fact that the feature structure (or, in LFG terminology, the functional structure) associated with the leftmost NP is the subject of the sentence (more exactly is the value of the feature 'subject').

$$S \rightarrow NP \quad VP^7$$
$$<S\ SUBJ> = <NP> \quad <S> = <VP>$$

In an LFG grammar, the equations associated with the rules serve to build up one complex feature structure for the whole sentence, its functional structure.

The f-structure of the sentence 'a girl handed the baby a toy' looks as

---

[7] This rule is a PATR-II version of the LFG rule

$$S \rightarrow NP_{(\uparrow SUBJ) = \downarrow} \quad VP_{\uparrow = \downarrow}$$

follows:

$$\begin{bmatrix} \text{SUBJ:} & \begin{bmatrix} \text{SPEC:} & \text{A} \\ \text{NUM} & : \text{SING} \\ \text{PRED:} & \text{'GIRL'} \end{bmatrix} \\ \text{OBJ} : & \begin{bmatrix} \text{SPEC:} & \text{THE} \\ \text{NUM} & : \text{SING} \\ \text{PRED:} & \text{'BABY'} \end{bmatrix} \\ \text{OBJ2:} & \begin{bmatrix} \text{SPEC:} & \text{A} \\ \text{NUM} & : \text{SING} \\ \text{PRED:} & \text{'TOY'} \end{bmatrix} \\ \text{TENSE} & \text{PAST} \\ \text{PRED} & \text{'HAND <(SUBJ) (OBJ2) (OBJ)>'} \end{bmatrix}$$

Such an f-structure expresses the predicate-argument relation and thus constitutes a good input into the semantic component. Furthermore the level of f-structure may serve for transfer in machine translation.[8]

In UG's features come from the lexicon or get introduced through rules. If a feature is introduced through a rule, which can be applied recursively, then the feature structure may become very complex. Take, for instance, the rule which introduces infinitival complements (vcomp). Kaplan, Bresnan (1982, p. 217) propose the following implied rule:

```
VP   -->    V , ... ,    VP'
            <VP  VCOMP> = <VP'>
VP'  -->    (to)        VP
            <VP'> = <VP>
```

The repeated application of these two rules may lead to an f-structure with a path like:

[vcomp: [vcomp: [vcomp: [pred: 'buy <SUBJ, OBJ>']]]]

An example of how linguistic generalisations are expressed with the help of such paths will be given beyond.

To what extent unification increases the generative power of a context-free grammar can best be appreciated by looking at a UG for the context-

---

[8] This is at least the working hypothesis of several projects in MT (e.g. see Kudo and Nomura (1986)).

sensitive language a"b"c". The feature structure in this grammar records the number of occurrences of a's, b's and c's; in other words, the feature structure simulates a counter.

LFG AND GPSG AS EXTENDED UNIFICATION-BASED FORMALISMS

In the preceding sections we gave an introduction to PATR. We now mention several extensions and/or restrictions which are found in LFG and GPSG and make some remarks about their implementation.

LFG

Completeness and coherence:
LFG uses grammatical functions like 'subject' or 'object' for subcategorization and for encoding the predicate-argument structure. All the grammatical functions referred to in a lexical entry (remember our example pred = 'kaufen <subj, obj>') must have values in the f-structure. In other words, the f-structure must be complete. No grammatical function other than these specified in the lexical entry may have a value in the f-structure, i.e., the f-structure must be coherent.

These two conditions are required only of the final f-structure. In an implementation completeness and coherence can only be checked at the end.

Existential constraints and Negation:
An existential constraint like ! (↑Tense) is used for an attribute without specifying the value (past, present or future). Existential constraints can only be checked at the end.

A negative existential constraint like -(↑Tense) expresses that the f-structure of the mother constituent may not contain the attribute 'Tense'. If negation is used for attributes that may have complex values, then it is not obvious how negation should be interpreted semantically.

Some researchers use disjunction and negation over attributes with complex values. The partiality of the f-structures renders the implementation extremely difficult.[9]

Regular expressions over features (functional uncertainty).

Regular expressions are used to describe constructions in which the object of a deeply embedded infinitive is separated from its verb, as it is the case in the famous Dutch cross-serial dependencies (see Gazdar, Netter and Zeevat, this volume),[10] or in the German sentence:

> Eine Eigentumswohnung wird Hans zu kaufen versuchen wollen.
> Hans may want to try to buy an apartment.

The noun phrase 'eine Eigentumswohnung' is the object of 'kaufen'. 'kaufen' depends on 'versuchen', which depends on 'wollen', which depends on 'wird'. The correct f-structure is produced by two paths, which are constructed through repeated unifications in different parts of the syntactic tree assigned to the sentence in question.

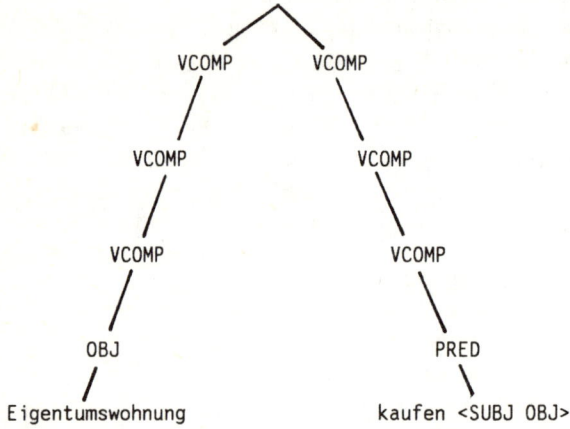

The three occurrences of the attribute 'vcomp' in the path that leads to the verb 'kaufen' are introduced through repeated applications of the VP-rule. The construction of the path, which points to the object 'eine

---

[9] For a recent overview see Pereira (1987).

[10] Bresnan, J., et al. (1982), 'Cross-serial Dependencies in Dutch', *Linguistic Inquiry* (13), pp. 613-635.

Eigentumswohnung', could be handled very simply with the equation

```
S -> ... NP ...
    <S VCOMP VCOMP VCOMP OBJ> = <NP>
```

However, in general one does not know how many occurrences of VCOMP will be produced in the (iterated) application of the VP rule. Kaplan therefore proposed to introduce regular expressions into equations. The new equation

```
<S VCOMP* OBJ> = <NP>
```

permits any number of 'vcomps' to be generated. Klaus Netter (this volume) uses this extension for the description of German infinitival constructions.

For English regular expressions over features are used in the analysis of unbounded dependencies. They replace the long-distance metavariables in Kaplan/Bresnan (1982).

The formal properties and the implementation of feature structures with negation, disjunction and regular expressions are now being studied extensively. At the Friedenweiler workshop the descriptive adequacy (from a linguistic point of view) of these extensions was discussed.

GPSG

Feature instantiation principles.

In GPSG the feature structures that can be built are heavily restricted. This restriction has consequences for the generative power of the theory. A language like anbncn cannot be generated by a GPS-grammar because the feature-structure cannot stimulate a counter (as in LFG or PATR).

GKPS in their textbook define subsumption (they use the term extension) and unification. The reader must keep in mind, however, that GPSG is a very restricted type of UG. Instead of equations like <VP agr> = <V agr>, GPSG has universal feature instantiation principles[11]: the foot feature principle (FFP), the control agreement principle (CAP), and the head feature convention (HFC). In addition there are feature

---

[11] See GKPS, chapter 5.

specification defaults (FSD) and feature cooccurrence restrictions (FCR). All these constraints are applied simultaneously, at least in theory. In practice, however, it turns out that there exists an implicit ordering of the principles. Shieber (this volume) shows that this ordering looks as follows:

$$CAP > FFP > FSD_{lex} > HFC > FSD_{nonlex}$$

He proposes to enlarge the GPSG formalism in such a way that equalities can be stated directly (like in LFG and PATR). Boguraev (this volume) also argues for the introduction of PATR-style equations into GPSG like:

$$<\text{mother feature}> = <\text{daughter feature}>.$$

Immediate dominance (ID) and linear precedence (LP)

ID rules are unordered context-free rules, i.e., they do not specify an order among the constituents of the right hand side of the rule. LP-rules specify the linear order of constituents of local trees. In implementing GPSG one can parse ID/LP statements directly (as in Shieber 1983) or compile the ID/LP rules into a set of linearised rules. Boguraev (this volume) discusses the merits of both approaches.

Metarules

Metarules generate new rules on the basis of existing rules.

LINGUISTIC THEORIES FOR NATURAL LANGUAGE PROCESSING?

At the Friedenweiler conference there was a consensus that (recent) linguistic theories are necessary for NLP. On the most elementary level implementing a linguistic theory like GPSG gives the possibility "to draw on the joint experience of a considerable number of linguists and take advantage of the linguistic research, both existing and likely to appear" (Boguraev, this volume). The linguist can write his rules and dictionary entries in a formalism that is familiar to him. The choice of LFG for the German BMFT project (EUROTRA-D Begleitforschung) was motivated by the same consideration.

Implementing linguistic theories is facilitated by a convergence of the goals of linguistics and NLP. The authors of GKPS (1985) state the following crucial methodological assumption: "A grammatical framework can and should be construed as a formal language for specifying grammars of a particular kind. The syntax and, more importantly, the semantics of that formal language constitute the substance of the theory or theories embodied in the framework." (p. 2).

If a grammatical formalism (i.e., the formalism in which a given linguistic theory is expressed) has a well defined syntax and semantics, it is much easier to find computational devices to implement the grammars expressed in this formalism. It is no accident that there exist many implementations for GPSG and LFG on the one side and only a few preliminary attempts to program GB. The grammatical formalism associated with GB has received much less attention than the unification-based formalisms. The same holds of some subparts of given linguistic theories.

Why is there no satisfactory implementation of coordination? Because neither GPSG nor LFG give a precise syntactic and semantic definition of the mechanisms involved in coordination. Implementing may elucidate some weak points of the theory. The papers by Boguraev and Shieber (this volume) illustrate this fact very well. They show that the principles of feature instantiation in GPSG need to be clarified. These results may lead to a change of the theory (for instance in the direction of HPSG).

The highest level of satisfaction a linguist can reach is the specification of a formal system that has universals as consequences. In the words of GKPS(p.2): "The most interesting contribution that generative grammar can make to the search for universals of language is to specify formal systems that have putative universals as *consequences*, as opposed to merely providing a technical vocabulary in terms of which autonomously stipulated universals can be expressed". An example are ID/LP statements. ID/LP grammars allow us to state generalizations that cannot be expressed in a traditional phrase structure grammar. This advantage of an ID/LP grammar over traditional phrase structure grammars should be preserved in an implementation. In other words, one should use an algorithm that uses ID/LP constraints directly without compiling them into a context-free "object grammar". Barton (1985) shows that, despite certain problems, the direct implementation of ID/LP constraints is more efficient than the alternative of parsing an expanded object grammar.

The case of ID/LP statements, however, is an exception. The usual situation looks like this: a linguist discovers a constraint like Ross's "wh-island constraint". This constraint says that no rule can move any element out of a clause introduced by a wh-phrase. An example where this constraint is violated is:

*The dog that Bill wonders who owns ___ .

This constraint can then be expressed in the formalisms associated with GB, LFG or GPSG. A parser which incorporates this constraint should be more efficient than a parser where the facts covered by this constraint have to be accounted for separately. In an LFG parser we can use the "island constraint" still in another respect. Consider the following sentence with an incomplete relative clause:

'The girl |who saw ___ | lives in Tübingen.'

The verb 'see' subcategorizes two grammatical functions, subject and object. Once the parser has analyzed the relative clause it knows that its f-structure is incomplete and that it can stop parsing. It need not go on working until the main clause has been analyzed. Completeness can be checked here because relative clauses are islands. There is no way to move information through unification into the f-structure of a relative clause. (In LFG constituents are not moved out of a position but functional information is moved into a certain structure through unification). Knowledge about the "island constraint" thus leads to greater efficiency in NLP. We believe that it is beneficial for NLP if the regularities, which have been discovered over the last thirty years, are taken into consideration. This may be done independently of the theory within which they were originally formulated.

To give just one more example to substantiate this claim, let's look at anaphoric pronouns. Why can the pronoun 'ihr' in sentence (a) denote the same person as 'Maria'? Why can 'ihr' and 'Maria' in sentence (b) never denote the same person?

(a) Hans hat ihr, obwohl Maria protestierte, das Wort entzogen.
 John cut Mary off, although she protested

(b) Man hat ihr vorgeschlagen, daß Maria nach Stuttgart gehen sollte.
It was proposed to Mary that she should go to Stuttgart.

The explanation seems to be that in (a) the subordinate clause is an adjunct, whereas in (b) it is an argument of the verb 'vorschlagen'. The distinction between adjunct and argument crucial for certain cases of anaphora resolution. Researchers in NLP just cannot ignore such results.

After this excursion into "real" linguistics let's go back to grammar formalisms and their implementation. Unification-based formalisms are easy to implement, because they were designed according to the principles used in the design of today's computer languages.

Furthermore, the notions of 'directed acyclic graph' and 'unification' have their counterparts in logic programming. Of course, there are important differences. But nevertheless for someone who is familiar with logic programming there exists an immediate connection between reentrancy in a graph and shared variables in PROLOG. First-order terms as partially specified objects in Definite Clause Grammars are similar to the feature structures in UG's. Since most of the participants in the Friedenweiler workshop work with PROLOG, the similarities between UG and concepts from logic programming were considered to be more important than the differences. Current research shows that the ties between the two fields are becoming even closer.

In order to understand a possible misunderstanding a word of caution is in order. We do not want to say that ease of implementation must be a crucial criterion for a linguistic formalism. Difficulties of implementation should not prevent linguists to invent new descriptive devices. Consider for instance disjunction and negation in feature structures. L. Karttunen (1984) has shown that these two operators are very useful for linguists. Their implementation, however, has lead to nearly insurmountable difficulties. Until now nobody seems to have managed to program unification with full disjunction and negation. A somewhat similar situation arose with the introduction of regular expressions in feature paths. The normal unification algorithm for equations in LFG can no longer be used, but this is no reason for rejecting this innovation, since it allows relevant linguistic generalisations to be expressed.

Our main conclusion may be wishful thinking, but nevertheless here it is: the best linguistic theory is the best basis for NLP.

SUMMARY OF THE CONTRIBUTIONS

Stuart M. Shieber, Separating Linguistic Analyses from Linguistic Theories

Shieber investigates the role of linguistic theories and their associated formalisms and analyses in the effort to develop NLP applications. After some terminological clarification the author describes on the one hand the goals for linguistic theories and their formalisms and the goals for NLP formalisms on the other. Comparing the goals he concludes: "those aspects of linguistic formalisms that support rigor, declarativeness, and linguistic felicity should be incorporated into NLP. However, those aspects of the formalisms that are geared towards restrictiveness should be eschewed - *unless*, of course, they provide auxiliary benefit by improving computational efficiency or simplifying analyses."

The main part of the paper is devoted to the question of which aspects of linguistic analyses are sparable from particular formalisms and at what cost. One way to show that an analysis can be separated from the formalism in which it was stated originally consists in reducing one formalism to another. To give a proof that one formalism is equivalent to another is very difficult. Such a proof presupposes that the syntax and the semantics of the formalisms in question are precisely specified, which is not usually the case in linguistics. The results of this paper should therefore be taken *cum grano salis*.

Shieber obtains his results by reducing the formalisms of functional unification grammar (FUG), LFG and GPSG to PATR. One of the reductions, that from GPSG to PATR, is presented in greater detail. Shieber argues that this reduction leads to a simpler grammar. In GPSG the principles for feature instantiation are stated in terms of *identities* of features. To avoid the combinatorial problems Shieber reformulates these principles in PATR type equalities. "Intrinsic in this conversion is the use of a unification-based grammar formalism, so that axioms can be stated schematically, without enumerating all of their possible instantiations. In fact, we would contend that defining the semantics of a GPSG grammar in this way yields a much simpler formulation. The need for such a reconstruction is evident to anyone who has studied the GKPS text."

The parts of GPSG that cannot be reduced are the metarules and the feature cooccurrence restrictions (FCRs). These devices are essential for formulating certain analyses.

Gerald Gazdar, Applicability of Indexed Grammars to Natural Languages

One of the aims of linguistic theories is to delimit the class of possible natural languages. A linguistic formalism should be *restrictive*, characterizing *only* the possible natural languages. This goal is not shared by people working in NLP. According to Shieber (this volume) restrictiveness is a characterisitc to be avoided wherever possible in the design of formalisms for NLP. As a linguist one would like to know where the natural languages are situated in the hierarchy of formal languages.

Indexed grammars are obtained by modifying the class of context-free phrase structure grammars in such a way that "(i) grammars are allowed to employ a single designated feature that takes stacks of items drawn from some finite set as its values, and (ii) rules are permitted to push items onto, pop items from, and copy the stack."

Indexed languages lie between context-free and context-sensitive languages. Gazdar shows what indexed grammars can do by giving examples from English and two potential natural languages Norwedish and Belgian. The English examples exhibit structures of the type {...cba abc...}:

(13) Jude is less$_b$ obviously as$_a$ nice as$_a$ Kim than$_b$ Chris is.

The next example (from Norwedish) concerns multiple unbounded dependencies without resumptive pronouns, i.e., hypothetical English sentences like "Who would you never vote for who supports ___ ? The last example exhibits dependencies of the type abcd abcd, which occur in the Dutch sentences treated in the LFG framework by Bresnan et al. (1982). Gazdar then considers two possible constraints on the power of indexed grammars and shows that there are linguistic data which cannot be accounted for if these constraints are adopted.

Branimir Boguraev, A Natural Toolkit: Reconciling Theory with Practice

This paper discusses the implementation of GPSG which is being carried out jointly by groups at the Universities of Cambridge, Edinburgh and Lancaster. The aim of this effort is to produce a computational grammar of English linked to a list of 5000 words, a morphological analyser and parser.

The author first explains the choice of GPSG as the theoretical framework for the project. GPSG was chosen because it seemed computationally tractable and because it offered the possibility to draw on the joint experience of linguists and to take advantage of linguistic research, both existing and likely to appear during the course of the project. The author then discusses in great detail the conflict between the declarative nature of GPSG and its procedural implementation. One of the sources of the computational complexity of GPSG is its theory of syntactic features. This complexity is already obvious to anyone who has taught a course with Gazdar et al. 1985 and who has asked his students to derive a few sentences on paper. Boguraev presents a special language for feature propagation (due to Thompson (1985)).In order to make feature propagation independent of the paper, one has to include equations in the style of PATR II like < mother f.> = < daughter f.>

A second proposal for feature propagation uses the mechanism of metarules in order to change the original rule by propagating features. The third proposal, which represents the solution adopted now, consists in propagating features by unification. The grammar writer can use ordinary Prolog variables in the the grammar rules and in the lexicon. These variables range over atomic values and get instantiated by unification at parse time.

Boguraev then describes the grammatical formalism, which tries to be faithful to the spirit of GPSG and yet provide an efficient and flexible implementation.The main idea ist to compile as much as possible into the object grammar before parsing.

The paper gives an excellent illustration of the difficulties one encounters in the implementation of a declarative linguistic theory. How many linguistic generalizations get lost (compiled away) in the passage from the "source" grammar (written by the linguist who doesn't know anything about implementations) to the "object" grammar, which is used in the actual parsing. Does the linguist who has to debug his grammar recognize his "source" grammar in the "object" grammar or have his elegant and simple rules been compiled into something that looks like a sequence of Chinese characters? Does the relation between "source" grammar and "object" grammar correspond to the relation between Lisp code and assembler code ?

Jörg Kindermann, Justus Meier, An Extension of LR-parsing for Lexical Functional Grammar

One of the areas of computer science which has influenced NLP is computer design. Thus F. Pereira uses shift-reduce parsing for the characterization of attachment preferences (Pereira 1985). S. Shieber shows that a shift-reduce parsing technique can help in sentence disambiguation (Shieber, 1983). LR parsing algorithms were also designed for compiler construction. An LR parsing algorithm is a shift-reduce algorithm which is deterministically guided by a parsing table indicating what action should be taken next. Tomita (1985) extended this standard algorithm with the idea of a graph-structured stack, so that it can handle ambiguous grammars. Kindermann and Meier apply Tomita's idea to the implementation of LFG.

The first part of the paper is a re-implementation of Tomita's parser. In the second part the implementation is adapted to the processing of LFG rules. Unification of f-structures is defined following Dörre and Eisele (1986). F-structures are built simultaneously, i.e., the parser solves equations as soon as possible, therefore sentences which have inconsistent f-structures can be eliminated as soon as possible. Since the parser is to be integrated into an experimental system for the development of LFG grammars the authors also provide debugging facilities.

Hans-Ulrich Block, Hans Haugeneder, An Efficiency-Oriented LFG Parser

This implementation of LFG is not part of an experimental system for grammar writers. It is intended to be used in a natural language consulting system. This intended application may explain the term "efficiency-oriented" in the title of the paper.

The authors identify three areas which contribute in a critical way to the overall performance of the parser: long-distance dependencies, the implementation of the merging algorithms, and the interaction of c-structure analysis and construction of f-structures. Only the first two points are discussed in the paper. The treatment of long-distance dependencies which the authors propose combines ideas from LFG and from GB. Displaced constituents (here *wh*-elements) are transported down the syntactic tree until they find a syntactic position where they can be consumed. The consuming position is restricted by suitable constraints. Empty productions thus become unnecessary. These ideas are built into an Earley parser, implemented in LISP. It is difficult to judge whether the treatment proposed is really more efficient than the method of 'gap threading' used in other implementations of long-distance dependencies in LFG (e.g. Frey/Reyle (1983)). In the next section the authors present a merge of algorithm that operates on shared structures. They then show its deficiencies and discuss possible improvements.

Eric Wehrli, Parsing with a GB-grammar

In "Syntactic Structures" (1957) Chomsky defines generative grammar as follows: "By a generative grammar I mean simply a system of rules that in some explicit and well-defined way assigns structural descriptions to sentences" (p.8). When Shieber defines the goals of linguistic theory (this volume) he had to go back to 1957 in order to find a passage where Chomsky uses the term "generative" in the sense of being explicit or rigorous. In GB at least there are only few attempts at explicit specification of grammars[12]. Someone who wants to write a GB parser is therefore in a more difficult position than someone who intends to implement LFG.

Wehrli is fully aware of this difficulty when he writes that the mere issue of "what counts as a GB-parser" is likely to be controversial. He states two conditions that the parser should fulfill: (a) return the set of S-structures

---

[12] The authors of GKPS state openly that in their opinion GB is not a generative grammar (p.6).

for a given sentence as specified by GB grammars, (b) reflect in some direct fashion the organization of the grammar.

Following the organization of the grammar the parser contains three components: the $\overline{X}$-component, the θ-component, and the binding component. The description of these components constitutes the main part of the paper. How the various components of the parser interact is illustrated by a full parse of the sentence "Quel livre est-ce que Jean a fait acheter à Paul?"

In the last section Wehrli argues that, although they may be much harder to implement, modular principle-based parsers present definite advantages over non-modular rule-based parsers in dealing with ambiguity and problems of word-order. Since the author does not present any algorithms, it is difficult to see how the parser really works. We hope that the efforts towards implementing GB will contribute to make the syntax and semantics of the associated formalism more precise. This would allow us to make computational use of the vast amount of papers on German syntax written in this framework. It would furthermore provide the possibility to evaluate claims like "the limitations on free word order in German are fully predicted by the theory of GB", which are made in the next paper.

Henk Zeevat, Combining Categorial Grammar and Unification

Zeevat presents a version of categorial grammar in which several insights from HPSG and PATR-II have been incorporated. The author uses three primitive categories: nouns, noun phrases and sentences. These primitive categories are further specified by features which correspond roughly to the features used in GPSG.

Derived categories are defined in the usual way. An important innovation is the use of variable categories. With the introduction of variable categories one can avoid making certain functor categories (like np) highly ambiguous.

If one is dealing with type-raised noun phrases, then a noun phrase looking for an intransitive verb would be of type s/(s/np). The noun phrase looking for a transitive and a ditransitve verb would have the form (s/np)/(s/np/np) and (s/np/np)/(s/np/np/np) respectively. The use of variables makes it possible to assign just one category to noun phrases:

X/(X/np)

where X is a variable ranging over categories.

The variable in the preceding example has an abbreviatory function: it stands for a finite number of possibilities that would be spelled out if necessary. In the last section, however, Zeevat uses variables that stand for possibly infinite disjunctions.

This new use of variables changes the generative power of the grammar. One can show the indexed languages (see Gazdar this volume) are within the expressive power of unification categorial grammars.

Zeevat illustrates this additional generative power with his treatment of Dutch infinitivals in subordinate clauses (see Bresnan et al., 1982). The possibility of treating cross serial dependencies in categorial grammar without invoking composition rules confirms Hans Uszkoreit's conclusion that often unification can be used to obtain the effect of composition (Uszkoreit, 1986).

P. J. Whitelock, A Feature-based Categorial-like Morpho-Syntax for Japanese

This paper gives a description of Japanese morpho-syntax based on categorial grammar. The categories are enriched with feature structures. Two categories may be combined to form a new category either by forward application or by backward application. The grammar is implemented in PROLOG. An earlier version was used in the generation component of an English-Japanese Machine Translation system. The present version can be used for both recognition and generation.

The data covered include case, tense, formation of adnominal constructions ('no' as a possessive marker and 'na'), infinitives, gerunds, passives and causatives. Whitelock presents some interesting data on a periphrastic construction which marks progressive or perfective aspect, ambiguously or not according to the meaning of the verb. For instance, punctual verbs can only be interpreted perfectively with this construction.

One may wonder why many linguists today combine unification grammar and categorial grammar? Is it more than an exercise to show how a traditional categorial analysis can be encoded declaratively in lexical entries and then used for parsing? If the categorial information is not used for the construction of semantic representations, why use categorial grammars?

Whitelock justifies his use of this framework with "the ease with which the morpho-syntactic behaviour of a diversity of lexical items can be subsumed under the two combination rules of a categorial grammar".

Furthermore the categorial viewpoint seems to provide "a natural characterization of what appears to be a common diachronic process - the grammaticalization of particular lexical items - as an operation of type-raising in the lexicon."

Christoph Schwarze, The Treatment of the French adjectif détaché in Lexical Functional Grammar

An 'adjectif détaché' is an apposition-like construction as illustrated by the example: "La pluie tombe, *vaporeuse*." (The rain falls, *steamy*).

The 'adjectif détaché' has variable word order. Schwarze analyses the 'adjectif détaché' as a controlled *X-adjunct*. The corresponding f-structure is straightforward. It is identical with the f-structure which Bresnan (1982, p.325) gives for the parallel English construction "Sure of winning, Mary entered the competition yesterday". In order to account for the different positions in which the 'adjectif détaché' may occur, Schwarze discusses two rules, one which leaves the acceptability of certain constructions to stylistics and one (more complicated) which does not.

There exists a second type of 'adjectif détaché' (more like a non-restrictive adjective) which immediately follows. An example would be: "Une femme, grand et belle ... " (a woman, tall and beautiful). If this construction is introduced by the rule

$$NP \rightarrow NP \qquad (AP)$$
$$\uparrow = \downarrow \qquad \downarrow \in (ADJ)$$
$$(\downarrow SUBJ) = \uparrow$$

then one gets a circular f-structure. One way out would be to postulate anaphoric control between the 'adjectif détaché' and its controller. (For an example of the corresponding f-structure, see Bresnan (1982) p.299, where she analyses the Walpiri version of the noun phrase "the small child".) However, such an analysis would contradict the arguments which the author advances in favour of functional control. The solution which the author finally adopts leaves open several questions and shows that further research on adnominal modifiers is necessary within the framework of LFG.

Dieter Wunderlich, Some Problems of Coordination in German

Coordination is one of the most difficult areas of natural language and so far there is no comprehensive treatment for constituent coordination, gapping, left deletion, right node raising, etc., neither in GB nor in LFG or GPSG. It is, therefore very commendable that Wunderlich dares to attack such a complicated topic. He begins with a rather irregular case of coordination which he illustrates with the following example: "In den Wald ging der Jäger und fing eine Hasen." ("Into the forest went the hunter and caught a hare.") The first conjunct is a complete sentence, the second conjunct must be analyzed as a verb phrase because the subject is missing. Starting with this missing subject Wunderlich investigates the general conditions of ellipsis in coordinate structures. He tries to find out by empirical generalizations from the grammatical and ungrammatical coordinate constructions what restrictions have to be observed. He summarizes the restrictions he found out in six points. The restrictions are illustrated with relevant grammatical and ungrammatical examples[13].

Wunderlich then examines how his special type of coordination in German could be accounted for within GB or GPSG. He concludes that, within the standard assumptions of the Chomsky tradition, no solution is available. GPSG, however, seems to offer the necessary technical apparatus.

Wunderlich proposes to introduce a modified version of the metarule which introduces main clauses (-SC stands for minus subordinate clause).

$$VP \longrightarrow W \Longrightarrow V_n \longrightarrow NP, W, V_n$$
$$-SC \quad\quad NOM \quad CONJ\alpha 2$$
$$+AC$$

---

[13] There seems to be some disagreement about the data concerning condition (E). A sentence like "*Den Korb hat die Tante ___ und der Onkel hat in den Hof den Sack geworfen" is rejected by most informants although the deleted element of the first conjunct is not in the topic position in the second conjunct. According to Wunderlich this sentence should be grammatically well-formed.

The output of this rule does not quite fit the coordination schema in GKPS. But since neither CONJ nor BAR are head features Wunderlich sees in his example an instance of the following generalized coordination schema:

$$Vn \longrightarrow V_0 \text{ CONJ}\alpha 1 \;,\; \ldots \;,\; VP \text{ CONJ}\alpha 2 \qquad \text{where } \alpha 1 = \text{NIL}$$

These two rules explain all the properties of the 'subject gap in fronted finite verb coordination', i.e., examples like the one with the hunter and the rabbit[14].

Gisbert Fanselow, German Word Order and Universal Grammar

The author describes German word order within the framework of GB. He first presents the basic facts about German word order. He shows that German has all the syntactic properties that are normally postulated for a non-configurational language. The basic facts are summarized as follows: "The X-bar-scheme generates SOV-orderings only, and there is a special instance of Move α, which we may tentatively identify as 'IP-internal reordering'(IIR), which optionally moves non-focus elements to some pre-IP position." Here, IP stands for INFL Phrase. A German clause like "weil den Mann niemand mag" (because nobody likes the man) is assumed to have the following structure

---

[14] It remains unclear to the editors how one could exclude sentences like
*Gestern ging er in den Wald und wurde ihm geholfen.
*Gestern hat es geschneit und könnte morgen regnen.
which these two rules also seem to generate.

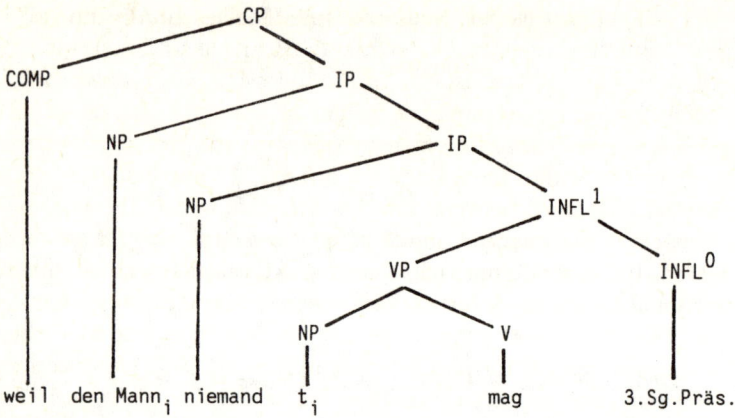

This special instance of Move α is examined more closely in section two, where the author shows that the domain of application of this rule is determined by the nature of the trace that is left in place. The author gives convincing arguments that his instance of Move α may create exactly those dependencies between trace and antecedent that are licensed for anaphoric binding in general.

In section three the author addresses two questions: why does the movement rule leave an anphoric trace, and why is it constrained to topic elements, in other words why is it impossible to apply the rule to focus elements. An ungrammatical example with a focus element preceding the subject would be "*weil im Hilton der Präsident wohnt". The answer is that focus elements cannot be preposed in the middle field because this would lead to a contradiction with the empty category principle. Section four is devoted to the treatment of some apparent counterexamples. In the last section the author examines the possible conssequences of this analysis for the description of free-word-order languages in general.

The main point of the paper is that GB provides independently motivated principles from which the facts of German word-order can be deduced.

Klaus Netter, Nonlocal-Dependencies and Infinitival Constructions in German

Drawing on the example of infinitival constructions in German this paper contrasts two different approaches to the treatment of non-local dependencies within the framework of Lexical Functional Grammar. The essential difference between the two accounts is that the first and older approach, Constituent Control (CC), operates on phrase structure, whereas the second approach, Functional Uncertainty (FU), operates on functional structure. A further difference between the two approaches is that FU does not require empty strings (as traces), which are indispensable in CC for purely technical reasons. This paper concentrates on the linguistic aspects rather than the mathematical properties of FU, arguing in favour of FU on the basis of linguistic data.

To compare the two approaches a small fragment of German infinitival constructions is described. The phenomena considered are primarily extraposition and 'wh-movement'.

A grammar for basic clauses is presented in section 1, which illustrates the underlying grammatical relations. It is argued that, given these basic assumptions, extraposition to the right must be treated as a kind of non-local dependency in German. To introduce and compare the mechanisms of CC and FU, the grammar is extended in section 2 for both mechanisms, to cover the extraposition phenomena. The simple case of extraposed infinitival clauses governed by verbs serves to show that for a CC-based analysis, an equivalent grammar based on FU can be constructed.

By expanding the grammar further to include infinitival clauses subcategorized for by nouns (section 3), evidence is presented which suggests that grammatical relations rather than the phrase structure configuration determine the grammatical process of extraposition. For these phenomena, the FU approach permits to capture certain generalizations more directly than the phrase structure oriented CC.

In section 4, a more classical type of non-local dependencies, wh-movement, illustrated by German relative clauses, is discussed. Certain restrictions on wh-movement with respect to its interaction with extraposition are described. It is shown that, given the correctness and adequacy of the generalizations outlined in the previous sections, FU allows the formulation of restrictions which cannot be expressed in the traditional approach of constituent control.

Christa Hauenschild, GPSG and German Word Order

Hauenschild starts from Uszkoreit's revised version of the linear precedence statements within GPSG. She discusses some problems of Uszkoreit's approach which result from the fact that in his account problems of word order are treated at the syntactic level only. She points out the LP statements in Uszkoreit (1986) do not account correctly for the relative position of direct and indirect pronominal objects. The unmarked order of direct and indirect pronominal objects is just the opposite of the unmarked order in case both objects are full nouns. Compare "Sie gab es ihm" (she gave it to him) with "Sie gab dem Mann das Buch" (she gave the man the book). Additional complications arise through the FOCUS feature. The pronoun 'es', for instance, cannot carry the intonation focus (which seems to be the interpretation of the FOCUS feature in Uszkoreit (1986).

Instead of introducing more complex relations between LP statements, Hauenschild argues for an alternative framework for the solution of word order. Under the influence of the Prague school of linguistics the author proposes to base the analysis of the thematic structuring of sentences and texts on a conception of functional sentence perspective. These ideas are to be incorporated into a model for machine translation. Preliminary research for this model of machine translation has already been undertaken at the University of Konstanz (Engelberg et al., 1984).

William R. Keller, Nested Cooper Storage: The Proper Treatment of Quantification in Ordinary Noun Phrases

"John seeks a unicorn" is probably the most famous sentence in formal semantics. It has two interpretations depending only on the scope assigned to the quantified noun phrase "a unicorn". Montague regarded such sentences as syntactically ambiguous. There are, however, no syntactic criteria to motivate this structural ambiguity.

R. Cooper designed a mechanism (called Cooper storage) which assigns correct scope without the need for otherwise unmotivated syntactic ambiguity. Unfortunately this technique tends to assign too many analyses for complex noun phrases like "*An agent of every company* arrived" or "They disqualified *a player belonging to every team*". In order to avoid such overgeneration Keller suggests a modification of Cooper's theory: nested Cooper Storage. Instead of simply putting the denotation of a noun phrase node into store, the revised rule creates a completely new store and places in it the whole interpretation for the noun phrase.

Nested Cooper Storage presents no particular difficulties with regard to implementation. A faithful implementation of nested Cooper storage seems to produce just the right number of readings. Of course it can make no claims with regard to preferred readings. Keller is not the only one to propose a modified version of Cooper storage. GKPS also work under the assumption that quantifier ambiguities should be handled by some variant of Cooper storage (p.15). They add, however, that the work of Kamp (1981) suggests that a comprehensive tratment of quantifiers and anaphora may require a form of representation, discourse representation structure, intermediate between syntactic representations and their natural-theoretic interpretations. This is the topic of the next paper.

Uwe Reyle, Compositional Semantics for LFG

The paper presents a modification of (typed) lambda-calculus which allows a functional application of the arguments of a relation to be made that is independent of the order of the arguments. Semantically, the independence is achieved by taking the denotation of e.g. a two place relation not to be a subset of the cartesian product UxU of the domain of individuals but to be a subset of a set of partial functions from a set of indices into the union of copies of U. The set of indices comprises natural numbers as well as names of grammatical functions. This allows, first, a direct interpretation of f-structures and, second, a formulation of a compositional semantics for LFG. With every LFG-rule that combines syntactic items to produce a new item, a corresponding semantic rule is associated which gives the meaning of the produced item from the meanings of the input terms. Finally it is shown how this lambda-calculus can be implemented directly within a unification framework that is enriched by a copying operation.

REFERENCES

Abney, S./Cole, J.(1985), A Government and Binding Parser, *Proceedings of the North Eastern Linguistic Society* XVI

Dörre, J./Eisele, A.(1986), A Lexical Functional Grammar System in Prolog, in: *Proceedings of Coling 1986*

Engelberg et al.(1984), Con^{3}Tra: ein prozedurales Modell des Textverstehens für die Übersetzung. *Papers of the Sonderforschungsbereich 99*, Konstanz

Frey, W./Reyle, U.(1983), A Prolog Implementation of LFG as a Base for a Natural Language Processing System, in: *Proceedings of the first Meeting of the European Chapter of the Association for Computational Linguistics*, Pisa 1983

Kamp, H.(1981), A Theory of Truth and Semantic Representation, in: Groenendijk et al. (eds.), *Formal Methods in the Study of Language*, Mathematical Centre Tract, Amsterdam, 1981

Kaplan, R./Bresnan, J.(1982), Lexical Functional Grammar: a Formal System for Grammatical Representation, in: Bresnan, J.(ed.) *The Mental Representation of Grammatical Relations*, MIT Press

Kay, M.(1979), Functional Grammar in: *Proceedings of the Fifth Annual Meeting of the Berkeley Linguistic Society*

Kudo, I./Nomura, H.(1986), Lexical Functional Transfer: A Transfer Framework in a Machine Translation System Based on LFG, in: *Proceedings of Coling* 1986

Pereira, F.(1985), A new Characterization of Attachment Preferences, in: Dowty,D. et al. (eds.), *Natural Language Parsing*, Cambridge University Press, 1985

Pereira, F.(1987), Grammars and Logics of Partial Information, in: *Proceedings of the International Conference on Logic Programming*, Melbourne, 1987

Shieber, S.(1983), Direct Parsing of ID/LP Grammars, *Linguistics and Philosophy* 7

Shieber, S.(1984), Notes from the Unification Underground, *Technical Note* 327, SRI International

Uszkoreit, H. (1986), Constraints on Order. To appear in: *Linguistics* 24/5

Tomita, M. (1986), *Efficient Parsing for Natural Languages: A fast Algorithm for Practical Systems*, Kluwer Academic Publishers, Boston, MA

STUART M. SHIEBER

ARTIFICIAL INTELLIGENCE CENTER
AND CENTER FOR THE STUDY OF
LANGUAGE AND INFORMATION
SRI INTERNATIONAL

SEPARATING LINGUISTIC ANALYSES FROM
LINGUISTIC THEORIES

1. INTRODUCTION[0]

Many of the papers in this volume stress the desirability of making computational use of insights from linguistics as an aid in the processing of natural language. Groups of researchers throughout the world are engaged in efforts that are often described as implementing a linguistic theory. In this paper I will start out by addressing the question of what *level* of linguistic practice is best for natural-language-processing (NLP) efforts[1], whether results from linguistic theory (LT) should be utilized by modeling a particular linguistic theory, interpreting a linguistic formalism,

---

[0] This research has been made possible by a gift from the System Development Foundation. I am indebted to John Bear, David Israel, Lauri Karttunen, Fernando Pereira, and Ray Perrault for their comments on earlier drafts of this paper and to Gerald Gazdar, Ivan Sag, Henry Thompson, and members of the Foundations of Grammar project at the Center for the Study of Language and Information for their helpful discussions during the development of this work. An earlier shorter version of this paper was presented at the Alvey/ICL Work shop on Linguistic Theory and Computer Applications, held at the University of Manchester Institute of Science and Technology, Manchester, England, in September 1985, and appears in the proceedings published by Academic Press. I thank the organizers of that workshop for permission to publish portions of that paper here.

[1] In this paper, I will use "NLP" specifically to refer to computer applications requiring the processing of natural language, and not to the important, but separate, issues of computational or mathematical approaches to linguistics.

or embodying a linguistic analysis. That is, I will investigate what the role of linguistic theories and their associated formalisms and analyses should be in the engineering discipline of developing NLP applications. In particular, I will contend that, because the goals and strategies of LT and NLP research differ, linguistic theories and formalisms may be inappropriate for importation into NLP applications.

Nonetheless, I will adopt the possibly controversial position that NLP efforts can benefit from insights expressed in linguistic analyses of particular languages.[2] For instance, in writing systems to interpret English sentences that include, say, the comparative construction, a system builder or grammar writer might find it beneficial to make use of one or another of the previously described linguistic analyses of this construction. Given that this is so, the question arises as to what sort of commitment to linguistic theories and formalisms this necessitates, that is, to what extent analyses are dependent on the particular formulations found in the linguistic literature. An instructive analogy can be drawn with the relationship of computer science to computer programming. Consider the following rewording of the previous paragraph:

> I will adopt the uncontroversial viewpoint that computer programming can benefit from using algorithms from computer science. For instance, in writing a system to, say, sort records in a database, a system builder or programmer might find it beneficial to make use of one or another of the previously described sorting algorithms. Given that this is so, the question arises as to what sort of commitment to programming languages this necessitates, that is, to

---

[2] That this view is controversial can be seen in an opinion shared by many NLP researchers, and voiced, for example, in Roger Schank's comments to the effect that "research on syntax should have stopped fifteen years ago" and that "the hard part of natural language is not the language" [20, p. 166]. Although it is true that there are exceptionally difficult problems in NLP research that are not traditionally dealt with by linguistics and about which "linguistic theory" as construed by linguists has little to say, it does not follow that those problems that are addressed by linguistics are straightforward or that linguists' expertise is not pertinent to NLP efforts.]

what extent algorithms are dependent on the particular formulations of them found in the computer science literature.

This latter question is easy to answer. Algorithms from computer science are not at all tied to the particular formulations in which they are described. Despite the fact that quicksort was first described in ALGOL, it can still be used by programmers writing in Pascal. Indeed, many algorithms were originally described only informally, e.g., Earley's algorithm. Nonetheless, any effective procedure has an implementation in some programming language, that is, if we believe Church. And since any program in a given programming language can be reduced to an equivalent program in any other programming language (of suffcient power), it follows that they have implementations in all programming languages. This ability to reduce one programming language to another thus demonstrates that the use of algorithms from computer science does not in theory tie us to any particular language for expressing algorithms.

Similarly, the issue of whether a particular linguistic analysis requires allegiance to a given language for expressing analyses, i.e., grammar formalism, can be at least partially elucidated by exhibiting *reductions* from one linguistic formalism to another. As a side effect, such reductions help establish exactly which differences among linguistic theories that use the formalisms are purely (though not merely) *notational*, and, on the other hand, which ones are *notional*.

Reductions from one formalism to another can convey several types of information of different degrees of granularity. At a coarse grain, a reduction from one formalism to another can precisely convey their relative computational power and complexity. Reductions showing the interreducibility of programming languages or NP-complete problems are of this type. This use of reductions gives evidence of what might be called the *absolute expressivity* of formalisms.

Second, the existence or nonexistence of certain reductions can give evidence at a finer grain of *functional expressivity*. Rather than deciding whether a problem in one formalism can be *encoded* in another, this type of inquiry determines whether the problem can be *directly stated* in the other formalism. In such a reduction, we disallow reencoding the problem statement in the language of the other formalism. Two formalisms that are expressively equivalent in the absolute sense may nevertheless not be equivalent in functional expressivity; the prime example of such a pair of systems is the simple and second-order typed lambda calculi. Although both calculi are Turing-equivalent, it can be shown that the second-order system can directly compute functions that can be computed only indirectly in a simply typed system [7].

Finally, a reduction from one formalism to another can elucidate their *notational expressivity*. Consider two programming languages, say, Pascal and Pascal', a minor variant that lacks the *while...do...* construct but is otherwise identical. Clearly, programs in either language can be reduced to equivalent programs in the other. The reduction from Pascal' to Pascal is, in fact, the identity reduction, whereas the reverse direction requires encoding of *while...do...* statements by means of some other construct, e.g., *repeat...until...* . That the latter reduction is more complex than the former shows the intuitively obvious fact that Pascal is more notationally expressive than Pascal' (though not more functionally or absolutely expressive). Though this example for programming languages is trivial, the use of the same technique for linguistic formalisms can be quite revealing, especially considering that the question of the precise relationships among the theories and formalisms has not been actively investigated. The details of reductions can show quite graphically just how close various formalisms are to one another. The simpler the reductions are, the closer the formalisms. In other words, reductions among formalisms can not only demonstrate what things can be expressed in the various formalisms, but how easy those things are to express.

The question of whether linguistic analyses are separable from their formulations within particular linguistic theories and formalisms is much less easily answered than its computer language analogue, even though the technique used--notational reductions--is the same. The answer depends first of all on *what* the distinctions are among the concepts of analysis, formalism and theory, concepts whose meanings are not always agreed upon, let alone made precise in the linguistics literature. Second, it requires serious research on exactly *how* formalisms and theories can be interreduced and what properties the reductions possess. Finally, even if such a separation could be demonstrated--by exhibiting certain complete or partial reductions among linguistic formalisms--it remains to be shown *why* this separation would aid in NLP efforts.

This paper will be divided, therefore, into three parts corresponding roughly to these three questions: what, why, and how. First, I will briefly discuss the notions of theory, formalism, and analysis as they are employed in linguistics and other fields in an effort to clarify the terminology. Second, I will provide some methodological justification for the attempt to separate analyses from their formal and theoretical underpinnings. Third, I will describe some work in progress on characterizing the relations among certain formalisms within theories of syntax. I will concentrate on syntax because it is the subfield of linguistics most familiar to me. In particular, I will stress the lexical-functional grammar (LFG) and generalized phrase structure grammar (GPSG) theories as these seem to be the major "contenders" for use by people interested in utilizing syntactic theories for NLP computer applications. The reductions I will discuss concern the formalisms found in LFG and GPSG, and certain formalisms from computational linguistics--namely, the functional unification grammar (FUG) formalism of Martin Kay [11], and the PATR formalism from SRI International [16].

2. WHAT: SOME TERMINOLOGY

Before discussing the separation of linguistic analyses from formalisms and theories, I need to make clear what I (and linguists themselves) mean by the terms *formalism*, *theory*, and *analysis*--especially because they are not always well differentiated in the linguistic literature and because they are used in linguistics in relatively nonstandard ways vis-à-vis other disciplines.

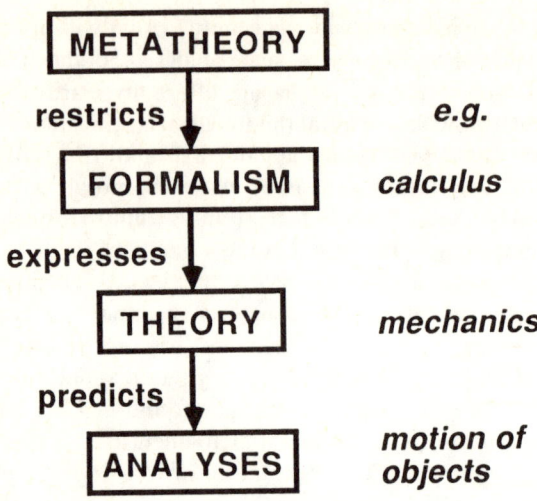

Figure 1: Relations Among Terms

In many scientific fields, the scientist is interested in building a *theory* of some observable phenomena (say, the laws governing the motion of objects). He may use a special notation or *formalism*--the calculus, for instance--to write down one of several possible theories of motion. These theories in turn predict *analyses* of certain specific observable phenomena (given appropriate contingent facts such as boundary conditions); for instance, the motion of a ball thrown into the air or of people jumping in elevators can be analyzed by a theory of kinematics. The notations for describing theories are typically designed to be as general as possible, thereby allowing a broad spectrum of theories to be stated and facilitating comparison among them. A graphic representation of the relations among the concepts is given in Figure 1.

The terminology is used differently in linguistics. As before, attempts to characterize observable data are generally thought of as *analyses* (e.g., the analysis of a particular English sentence). But a description of an entire language (what would be referred to in nonlinguistic terminology as a theory of the language) usually falls under the label *analysis* as well (e.g., an analysis of English syntax). These analyses predict the observable phenomena, e.g., the LFG analysis of English predicts the grammaticality and ambiguity properties of English sentences. The term *theory* is primarily reserved for a characterization of general properties of or relationships among analyses in this latter sense--what in other fields would be considered a *metatheory*. For instance, the study of possible geometries is not a theory of space, but a theory of theories of space, of which Euclidean geometry and Riemannian geometry are but two. There are metatheories in other fields as well, but in linguistics, unlike other fields, the metatheory is the subject's *raison d' être*.[3] A summary of the relations for linguistic terminology is pictured in Figure 2.

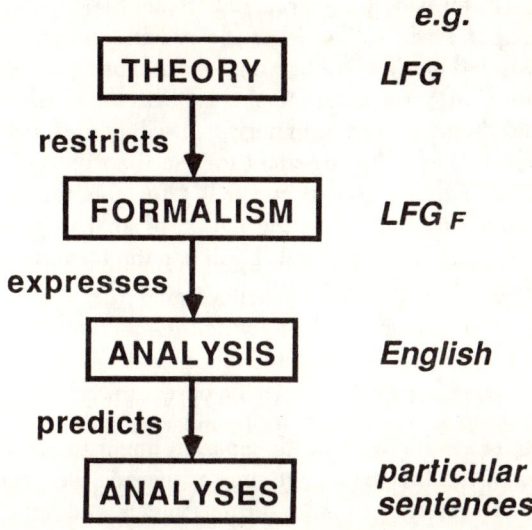

Figure 2: Relations Among Terms in Linguistics

The differences, of course, are only in the words used to express the structure of the disciplines; the ideas themselves are much the same. But terminological differences like these can be confusing. For example, in other fields, theories are *expressed* in formalisms. In linguistics, analyses are expressed in formalisms and theories are expressed *alongside* formalisms. Since the primary objective of research in each case is development of a "theory", this distinction is important. The relationship

---

[3] One important exception is the field of mathematical logic. Since the discovery of the paradoxes, the metatheory of logic has been the primary study of logicians.

between formalisms and the object of study in the two cases is quite different. In one case it is primarily a tool, in the other a theoretical device.[4]

This analogy between the terminologies of linguistics and other sciences is not the only one that could be made. Linguistic theories do, for instance, share with physical theories the property of being unitary explanations for actually realized phenomena, a property that metatheories of physics would not share. The important point is that the various terms--metatheory, formalism, theory, analysis--are not interchangeable and can differ widely from one field to another.

In the rest of this paper I will follow linguistic practice in using the words *theory*, *formalism*, and *analysis*, rather than *metatheory*, *formalism*, and *theory*, respectively. Furthermore, to make explicit the distinction between formalisms and theories used in linguistics, I will henceforth use the acronym of the theory (say, LFG) to stand for the theory itself, and the acronym subscripted with an F (as in LFG_F) for the formalism associated with the theory. Note also that the notion of analysis is used ambiguously in linguistics jargon. In general, I will use the term *analysis* as vague (not ambiguous) between the two interpretations.

3. WHY: METHODOLOGICAL MOTIVATION

I now turn to the rationale for wanting to separate linguistic analyses from linguistic theories in the first place. Of course, there is the obvious intellectual advantage of thereby gaining a firmer understanding as to which differences among theories are intrinsic as opposed to emergent from notational aspects of the respective formalisms (i.e., which theoretical concepts from one formalism are difficult or impossible to state in another). But I am here concerned with the application of linguistic theory to NLP. In such an application, why not just incorporate into an NLP system an entire theory of linguistics, with its associated

---

[4] Metatheoretic restrictions are of course embodied in the formalism used in stating theories in other sciences as well. Use of the calculus, for instance, presupposes that one's theory of space will have certain properties of continuity of fundamental magnitudes. However, such restrictions are seldom made explicit or studied in their own right outside of linguistics.

formalisms and analyses?

The reason is that the traditional methodological goals and strategies of research in linguistic theory and NLP are in direct conflict, and this conflict is reflected in actual practice in the two disciplines. In deciding whether to incorporate a linguistic theory wholesale into an NLP system, we need to have an understanding of what the respective goals of LT and NLP are. Then, insofar as the goals of LT are consistent with and aid those of NLP, devices from the former can beneficially be incorporated into an NLP system. Where the goals are conflicting, however, the associated techniques should be avoided.

In this section, I identify these goals and strategies and show where they differ. In particular, I demonstrate that the goals linguists adhere to in their design of theories and their evaluation of formalisms diverge from those researchers desire for natural-language-processing purposes especially in the role of expressiveness of the theoretical constructs, and consider some implications of this divergence.

3.1 Goals for Linguistic Theories and Formalisms

3.1.1 Goals for Linguistic Theory

For reasons usually motivated by the problem of language acquisition, linguists have traditionally been interested specifically in universal properties of language. Chomsky summarizes the goals of research in linguistic theory thus:

> Let us recall the basic character of the problem we face. The theory of UG must meet two obvious conditions. On the one hand, it must be compatible with the diversity of existing (indeed, possible) grammars. At the same time, UG must be sufficiently constrained and restrictive in the options it permits to account for the fact that each of these grammars develops in the mind on the basis of quite limited evidence. [6, p. 3]

That is, a theory of linguistics should *characterize all and only the possible natural languages*. I have chosen a quite recent quotation to this effect, but, of course, the idea has pervaded the practice of linguistics since the appearance of *Syntactic Structures*.

Secondarily, of course, other requirements are usually imposed on the task, three examples of which I discuss here. First, it is typically desired that the characterization be "generative" in the sense of being explicit or rigorous. Chomsky defines the term thus:

> By a generative grammar I mean simply a system of rules that in some explicit and well-defined way assigns structural descriptions to sentences. [5, p. 8]

Second, Occam's razor tends to cut in favor of theories that admit relatively simple, elegant analyses. Although such a comparison is perforce based on aesthetic or subjective standards, it is hard to imagine any other criterion that could serve for comparison of theories that have the same expressive power.[5] Certainly, simplicity as a criterion for choosing theories is a common standard in other fields of research.[6]

In fact, we see this criterion of "linguistic felicity" used at least implicitly in linguistics. Gazdar notes its importance in choosing between base-generated and transformational approaches:

> If to do things exclusively by direct phrase structure generation was to lead inevitably to aesthetic disaster (re simplicity, economy, generality, empirical motivation, etc.) whilst competing transformational analyses were paragons of elegance and enlightenment, then one might reasonably feel inclined to reject the former in favour of the latter. [8, p. 134]

Finally, current practice seems to place a value on the declarative (or order-independent, or order-free) nature of the characterization. Kaplan

---

[5] By expressive power, I mean to include not only absolute expressivity limitations, but notational expressivity as well, not only formal limitations on expressivity, but theoretical, noformal limitiations, whatever they might be.

[6] This notion of simplicity should not be confused with the sort of "simplicity metric" that, according to Chomskyan linguistics, governs a child's choice among grammars. Simplicity metrics of this sort, as Chomsky himself notes, cannot be used to choose among different theories.

and Bresnan write:

> *The constraint of order-free composition* is motivated by the fact that complete representations of local grammatical relations are effortlessly, fluently, and reliably constructed for arbitrary segments of sentences. [3, p. xlv]

Regardless of the soundness of this reasoning, the goal of declarativeness is shared by at least LFG, GPSG, and government-binding theory (GB). These theories all define sentential grammaticality in terms of simultaneous well-formedness constraints, rather than procedures for recognition.

To summarize, then, the goals linguists pursue in designing their theories are, first and foremost, *completeness* (characterizing *all* the possible natural languages), and *restrictiveness* (characterizing *only* the possible natural languages); secondarily, they pursue such goals as *rigor*, *simplicity*, *elegance*, and *declarativeness*.

3.1.2 Goals for Linguistic Formalisms

These are the goals linguists have for their theories, but what of the goals they pursue in designing the associated formalisms? Current linguistic theories are usually most precise in the descriptions of their formalisms, in contradistinction to the unformalized "substantive" portion of the theory. It is generally impossible to determine if a computer system correctly and soundly realizes theoretical constructs that are not rigorously stated. Consequently, efforts to "implement a linguistic theory" typically, and for good reason, concern themselves only with that aspect of the theory embodied in, not stated with, the formalism. The question of what goals are pursued in the design of the formalisms therefore becomes especially important. The answer to this question is complicated by the fact that the relationship between theory and formalism differs from theory to theory. One common notion is that the theory is fully determined by the formalism, that is, that the formalism itself should embody all the constraints on universal grammar. This view is explicitly propounded by the originators of GPSG:

> A grammatical framework can and should be construed as a formal language for specifying

> grammars of a particular kind. The syntax, and, more importantly, the semantics of that formal language constitute the substance of the theory or theories embodied in the framework. [9, p. 2]

The same view is also at least intimated by Bresnan and Kaplan:

> The lexical theory of grammar provides a formally explicit and coherent theory of how surface structures are related to representations of meaningful grammatical relations. [3, p. 4]

On the other hand, a view of grammar could be propounded in which the formalism is but one part of the theory. Constraints supplied by formal limitations (i.e., limitations of the formalism) would indeed constitute universal claims, but so would other constraints that, while not incorporated in the formalism, are nonetheless essential to the theory. This, I take it, is Bresnan's view, as expressed in the following excerpt:[7]

> Having no formal theory at all will lead to vague and inconsistent formulations at both the theoretical and descriptive levels. Despite its importance, however, a formal theory of grammar is only one step in the construction of a substantive linguistic theory of universal grammar. The present work adds to the theory of LFG a set of substantive postulates for a universal theory of control and complementation. [3, p. 282]

Thus, Bresnan distinguishes formal and substantive constraints in a theory,[8] whereas Kaplan [10] and Gazdar *et al.* would require all constraints to be formal. But, in either case, at least part of the burden of restrictiveness is placed on the formalism itself, that is, more restrictive

---

[7] I have assumed in interpreting this quotation that Bresnan uses the term "formal theory" to mean theoretical constraints embodied in the formalism.

[8] Chomsky also distinguishes notions of "formal" and "substantive"; however, these are slightly different in scope from Bresnan's usage. Though I find the choice of the term "substantive" unfortunate--formal constraints seem to me to be as substantive as any--I will continue to use Bresnan's terminology.

formalisms are historically favored over less restrictive ones. If this were not so, arguments against LFG, say, on the basis of the overexpressiveness of LFG_F (cf. [2]) would have no force. Thus, the same criteria of restrictiveness, completeness, simplicity, rigor, and declarativeness that linguists apply to their theories are applied to their formalisms as well.

3.2 Goals for NLP Formalisms

What, then, of the goals of natural-language-processing efforts in computer applications? Simply put, such efforts aim to *characterize computationally one or a small number of languages*. As mentioned earlier, the grammar formalism, in this case at least, is of paramount importance, since substantive theory typically finds little place in computer application. For this reason, I will be concentrating on the desired characteristics of formalisms used in NLP systems, that is, on the question of which design strategies NLP formalism designers should pursue.

Obviously, formalisms intended for NLP should be designed to facilitate such a computational characterization. They must therefore be at least expressive enough to characterize the subset of natural languages relevant to the application; we might call this criterion *weak completeness*. On the other hand, they are constrained by limitations of computational effectiveness, not only in the technical sense as used in the term "effective procedure", but in the informal sense of "usable under current technology" as well.

On a secondary level, of course, other characteristics are important. For instance, to aid in articulating the grammars of natural language and changing them as new consequences of a grammatical analysis are revealed, they should be as flexible and expressive as possible. To make implementation and verification of correctness easier, they should be kept simple, with a firm mathematical foundation. In short, they should obey all the rubrics of a good computer language as commonly construed in current computer science. Computer-language designers are increasingly putting forward concepts of rigorous mathematical foundations, declarativeness, simplicity, expressivity[9], and flexibility. These criteria

---

[9] Clearly, since virtually all programming languages are equivalent in absolute expressive power, what I (and others) have in mind here is notational expressivity, in the sense introduced in Section 1.

seem to be so well accepted in computer-language design that it seems almost ludicrous to call attention to them at all. They serve as the motivating influence, for instance, in current research efforts in programming-language design issues such as the theory of data types, functional and logic programming and explicit programming-language semantics; research in all these fields and others attests to the importance of such factors in the design of computer languages. In fact, these same criteria apply equally well, and for identical reasons, to computer languages for encoding linguistic information, namely, to grammar formalisms.

In sum, the characteristics of grammar formalisms promoted by the goals of NLP are, first of all, *weak completeness* and *computational effectiveness*. Secondarily, they are the goals of computer language design in general: *expressivity, simplicity, declarativeness, rigor*, etc.

3.3 Comparing the Goals

As is apparent from the foregoing discussion, there is a great deal of overlap between the goals for linguistic theory and the strategies for the design of NLP systems. For instance, both require formalisms that are rigorous and preferably declarative, and that allow simple and elegant formulation of grammars. The main differences are found in their view of whether expressivity should be constrained or promoted.

Linguistic-theory design is characterized by a dialectic counterposing completeness and restrictiveness. In NLP, the dialectic is between generality, on the one hand, and the constraints of computational effectiveness and practical felicity, on the other. Restrictiveness is not only not a primary goal, it is a characteristic to be avoided wherever possible. Again, consider an analogy with computer programming. If restrictiveness were a criterion in choosing a computer language for solving a problem, then someone planning to write a program to perform matrix multiplication should be attracted to a language in which only matrix multiplication programs could be written. Such an idea is patently ridiculous, for not only is such a restriction unnecessary, but the process of changing, augmenting, and maintaining programs practically guarantees that today's matrix multiplication program will be tomorrow's general statistical package. Similarly, choosing a grammar formalism because it is restrictive hobbles a grammar writer during the inevitable period of debugging, changing, rewriting and maintaining grammars. Unless one believes that linguists have designed the ultimately correct formalism and that grammar writers never make mistakes in its application, it is merely bad engineering to choose a restrictive formalism for restrictiveness' sake.

Thus, insofar as possible, those aspects of linguistic formalisms that support rigor, declarativeness, and linguistic felicity should be incorporated into NLP. However, those aspects of the formalisms that are geared towards restrictiveness should be eschewed--*unless*, of course, they provide auxiliary benefit by improving computational efficiency or simplifying analyses. Finally, aspects of the formalisms designed to aid the goal of completeness may or may not be pertinent to NLP, depending on the weakness of the particular application's completeness requirement.

Some examples of this sort of reasoning are in order. Certain particular formal constraints in the linguistic theories may be detrimental in a formalism for NLP if their inclusion decreases the expressivity of the formalism without serving to simplify analyses. For instance, the functional locality principle of LFG falls into this class. By requiring that "designators in lexical and grammatical schemata may specify no more than two function-applications" [3, p. 278], the generality of the formalism is reduced in such a way that grammars become more, not less, complex. I am not arguing here against this formal restriction as a grammatical universal, but only against its inclusion as a device in NLP systems.

On the other hand, the head feature convention (HFC) of GPSG might be usefully added to an NLP formalism on the grounds that it makes the job of grammar writing simpler. It is no coincidence that typical implementations of LFG do not include functional locality, whereas those of GPSG do include the HFC. Ideally, however, we would want an even more general formalism--one in which the head feature convention or similar devices could be stated as a formal construct, as Martin Kay has argued for FUG.

4. HOW: SEPARATING ANALYSES FROM FORMALISMS

Thus, we see that the goals of NLP and LT, though sharing many factors, nevertheless differ in certain key places, especially as regards the notion of restrictiveness. Since the constraints and restrictions in LT play such an important role, this brings us back to the question of how separable the analyses in the theories are from their theoretical and formal commitments. Is there a way of expressing such analyses in a formal language that is more consonant with the goals of NLP, less restrictive, simpler, more flexible? Reviewing the previous argument, the displaying of notational reductions from one formalism to another gives us a tool for deciding such questions. In this section I will discuss several such reductions which can shed light on the question of which aspects of analyses are separable from particular formalisms and at what cost. These are the results of some research being carried out by a group at the Center for the Study of Language and Information, in which I have been participating, to find such reductions and their properties. The project is an attempt to extract and compare the main ideas in the various formalisms, theories, and analyses. To facilitate this enterprise, I will make use of certain formalisms that are not part of any linguistic theory--namely FUG and PATR. These formalisms are quite simple and expressive, and thus serve ideally as both targets and sources of reductions. Though FUG and PATR were designed from the outset to be tools satisfying some of the goals of NLP rather than those of linguistic theory, the reductions in which they are involved do *not* show, nor are they intended to show, that the analyses can be stated in a formalism appropriate for an NLP system. Rather, they merely open up this abstract possibility by demonstrating that analyses can often, in principle at least, be separated from the formalisms in which they are traditionally stated.

It is also important to note that the research outlined here is necessarily programmatic to a great extent. Proving the correctness of a reduction of one formal system to another--Turing machines to Post machines, say--is only possible because the *meaning* of a Turing or Post machine program (i.e. a specification of its behavior) is well-defined by virtue of an explicit semantics for the machines. The grammar formalisms used in linguistics for the most part have never been given precise semantics. Indeed, of the languages discussed here, only PATR has had a mathematical semantics defined for it [12]. Therefore, we must rely on intuitive understandings of the semantics of these complex formalisms to convince ourselves of the correctness of the reductions. Since without a precise semantics, many facets of the interpretation of the formalisms are left to judgment, this program of reducing one formalism to another is prone to difficulties. Nonetheless, as the following sections should demonstrate, much useful information can be gleaned from these attempts, despite their frailties, even if the results can never be as rigorous as we might like.

The chart in Figure 3 summarizes the reductions that are at least currently proposed. I will give a brief overview of results for these reductions without presenting the reductions themselves. The claims in this section will be substantiated by a case study exemplifying the type of analysis and conclusions that this research leads to; to this end, I will present one of the reductions, that from $GPSG_F$ to PATR, in greater detail in Section 4.2. Throughout these sections, I will assume a familiarity with all of the formalisms mentioned so far.

4.1 An Overview of Some Reductions

4.1.1 PATR and FUG

I start with the reductions between PATR and FUG because these are the simplest of the reductions, yet they provide a good example of the role reductions can play in clarifying the differences among formalisms and theories.

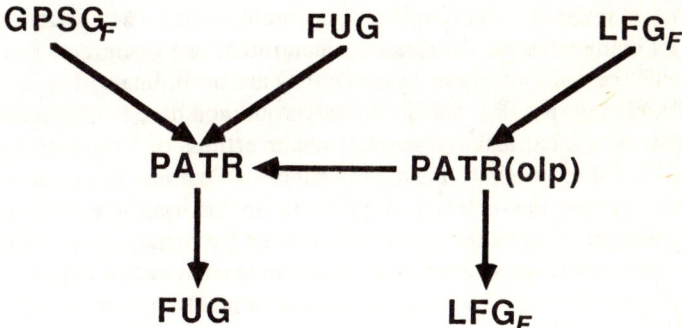

olp = off-line parsable

Figure 3: Proposed Reductions

PATR grammars use rules that simultaneously constrain string concatenation and directed-graph unifications. They can be viewed as FUG grammars with the following properties:

- They are in disjunctive normal form.

- No embedded *cset* features are allowed.

- No embedded *pattern* features are allowed.

- All values of the *pattern* features are of the following simple form: a sequence of *cset* elements.

This observation can be used as the basis of a simple notational reduction from PATR to FUG. The reduction thus engendered is *nonoptimal*, in the sense that it does not make full use of the FUG notation. It is this difference in expressivity that is exploited in the ability to implement (relatively) efficient parsers for PATR. The reduction is also *linear*, in the sense that the FUG grammar is related linearly in size to the PATR grammar. Finally, the reduction is itself declarative, in the sense that it can be stated independently of a procedure for building an FUG rule from a PATR rule.

In the reverse direction, any FUG can be converted to a PATR grammar by converting it to disjunctive normal form and somehow dealing with the special *ANY* values that FUG allows as existential constraints. The question of *ANY* values, along with constraint equations in general, will be touched upon again later. For the moment, I merely note that PATR is expressive enough to model them indirectly through a reduction that is not particularly perspicuous or attractive. This is thus a clue that *ANY* values constitute a true notional difference between the formalisms. The conversion to disjunctive normal form, it should be mentioned, is not a linear transformation; it is in fact exponential [1, 14, 15]. Thus, the difficulty in reducing FUG to PATR relative to the converse reduction lends support to the intuitive conclusion that PATR is a notational subset of FUG. Note that this conclusion holds even in the face of the formal equivalence of the two formalisms (since they are both Turing-equivalent).

4.1.2 LFG$_F$ and PATR

The LFG$_F$ formalism is a unification-based formalism quite similar to PATR in its overall design, though with certain extra devices and at least two additional well-defined formal constraints. It is not surprising, therefore, that most of the PATR formalism can be directly reduced to LFG. The main problems arise in overcoming the constraints of *off-line parsability*[10] [13] and *functional locality*. The former is provably impossible, in that the constraint diminishes the generative capacity (i.e. absolute expressivity) of LFG to a level below that of PATR. The use of extra features, however, allows PATR grammars to be reduced in such a way that functional locality is observed. Thus, off-line-parsable PATR grammars can be translated into LFG quite simply.

The reverse reduction, i.e., reducing LFG grammars to PATR, is more difficult because such extensions as set values, disjunction, negation, semantic forms, functional completeness, and constraint equations need to be modeled. I will briefly discuss only the latter three devices here as disjunction has been mentioned previously and the semantics of negation and set values is sufficiently complex and indeterminate that much further work is required. Semantic forms are easily modeled with the standard PATR logical-form encoding. Constraint equations have been shown by Kelly Roach to be reducible to *ANY* values. Functional completeness can be modeled with *ANY* as well. Perhaps more surprisingly, Mark Johnson has demonstrated that both *ANY* values and constraint equations in general can be modeled in a purely monotonic system such as PATR. The reduction, as mentioned before, is reasonably complex and obscure, involving modeling a "memory" within the feature structures using unification, and replacing certain constraints with "assignments" to the memory.[11]

Similar arguments show that many aspects of LFG are directly embeddable within the PATR formalism. But the fact that the encoding of constraint equations and *ANY* is difficult, even though both are easily interreducible, points to another important notion in these grammar

---

[10] The constraint of off-line parsability disallows LFG$_F$ grammars whose context-free base admits derivations of the form $A => ^+ A$ for some nonterminal A.

[11] These results are at present unpublished. They have been presented at meetings of the Foundations of Grammar group at CSLI.

formalisms that is missing in PATR--the notion of nonmonotonic modes of combining information. Once again, the technique of reducing grammar formalisms has yielded an observation about what is notionally important in the formalisms.

4.2 A Case Study: GPSG$_F$ and PATR

As a case study of the detailed analysis of a formalism through the development of notational reductions, I will consider in greater detail a reduction from the GPSG$_F$ formalism to PATR.[12] I demonstrate that reductions can provide not only a more abstract understanding of the underlying ideas in the formalism, but can also lead to a simplification of the formalism's semantics. Readers uninterested in the technical details of the reduction should proceed to Section 4.2.4.

4.2.1 Overview

Like the other linguistic theories discussed here, the theory of generalized phrase structure grammar has described language axiomatically, that is, as a set of universal and language-specific constraints on the well-formedness of linguistic elements of some sort. In the case of GPSG, these elements are trees whose nodes are themselves structured entities from a domain of *categories* (a type of *feature structure* [17]). The proposed axioms have become quite complex, culminating in the ambitious recent volume by Gazdar, Klein, Pullum, and Sag entitled *Generalized Phrase Structure Grammar* [9] (henceforth GKPS). The coverage and detailed analysis of English grammar in this work are impressive, in part because of the complexity of the axiomatic system developed by the authors.

I examine the possibility that simpler descriptions of the same theory can be achieved through a slightly different, albeit still axiomatic, method. Rather than characterize the well-formed trees axiomatically, we progress in two stages by procedurally characterizing the well-formedness axioms themselves, which in turn characterize the trees; this characterization is given by a reduction procedure that converts GPSG grammars into

---

[12] This section is derived from an earlier paper on simplifying GPSG through compilation into PATR [18].

grammars written in the PATR formalism.[13] PATR has its own declarative semantics, and can therefore be viewed as an axiomatization of string well-formedness constraints.

The characterization of GPSG thus obtained is simpler and better defined than the version described by GKPS. The semantics of the formalism is given directly through the reduction to PATR. Also, the PATR axiomatization has a clear constructive interpretation, unlike that used in GKPS, thus making the system more amenable to computational implementation. Finally, as we have mentioned previously, the characteristics of the reduction--the difficulty or ease with which the various devices can be encoded in PATR--can provide a measure of the relative expressiveness and indispensability of these devices.

4.2.2 The GPSG Axioms

A Summary of the Principles

GPSG describes natural languages in terms of various types of constraints on local sets of nodes in trees. Pertinent to the ensuing discussion are the following:

- ID (immediate dominance) rules, which state constraints of *immediate dominance* among categories;

- metarules, which state generalizations concerning classes of ID rules;

- LP (linear precedence) rules, which constrain the linear order of sibling categories;

- feature cooccurrence restrictions (FCR), which constrain the feature structures as to which are permissible categories;

---

[13] However, a caveat is in order. A detailed analysis from this perspective of linear precedence (LP) rules, and feature cooccurrence restrictions is not discussed fully here, nor do I completely understand them. (See Section 4.2.3.) While in a confessional mood, I should add that the algorithm given here has not actually been implemented.

> – feature specification defaults (FSD), which provide values for features that are otherwise unspecified;

and, most importantly,

> – universal feature instantiation principles, which constrain the allowable local sets of nodes in trees; these feature instantiation principles include the head feature convention (HFC), the foot feature principle (FFP), and the control agreement principle (CAP).

In GPSG all of these constraints are applied simultaneously. A local set of nodes in a tree is admissible under the constraints if and only if there is some base or derived ID rule (which we will call the *licensing rule*) for which the parent node's category is an extension of the left-hand-side category in the rule, and the children are respective extensions of right-hand-side categories in the rule, and, in addition, the set of nodes simultaneously satisfies all of the separate feature instantiation principles, ordering constraints, etc. By *extension*, we mean that the constituent has all the feature values of the corresponding category in the licensing rule, and possibly some additional feature values. The former type of value is called *inherited*, the latter *instantiated*.

The feature instantiation principles are typically of the following form: if a certain feature configuration holds of a local set of nodes, then some other configuration must also be present. For instance, the antecedent of the control agreement principle is stated in terms of the existence of a *controller* and *controllee*, which notions are themselves defined in terms of feature configurations. The consequent concerns identity of agreement features.

Interaction of Principles

Much care is taken in the definitions of the feature instantiation principles (and their ancillary notions such as controller, controllee, free features, privileged features, etc.) to control the complex interaction of the various constraints. For instance, the FFP admits local sets of nodes with *slash* feature values on parent and child where no such values occur in the licensing ID rule, i.e., it allows *instantiation of slash features*. But the CAP's aforementioned definition of control is sensitive to the value of the *slash* feature associated with the various constituents. A simple definition of the CAP would ignore the source of the slash value, whether inherited, instantiated by the FFP, or instantiated in some other manner. However, the appropriate definition of control needed for the CAP must ignore *instantiated* slash features, but not *inherited* ones. According to GKPS:

> We must modify the definition of control in such a way that it ignores perturbations of semantic type occasioned by the presence of instantiated *FOOT* features. [9, p. 87]

Thus, the CAP is in some sense blind to the work of the FFP. As GKPS note, this requirement makes stating the CAP a much more complex task.

The increased complexity of the principles resulting from this need for tracking the origins of feature values is evident not only in the CAP, but in the other principles as well. The head feature convention requires identity of the head features of parent and head child. The features *agr* and *slash*--features that can be inherited from an ID rule or instantiated by the CAP or FFP, respectively--are head features and therefore potentially subject to this identity condition. However, great care is taken to remove such instantiated head features from obligatory manipulation by the HFC. This is accomplished by limiting the scope of the HFC to the so-called *free* head features.

> Intuitively, the *free* feature specifications on a category [the ones the HFC is to apply to] is the set of feature specifications which can legitimately appear on extensions of that category: feature specifications which conflict with what is already part of the category, either directly, or in virtue of the FCRs, FFP, or CAP, are not *free* on that category. [9, p. 95]

That is, the FFP and CAP take precedence (intuitively viewed) over the HFC.

Finally, all three principles are seen to take precedence over feature specification defaults in the following quotation:

> In general, a feature is exempt from assuming its default specification if it has been assigned a different value in virtue of some ID rule or some principle of feature instantiation. [9, p. 100]

GKPS accomplish this by defining a class of *privileged* features and excluding such features from the requirement that they assume their default value. Of course, instantiated head features, slash features, and so forth are all considered privileged. However, a modification of these exemptions is necessary in the case of lexical defaults, i.e., default values instantiated on lexical constituents. I will not discuss here the rather idiosyncratic motivation for this distinction, but merely note that lexical-constituent defaults are to be insensitive to changes engendered by the HFC, as revealed in this excerpt:

> However, this simpler formulation is inadequate since it entails that lexical heads will always be exempt from defaults that relate to their HEAD features. ... Accordingly, the final clause needs to distinguish lexical categories, which become exempt from a default only if they covary with a sister, and nonlexical categories, which become exempt from a default if they covary (in relevant respects) with *any* other category in the tree. [9, p. 103]

Thus, the interaction of these principles is controlled through complex definitions of the various classes of features they are applicable to. These definitions conspire to engender the following implicit precedence ordering on the principles;[14] principles earlier in the ordering are blind to the instantiations from later principles, which are themselves sensitive to (and exempt from applying to) features instantiated by the earlier principles.[15]

$$CAP > FFP > FSD_{lex} > HFC > FSD_{nonlex}$$

Of course, all ID rules, both base and derived, are subject to all these principles; yet metarule application is not contingent on instantiations of the base ID rules. Conversely, LP constraints are sensitive to the full

---

[14] Current efforts by at least certain GPSG practitioners are placing the GPSG type of analysis directly in a PATR-like formalism. This formalism, Pollard's head-driven phrase structure grammar (HPSG) variant of GPSG, uses a run-time algorithm similar to the one described in this paper. Highly suggestive is the fact that the HPSG run-time algorithm also happens to order the principles in substantially the same way.

[15] We use the symbol > to denote one principle "taking precedence over" another.

range of instantiated features. The precedence ordering can thus be extended as follows:

$$\text{META} > \text{CAP} > \text{FFP} > \text{FSD}_{lex} > \text{HFC} > \text{FSD}_{nonlex} > \text{LP}$$

The existence of such an ordering on the priority of axioms is of course not a necessary condition for the coherence of such an axiomatic theory. Undoubtedly, this inherent ordering was not apparent to the developers of the theory; its existence may even be the source of some surprise to them. Yet, the fact that such an ordering does exist and is strict leads us to a substantial simplification of the system. Instead of applying all the constraints simultaneously, we might do so sequentially, so that the precedence ordering--the blindness of earlier principles in the ordering to the effects of later ones--emerges simply because the later principles have not yet applied.

This solution harkens back to earlier versions of GPSG in which the semantics of the formalism was stated in terms of compiling the various principles and constraints into pure context-free rules. This compilation process can be combinatorially explosive, yielding vast numbers of context-free rules. Indeed, the whole point of the GPSG decomposition is to succinctly express generalizations about the possible phrasal combinations of natural languages. However, by carefully choosing a system for stating constraints on local sets of nodes--a formalism more compact in its representation than context-free grammars--we can compile out the various principles and constraints without risking this explosion in practice.[16]

The GPSG principles are stated in terms of identities of features. If we are to avoid the combinatorial problems of pure CF rules, we must have a formalism in which such equalities can be stated directly, without generating all the ground instances that satisfy the equalities. What is needed, in fact, is a unification-based grammar formalism [17]. As stated previously, I will use a variant of PATR [16] as the formalism into which GPSG grammars are compiled. In particular, I assume a version of PATR that has been extended by the familiar technique of decomposition into an immediate-dominance and linear-precedence component. This will allow us to ignore the LP portion of GPSG for the nonce.

---

[16] Of course, even this compilation technique is exponential in the worst case.

PATR is ideal for two reasons. First, it is the simplest of the unification-based grammar formalisms, possessing only the apparatus that is needed for this exercise. Second, a semantics for the formalism has been provided, so that, by displaying this compilation, we implicitly provide a semantics for GPSG grammars as well.

4.2.3 The Compilation Algorithm

I postpone for the time being discussion of the metarules, LP constraints, and feature cooccurrence restrictions, concentrating instead on the central principles of GPSG, those relating to feature instantiation. The following nondeterministic algorithm generates well-formed PATR rules from GPSG ID rules. A GPSG grammar is compiled into the set of PATR rules generated by this algorithm.

Preliminaries

First, observe that a GPSG ID rule is only notationally distinct from an *unordered* PATR rule. Thus, the first step in the algorithm is trivial. For example, the ID rule

$$S \rightarrow X^2; H[-subj] \tag{R_1}$$

is written in unordered PATR as

$$\begin{aligned}
X_0 &\rightarrow X_1, X_2 \\
&\langle X_0\ n \rangle = - \\
&\langle X_0\ v \rangle = + \\
&\langle X_0\ bar \rangle = 2 \\
&\langle X_0\ subj \rangle = + \\
&\langle X_1\ bar \rangle = 2 \\
&\langle X_2\ subj \rangle = -
\end{aligned} \tag{R_2}$$

Note that abbreviations (like S for $[-n; +v; bar2; +subj]$) have been made explicit.

In fact, we will make one change in the structure of categories (to simplify our restatement of the HFC) by placing all head features under the single feature *head* in the corresponding PATR rule. We do not, however, add an analogous feature *foot*.[17] Thus, the preceding rule

---

[17] But recall that *slash* is a head feature and thus would fall under the path <*head*

becomes

$$X_0 \rightarrow X_1, X_2$$
$$\langle X_0 \text{ head } n \rangle = -$$
$$\langle X_0 \text{ head } v \rangle = +$$
$$\langle X_0 \text{ head bar} \rangle = 2$$
$$\langle X_0 \text{ head subj} \rangle = +$$
$$\langle X_1 \text{ head bar} \rangle = 2$$
$$\langle X_2 \text{ head subj} \rangle = - \tag{R_3}$$

We use an operation add_c (read "add conservatively"), which adds an equation to a PATR rule conservatively, in the sense that the equation is added only if the equations are not thereby rendered unsolvable. If addition would cause unsolvability, a weaker *set* of unifications is added (conservatively) instead--one for each feature in the domain of the value being equated. For instance, suppose that the operation add_c ($\langle X_0 \text{ head} \rangle = \langle X_1 \text{ head} \rangle$) is called for, where the domain of the head feature values (i.e., the various head features) consists of the features a, b, and c. If the equations in the rule already specify that $\langle X_0 \text{ head } a \rangle \neq \langle X_1 \text{ head } a \rangle$, then this operation would add only the two equations $\langle X_0 \text{ head } b \rangle = \langle X_1 \text{ head } b \rangle$ and $\langle X_0 \text{ head } c \rangle = \langle X_1 \text{ head } c \rangle$, since addition of the given equation itself would cause rule failure. Thus, the earlier constraint of values for the a feature is given precedence over the constraint to be added.

In the description of the algorithm, a nonempty path p is said to be defined for a feature structure X if and only if p is a unit path $\langle f \rangle$ and $f \in dom(X)$ or $p = \langle f p' \rangle$ and p' is defined for $X(f)$. Our notion of a feature's being defined for a constituent corresponds to the GPSG concepts of being instantiated or of covarying with some other feature.

As in the previous definition, we will be quite lax with respect to our notation for paths, using $\langle \langle a \ b \rangle \ c \rangle$ and $\langle a \ \langle b \ c \rangle \rangle$ as synonymous with $\langle a \ b \ c \rangle$. Also, we will consistently blur the distinction between a set of equations and the feature structure it determines.[18]

---

slash>.

[18] See my paper [19] for details of the mapping that makes this possible.

The Algorithm Itself

Now our algorithm for compiling a GPSG grammar into a PATR grammar follows:

For each ID rule of GPSG (basic or derived by metarule) $X_0 \rightarrow X_1,...,X_n$:

CAP If X_i controls X_j (determined by $Type(X_i)$ and $Type(X_j)$), then add_c ($<X_i\ con> = <X_j\ con>$), where

$$con = \begin{cases} <head\ slash> & \text{if } <head\ slash> \text{ is defined for } X_i \\ <head\ agr> & \text{otherwise} \end{cases}$$

FFP For each foot feature path p (e.g., $<head\ slash>$), if p is not defined for X_0, then $addc$ ($<X_i\ p> = <X_0\ p>$) for zero or more i such that $0 < i \leq n$ and such that p is not defined for X_i.[19]

FSD$_{lex}$ For all paths p with a default value, say, d, and for all i such that $0 < i \leq n$, if $<X_i\ bar> = 0$ and p is not defined for X_i, then add_c ($<X_i\ f> = d$).

HFC For X_i the head of X_0 and for each head feature f, add_c ($<X_i\ f> = <X_0\ f>$).

FSD$_{nonlex}$ For all paths p with a default value, say, d, and for all i such that $0 < i \leq n$, if $<X_i\ bar> \neq 0$ and p is not defined for X_i, then add_c ($<X_i\ f> = d$).

---

[19] Actually, the operation add_c is superfluous here. The equation can simply be added directly, since we have already guaranteed that the pertinent features are not yet instantiated. By a similar argument, we can conclude that only the add_c operations in the CAP and HFC are really necessary. We will use add_c, however, for uniformity. Note also that it is the FFP portion of the algorithm that is responsible for its nondeterminism.

An Example

Let us apply this algorithm to the preceding rule R_1.[20] We start with the PATR equivalent R_3. By checking the existing control relationships in this rule *as currently instantiated*, we conclude that the subject X_1 controls the head X_2. We conservatively add the unification $<X_2\ head\ agr> = <X_1>$. This can be safely added, and therefore is.

Next, the FFP step in the algorithm can instantiate the rule further. Suppose we choose to instantiate a slash feature on X_2. Then we add the equation $<X_0\ head\ slash> = <X_2\ head\ slash>$. Lexical default values require no new equations, since no constituents in the rule are given as bar level 0 at this point.

The HFC conservatively adds the equation $<X_0\ head> = <X_2\ head>$, as X_2 is the head of X_0. But this equation, as it stands, would lead to the unsolvability of the entire set of equations, since we already have conflicting values for the head feature *subj*. Thus, the following set of unifications is added instead:[21]

$<X_0\ head\ n> = <X_2\ head\ n>$
$<X_0\ head\ v> = <X_2\ head\ v>$
$<X_0\ head\ bar> = <X_2\ head\ bar>$
$<X_0\ head\ agr> = <X_2\ head\ agr>$
$<X_0\ head\ inv> = <X_2\ head\ inv>$
...

Finally, nonlexical defaults are introduced for features not in the domains of constituents.[22] Since the path $<head\ inv>$ is defined for the constituents X_0 and X_2,[23] the default value (i.e., '.-' according to FSD 1 in

---

[20] We do not include here the effect of the rule on every feature postulated by GKPS but only a representative sample.

[21] A more efficient representation of such sets could be achieved by the introduction of nonmonotonic operations such as overwriting or priority union. But such notational efficiency considerations need not concern us here.

[22] I have made the simplifying assumption that feature specification defaults are stated in terms of simple default values for features, rather than the more complex boolean conditions used in the GKPS text. The modifications to allow the more complex FSDs are probably complex leading to an exponential nondeterminism in this phase of compilation.

[23] The value of the feature *head* on the constituent X_0 has the feature *inv* in its domain because the unification $<X_0\ head\ inv> = <X_2\ head\ inv>$ gives as value to $<X_0\ head\ inv>$

GKPS) is not instantiated on either constituent. Similarly, the *case* default value (*acc*, FSD 10) is not instantiated on the subject NP. But the *conj* feature default[24] ('~') will be instantiated on all three constituents with the equations

$$\langle X_0 \; conj \rangle = \sim$$
$$\langle X_1 \; conj \rangle = \sim$$
$$\langle X_2 \; conj \rangle = \sim$$

The (partial) generated rule is the following:

$$X_0 \rightarrow X_1, X_2$$
$$\langle X_0 \; head \; n \rangle = -$$
$$\langle X_0 \; head \; v \rangle = +$$
$$\langle X_0 \; head \; bar \rangle = 2$$
$$\langle X_0 \; head \; subj \rangle = +$$
$$\langle X_1 \; head \; bar \rangle = 2$$
$$\langle X_2 \; head \; subj \rangle = -$$
$$\langle X_2 \; head \; agr \rangle = \langle X_1 \rangle$$
$$\langle X_0 \; head \; slash \rangle = \langle X_2 \; head \; slash \rangle$$
$$\langle X_0 \; head \; n \rangle = \langle X_2 \; head \; n \rangle$$
$$\langle X_0 \; head \; v \rangle = \langle X_2 \; head \; v \rangle$$
$$\langle X_0 \; head \; bar \rangle = \langle X_2 \; head \; bar \rangle$$
$$\langle X_0 \; head \; agr \rangle = \langle X_2 \; head \; agr \rangle$$
$$\langle X_0 \; head \; inv \rangle = \langle X_2 \; head \; inv \rangle$$
...
$$\langle X_0 \; conj \rangle = \sim$$
$$\langle X_1 \; conj \rangle = \sim$$
$$\langle X_2 \; conj \rangle = \sim$$
...

(R₁)

---

a variable, the same variable as the value for $\langle X_2 \; head \; inv \rangle$. Thus, the path $.\langle head \; inv \rangle$ is defined for X_0 and, similarly, for X_2.

[24] I assume here, contra GKPS, that '~' is a full-fledged value in its own right, at least as interpreted in this compilation. Since this value fails to unify with any other, e.g., '+' or ' ', it has exactly the behavior desired, namely, that the feature is prohibited from taking any of its standard values.

Problems and Extensions

Several problems have been glossed over in the previous discussion. First, I have not mentioned the role of LP rules. Two possibilities are available for their interpretation: a "run-time" and a "compile-time" interpretation. We can augment the PATR formalism with LP rules in the same way as GKPS, providing for local sets of nodes to satisfy an ID PATR rule if and only if the nodes are extensions of elements in the ID rule such that the LP rules are all satisfied. Alternatively, we can generate at compile time all possible rule linearizations compatible with the LP statements, but this leads us into the problem of interpreting LP statements relative to partially instantiated categories, an issue beyond the scope of this paper.

Second, feature cooccurrence restrictions were ignored in the previous discussion. One alternative is to modify the lattice of categories relative to which unification is defined[25] in such a way that all categories violating the FCRs are simply removed. Then unification over this revised lattice would be used instead of the simpler version and FCRs will automatically always be obeyed. Unfortunately, the possibility exists that unification over the revised lattice may not bear the same order-independence properties that characterize unification over the freely generated lattice. Of course, if this turned out to be the case, it would cast doubt on the well-foundedness of the original GKPS interpretation of FCRs as well, and thus is an interesting question to pursue.

Another alternative involves checking the FCRs at every point in the algorithm, throwing out any rules which violate them at any point. In addition, FCRs would be required to be checked during run time as well. This alternative, though more direct, violates the spirit of the enterprise of giving a compilation from the complex GKPS formulation to a simpler system.

A final problem concerns the ordering of the HFC and the CAP. The definitions of controller and controllee necessary for stating the CAP depend on the assignment of semantic types to constituents, which in turn depend on the configuration of features in the categories. We have already noted that the features pertinent to the definition of semantic type

---

[25] For the technical background of such a move, see the discussion by Pereira and me [13].

(and hence control) do not include instantiated foot features. Indeed, GKPS claim that "it is just HEAD feature specifications (other than those which are also FOOT feature specifications) and inherited FOOT feature specifications that determine the semantic types relevant to the definition of control" [9, p. 87]. Unfortunately, the ordering we have given precludes instantiated head features from participating in the definition of semantic type and hence in the CAP.[26] It seems that the HFC must apply before the CAP for the definition of semantic type, but after the CAP so that the CAP instantiations of head features take precedence. Thus, our earlier claim of strict ordering may be falsified by this case.

However, the class of head features necessary for type determination and the class that must be instantiated after the FFP are disjoint. This can be seen from the parenthetical comment in the previous quotation. Consequently, we can merely split the application of the HFC in two, instantiating the former class before the CAP and the latter class after the FFP, as originally described. Alternatively, it might be possible merely to notate head features on the head constituent rather than on the parent as is conventionally done. In this case, the information needed by the CAP consists of inherited, not instantiated, head feature values, and is thus not subject to the ordering problem.

On the other hand, if the sets had not been disjoint, this would have presented a problem for our algorithmic analysis, though not necessarily for the definition of GPSG given by GKPS. Suppose that the HFC determines types in such a way that the CAP is required to apply and it instantiates head features thereby overriding the original values (since the CAP takes precedence) and changing the type determination so that the CAP does not apply. We would thus require the CAP to apply if and only if it does not apply. This paradox would appear as an ordering cycle in our algorithm.

4.2.4 Conclusion

The axiomatic formulation of generalized phrase structure grammar by GKPS is a quite subtle and complex system. Yet, as we have shown, GPSG grammars can be substantially converted to grammars in a simpler,

---

[26] I am indebted to Roger Evans ans William Keller for pointing this problem out to me and for helpful discussion of alternative solutions.

and constructive, axiomatic system through a straightforward (albeit procedural) mapping. Intrinsic in this conversion is the use of a unification-based grammar formalism, so that axioms can be stated schematically, without enumerating all of their possible instantiations. In fact, we would contend that defining the semantics of a GPSG grammar in this way yields a much simpler formulation. The need for such a reconstruction is evident to anyone who has studied the GKPS text.

Furthermore, the characteristics of the reduction--for instance, the location of nondeterminism in the compilation algorithm and the complexity of that nondeterminism--provides a measure of the relative notational expressivity of the formalisms. The exponentiality of metarule compilation and the pervasive nature of FCRs, for example, indicate that exactly those portions of $GPSG_F$ are truly essential for stating certain analyses, i.e., that analyses using those formal devices do so necessarily.

5. SUMMARY

These arguments are not proofs of the equivalence of formalisms. Rather, they are informal demonstrations that some of the formalisms commonly employed in linguistics today share key concepts. To the extent that this is so, analyses from one formalism can be stated within another. For instance, the type of subcategorization analysis applied in many PATR grammars and used exclusively by HPSG, involving lexical encoding of complements in terms of lists of complements rather than sets of grammatical functions, could be embedded within the LFG_F formalism or FUG. Similarly, LFG-style analyses based on the lexical encoding of subcategorization with grammatical functions are easily embeddable in FUG or in PATR augmented with some nonmonotonic device (but less easily without one); furthermore, we learn that the choice of nonmonotonic device is not particularly critical.

Once this view of the mutual independence of analysis and formalism takes hold, we can start looking for the key ideas that are shared across analyses, across formalisms, and across theories, ideas which allow for simple reduction of one formalism to another. Such shared ideas include the structuring of expressions and association of expressions with partial information, constraints of equality over information structures, lexical encoding of phrasal combinatorics, and so forth. Conversely, those devices that engender complex reductions can be pinpointed as important notional extensions, and can be investigated in the abstract, independent of their instantiation in a particular formalism. As we have seen, notions such as disjunction, various nonmonotonic types of constraints, and complex constraints such as feature cooccurrence restrictions are examples of devices that engender intrinsic differences among the formalisms.

These reductions demonstrate that analyses from many current linguistic theories all share basic properties. This commonality shows a remarkable convergence of syntactic theories, echoed in the similarity of their associated formalisms. Certainly, NLP systems should take advantage of this convergence, especially as they are thereby enabled to use analyses from any and all of the theories.

6. PREVENTING SOME MISCONCEPTIONS

In an attempt to forestall certain inevitable questions concerning the points made in this paper, I would like to mention certain misconceptions to be avoided.

First of all, linguists might complain that I am ascribing too much significance to the notion of formalism in linguistic theory. On the contrary, by precisely delimiting the role formalisms play in furthering the goals of linguistic theory (for instance, by means of notational reductions) I believe that this work has demonstrated that differences among the various formalisms are considerably less than is commonly thought. In this sense, the research seems to put formalisms in their proper place, as particular notations for very general ideas that transcend the formalisms themselves.

Second, I would like to make it clear that I am not recommending PATR (or FUG for that matter) as a formalism in which to write LFG grammars or GPSG grammars. PATR is an egregious notation for LFG compared to LFG_F. In fact, the pure PATR formalism was never intended to serve as a formalism in which a grammar writer actually composes any kind of grammar at all.

> Clearly, the bare PATR-II formalism ... is sorely inadequate for any major attempt at building natural-language grammars ... . However, given a simple underlying formalism, we can build more efficient, specialized languages on top of it, much as MACLISP might be built on top of pure LISP. And just as MACLISP need not be implemented (and is not implemented) directly in pure LISP, specialized formalisms built conceptually on top of pure PATR-II need not be so implemented. [16, p. 364]

Thus PATR is playing the same role here as kernel languages in computer science. Cardelli and Wegner have summarized the idea nicely:

> Although we have used a unified language throughout the paper, we have not presented a language design. In language design there are many important issues to be solved concerning readability, ease of use, etc. which we have not directly attacked. We propose [the unified language] as a framework to classify and compare existing languages. We do not propose it as a programming language, as it may be clumsy in many areas, but it could be the basis of one. [4, p. 41]

The claim here is that very general languages like PATR or FUG can serve as the bases of particular computer languages for encoding linguistic information--languages that can employ analyses from different syntactic theories. Furthermore, the conflicting goals of linguistic theory and natural-language processing make such an enterprise eminently desirable. Finally, research in this area can help to elucidate theoretical questions from linguistics concerning the true nature of constraints in theories, to determine whether they inhere in the formalism or require substantive restrictions.

REFERENCES

1. Barton, G. Edward, Robert C. Berwick and Eric Sven Ristad. Agreement and Ambiguity In *Computational Complexity and Natural Language*. MIT Press, Cambridge, Massachusetts, 1987.

2. Robert Berwick and Amy Weinberg. *The Grammatical Basis of Linguistic Performance: Language Use and Acquisition.* MIT Press, Cambridge, Massachusetts, 1984.
3. Joan Bresnan, editor. *The Mental Representation of Grammatical Relations.* MIT Press, Cambridge, Massachusetts, 1982.
4. Luca Cardelli and Peter Wegner. Understanding types, data abstraction and polymorphism. Draft paper, 1985.
5. Noam Chomsky. *Aspects of the Theory of Syntax.* MIT Press, Cambridge, Massachusetts, 1965.
6. Noam Chomsky. *Lectures on Government and Binding.* Foris Publications, Dordrecht, Holland, 1982.
7. Steven Fortune, Daniel Leivant, and Michael O'Donnell. *The Expressiveness of Simple and Second Order Type Structures.* Research Report RC 8542, IBM Thomas J. Watson Research Center, Yorktown Heights, New York, 1980.
8. Gerald Gazdar. *Phrase Structure Grammar,* pages 131-186. D. Reidel, Dordrecht, Holland, 1982.]
9. Gerald Gazdar, Ewan Klein, Geoffrey K. Pullum, and Ivan A. Sag. *Generalized Phrase Structure Grammar.* Blackwell Publishing, Oxford, England, and Harvard University Press, Cambridge, Massachusetts, 1985.
10. Ronald Kaplan. Personal communication, 1985.
11. Martin Kay. *Unification Grammar.* Technical Report, Xerox Palo Alto Research Center, Palo Alto, California, 1983.
12. Fernando C. N. Pereira and Stuart M. Shieber. The semantics of grammar formalisms seen as computer languages. In *Proceedings of the Tenth International Conference on Computational Linguistics,* Stanford University, Stanford, California, 2-7 July 1984.
13. Fernando C. N. Pereira and David H. D. Warren. Parsing as deduction. In *Proceedings of the 21st Annual Meeting of the Association for Computational Linguistics,* pages 137-144, Massachusetts Institute of Technology, Cambridge, Massachusetts, 15-17 June 1983.
14. Ritchie, Graeme. The Computational Complexity of Sentence Derivation in Functional Unification Grammar. In *Proceedings of the 11th International Conference on Computational Linguistics,* pages 584-586, University of Bonn, Bonn, West-Germany, August 1986.
15. William C. Rounds and Robert Kasper. A Complete Logical Calculus for Record Structures Representing Linguistic Information. In *Proceedings of the 15th Annual Symposium on Logic in Computer Science,* Massachusetts Institute of Technology, Cambridge, Massachussetts, June 1986.
16. Stuart M. Shieber. The design of a computer language for linguistic information. In *Proceedings of the Tenth International Conference on Computational Linguistics,* Stanford University, Stanford, California, 2-7 July 1984.
17. Stuart M. Shieber. *An Introduction to Unification-Based Approaches to Grammar.* Volume 4 of Lecture Note Series, Center for the Study of Language and Information, Stanford, California, 1986.
18. Stuart M. Shieber. A simple reconstruction of GPSG. *In Proceedings of the 11th International Conference on Computational Linguistics,* University of Bonn, Bonn, West Germany, 25-29 August 1986.
19. Stuart M. Shieber. Using restriction to extend parsing algorithms for complex-feature-based formalisms. In *Proceedings of the 22nd Annual Meeting of the Association for Computational Linguistics,* University of Chicago, Chicago, Illinois, July 1985.
20. Patrick H. Winston and Karen A. Prendergast. *The AI Business: Commercial Uses of Artificial Intelligence.* MIT Press, Cambridge, Massachusetts, 1984.

GERALD GAZDAR

UNIVERSITY OF SUSSEX

SCHOOL OF SOCIAL SCIENCES

BRIGHTON

APPLICABILITY

OF INDEXED GRAMMARS

TO NATURAL LANGUAGES

1. INTRODUCTION*

If we take the class of context-free phrase structure grammars (CF-PSGs) and modify it so that (i) grammars are allowed to make use of finite feature systems and (ii) rules are permitted to manipulate the features in arbitrary ways, then what we end up with is equivalent to what we started out with. Suppose, however, that we take the class of context-free phrase structure grammars and modify it so that (i) grammars are allowed to employ a single designated feature that takes stacks of items drawn from some finite set as its values, and (ii) rules are permitted to

---

* This paper originates in a talk given to the Workshop on Scandinavian Syntax and the Theory of Grammar held in Trondheim in the Summer of 1982 and organized by Lars Hellan. I am indebted to Jens Erik Fenstad for drawing my attention to an error in my presentation there. A subsequent version was given to the Santa Cruz Workshop on the Mathematics of Grammars and Languages organized by Geoffrey K. Pullum in June 1985. I am grateful to Fernando Pereira, Carl Pollard, and Stuart Shieber for relevant conversations, to Bill Marsh and Geoff Pullum for their detailed comments on earlier drafts, and to Dikran Karageuzian and his colleagues for the work they did on the diagrams and figures found below. Support for work on this paper was provided by the ESRC (UK), by grants to Stanford University from the National Science Foundation (BNS-8102406) and the Sloan Foundation, by the Center for the Study of Language and Information, and by grants from the Sloan Foundation and System Development Foundation to the Center for Advanced Study in the Behavioral Sciences.

push items onto, pop items from, and copy the stack. What we end up with now is no longer equivalent to the CF-PSGs but is significantly more powerful, namely the indexed grammars (Aho, 1968). This class of grammars has been alluded to a number of times in the recent linguistic literature: by Klein (1981) in connection with nested comparative constructions, by Dahl (1982) in connection with topicalised pronouns, by Engdahl (1982) and Gazdar (1982) in connection with Scandinavian unbounded dependencies, by Huybregts (1984) and Pulman and Ritchie (1984) in connection with Dutch, by Marsh and Partee (1984) in connection with variable binding, and doubtless elsewhere as well.

Indexed grammars fall in between CF-PSGs and context-sensitive grammars in their generative capacity. Every context-free language (CFL) is an indexed language (IL), but not conversely. Thus $a^n b^n c^n$ is an IL, for example, but it is not a CFL. And every IL is a context-sensitive language, but not conversely. Until recently, there were no good arguments to suggest that the natural languages (NLs) fell outside the CFLs (see Pullum and Gazdar, 1982, for defense of this claim), but work by Culy (1985), Huybregts (1984) and Shieber (1985) does now indicate rather strongly that they do. However, no NL phenomena are known which would imply that NLs exist which fall outside the indexed class (see Gazdar and Pullum, 1985, for a survey).

Hopcroft and Ullman write that "of the many generalizations of context-free grammars that have been proposed, a class called 'indexed' appears the most natural, in that it arises in a wide variety of contexts" (1979:389). One purpose of the present paper is to make indexed grammars more accessible to linguists and computational linguists, and more directly relevant to their concerns. It assumes some passive competence in mathematical linguistics, but not very much. In accord with the purpose just mentioned, I shall present grammars informally as sets of rules, rather than as the official n-tuples. The start symbol will always be "*S*" or "*S'*" and the relevant sets of terminals, indices, and nonterminals can simply be inferred from looking at what appears in the rules.

2. THE FORM OF RULES: A STACK-ORIENTED NOTATION

In exhibiting schematic rules and trees below, I shall maintain a number of orthographic conventions: nonterminal symbols are indicated by upper case letters (*A, B, C*), terminal symbols by lower case letters (**a, b, c**), possibly empty strings of terminals and nonterminals by *W*, W_1, W_2, etc., indices by lower case italic letters (*i, j, k*), and stacks of indices by square brackets and periods ([], [..], [*i*,..]) where [*i*,..] is a stack whose topmost index is *i*, [] is an empty, and [..] is a possibly empty stack of indices. As for the rules themselves, Aho (1968) uses one notation, and Hopcroft and Ullman (1979) use another. The notation used below is essentially just a redundant, and intendedly more perspicuous, variant of that employed by Hopcroft and Ullman.

In the standard formulations, an indexed grammar can contain rules of three different sorts:

(1) i.   *A*[..]   ->   *W*[..]
    ii.   *A*[..]   ->   *B*[*i*,..]
    iii.   *A*[*i*,..]   ->   *W*[..]

I shall refer to rules that have one or other of these three forms as H&U rules. The first type of rule simply copies the stack to all nonterminal daughters. The second type of rule pushes a new index onto the stack handed down to its unique nonterminal daughter. And the third type of rule pops an index off the stack and distributes what is left to its nonterminal daughters. In the rules, *A* and *B* are nonterminal symbols (not necessarily distinct) and *W* is a string of terminal and/or nonterminal symbols. A compound symbol of the form *A*[..] means that the nonterminal *A* bears the stack [..]. A compound symbol of the form *W*[..] stands for a string of terminal and/or nonterminal symbols each nonterminal symbol of which bears the stack [..]. Terminal symbols cannot bear stacks. Thus, if *W* = *BcDe*, then *W*[..] = *B*[..]c *D*[..]e. Stacks of indices are thus associated with nonterminals and transmitted by rules. Indeed, the ILs are exactly characterised by a class of automata known as (one-way nondeterministic) nested stack automata (Aho, 1969). The indices that make up stacks are drawn from some finite vocabulary though the stacks themselves are not bounded in size. Any upper bound on the size of stacks restricts the class of grammars to the context-free class.

The types of rule shown in (1) are just those permitted in Hopcroft and Ullman's definition of the class of grammars--what I shall refer to as the standard definition. Notice that this definition (a) copies all or most of the stack to all nonterminal daughters in all rule types, and (b) restricts additions to the stack to cases where the mother category has but a single daughter. Neither aspect of the definition appears to be essential, and things are probably only done that way in order to facilitate doing proofs. Suppose we allow the rule types shown in (2) in addition to those listed in (1):

(2) i. $A[..] \to W_1[] B[..] W_2[]$
   ii. $A[..] \to W_1[] B[i,..] W_2[]$
  iii. $A[i,..] \to W_1[] B[..] W_2[]$

Rules of type (2.i) would allow the stack to be carried down onto a single nonterminal designated daughter, and rules of type (2.ii) and (2.iii) would also allow such a designated daughter to have its stack incremented or decremented, respectively. As shown in the appendix, permitting such additional rule types has no consequences for the class of languages such grammars can generate.

3. SOME EXAMPLE GRAMMARS

The best way to see how indexed grammars work is to look at an example, such as (3), which shows a grammar for $a^n b^n$.

(3) $S[..] \to a A[z,..]$
      $A[..] \to a A[a,..]$
      $A[..] \to B[..]$
      $B[a,..] \to b B[..]$
      $B[z,..] \to b$

This looks more complicated than it actually is. All it does is generate trees such as that shown in (4):

(4)
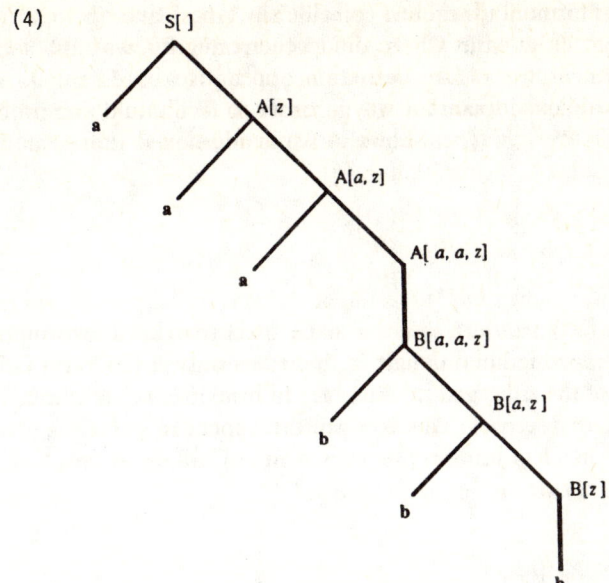

As we go down the tree, nonterminal as are produced, and index as are loaded onto the stack. When we get to the middle, signalled by the change of category from *A* to *B*, then nonterminal bs are produced, and index as are removed from the stack. The stack thus records how many nonterminal as were originally produced, and this record can then be used to produce exactly as many nonterminal bs. One slight complication is the use of the end-marker index z. This is necessary because the standard formulations of index grammars allow a non-empty stack to simply disappear if the category the stack appears on only has terminal daughters. We could avoid the need for end-marker indices of this kind by requiring that the stack distributed over daughters must be empty when every daughter is nonterminal. As shown in the appendix, such a constraint would not affect the class of languages generated, but it does simplify the formulation of certain kinds of grammar. Thus we could simplify the grammar in (3) above by replacing each occurrence of z with *a*. When I come to discuss certain abstract tree configurations later in the paper, I shall simply ignore end-marker indices.

Notice that (4) is a right-linear (and hence finite state) tree, and that

$a^n b^n$ is a CFL. This is not merely a coincidence: Aho (1968:667-669) was able to prove that exactly the CFLs could be generated down sets of left-linear or right-linear trees. Of course, since $a^n b^n$ is a CFL, we do not need to use an indexed grammar to generate it. We could generate it either with a CF-PSG or (equivalently) with an indexed grammar that made no use of indices, such as that in (5):

(5) $S[..]$ -> a $S[..]$b
       $S[..]$ -> a b

But the grammar shown in (3) has the advantage, in the present context, of illustrating how stacks of indices can be used to record information about what has happened in one part of the tree, transmit the information to another part of the tree, and then use the information to determine the form of that other tree-part. This is a powerful mechanism. Thus a very slight modification of grammar (3), shown in (6), allows $a^n b^n c^n$ to be generated, and the latter is not, of course, a CFL.

(6) $S[..]$ ->   a $A[z,..]$
       $A[..]$ ->   a $A[a,..]$
       $A[..]$ -> $B[..]$
       $B[a,..]$ ->   b $B[..]$c
       $B[z,..]$ ->   b c

A further modification, equally slight, allows us to get $a^n b^n c^n d^n$ (likewise not a CFL).

(7) $S[..]$ ->   a $A[z,..]$d
       $A[..]$ ->   a $A[a,..]$d
       $A[..]$ -> $B[..]$
       $B[a,..]$ ->   b $B[..]$c
       $B[z,..]$ ->   b c

As a final illustration, (8) shows a grammar for a simple XX language (where XX is in $\{a, b, c\}^+$).

(8) $S[..]$ -> **a** $A[x,..]$
    $S[..]$ -> **b** $A[y,..]$
    $S[..]$ -> **c** $A[z,..]$
    $A[..]$ -> **a** $A[a,..]$
    $A[..]$ -> **b** $A[b,..]$
    $A[..]$ -> **c** $A[c,..]$
    $A[..]$ -> $B[..]$
    $B[a,..]$ -> $B[..]$**a**
    $B[b,..]$ -> $B[..]$**b**
    $B[c,..]$ -> $B[..]$**c**
    $B[x,..]$ -> **a**
    $B[y,..]$ -> **b**
    $B[z,..]$ -> **c**

This grammar can be radically simplified if we adopt a couple of transparent rule-collapsing conventions together with the constraint on rule application which permits the elimination of end-markers (in (8) the end-marker indices are $x, y,$ and z):

(9) $S[..]$ -> $\phi\, S[\phi,..] \mid B[..]$
    $B[\phi,..]$ -> $\phi \mid B[..]\, \phi$
    where ϕ is in $\{a,b,c\}$.

WHAT INDEXED GRAMMARS CAN DO

In this section, we look at some abstract tree configurations that indexed grammars can generate, and consider their potential relevance to three natural languages, English, Norwedish, and Belgian. We first consider the mirror-image languages. CF-PSGs can generate these, but only with a tree structure that employs center-embedding, as in (10), for example:

(10)

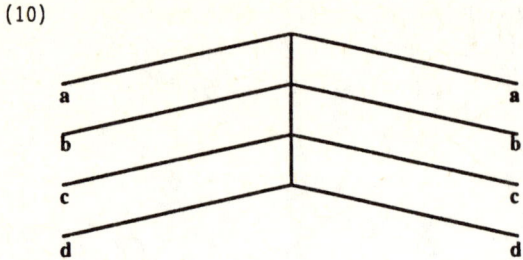

Suppose, however, that we want this kind of string set, but we also want it to be associated with a tree set which does not nest in the center, but rather at the the left or right periphery, as in (11) or (12):

(11)

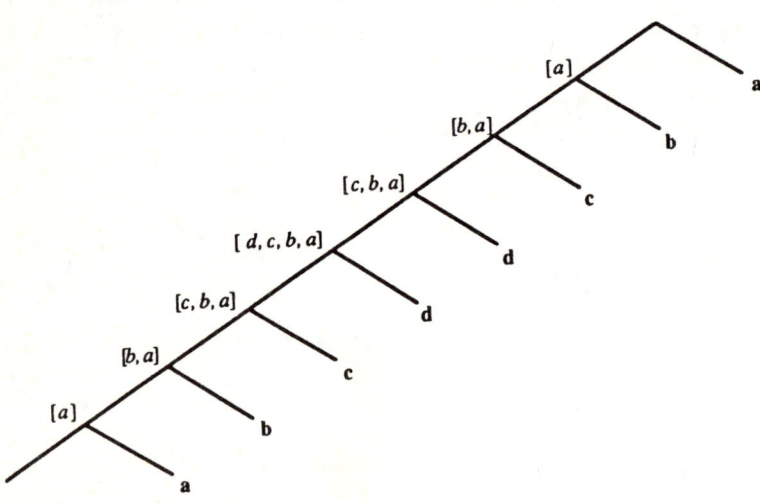

(12)

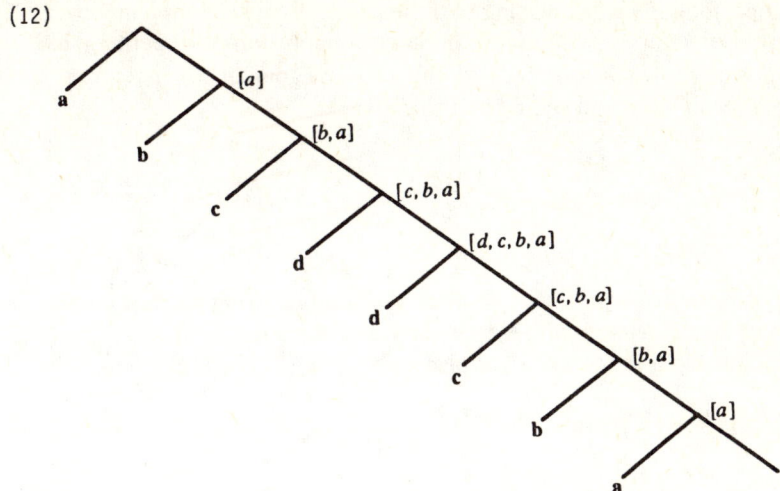

A CF-PSG will not be able to help us here (unless there is an upper bound on the length of the mirror-image constituent), but an indexed grammar can. We simply stack information as to the nature of the first half of the string as we go up (or down) the tree, then we change tack and start unstacking it in order to create the reverse image.

Is this potentially linguistically useful? Well, consider the following examples, the first two due to Klein (1981) and the third to Bowers (1975) [but cited by Klein].

(13) Jude is |less|$_b$ obviously |as|$_a$ nice |as|$_a$ Kim |than|$_b$ Chris is.

(14) You are |as|$_b$ much tall|er|$_a$ |than|$_a$ me |as|$_b$ I expected.

(15) This fence is |so much|$_c$ |too much|$_b$ high|er|$_a$ |than|$_a$ that one |for|$_b$ me to even consider climbing it |that|$_c$ it's simply incomprehensible to me that Mary would try to get me to do it.

Arguably, these examples exhibit a structure like that shown in (11), above, at least in relevant respects. And it is probably uncontroversial to assert that they do not have a structure along the lines of (10). Although (15), which involves the reflection of three items, is teetering on the edge of unacceptability, there is no reason to think that there is a grammatical upper-bound on the nesting of these paired English complementizers. The correct analysis of these examples probably looks something like that shown in (16) [the details of category assignment are irrelevant to the matter in hand and should be ignored].

(16)
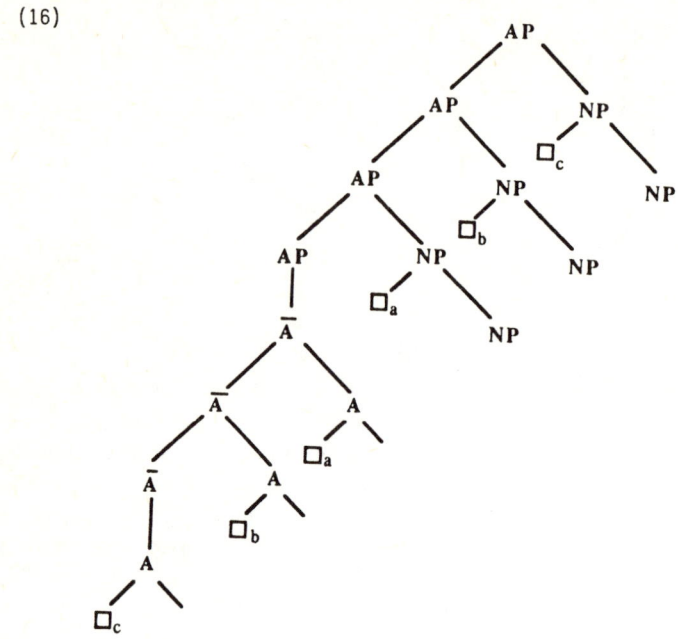

Of course, the pattern in something like (15) is not exactly **cbaabc**, but there is a homomorphism that will give you that sequence.

So we have some data that suggests that structures like (11) may be found in natural languages. What about the reflection of (11), namely (12)? Here we will need to turn to a hypothetical Scandinavian language called Norwedish. Norwedish is like other Scandinavian languages in that it permits multiple unbounded dependencies into a single structure (see Engdahl, 1980; Maling and Zaenen, 1982), but it differs from them in that it does not permit resumptive pronouns. It is similar to Icelandic in having a range of cases that are idiosyncratically governed by verbs, and it differs from Norwegian in that all its unbounded dependency pairings must be nested. Here is the structure of a typical Norwedish sentence involving three unbounded dependencies:

(17) Norwedish

[tree diagram showing nested S → NP S, S → NP VP, VP → V S recursion, with dependency lines labeled a, b, c connecting displaced NPs to lower verbs, terminating in V PP]

We can pair the displaced NPs with the verbs in the manner indicated thanks to the Icelandic-style case-marking that is so prevalent in Norwedish. So, formally speaking, what we have here is the same as the English paired complementizer case, except in mirror image. Now why is this? What makes one the reflection of the other? How would their grammars have to differ? These questions are best answered by reference to the charts below.

For simplicity, this chart is restricted to binary branching rules in which one branch increments or decrements the stack. As can be seen from (18a), under these restrictions, there are four possible configurations: the cross of increment vs. decrement by stack-on-left vs. stack-on-right. A class of tree structures that uses the stack to some end will minimally need to employ one of the stack-increment rules and one of the stack-decrement rules. Let us therefore refer to a class of tree structures that only uses one kind of stack-increment rule and one kind of stack-decrement rule as a minimal possibility. Two of the four minimal possibilities are shown in (18b), the one on the left giving rise to structures like (11), and hence, potentially, to the English paired complementizer construction, and the one on the right giving rise to structures like (12), and hence, potentially, to Norwedish unbounded dependencies. However, as (18c) and (18d) show, there are two further minimal possibilities. These will generate trees of the general form shown in (19) and (20), respectively.

(18)

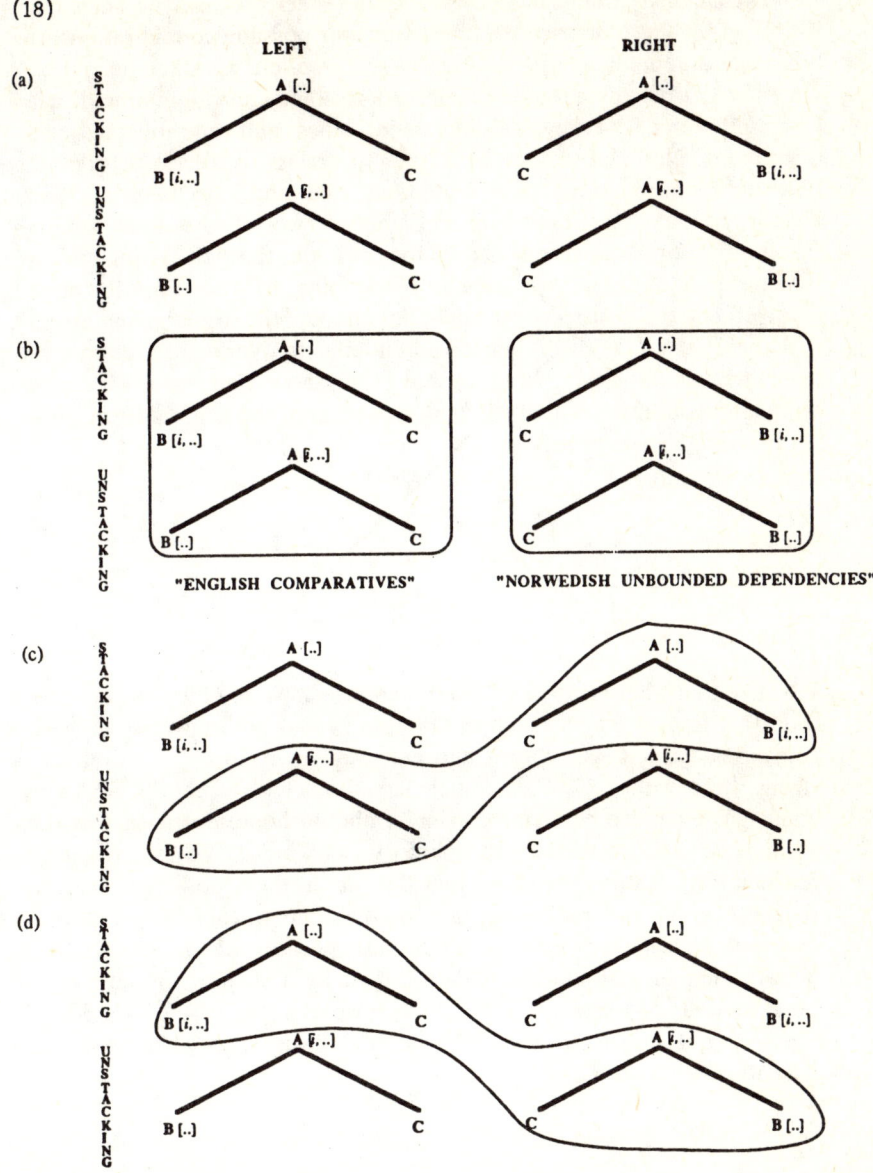

(19)

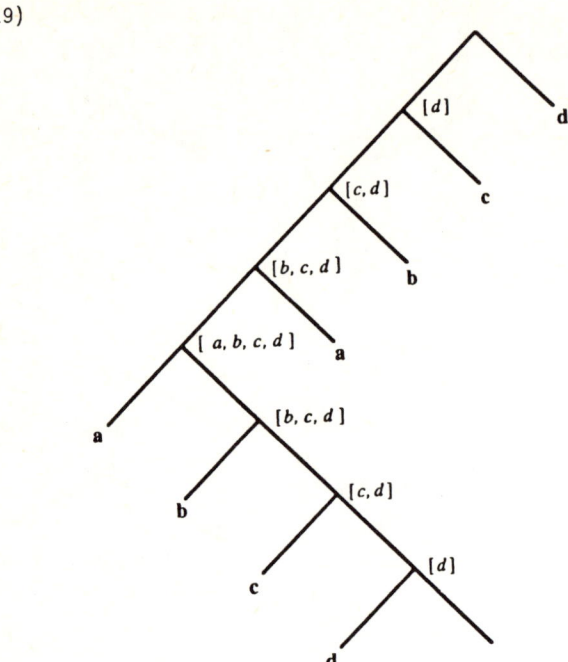

Notice that whereas the rule combinations shown in (18b) both give rise to mirror image strings, those in (18c) and (18d) both give rise to string-copying constructions, so we could not even generate the relevant set of strings here with a CF-PSG, much less the set of trees. So do natural languages ever exhibit string-copying (modulo homomorphism) in their syntax (as opposed to their morphology--see Culy (1985) for discussion relevant to the latter)? It seems that they do: in the hypothetical language Belgian, as in the real language Swiss German (Shieber, 1985), for example, all speakers use a class of verb phrases which consists of an initial string of case-marked NPs followed by a string consisting of the same number of verbs where the ith verb governs the case on the ith NP. The next question is: do these Belgian VPs have either of the structures indicated by (19) or (20)?

(20)

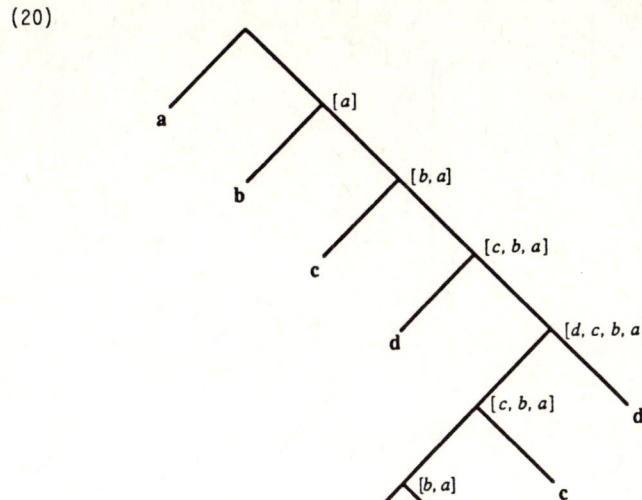

Unfortunately, the difficulties of doing informant work on a hypothetical language make it hard to get evidence that bears directly on this question. However, the available work on a closely related language, Dutch, suggests that the answer is likely to be "no" (see Bresnan, Kaplan, Peters and Zaenen, 1985). Must we then conclude that even indexed grammars are inadequate to the task of providing structural descriptions for the sentences of at least some natural languages? Well, no. Notice that we have been assuming throughout this section that only one daughter gets to carry the stack. And this appear to be what we want for the English and Norwedish constructions discussed above. But the formalism of indexed grammars allows, and the H&U formalism encourages, more than one daughter to carry the stack. So our Belgian VPs can, if we wish, be provided with structural descriptions of the form shown in (21):

(21) Belgian Verb Phrases

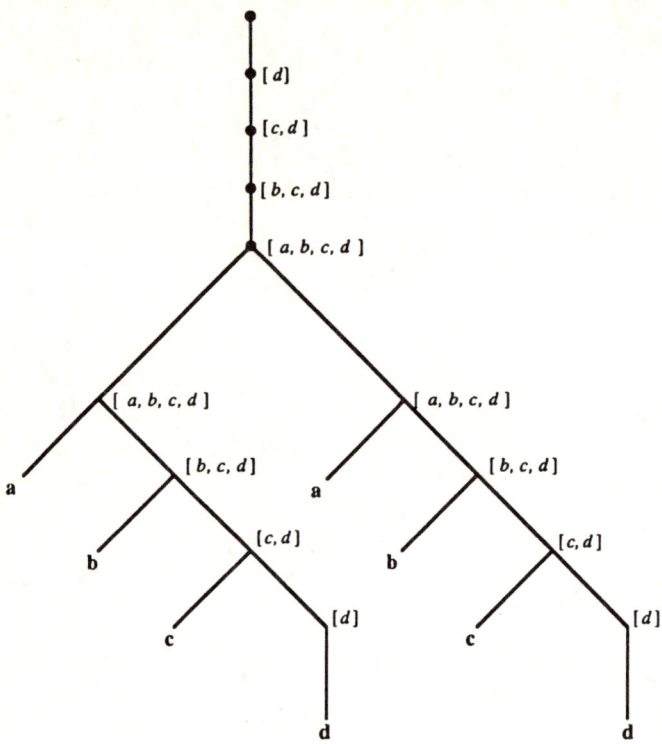

And this, modulo a couple of probably irrelevant details, is the structure that Bresnan, Kaplan, Peters and Zaenen argue for in the case of Dutch (cf. also Pulman and Ritchie (1984) who provide a simple indexed grammar for the Dutch construction).

At first sight, it looks to be rather a pity that the facts of Belgian (and related languages) force us into the use of branching stacks. Suppose that one of the structures (19) or (20) had been correct. Then we might have postulated a constraint on NL-applicable indexed grammars to the effect that no rule may copy the stack (or the tail of the stack) to more than one daughter. This constraint amounts to defining the class of permissible grammars in terms just of the rule forms in (2), not the union of those in

(1) and (2) as we have been supposing so far. This constraint is attractive because it seems likely to have substantive language-theoretic content giving us grammars that define a proper superset of the CFLs and a proper subset of the ILs[1]. Certainly the set of structural descriptions would be constrained--we would not be able to get (21), for example. And Bill Marsh (personal communication) conjectures that it would not be possible to generate the languages $a^n b^n c^n d^n e^n$ or $\{WWW: W$ is in $\{a, b\}^+\}$, both of which are ILs, given the constraint envisaged above.

Unfortunately, this constraint is a non-starter if our goal is the description of natural languages. And the reason can be given in one word: coordination. The relevant generalization about natural language coordination is as follows: a conjunct category has all the syntactic properties of the category which immediately dominates it (see Sag *et al.* for extensive discussion). Hence if the dominating category has a particular stack associated with it, then each conjunct will also have to carry that stack. But, by definition, coordination involves more than one conjunct, and the construction will force the use of branching stacks. Thus, for example, in Scandinavian languages, if we take some embedded sentential complement that has three unbounded dependencies reaching into it and coordinate it with another sentential complement, then the result will be grammatical just in case the latter can also be construed syntactically as having the same three unbounded dependencies reaching into it (Engdahl, 1980; Zaenen, Engdahl and Maling, 1981; Maling and Zaenen, 1982). In other words, both conjuncts must have the same stack.

WHAT INDEXED GRAMMARS CANNOT DO

As one moves further up the Chomsky hierarchy, it becomes harder and harder to find easily describable languages that the classes of grammar cannot generate. In the highest reaches, one works with diagonalizations or Turing machine encodings and the like. But it has taken linguistics 30

---

[1] Aho's discussion of RIR, LIL, RIL and LIR grammars (1968:667-670). His results on these restricted types of indexed grammar do not immediately carry over, however, since we have not been assuming that rules may contain at most one nonterminal in their expansion. See also his notion of "intermediate" categories (1968:670)--these are nonterminals that do not allow the introduction of new indices.

years to even find convincing examples of XX phenomena (unbounded reduplication). We have no reason whatsoever for believing that natural language grammars are not (equivalent to) a proper subset of the indexed grammars. However, we should at least know what such a reason might look like. There are two kinds of data we might adduce: (i) sets of strings, and (ii) sets of structural descriptions.

Let us consider the stringset case first. We know from Hayashi (1973) that languages such as $\{a^{n!}: n \geq 1\}$ and $\{(\$w)^{|w|}: w \text{ is in } \{a, b\}^*\}$ are not indexed. But it seems inconceivable that we will find (homomorphic) natural language counterparts to either of these, for reasons having little to do with mathematical linguistics. Marsh and Partee (1984) discuss a first-order logical language that they conjecture not to be indexed, but this example seems likely only to be relevant to the languages we might use to describe (the meanings of) natural language strings, not to the natural language strings themselves. The best potential exemplar that has yet emerged is called MIX: MIX consists of all strings containing the same number of as, bs and cs in any order[2] It is easy to show that MIX is not a CFL, and Marsh (1985) conjectures that it is not an IL either, though as yet he has no proof of this. Even assuming that MIX is outside the ILs, it seems rather unlikely that any natural language will turn out to have a MIX-like characteristic on which a proof of non-ILness could be based. However, at least it is easy to see what a natural language would need to be like in order to be like MIX.

It seems marginally more likely that languages will exhibit certain patterns of structural description that may turn out to be outside the scope of indexed grammars. Consider the following sample trees (and reflections thereof):

---

[2] MIX was originally described by Emmon Bach and was so-dubbed by students in the 1983 Hampshire College Summer Studies in Mathematics. Pullum (1983) uses the expression "Bach languages" to refer to MIX-like stringsets.

Applicability Of Indexed Grammars

(22)

*

(23)

*

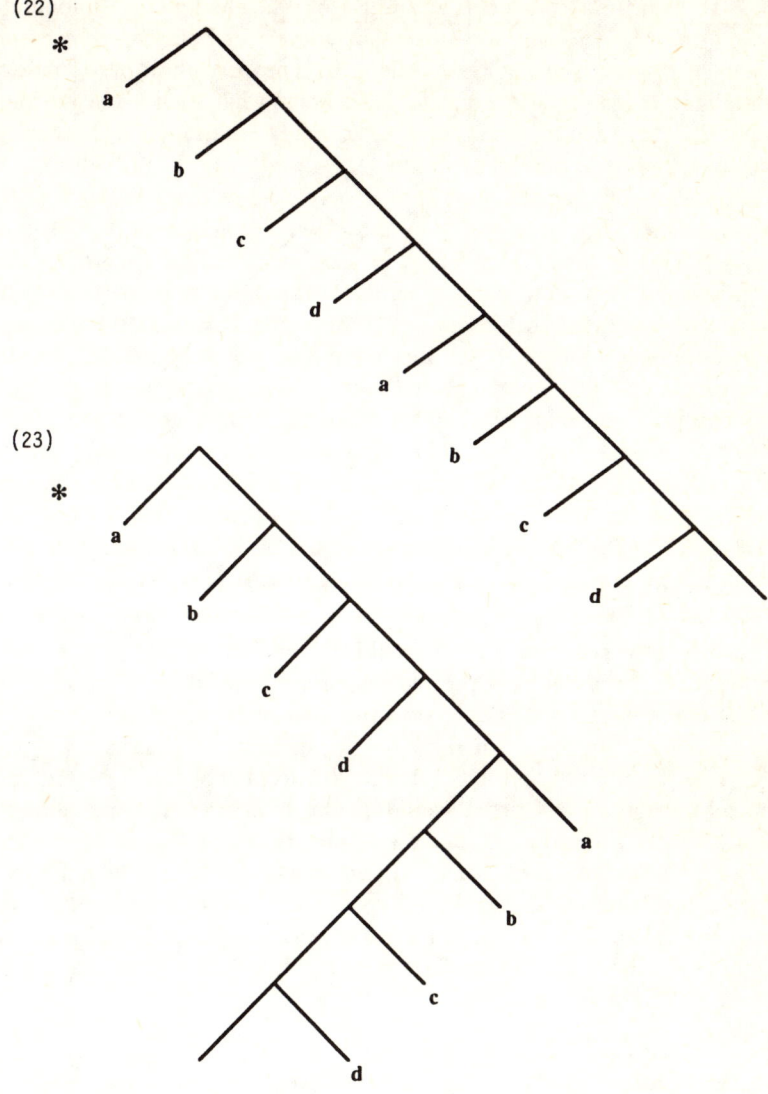

(24)

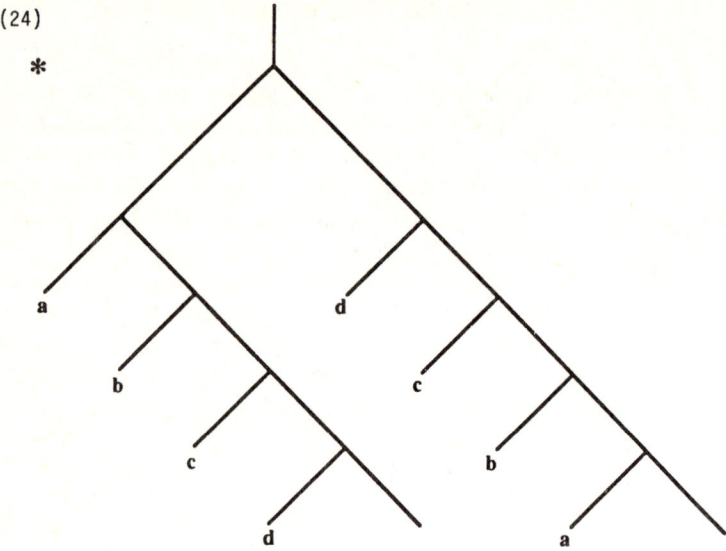

As far as I can see, none of the three infinite families of trees of which these would be typical members could be generated by an indexed grammar. I do not have a proof of this in the case of (23) or (24), but if the reader works out how the indices would have to go in order to get these structures, then they will come to share my intuition[3]. It is easy to see what a natural language would be like if it had such structures: a language that was structurally just like Norwedish except that the NPs and verbs matched up in an XX order would exhibit structures like that shown in (22)[4], whereas a language that was structurally just like Belgian except that the *NP*s and verbs paired up in a nested fashion would exhibit structures like that shown in (24). Neither possibility seems *a priori* implausible. If they occur, then I conjecture that indexed grammars cannot describe them. If they do not occur, then that is an interesting fact about natural languages.

---

[3] The impossibility of the (22)-type case follows from Aho's proof, noted above, that only CFLs can be generated down sets of left-linear or right-linear trees.

[4] Philip Miller has pointed out to me that Norwegian may be such a language - see Maling and Zaenen 1982, p.237.

CONCLUDING REMARKS

This paper has considered only one possible constraint on the power of indexed grammars (to a single stack-carrying daughter) and found it linguistically wanting. Engdahl (1982b: 25-26) in effect considers another (finite upper bounds on stack size) and finds that linguistically wanting also. But there are a number of other avenues worth exploring (e.g., that pursued in Pollard, 1985) and theoretical computer scientists, notably those based in Europe (e.g., Maibaum, 1974; Bertsch, 1975; Engelfriet and Schmidt, 1977/78; Damm, 1982; Parchmann, Duske and Specht, 1980a, 1980b) are continuing to produce relevant work. Given the current interest in the use of stack-valued features among those using unification-based syntactic formalisms, and the possibly equivalent mechanisms evident in some recent generalizations of categorial grammar, the need for such further exploration is a matter of some priority.

APPENDIX

The first half of this appendix presents an informal proof of the language-theoretic equivalence of ordinary indexed grammars to those augmented with the rule types shown in (2). The second half shows that the constraint which permits the elimination of end-markers has no language-theoretic consequences.

1. Obviously the augmented grammars can generate everything that the unaugmented ones can, so the only question we have to concern ourselves with is whether the unaugmented grammars can generate every language allowed by the augmented ones. It is fairly easy to show that they can.

(1) i. $A[..] \rightarrow W[..]$
    ii. $A[..] \rightarrow B[i,..]$
    iii. $A[i,..] \rightarrow W[..]$

(2) i. $A[..] \rightarrow W_1[] B[..] W_2[]$
    ii. $A[..] \rightarrow W_1[] B[i,..] W_2[]$
    iii. $A[i,..] \rightarrow W_1[] B[..] W_2[]$

Consider an H&U indexed grammar augmented with rules of type (2.i), as exhibited in (A1):

(A1) $A[..] \rightarrow W_1[] B[..] W_2[]$

We will assume that the grammar contains n rules of this form, numbered from 1 to n. Replace each such rule r, where $1 \leq r \leq n$, with the following three H&U rules:

(A2) i. $A[..] \rightarrow A^r[|,..]$
 ii. $A^r[..] \rightarrow W[..]$, where $W = W_1 B^r W_2$
 iii. $B^r[|,..] \rightarrow B[..]$

Here A^r and B^r are categories that are not mentioned elsewhere in the grammar, and $|$ is an index that is not mentioned elsewhere in the grammar. Since the H&U rules do not permit the specification of empty stacks, the function of the index $|$ is to put a 'bottom' on the stack. The grammar that results now consists entirely of H&U rules, but will it generate the same language as the original grammar? To see that it will, imagine walking down the tree: (A1) will allow you to walk directly from $A[..]$ to $B[..]$ in one step, whereas (A2) forces you to go from $A[..]$ to $A^r[|,..]$ to $B^r[|,..]$ to $B[..]$, but you end up in the same place. What about the material to the left and right of $B[..]$? In the grammar using (A1) it will be $W_1[]$ and $W_2[]$, i.e., strings of terminals and nonterminals none of which carry a nonempty stack. In the grammar using (A2) it will be $W_1[|,..]$ and $W_2[|,..]$, i.e. the same strings of terminals and nonterminals, but where the nonterminals carry stacks whose topmost index is $|$. However, these stacks might as well be empty, since, ex hypothesi, the only rule that will permit the $|$ to be unpacked is (A2.iii) and the only rule in the grammar which introduces B^r as a daughter is rule (A2.ii) which itself can only apply expand the daughter introduced by (A2.i), and the latter introduces the $|$ which (A2.iii) subsequently unpacks. So the presence of $|$ in $W_1[|,..]$ and $W_2[|,..]$ merely seals the stacks up: the $|$ and everything beneath it can do no further work in the expansion of the nonterminals in W_1 and W_2.

Consider an H&U indexed grammar augmented with rules of type (2.ii), as exhibited in (A3):

(A3) $A[..] \rightarrow W_1[] B[i,..] W_2[]$

Given a parallel numbering assumption to that adopted above, and a convention that 'R' and 'r' are distinct numerical representations (arabic and roman, say) of a number r, we replace each such rule r with the following four H&U rules:

(A4) i. $A[_{..}] \rightarrow A^R[i,..]$
    ii. $A^R[..] \rightarrow A^r[\,|,..]$
    iii. $A^r[..] \rightarrow W[..]$, where $W = W_1 B^r W_2$
    iv. $B^r[\,|,..] \rightarrow B[..]$

Here A^R, A^r and B^r are categories that are not mentioned elsewhere in the grammar, and $|$ is an index that is not mentioned elsewhere in the grammar. The grammar that results now consists entirely of H&U rules, and the proof that it will generate exactly the same language as the original grammar is basically the same as the proof for (2.i) type rules sketched above.

Finally, consider an H&U indexed grammar augmented with rules of type (2.iii), as exhibited in (A5):

(A5) $A[i,..] \rightarrow W_1[]\, B[..]\, W_2[]$

We carry over our existing numbering conventions and replace each such rule r with the following four H&U rules:

(A6) i. $A[i,..] \rightarrow A^R[..]$
    ii. $A^R[..] \rightarrow A^r[\,|,..]$
    iii. $A^r[..] \rightarrow W[..]$, where $W = W_1 B^r W_2$
    iv. $B^r[\,|,..] \rightarrow B[..]$

As before, A^R, A^r and B^r are categories that are not mentioned elsewhere in the grammar, and $|$ is an index that is not mentioned elsewhere in the grammar. The grammar that results now consists entirely of H&U rules, and an equivalence proof is a trivial variant of that for (2.ii) type rules.

2. We turn now to the question of constraining the application of indexed grammar rules so as to reduce the need for end-markers. We shall call grammars constrained in this way "non-wasteful".

> (A7) The interpretation of an indexed grammar is **non-wasteful** if and only if admissible trees are required to satisfy the following condition: if a nonterminal does not dominate another nonterminal, then its stack must be empty.

The question we are addressing then is this: do indexed grammars under a non-wasteful interpretation generate exactly the indexed languages? The cases we have to consider are the H&U rules of types (1.i) and (1.iii) in the situation where W_1 and W_2 contain no nonterminal symbols. And the constraint on rule application that we want can be stated as follows:

(A8) Suppose i. $A[..]$ -> $W[..]$,
        or ii. $A[i,..]$ -> $W[..]$,
where W is in T^+, and where T is the set of terminal symbols. Then $A[..]$ or $A[i,..]$ may dominate $W[..]$ just in case $[..] = []$, i.e., the stack contains no indices.

Does such a constraint either reduce or enlarge the class of languages that the grammars can generate? The reduction question amounts to a question of whether we can circumvent the constraint against throwing away non-empty stacks that is imposed by (A8). This turns out to be easy to do. Replace each rule r of type (A8) with the following set of rules:

(A9)   i. $A[..]$ -> $A^r[..]$ (for (A7.i) rules only)
      ii. $A[i,..]$ -> $A^r[..]$ (for (A7.ii) rules only)
      iii. $\{A^r[j,..] \rightarrow A^r[..] : j \text{ is in } I\}$
      iv. $A^r[..]$ -> $W[..]$
where A^r is a new nonterminal not employed elsewhere in the grammar and I is the set of indices in the grammar.

As can be seen, repeated use of rules provided by (A9.iii) will allow the stack to be emptied before (A9.iv) is invoked. Thus application of the latter can satisfy (A8). So the constraint (A8) does nothing to reduce the class of languages we can generate. But does it enlarge it? To show that it does not, we need to show that we can convert any grammar that obeys the constraint into an equivalent H&U indexed grammar that does not. This can be done as follows: augment the set of indices I with one new index z, then replace every rule of type (A8.i) with a rule of the form shown in (A10),

(A10) $A[z,..]$ -> W

        and replace every rule r of type (A8.ii) with a pair of rules having the following form,

(A11) i. $A[i,..] \rightarrow A'[..]$
ii. $A'[z,..] \rightarrow W$

where B' is a new nonterminal not employed elsewhere.

Now replace the grammar's start symbol S with a new start symbol S', where S' is a nonterminal not used elsewhere in the grammar, whilst leaving any rules that employ S unchanged (i.e., do not map S into S'). Finally, add the following rule to the grammar:

(A12) $S'[..] \rightarrow S[z,..]$

We have now arrived at an indexed grammar that will generate exactly the same language as the one we started out with, regardless of whether we impose (A8) or not. The rules in (A10) and (A11.ii) cannot help but meet the constraint since z will always be the last index on the stack, in virtue of its introduction by (A12). This shows that (A8) does not enlarge the class of languages: for every grammar adopting the constraint there is an equivalent indexed grammar to which the constraint is irrelevant. Hence adoption of (A8) has no consequences for the class of languages generated.

REFERENCES

Aho, Alfred V. 1968. Indexed Grammars. *Journal of the Association for Computing Machinery* 15:647-671.
Aho, Alfred V. 1969. Nested Stack Automata. *Journal of the Association for Computing Machinery* 16:383-406.
Bresnan, Joan W., Ronald M. Kaplan, P. Stanley Peters, and Annie Zaenen. 1982. Cross-serial Dependencies in Dutch. *Linguistic Inquiry* 13:613-635.
Bertsch, Eberhard. 1975. Two Thoughts on Fast Recognition of Indexed Languages. *Information and Control* 29:381-384.
Bowers, John S. 1975. Adjectives and Adverbs in English. *Foundations of Language* 13:529-662.
Culy, Christopher. 1985. The Complexity of the Vocabulary of Bambara. *Linguistics and Philosophy* 8:345-351.
Dahl, Osten. 1982. Bound Pronouns in Dislocated Constituents. Manuscript, University of Stockholm.
Damm, Werner. 1982. The IO- and OI-hierarchies. *Theoretical Computer Science* 20:95-207.
Engdahl, Elisabet. 1980. The Syntax and Semantics of Questions in Swedish. PhD dissertation, University of Massachusetts at Amherst.
Engdahl, Elisabet. 1982. Restrictions on Unbounded Dependencies in Swedish. In Elisabet Engdahl and Eva Ejerhed (Eds.), *Readings on Unbounded Dependencies in Scandinavian*. Stockholm: Almqvist and Wiksell, 151-174.

Engelfriet, Joost and Erik Meineche Schmidt. 1977/78. IO and OI. *Journal of Computer and System Sciences* 15:328-353; 16:67-99.
Gazdar, Gerald. 1982. Phrase Structure Grammar. In Pauline Jacobson and Geoffrey K. Pullum (Eds.), *The Nature of Syntactic Representation*. Dordrecht: Reidel, 131-186.
Gazdar, Gerald and Geoffrey K. Pullum. 1985. Computationally Relevant Properties of Natural Languages and Their Grammars. *New Generation Computing* 3:273-306. [Also appeared as CSLI Report CSLI-85-24, Stanford, May 1985.]
Hayashi, Takeshi. 1973. On Derivation Trees of Indexed Grammars--an Extension of the uvwxy Theorem. Publ. RIMS (Kyoto University) 9:61-92.
Hopcroft, John and Jeffrey Ullman. 1979. *Introduction to Automata Theory, Languages, and Computation*. Reading, Massachusetts: Addison-Wesley.
Huybregts, Riny. 1984. The Weak Inadequacy of Context-free Phone Structure Grammars. In Ger de Haan, Mieke Trommelen and Wim Zonneveld. (Eds.), *Van Periferie naar Kern*. Dordrecht: Foris
Klein, Ewan. 1981. The Syntax and Semantics of Nominal Comparatives. In M. Moneglia (Ed.), *Atti de Seminario su Tempo e Verbale Strutture Quantificate in Forma Logica*. Florence: Presso l'Accademia della Crusca
Maibaum, T. S. E. 1974. A Generalized Approach to Formal Languages. *Journal of Computer and System Sciences* 8:409-439.
Maling, Joan and Annie Zaenen. 1982. A Phrase Structure Account of Scandinavian Extraction Phenomena. In Pauline Jacobson and Geoffrey K. Pullum (Eds.) *The Nature of Syntactic Representation*. Dordrecht: Reidel. 229-282.
Marsh, William E. 1985. Some Conjectures on Indexed Languages. Paper presented to the Association for Symbolic Logic Meeting, Stanford University, July 15-19, 1985.
Marsh, William E. and Barbara H. Partee. 1984. How Non-context-free is Variable Binding? In Mark Cobler et al. (Eds.), *Proceedings of the Third West Coast Conference on Formal Linguistics*. Stanford: Stanford Linguistics Association, 179-190.
Parchmann, R., J. Duske and J. Specht. 1980a. On Deterministic Indexed Languages. *Information and Control* 45:48-67.
Parchmann, R., J. Duske and J. Specht. 1980b. Closure Properties of Deterministic Indexed Languages. *Information and Control* 46:200-218.
Pollard, Carl J. 1984. Generalized Phrase Structure Grammars, Head Grammars, and Natural Languages. Phd thesis, Stanford University.
Pollard, Carl J. 1985. Some Extensions of Context-free Grammars and Their Time Complexity. Paper presented to the Santa Cruz Workshop on the Mathematics of Grammars and Languages, June 25-28, 1985.
Pulman, Stephen G. and Graeme D. Ritchie. 1984. Indexed Grammars and Intersecting Dependencies. Unpublished paper, University of Cambridge.
Pullum, Geoffrey K. 1983. Context-freeness and the Computer Processing of Human Languages. *Proceedings of the 21st Annual Meeting*, Association for Computational Linguistics, Menlo Park, CA, 1-6.
Pullum, Geoffrey K. and Gerald Gazdar. 1982. Natural Languages and Context-free Languages. *Linguistics and Philosophy* 4:471-504.
Sag, Ivan A., Gerald Gazdar, Thomas Wasow and Steven Weisler. 1985. Coordination and How to Distinguish Categories. *Natural Language and Linguistic Theory* 3:117-171.
Shieber, Stuart M. 1985. Evidence Against the Context-freeness of Natural Language. *Linguistics and Philosophy* 8:333-343.
Zaenen, Annie, Elisabet Engdahl and Joan Maling. 1981. Resumptive Pronouns can be Syntactically Bound. *Linguistic Inquiry* 12:679-682.

BRANIMIR BOGURAEV
UNIVERSITY OF CAMBRIDGE
COMPUTER LABORATORY
CAMBRIDGE, ENGLAND

A NATURAL LANGUAGE TOOLKIT:
RECONCILING THEORY WITH PRACTICE

ABSTRACT

Generalized Phrase Structure Grammar (GPSG) is a highly restrictive theory of natural language syntax, characterised by complex interaction between its various rule types and constraints. Motivated by desire for declarative semantics, the theory defines these as applying simultaneously in the process of licensing local trees. As a result, as far as practical implementations of GPSG are concerned, the theory loses its apparent efficient parsability and becomes computationally intractable. This paper describes one aspect of an UK collaborative effort to produce a general purpose morphological and syntactic analyser for English within the theoretical framework of Generalized Phrase Structure Grammar, namely the development of a tractable grammatical formalism with clear semantics, capable of supporting the task of writing a substantial grammar. The paper outlines the intellectual and pragmatic background of the development effort and traces the incremental evolution of this formalism, following discussions concerning the fundamental issues of rules interpretation, feature system, grammar organisation, parser strategy, environment for grammar writing and support, and the construction of a lexicon linked to the grammar. Particular emphasis is placed on the quesiton of how theoretical standpoints have been reconciled with practical constraints, and how the commitment to deliver a functional morphological and syntactic analyser of wide scope and coverage of English has influenced the current state of the grammatical formalism.

1. INTRODUCTION

The Alvey Programme of advanced information technology (IT) research and development was established in 1983 in the UK, with the primary objective of stimulating British IT research through a programme of collaborative research projects aimed at several enabling key technologies. Within the larger framework of the Alvey Intelligent Knowledge Based Systems (IKBS) programme, a coordinated effort to build a natural language parsing toolkit for the use by academic and industrial community is currently under way; the work is being carried out jointly by groups at the Universities of Cambridge, Edinburgh and Lancaster.

Three closely related projects are aimed at producing directly compatible software and rules, thus resulting in an integrated system for morphological and syntactic parsing of text within a substantial subset of the English language. The projects will deliver, respectively, *a computational grammar of English* linked to a 50,000 strong word-list, *a morphological analyser* embedded in a program capable of handling large quantities of dictionary information within natural language processing systems, and a *parser* which will provide a complete lexico-syntactic language processing facility when combined with the Dictionary Access and the Grammar tools. The work is being carried out within the theoretical framework of Generalized Phrase Structure Grammar (henceforth GPSG; Gazdar et al., 1985).

The morphology / dictionary project is described in more detail in Russell et al. (1986). Overall, its aims are to develop a morphological analyser of English capable of dealing with inflectional and derivational morphology and associated software for efficient handling of large quantities of lexical information of relevance to natural language processing systems. Background is provided by recent work of Koskenniemi (1983) which develops a general model for two-level morphology employing a finite-state grapheme-to-phoneme transducer. The resulting system offers a perspicuous, rule-based, notation for describing a variety of morphological phenomena, a hand-crafted "core" lexicon of English, and dictionary access software which efficiently breaks a word into morphemes and delivers a structure indicating how it relates to a root form stored in the lexicon.

Some aspects of the parser project are described in Phillips and Thompson (1986a, 1986b). The aim there is to build on previous work on parsing within the GPSG framework (see, in particular, Phillips and Thompson, 1985) and to construct a chart parser augmented with unification, suitably interfaced with the lexicon access system and capable of efficiently interpreting the grammar developed by the grammar project.

It is envisaged that the complete integrated toolkit will be used by a number of research and development groups, as a base component for a range of applications. Morphosyntactic analysis of text is clearly of importance to any subsystem attempting to use natural language in some way, whether for access to a back end computational system, for dialogue with an expert or advisory system, for document scanning, or for speech synthesis from written sources, to name but a few tasks. The requirements of such a potentially diverse user community motivate the need for efficiency and wide coverage by the integrated morphological and syntactic analyser. In particular, the grammar project is committed to developing a "core" grammar of English, offering treatment of declaratives of all the major verbal and adjectival complement types and all the transformational variants of these, yes/no and wh- questions, imperatives, restricted relative clauses, prepositional phrases, comparatives, coordination and complete coverage of noun phrases.

The need for such a comprehensive parsing capability imposes strong connectivity between the three projects. For example, the processing model adopted by the parser would influence the lexicon access strategy. The feature sets and defaults used in the grammar and in the lexicon must be compatible, and there is clearly going to be substantial overlap between their respective declarations and default specifications. Issues of parsability and efficiency impose constraints on the parsing model adopted. Most importantly, a clear grammar formalism and well understood interpretation of it are critical for the design of the parser, as well as for the development of a consistent, coherent and comprehensive grammar.

This paper will outline the intellectual and pragmatic background of the

Tools Projects and will trace the development of issues including choice of grammatical formalism, feature system, parser strategy, grammar support and development environment, and lexicon build-up and its linking to the grammar. Some consideration will be given to the question of how theoretical standpoints have been reconciled with practical constraints, and how the commitment to deliver a functional morphosyntactic analyser of wide scope and coverage of English has influenced the current state of the grammar formalism.

We first discuss the initial set of considerations influencing the choice of grammatical theory and defining the overall shape of the project. Then, as an example of a particular conflict between the declarative nature of the GPSG theory of Gazdar et al. (1985) (henceforth GPSG85) and its procedural implementation, we present two proposals aimed at reducing one of the major sources of the computational complexity of GPSG, namely its feature propagation regime as defined by the theory of syntactic features, by introducing explicit control of feature propagation. We then describe the current state of the grammatical formalism, incorporating a notation true to the spirit of GPSG, but allowing realistic implementation while still offering the grammar writer efficiency and flexibility. The organisation of the grammar, necessarily different from the one proposed in GPSG85, is described next. Finally, the paper outlines the computational environment in which a theoretical linguist can exploit the flexibility of the grammatical notation and sketches a strategy for constructing a substantial lexicon and linking it to the grammar. The paper assumes some prior knowledge of GPSG.

2. A RETROSPECTIVE VIEW ON THE GRAMMAR / PARSER DEVELOPMENT

2.1 In the beginning

The choice of GPSG as a theoretical framework for the development of the toolkit was influenced by several factors. Firstly, there was the seeming computational tractability of the grammatical theory. A range of early systems (eg. Thompson, 1981, 1982; Gawron et al., 1982; see also

Gazdar, 1984, for an extensive list of implementations of phrase structure grammars) indicated that realistic parsing could be achieved within the early framework of GPSG (Gazdar and Pullum, 1982). The later version of GPSG (presented in Gazdar et al., 1985) was developed even more formally and precisely, thus offering promise of a serious implementation. Secondly, there was already commitment to GPSG in the dictionary project (a word grammar describing rules for derivational morphology was being written in a related notation) and the parser project (where the intention and long term strategy was to build on existing experience and tools for developing chart parsers for PSGs). Finally, it was considered of great value to be able to draw on the joint experience of a considerable number of linguists and take advantage of the linguistic research, both existing and likely to appear during the course of the project, offering treatment of various phenomena within the GPSG framework.

At the same time, it was felt that the projects ought to remain moderately flexible and uncommitted to any particular version of the theory. From a very practical point of view, the development of a complete morphosyntactic analyser would need flexibility --- both for eventual incorporation of future developments in the formal theory and for ensuring that the version adopted for the delivery product was implementable in a reasonably efficient way. Also, given the formal precision and complexity of GPSG, it was decided to build a special purpose software system to aid the linguist in the process of grammar development. Some of the original considerations concerning the formalism to be adopted are detailed below.

The grammar writer should not assume, nor the parser specifically implement, any particular versions of the Head Feature Convention (HFC) and Foot Feature Principle (FFP). Instead, feature propagation regimes should be stated separately to the parser in a specially designed notation, which allows explicit control over the feature propagation within local trees. Feature instantiation would then be done by the parser "on the fly". The formalism would employ the immediate dominance / linear precedence (ID/LP) format of GPSG. Notwithstanding the results reported by Shieber (1984a) and, in particular, Barton (1985), who suggest that direct parsing of an ID/LP grammar is better than the alternative of parsing with an expanded object grammar, it was decided to have the grammar development environment accept ID/LP format, but design the parser to operate on linearised rules. This decision was prompted partly by the fact that the expansion of ID rules under linear precedence would not be large for English. In addition, if metarules are also applied before parse time (see eg. Thompson, 1982), then separating the grammar expansion and compilation machinery from the parser proper would leave more scope for experimentation with different grammar architectures. This was particularly desirable at the time, given that at the very beginning of the grammar project the exact potential and scope of the GPSG metarules mechanism was not entirely clear in all its practical implications.

The grammar formalism should employ, and, in the long run, the parser should understand, aliases (in the style of Evans' ProGram: Evans, 1985). The end product of the grammar project would be indexed to a substantial word list. Subcategorisation was to be regarded, following GPSG, as part of the feature system, but instead of numerical indices on preterminal symbols a feature TAKES would be employed taking values from a set of more mnemonic labels (eg. NP_INF, NP_PPLOC, BASE_VP and so forth). In addition, in order to facilitate subsequent semantic processing, additional features would be introduced in the lexicon describing, where relevant, the semantic type of a lexical item: these would have, in the style of PATR-II (Shieber, 1984b), labels like SUBJECT_RAISING, OBJECT_CONTROL, and so forth. Likewise, unique rule identifiers would be assigned to grammar rules, to be used as attachment points for companion semantic interpretation rules. On the whole, however, none of the projects would attempt to provide any semantics, apart from offer convenient handles where special purpose semantic procedures, relevant to particular tasks and applications, could be incorporated for making use of the results of morphosyntactic analysis.

An important consequence of the lack of semantics for the grammar development was that the Control Agreement Principle (CAP) of GPSG, which depends on the semantic types of the categories involved, could not be incorporated in the grammar. Instead, agreement would be handled along the lines presented in Gazdar and Pullum (1982), making use of feature matching in a more straightforward way (see below).

The division of labour between the grammar development environment and the parser was then as follows. The parser would operate on an expanded, "object", grammar, derived after ID/LP and metarule expansion. Since there was the possibility of some metarules adding features to categories in ID rules, the process of grammar compilation would have to check feature cooccurence restrictions (FCRs). Feature instantiation, however, was to be handled at parse time.

This differs somewhat from previous implementations for GPSG (for instance those of Kilbury, 1984; Phillips and Thompson, 1985; and Evans, 1985) in that an explicit attempt is made to compile as many as possible of the various grammar components into an expanded grammar prior to parsing. The parser then would operate on a set of phrase structure grammar rules with categories defined as feature bundles, and apart from moderately straightforward context-free parsing, it would be responsible for applying the set of criteria stipulated within the GPSG theoretical framework for licensing local trees.

Such an organisation of the complementary processes of grammar interpretation and parsing proper is clearly motivated by the desire for efficiency of the final morphosyntactic analyser. As indicated above, unlike systems in the style of ProGram and GPSGP (Phillips and Thompson, 1985), which were designed and intended to be used as linguists' workbench, the primary users of the toolkit described here are expected to incorporate a specific analyser configuration, and in particular a specific grammar, into a larger system. They are not going to experiment with a variety of different grammars or grammar formats. In such an environment, as Phillips and Thompson (1986a) point out, the compilation of the source grammar into an expanded form can take as much time as necessary --- this is going to be a one-off process and will not affect the end user, whose primary concern is going to be for fast response of the parser when presented with a sentence.

On the other hand, for the benefit of both the grammar writer and the parser designer, the formalism employed ought to be flexible enough to allow for, and perhaps experiment with, different styles of feature propagation. The motivation for this requirement was twofold. Firstly, as stated earlier, with an evolving theory such as GPSG it would be bad management if a project based on the theory did not take precautions to remain uncommitted to a particular version of the theory and to be capable of following and profiting from any developments in it. Secondly, as anticipated and demonstrated by experience with a range of GPSG implementations (Phillips and Thompson, 1986a; Kilbury, 1986; Shieber,

1986) it would seem that by far the most difficult aspect of GPSG to implement is the mechanism which coordinates and applies the intricately linked processes of applying the various feature propagation conventions, enforcing feature coccurence restrictions, and checking feature specification defaults (FSDs) as local trees are being scrutinised for consistency by the parser. Having the option for explicit control over feature propagation seemed like a step in the right direction for trying to gain better understanding of the practical implications of the most complex, and at the same time least stable, area of GPSG. Instead of a system designed and built for a particular interpretation of the GPSG formalism, the aim would be to provide what is essentially an interpreter for a number of different ways of using the formal apparatus of GPSG.

At that point, the organisation and the flow of information and control between the grammar and parser projects could be described as follows (see Figure 1). The source grammar would be developed and written in a metagrammatical notation, drawing heavily on GPSG and following the guidelines described above. This would then, after the expansion of aliases and the application of metarules, induce a base grammar, with most of the GPSG components compiled into it and distributed over a set of phrase structure rules with fully expanded categories. Before linearising the resulting base grammar, it would undergo a separate process of compiling particular versions of the Head Feature Convention, the Foot Feature Principle and the feature specification defaults into it. The final, "object", grammar thus produced would be the one used directly by the parser.

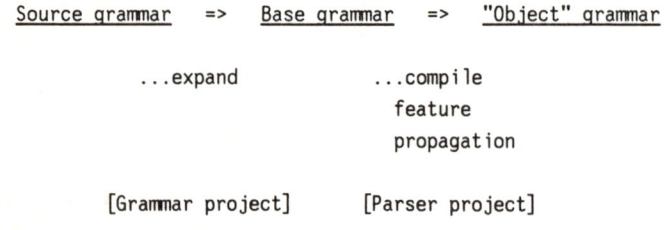

Figure 1

The following sections describe briefly two different mechanisms for explicitly specifying feature defaults and propagation regimes; for more details the reader is referred to Phillips and Thompson (1986a).

2.2 A language for feature propagation

The first proposal to provide explicit interpretation for some of the constraints on local tree admissability, namely feature propagation regimes, is due to Thompson (1985). A simple "language" (feature propagation regime specification language; henceforth FPRSL) would be used to indicate to the parser the following types of information: the particular context in a local tree to trigger some explicit manipulation of features, what this manipulation ought to be, and to which features it ought to apply. Figure 2 gives an example of two connected statements which together define a simple version of the Head Feature Convention. **Hfc1** can be read as follows: for every feature in the list specifying the domain of the propagation rule, apply the rule as defined by PropRuleDef to every head daughter (i.e. every daughter which is an extension of [+HEAD]); the rule itself stipulates that in local trees where pairs of mother and daughter nodes do not share a feature, the feature ought to be copied, in the relevant direction, together with its value.

```
PropRuleDef:   hfc1
    (cond
        ((and df (not mf)  (setf mf df)))
        ((and mf (not df)  (setf df mf))))

PropRule:      hfc1
    [+HEAD]    {ADV AUX BAR INV N PAST ........}
```

Figure 2

Hfc1 offers no indication what to do should a feature be instantiated (on a mother or a daughter) during parsing. An additional pair of statements would be needed to ensure that in such cases the feature must have the same value on the mother and the daughter (Figure 3). What YOKE in the definition of **hfc2** does is essentially introduce variable-valued features both on the mother and daughter nodes, which would be treated specially during the parsing process to ensure that whenever one of two features yoked together gets instantiated (a variable-valued feature will match any feature with the same name), the value gets copied across to the other. It turns out that, if applied to all daughters for the foot features SLASH, RE and WH, the definition of **hfc2** is adequate for specifying the Foot Feature Principle as well (see Figure 3).

```
PropRuleDef:    hfc2
   (cond
       ((and (not df) (not mf)    (yoke))))


PropRule:    hfc2   [+HEAD]    {ADV AUX BAR INV N PAST .....}



. . . . . . . . . .


PropRule:    hfc2   []    {RE SLASH WH}
```

Figure 3

The same notation can be used to encode feature specification defaults. Propagation rules for setting feature values appropriately can be defined fairly easily (see Figure 4). With the additional introduction of special feature values, "++" to match any other value, and "--" which will match iff no match is present for the feature, statements like "all verbal categories are by default -INV" and "if a PFORM specification is present, then the default BAR value is 0" can be expressed as shown in Figure 4.

```
PropRuleDef:    fsd+
   (cond ((and (not df)  (setval df  "+"))))

PropRuleDef:    fsd-
   (cond ((and (not df)  (setval df  "-"))))

PropRuleDef:    fsd0
   (cond ((and (not df)  (setval df  0))))



PropRule:    fsd-    [+V -N]    {INV}
PropRule:    fsd0    [PFORM ++]    {BAR}
```

Figure 4

In fact, the semantics of YOKE is not as simple and clean as it seems. In order to enforce correct behaviour during propagation, in particular when the introduction of new features into a local tree begins to interact closely with the feature cooccurence restrictions, the notation ought to be augmented to allow the concepts of optional and conditional features. Optionality stipulates that should a feature appear on a node, then its value must conform to the rule; however, the presence of the feature is not enforced. On the other hand, conditional features are introduced in local trees only when this would not violate any feature cooccurence restrictions. In order to achieve faithful implementation and interpretation of the Head Feature Convention and the Foot Feature Principle in this language, YOKE now must take two additional arguments which indicate the exact status of a feature that a rule like **hfc2** above is applied to.

While the definition of **hfc1** above is purely declarative within the FPRSL formalism, **hfc2** is procedurally oriented, in particular with the conditional / optional markings on YOKE. The semantics of optional / conditional features, as introduced here, cannot be described in isolation from the underlying mechanisms for parsing. Apart from adding to the currently active discussion on the merits of declarative vs. procedural grammar formalisms (see eg. Shieber, 1986a; Thompson, 1986 and Kaplan, 1986), the immediate problem in this context is that without being able to say, in the style of PATR-II, something like

   [MF] = [DF]

and expect this to achieve the correct result by proper interpretation of the feature propagation notation, there is the serious danger of ending up with a parser which only parses one way; or even worse --- a parser which parses differently, say, top down from bottom up.

2.3 Propagation rules as metarules

In search of more declarative semantics, where the interpretation of the propagation statements should not have to appeal to the parsing model, the next proposal (see Phillips and Thompson, 1986a, for more details) follows a suggestion of Shieber. A mechanism which is an integral part of GPSG, namely that of metarule expansion, is used to a somewhat different effect from its original, and conventional, purpose. Metarules in GPSG produce new rules, which are added to the original grammar. In contrast, Phillips and Thompson propose to employ the same mechanism, but with the effect of changing the original rule by propagating features.

The notational device they use is related to the "possible daughters of" notation for metarules (Gazdar et al., 1985), augmented with the concept of *modification* of a category. Modification of a category involves changes in its feature structure, introduced either by adding new features or by destructively changing the values of existing features, and is the mechanism which ultimately achieves the feature propagation within local trees. Without going into detailed exposition of the alternative notation for metarules, an example of its use is illustrated in Figure 5. The notation allows the specification of a pattern, a modification and an operation together with its argument(s). The metarule matches any ID rule in the source grammar whose left hand side is an extension of the pattern VP[+AUX]. The matching category is modified by [+INV, +SUBJ, +FIN]. A new ID rule is generated by the metarule by adding to the original (and already modified, as appropriate) ID rule an NP daughter. The example thus illustrates the representation of the subject-auxiliary inversion metarule (see also Figure 14 in section 4.1) in this formalism. Figure 5 also shows the effect of this metarule when applied to a particular ID rule.

Subject-auxiliary inversion:

VP [+AUX], [+INV, +SUBJ, +FIN] + NP.

VP [+AUX, +FIN] ->
    H [TAKES BASE_VP], VP[BSE].

↓

S [+INV, +FIN] ->
    H [TAKES BASE_VP], VP[BSE], NP.

Figure 5

A NATURAL LANGUAGE TOOLKIT

The formalism employs further notational extensions. Among these are the use of variables to match feature values (eg. @NUMBER will match any existing NUMBER specification), the symbol "~" (~NUMBER will match in the absence of a NUMBER feature, "meta-features" (the symbol "F" may range over feature sets) and an extended list of possible operators (with associated semantics) used to produce new ID rules from old. Thus "+" adds its argument as a daughter to the original ID rule (as in the example above), while "!" modifies each daughter in the input rule which is an extension of its first argument with its second argument. Figure 6 shows an implementation of the feature specification default [-INV] for verbal categories.

$$X \, ! \, [+V, -N, \sim INV], [-INV].$$

Figure 6

Using this notation then a simple propagation statement to copy a named feature from a head daughter to the mother would be as follows (Fig 7).

$$[+N, -V, \sim NUMBER], [@NUMBER] \, ! \, [@NUMBER].$$

Figure 7

The three rules in Figure 8, ranging over F = {N V BAR SLASH}, implement the Head Feature Convention of GPSG as it applies to some general features. The rules represent, respectively, instructions to copy instantiated features from mother to head daughter, from head daughter to mother, or to introduce a feature missing altogether to both, giving it (the same) variable value.

$$X \, [@F] \, ! \, H \, [\sim F], \, [@F].$$
$$X \, [\sim F], \, [@F] \, ! \, H \, [@F].$$
$$X \, [\sim F], \, [@F] \, ! \, H \, [\sim F], \, [@F].$$

Figure 8

Phillips and Thompson (1986a) demonstrate how the notation can be used to develop a grammar mimicking approximately the system described in Gazdar et al. (1985).

2.4 Towards a more declarative grammar formalism

A family of parser prototypes have been developed in Edinburgh implementing the propagation schemes discussed above (see Phillips and Thompson, 1986a, for more details). All of them are built on top of Thompson's chart parsing framework (MChart: Thompson, 1983), employ a bottom up parsing strategy and incorporate a range of local mechanisms designed specifically for speeding up the parsing process and of no particular theoretical importance.

A common property of these schemes is the move to compile just about everything into the grammar prior to parsing. The only component of GPSG left out of this process is the feature cooccurence restrictions --- these are still quite tricky to compile ahead and remain to be checked during parse time. (One prototype parser was developed especially from the premise that FCRs are abandoned --- an assumption made more practical if propagation rules are allowed to apply to restricted and named feature sets, as illustrated above). Using metarules for describing propagation regimes still made it necessary to introduce optional / conditional markings on features. Even without FCRs, when the need for conditional marking on features no longer exists, a faithful rendering of the Foot Feature Principle would seem to require that optional marking on features be retained. The notation was thus again lacking in purely declarative flavour, and consequently such an approach seemed to work provided that both the lexicon and grammar were written by the parser implementor: a state of affairs unacceptable for a coordinated and distributed effort like ours.

From the point of view of the whole toolkit effort, where the overriding objective is to find a compromise between a perspicuous and expressive grammar formalism in the spirit of GPSG and building a reasonably efficient parser for it, experimentation with the prototypes raised more issues than it answered. The question of existence and specification of an interpretation language for a particular notational framework which allows flexibility in its interpretation and at the same time strictly adheres to the spirit of the formalism is currently an active issue among computational linguists. It is interesting, and in the long run of enormous practical utility, to investigate ways of achieving this goal. In the short term, however, the aim is to develop and deliver a working morphosyntactic analyser for a considerable subset of English. Therefore, the grammar project is, in fact, using a different formalism; this, and the motivation behind adopting it, are discussed in the next section.

3. THE PRESENT DAY WISDOM

In addition to the problems with the schemes for explicit treatment of propagation regimes discussed above, it was felt undesirable to use the same notation --- that of metarules --- to handle two essentially very different phenomena. On the one hand there would be the conventional metarules used to generate and add new ID rules to the grammar. Then there would be the propagation statements which would either modify existing, or add new, ID rules. It is not clear what the consequences of mixing these together would be in the long run. There are at least two issues to be addressed when using metarules in the grammar notation. Firstly, there is the question of the order in which metarules ought to apply. Secondly, there is the general strategy towards closure of the grammar under metarules. It is far from easy to visualise the interaction between the two different kinds of metarule, so that a reasonable attitude towards such issues could be adopted. While Phillips and Thompson postulate ground principles for handling the two different kinds of rule, the implications of any particular strategy for the development of the core grammar could only be determined incrementally over a period of time.

Moreover, the move from feature instantiation via specific conventions to metarules appears to be in the opposite direction to recent developments in theoretical linguistics. Generally, metarules are a very powerful device, whose side effects are occasionally difficult to foresee and restrict, and this is certainly deemed to be undersirable from a theoretical linguist's point of view. While such power is usually welcomed by practicing "engineers", it is questionable if it was going to be of any help in this particular case. For the purposes of developing a large grammar for practical use, it might be occasionally useful to get "behind the scenes" and smooth any remaining sharp edges by hand; the metarule notation would have been far too opaque to allow this. From the point of view of feature instantiation regimes, it would seem that a system using metarules to implement feature propagation is likely to solve less problems than intended in the long run.

None of this, however, offered any significant insights into what the effects of "run-time" interaction between feature cooccurence restrictions, feature default specifications and propagation statements would be once a considerable grammar was developed. On the other hand, such a considerable grammar could not be developed and debugged without a serious parser as an integral part of the grammar development environment. In the absence of enough empirical data, questions like, for example, what would be a faithful implementation of "default" in GPSG85 (which distinguishes between categories not being specified for a feature, being negatively specified for a feature and not being able to be specified for a feature) remained open. In an attempt to arrive at a simpler, and yet flexible, system of features with explicit control over propagation, the present state of the grammar formalism represents an explicit move from the set theoretic apparatus of GPSG85 towards a unification-based treatment of linguistic phenomena.

3.1. Feature propagation by unification

It is important to note that from the very beginning of the project, a back door was opened for variable valued features. The initial motivation was due to the fact that agreement in GPSG85 is essentially semantically driven, while, on the other hand, no real provision for semantics was going to be made by any of the projects. Thus, while the handling of the head and foot features and cooccurence restrictions were going to be, one way or another, the parser's responsibility, some approximation of the Control Agreement Principle ought to be handled through the grammar. Variable valued features would provide the necessary apparatus for such a treatment, and what amounted essentially to unification would provide the mechanism for emulating an earlier treatment for CAP (in the style of Gazdar, 1982).

Adopting unification then was not going to be a dramatic step; in fact, given that it was to be supported by the parser, it made sense to attempt to investigate how much of the complex machinery of GPSG85 could be reinterpreted as a notation from which to induce a unification grammar. As long as it was clear that there was no intention to develop another general purpose linguists' workbench (in the style of PATR-II), unification could be regarded simply as a primitive operation with certain desirable properties. This view is, in fact, in line with Shieber (1984b), who looks at "pure" languages in theoretical computer science as opposed to specialised languages for practical purposes and draws a parallel which suggests that even though PATR-II emulates a virtual linguistic machine, specialised formalism for a given linguistic theory need not necessarily be implemented within it.

Unification can now be implemented quite efficiently (see for example Karttunen and Kay, 1985, and Pereira, 1985); a recent experiment in unification-based parsing (Alshawi et al., 1986) suggests that after translating phrase structure rules into Prolog clauses, complex feature-based categories can be processed directly by the optimised unification mechanism. If the variables standing for feature values are coerced to ordinary Prolog variables (in a style reminiscent of Pereira and Warren's Definite Clause Grammars --- see Pereira and Warren, 1980), an efficient programming system (such as, for instance, the New Implementation of Prolog --- Chung et al., 1985) can dramatically improve the performance of a parser built on top of it.

Thus in addition to the feature values as defined in the standard theory, variables now can be introduced by writing them directly into grammar rules. Variables will also be introduced by the lexicon --- the lexical access component employs the notion of Entry Completion Rules (see Russell et al., 1986), which can be used to simulate default lexical rules whose effect will be to flesh out word entries with all features relevant to the appropriate lexical category and assign sensible defaults or variable values to them. Variables range over atomic values and get instantiated by unification *at parse time*. Simple propagation statements (described in detail in section 3.2 below) are used to specify allowed propagation of features. In order to be able to specify different behaviour for different classes of features, explicit declaration of feature sets is supported. This allows the grammar writer to restrict the instantiation of variables in the rules and to achieve finer control over contexts to which propagation statements apply.

The existence of variables in the phrase structure rules of the object grammar is one of the crucial differences between the grammatical notation employed here and the theory of GPSG. Gazdar et al. (1985) view the grammar as describing a set of legal, and *fully instantiated*, local trees, defined declaratively by the simultaneous application of the various GPSG components. In contrast, this project regards the object, unification, grammar as specifying a set of *partially instantiated* phrase structure rules with considerably simpler semantics.

Further driven by the desire for simplicity, the current view on grammar formalism dispenses with the feature specification defaults and feature cooccurence restrictions of GPSG85. While such a seemingly drastic move appears to place the onus of ensuring consistency of feature bundles directly on the grammar writer, the organisation of the grammar now does not assume free instantiation of features, thereby reducing the danger of inconsistent feature clusters being introduced at parse time. In addition, the propagation rules themselves have a default status and can be overruled by explicit naming of feature values. To cover the very few cases where the effects of explicit feature propagation might have to be overridden, notional feature cooccurence restrictions are "hard-wired" into the grammar development environment. For example, the FCR in Figure 9 is applied during the process of ID rules normalisation, which entails copying of all the MAJOR (see below) features from the mother to each head daughter (the method for computing the head(s) of rules is built into the grammar compiler).

$$... : [BAR\ 0] \implies ([SUBCAT] \lor [TAKES]) \land [<major\ features>].$$

Figure 9

In this way the grammar development environment together with the particular grammar formalism as defined below represent a system which, while notationally quite close to the spirit of GPSG, still offers scope for freedom and experimentation. The freedom only goes insofar as it is now possible to exploit a range of different grammatical theories within one particular broad linguistic framework, namely that of GPSG. Thus the system we have developed is not a system like the core linguistic engine discussed by Shieber (1986a), which would offer a general facility within which to implement and compare different linguistic theories. Nonetheless, the grammar writer has the option to specify explicitly certain parameters of the grammar expansion process, or to abandon some of the more abstract theoretical apparatus of GPSG, without losing the ability to capture linguistic generalisations; in addition, she now has the option of explicitly specifying direct treatment of certain aspects of the theory --- for example, the assignment of bar levels during ID rules normalisation or achieving the effect of the Foot Feature Principle.

3.2 Grammar formalism

The current version of the grammar formalism comprises eight types of statement, roughly divided into *declarations* and *rules*. As far as possible, notational conventions introduced in Gazdar et al. (1985) are observed (however, as already noted, there are important differences in the interpretation of the notation). We have retained the GPSG *feature declarations, ID/LP rules* and *metarules* (but see below). The new grammar components are *feature set declarations, feature default rules* and *feature propagation rules*. The grammar development environment also supports *alias declarations*, as in Evans (1985). Figures 10 and 11 show examples of the different types of declarations and rules used in the grammar.

```
Feature:    VFORM    {BSE, ING, EN, TO}
Feature:    SUBCAT   {and, both, ...
                     either, for, that, ... whether}

Alias:      H = [H +, BAR 0].
Alias:      VP = [N -, V +, BAR 2, SUBJ -].
Alias:      EN = [VFORM EN].

Set:        VERBALHEAD = {PRD, FIN, AUX,
                     VFORM, PAST, NEG, INV}.
Set:        MAJOR = {N, V}.
```

Figure 10

```
IDRule VP/DITR:   VP ->      H [TAKES NP_NP], N2, N2.

LPRule LP4:       [SUBCAT] < [SUBCAT].

PropRule AGR/SPEC_N_1:
         N2  ->  DetN, [H +].
                 F (1) = F (2),    F in {PLU, COUNT}.

DefRule RHS_N1:   N1 ->   [H +], U.  F (1) = - ,   F in
                                                  {PRO, PN}.

MetaRule PASS:  VP ->    W, N2.  ==>  VP [+PRD, EN] ->
                                             W,(P2[by]).
```

Figure 11

Propagation and default rules employ similar formats and are subject to similar interpretations. For every ID rule which matches (in the same sense that a metarule pattern "matches") the pattern specified, the system ought to ensure that the feature equation associated with the propagation or default rule holds. Feature equations are defined in terms of features, either explicitly named (eg. FIN in Figure 15; section 4.1 below) or implicitly specified by ranging over feature sets (eg. F in VERBALHEAD; see Figure 15 and VERBALHEAD as declared above). Numeric indices in feature equations refer to the category specifications in the rule pattern; the rule categories are implicitly numbered from left to right.

For every feature specified by the feature equation, the interpretation of propagation rules is as follows. If it is present on only one of mother or daughter but not the other, its value is copied across; and if it is absent from both, it is added, with a variable value, to both. Values will get instantiated, by unification, at parse time. Thus the rule **AGR/SPEC_N_1** (Figure 11) ensures agreement between the determiner and the nominal head in a noun phrase, while the rule **HFC_VERBAL** (Figure 15) implements the HFC for verbal categories. Feature propagation rules serve the purpose of variable binding or feature instantiation in rules of the object grammar; however, since the propagation regimes they implement are "soft" (i.e. not hard-wired into the formalism or the parser), they offer flexibility and scope for experimentation in the process of grammar development, without in any way reducing the perspicuity of the grammar formalism.

Feature propagation rules have a certain default flavour, since their effect can be overridden by explicit introduction of values for a particular feature on the mother and any one daughter. Feature default rules are applied after propagation rules; their effect is to add features with particular values to specified categories in an ID rule. For example, the rule **RHS_N1** (Figure 11) defaults -PRO and -PN on N^1 to prevent it from dominating pronouns or propernames.

The descriptive device of feature default rules employed here differs from the feature specification defaults of GPSG in that it gives the grammar writer the option of specifying defaults on categories in the particular context of a local tree. FSDs are defined over categories only and lack the power of specifying a "don't care" value for a feature. For example, a notional default assigning -POSS to a [+N, -V] category is going to block any N^2 or N^1 rules matching a suitable lexical item which is marked +POSS in the lexicon. A feature default rule, on the other hand, can enforce an interpretation for such a default which only applies to N^2 categories participating in the right hand side of an ID rule and not explicitly marked +POSS. With similar motivation in mind --- namely seeking the expressive power to specify constraints on cooccurence of categories within local trees --- Kilbury (1986) introduces the notion of Category Cooccurence Restrictions, which allow him to dispense with metarules and still capture linguistic generalisations currently outside the scope of GPSG85. It is interesting to note the similarities between Kilbury's CCRs and the propagation and, in particular, the default rules discussed here.

With explicit control over feature propagation, it is now necessary for the grammar writer to have a clear idea of what counts as a well-formed category of major type. GPSG85 achieved this by the interplay of FCRs and FSDs; since we are using unification, the grammar now must be much more explicit on this account, especially if unification is taken to be strict, and not by extension (see section 3.3 below). The feature sets NOMINALHEAD, VERBALHEAD, ADJHEAD and PREPHEAD define which features may legitimately appear in the respective categories; appropriate default and propagation rules ensure the correct distribution of these within local trees.

The grammar formalism retains the GPSG metarules, with the following notational extensions. The multiset variable can be denoted by W or U; in the former case the metarule is taken to apply only to lexical ID rules, in the latter (as well as when it contains no variable) it is unrestricted in scope and thus can apply to non-lexical rules too. Furthemore, the category separators in the metarule pattern and target may be either a comma or a space, signifying whether the rule is to be applied to ID rules or linearised phrase structure rules. This was a decision adopted in the very early stages of the project, when it was thought that the conditions for metarules applicability would have to be weakened to account for constructions involving rightward movement, "heavy" NP shift and so forth. For instance, the current treatment of unbounded dependencies in the grammar relies on encoding, via non-lexical metarules, general facts about slash propagation, namely that a slash on the mother of a non-lexical ID rule will pass to the head (when it is [BAR 2] or [BAR 1]), otherwise in a lexical ID rule the slash will pass over to some sister of the lexical head.

As a consequence of these proposals for grammar formalism, it is necessary to adopt a different view on the way the different components interact to induce the object grammar. In particular, the reinterpretation of the components of GPSG85 retained here and the introduction of new declarations and rule types was motivated by the desire to provide a well defined order for their application in the process of inducing the object unification grammar, and constitutes another area where the interpretation of the formalism adopted by this project differs from the declarative semantics of GPSG85.

As discussed above, the default rules are introduced as a device for handling a common situation where a particular feature has been left unspecified in ID rules and yet must be taken to have an implicit, default, value. Leaving feature cooccurence restrictions out of the grammar altogether must be balanced by specifying finer grain of detail in the metarule patterns to avoid spurious matches. This suggests that default and propagation rules must be applied before metarule expansion --- to flesh out ID rules sufficiently so that appropriate metarules can then be identified and fired. Once a metarule has fired, however, there is a potential for a situation where a newly introduced feature might have to be propagated on its own right (eg. the [VFORM EN] introduced in the VP by the **PASS** metarule in Figure 11 needs to be propagated down to the head), or where it would overwrite an existing default. This latter case might be embarrassing for certain features; however, our grammar development effort (see below) has not yet uncovered a metarule which provokes such a situation. In any case, the interpretation of propagation rules built into the grammar compiler ensures that the output ID rule is not modified by them.

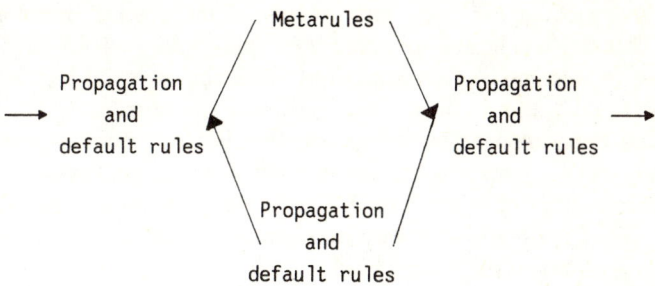

Figure 12

In order to achieve the desired overall effect for the object grammar, the output of the metarule expansion phase needs to be piped back into the default and propagation rules. Grammar expansion under metarules then involves them being applied in turn, their application separated by feeding the ID rules resulting from the last cycle into the default and propagation rules and adding that result to the original set of ID rules, to which the next metarule is applied, and so on (see Figure 12). Linearisation applies to the complete set of ID rules generated by the grammar, and there is a final cycle of linear metarule expansion followed by defaults assignment and propagation. Figure 13 illustrates the flow of control during the process of grammar expansion and compilation.

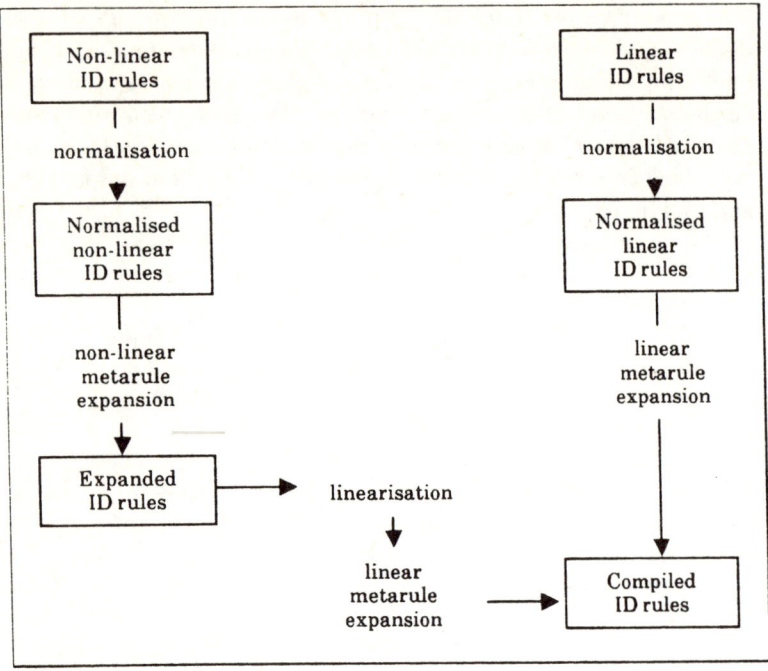

Figure 13

3.3 The grammar development environment

The organisation of the grammar is represented in the programming system built to support the grammar formalism outlined above. By analogy with present day programming environments (Barstow et al., 1984) where software development is supported by powerful interactive programming tools, the grammar writer has at her disposal a set of tools for grammar development (for detailed description see Carroll, 1986).

Grammar constructs (eg. feature sets, ID rules, propagation statements, or lexical item definitions) can be stated via a specialised input facility which incorporates a structure editor and performs dynamic checking of the declarations syntax. Explicit manipulation of the grammar items is supported; this includes display, editing and deletion. Depending on the item in focus, further options exist for monitoring the effects grammar expansion and compilation have on arbitrary fragments of the grammar. Thus individual rules can be piped through normalisation or linearisation, metarules applied explicitly to selected ID rules, or lexical items fully instantiated after the application of default and propagation rules.

In order to be able to evaluate fragments of grammar, as they are being developed, the grammar development environment (GDE) incorporates a parser with a range of user settable options. For instance, text can be analysed under specific grammar categories, different levels of detail in the analyses can be requested as an output from the parser, or run-time tracing of different parsing components can be switched on and off. A separate flag toggles between parsing with strict unification and unification by extension. Further means of grammar debugging is provided by a special purpose built generator.

Facilities exist for saving new and altered rules permanently, after they have been debugged to the linguist's satisfaction. Likewise, it is possible to swiftly change context by saving and restoring the current state of grammar being worked on. As the grammar grows in size and coverage, it is necessary and important to maintain upwards compatibility by making sure that no "ripple effects" are introduced by adding new rules to the existing set. Briscoe et al. (1986) discuss the use of a substantial corpus of English (Garside and Leech, 1982) for continuous monitoring of the state of the grammar.

In addition to being the essential and primary tool for grammar development and debugging by encouraging interactive and incremental rule elicitation, the GDE also provides a facility for expanding the source grammar and compiling it into a set of partially instantiated phrase structure rules which is then taken to be the input to the parser. Experimenting within the GDE with the two different modes of parsing --- by strict unification and by unification by extension --- made it clear that even though a grammar written for strict unification must make heavy (and careful) use of default and propagation rules in order to achieve complete and correct category instantiation, this is a more viable option both for grammar development and realistic parsing. Allowing categories to match by extension makes it far too easy to generate spurious analyses, in great numbers and at the cost of dramatically deteriorating performance.

The GDE software is now complete and stable, insofar as the grammar notation is stable and not required to change again. Satisfactory progress to date with the grammar, as well as real time constraints on the project (i.e. a completion date), make major changes in the formalism unlikely. Future work will be mostly aimed at the development of the grammar and the generation of a word list indexed to it.

4. CURRENT STATE AND FUTURE DEVELOPMENTS

4.1 A grammar example

Below is an example of a fragment of the grammar under development, extracted and slightly modified from Briscoe et al. (1986) (see also Grover, 1986). This presents an almost complete treatment of the English auxiliary verb system. Modals (Figure 14) require that their complement be BSE. "Do" and "ought", when modals, can only be finite. "Do" requires its complement to be -AUX, hence its different TAKES value from other modals. The propagation and default rules relevant to this fragment are illustrated in Figure 15. **HFC_VERBAL** was discussed above; **VP_VFORM** makes VPs in rules with VFORM value default to -FIN thus preventing, instance, a finite verb [+FIN, VFORM @] to match a VP [VFORM BSE]. Figure 16 gives some lexical entries with their feature specifications as they appear in the lexicon and shows how they will interact with the auxiliary grammar fragment.

```
                    ID rules:

    IDRule VP/MODAL:
    VP [+AUX,+FIN]    ->      H [TAKES BASE_VP], VP [BSE].

    IDRule VP/DO:
    VP [+AUX,+FIN]    ->      H [TAKES DO_COMPL],VP
                                             [AUX-, BSE].
```

```
IDRule VP/OUGHT:
VP [+AUX,+FIN]    ->        H [TAKES INF], VP [TO, +AUX].

IDRule VP/TO:
VP [+AUX, TO]     ->        H [TAKES BASE_VP], VP [BSE].

IDRule VP/BE_AUX:
VP [+AUX]         ->H [TAKES PRED], VP [+PRD].

        "Subject-Auxiliary inversion" metarule:

MetaRule SAI:
VP [+AUX] -> W. ==> S [+INV, +FIN] -> W, N2.
```

Figure 14

```
    Propagation and default rules for AUX grammar fragment:

PropRule HFC_VERBAL:
[N -, V +] -> [H +], U.F(0) = F(1), F in VERBALHEAD.

DefRule VP_VFORM:
[]              -> VP [VFORM], U.  FIN(1) = -.
```

Figure 15

```
        Sample lexical entries:

    does :   V [+AUX,+FIN, TAKES DO_COMP, -PAST].
    ought:   V [+AUX,+FIN, TAKES INF, -PAST].
    have :   V [+AUX, BSE, TAKES PSP, -FIN].
    has  :   V [+AUX,+FIN, TAKES PSP, -PAST].
    be   :   V [+AUX, BSE, TAKES PRED, -FIN].
    been :   V [+AUX, EN, -PRD, TAKES PRED, +PAST].
    can  :   V [+AUX,+FIN, TAKES BASE_VP, -PAST].
    put  :   V [+AUX,+FIN, TAKES PSP, +PAST].
```

Figure 16

The grammar of English for the natural language toolkit is currently under development in Lancaster (see Briscoe et al., 1986, for more details). In its present version it offers a central fragment with coverage of major clause and verb phrase types. This interacts with additional grammar fragments, and is used as a skeletal framework within which separate efforts have resulted in fleshing out the treatment of auxiliary verb structures, unbounded dependencies, and more recently, noun phrases and prenominal modifiers (see Grover, 1986), as well as ordinary, zero an free relatives, NP complements, VP and PP modifiers and topicalisation. There is no unified treatment of agreement as yet: the noun phrase fragment has propagation rules for specifier-noun agreement, likewise propagation rules exist for agreement between preposed categories and the category value of SLASH; agreement between noun and verb phrases at clause level is equally trivial.

4.2 The word list and its indexing to the grammar

Presently the grammar development environment incorporates preliminary versions of the lexicon and parsing systems developed by the other Tools Projects. In particular, in addition to the word definition facility used for immediate testing of grammar rules, the GDE allows independent interface and access to a hand-crafted lexicon of approximately 3,500 items, developed for the purposes of the dictionary project. On completion, the project will have developed appropriate software for loading a user supplied lexicon and interfacing to that with the aim of extracting information relevant to natural language processing programs.

For the purposes of the morphological and syntactic analyser which is jointly the ultimate objective of the Tools Projects, the development of the grammar will proceed essentially in parallel with the development of a substantial word list indexed to it. As a necessary prerequisite, the feature set and default rules used by the grammar and the lexicon are compatible with each other. From a purely methodological point of view, it is clear that since the complete system will be relying on the lexicon component to deliver fully specified lexical items, the elicitation of the overall feature set and the development and debugging of the default rules must be done in close cooperation between the two projects; in much the same way in which the design of a grammar formalism must be done with considerations relating both to the grammar and the parser projects alike.

However, once a stable system for encoding lexical information through syntactic features has been developed, it still remains to be applied to a lexicon of realistic size.

Given the availability of machine readable versions of published dictionaries, it is natural to approach the problem of deriving such a substantial word list from a suitable source. Most dictionaries offer conventional labels for broadly categorising words by their parts of speech. Thus it would be possible to extract general information of this sort without too much difficulty. In addition, the dictionary project has developed software for performing morphological analysis on inflected words, as a result of which a given lexical entry will acquire the relevant feature specifications for features like PAST, FIN, AGR, PLU and so forth, required for parsing. This leaves open the problem of associating detailed and correct subcategorisation information with the majority of the words in the lexicon.

Such information is not readily found in a published dictionary; a notable exception is the *Longman Dictionary of Contemporary English* (Procter, 1978, henceforth LDOCE). It is a dictionary with certain rare, and even unique, properties; what makes it particularly relevant to this project is the fact that among other things it offers, through a highly elaborate and semi-formal system, a finer grain of detail about the grammatical behdetail about the grammatical behaviour of individual words. Even though the grammar coding system in LDOCE is not GPSG specific, it encodes just the type of information which GPSG assumes relating to the subcategorisation classes in the lexicon. The Longman lexicographers have developed a representational system which is capable of describing compactly a variety of data relevant to the task of indexing a word list to a grammar: eg. distinctions between count and mass nouns (DOG vs. DESIRE), predicative, postpositive and attributive adjectives (ASLEEP vs. ELECT vs. JOCULAR), noun complementation (FONDNESS, FACT) and, most importantly, verb complementation and valency.

LDOCE grammar codes typically contain a capital letter, followed by a number and, occasionally, a small letter, for example [T5a] or [V3]. The capital letters encode information "about the way a word works in a sentence or about the position it can fill" (Procter, 1978: xxviii); the numbers "give information about the way the rest of a phrase or clause is made up in relation to the word being described" (ibid.). For example, "T" denotes a transitive verb with one object, while "5" specifies that what follows the verb must be a sentential complement introduced by *that*. (The small letters, in the case above "a", provide further information typically related to the status of various complementisers, adverbs and prepositions in compound verb constructions: eg. "a" indicates that the word *that* can be left out between a verb and the following clause.) "V3" introduces a verb followed by one object and a verb form (V) which must be an infinitive with *to*.

       believe *v* ....3 [T5a,b;V3;X *(to be)* 1, *(to be)* 7] to hold as an opinion; suppose: *I believe he has come.* | *He has come, I believe.* | "*Has he come*" "*I believe so.*" | *I believe him to have done it.* | *I believe him (to be) honest* ....

    Figure 17

   Within the framework of the grammar project, a system has been developed which is capable of "parsing" the grammar codes associated with individual verb senses from LDOCE word entries and deriving from them relatively theory-neutral representations of lexical entries utilisable by most theories of generative grammar. Thus, for example, from the grammar coding of the third verb sense of BELIEVE (see Figure 17), the program automatically generates the lexical entry in Figure 18 incorporating information about the grammatical category, syntactic subcategorisation frames and semantic type of the verb (for instance, a label like (Type 2 ORaising) indicates that under the given sense the verb is a two-place predicate; furthermore, if it occurs with a syntactic direct object, this will function as the logical subject of the predicate complement). Details concerning the way the program achieves this transformation and the justification for it can be found in Boguraev and Briscoe (1987). What is important here is that a generic lexical entry of the form above can now be directly mapped into a feature cluster within the features and feature set declarations used by the lexicon and grammar projects.

```
(believe   Verb    (Sense 3)

   ((Takes NP SBar)    (Type 2))

   ((Takes NP NP Inf)    (Type 2 ORaising))

   ((or  ((Takes NP NP NP)     (Type 2 ORaising))
         ((Takes NP NP AuxInf)    (Type 2 ORaising))))

   ((or  ((Takes NP NP AP)     (Type 2 ORaising))
         ((Takes NP NP AuxInf)    (Type 2 ORaising)))))
```

Figure 18

This mapping process can be applied with similar results to the noun, adjective and adverb definitions in LDOCE. These, together with the core lexicon containing most closed class items as well as modals, auxiliaries and other "difficult" words, will make the bulk of the target word list. While it is unrealistic to expect a direct and error-free mapping for all dictionary entries into corresponding word list items, the information contained in the dictionary can be used as a very good "first approximation" and thus considerably speed up the process of deriving lexical entries for our particular parsing framework. New entries automatically generated form their dictionary counterparts can be evaluated immediately by testing them against the grammar (Boguraev et al., 1987). The system described here can thus be seen as another component in the overall development effort, further promoting the interactive and incremental approach we have adopted for the whole project.

5. CONCLUSION

The work described here, and in particular the effort aimed at the development of a computational grammar of English within the overall framework of GPSG, falls under what might be called linguistic engineering, rather than original research into linguistic theory. Our aims are to make computational sense of a particular theory of grammar for the practical purposes of delivering a product to a wide user community. In such context we cannot afford to spend too much time seeking elegant solutions and trying to capture linguistic generalisations; we also need an implementation of the theory capable of meeting the demands of realistic processing time for morphosyntactic analysis.

The joint experience of the Tools Projects would seem to indicate that the "canonical" version of GPSG, as stated in Gazdar et al. (1985), while a long way from notational devices used for grammar development less than a decade ago, falls short on the count of having clearly stated semantics for its highly formalised, and therefore computationally attractive, notation. Furthermore, our experience is in line with a more general feeling that if taken to extremes, attempting to capture linguistic generalisations in a concise and "elegant" manner tends to lead to a grammar which is difficult to understand, and consequently to develop and debug. Thus, independently of issues such as the de facto internal consistency of GPSG, or the real generality of the generalisations that it attempts to capture, a project with a practical goal like ours must strike the right balance between attempting to benefit from the overall framework of a particular theory and aiming to produce a simple and clean object, easy to understand, maintain and extend.

Such a view led us to regard the target, object, set of phrase structure rules as the real grammar under development. The grammar formalism evolved in the course of the project should be viewed then not as a theory of grammar, but as a notational device with two primary purposes. Firstly, it allows latitude in experimenting with different interpretations of certain aspects of the overall grammatical framework. Thus, for example, explicit propagation rules make it possible to investigate alternative feature propagation regimes. Secondly, it offers the grammar writer a means of working quickly and efficiently. Components of the grammar notation, such as aliases and, in particular, feature propagations rules and metarules, not only reflect deep linguistic insights, but also function as higher level constructs in a specialised programming language designed to aid linguists at their work, and implemented within the grammar development environment.

Grammar writing, particularly where grammars of considerable size are concerned, is inherently experimental. It is impossible to design a grammar from scratch and get it right the first time. We hope, however, that with the right combination of theoretical framework, flexible notation and dynamic development environment, the task of the grammar writer in the long run will be made feasible, as well as easier.

ACKNOWLEDGEMENTS

This paper draws heavily on eighteen months of discussions between the members of the three Alvey Tools projects; large fragments of it can ultimately be traced back to internal memos, circulars, working papers and (interim versions of) user manuals. The grammar formalism described here evolved incrementally following joint sessions between Ted Briscoe, John Carroll, Claire Grover, Robert Moore, John Phillips, Steve Pulman, Graham Russell, Henry Thompson and the author (who claims no credit for linguistic insights, but the responsibilty for any errors and misrepresentation). I am particularly grateful to Hiyan Alshawi, Ted Briscoe and Steve Pulman for their comments on the first draft.

The work described here was supported in part by a research grant from the UK Science and Engineering Research Council (GR/D 05554) under the Alvey Programme and was carried out during the author's tenure of a SERC Research Fellowship. We are grateful to Longman Group Limited for kindly allowing the use of the headword and grammar code information on the typesetting tape of LDOCE for the purposes of deriving the word list indexed to the grammar.

BIBLIOGRAPHY

[1] Alshawi, Hiyan; Moore, Robert; Sparck Jones, Karen; and Pulman, Steven (1986). *Final report: Feasibility study for a research programme in natural-language processing.* SRI Technical Note, SRI International, Cambridge, UK.

[2] Barstow, David; Shrobe, Eric; and Sandewall, Erik (1984). *Interactive programming environments.* New York: McGraw Hill.

[3] Barton, G. Edward (1985). On the complexity of ID/LP parsing. *Computational Linguistics*, 11(4), 205-218.

[4] Boguraev, Bran and Briscoe, Ted (1987, Forthcoming). Large lexicons for natural language processing: exploiting the grammar coding system of LDOCE. *Computational Linguistics.*

[5] Boguraev, Bran; Briscoe, Ted; Carroll, John; Carter, David and Grover, Claire (1987). The derivation of a grammatically indexed lexicon from the Longman Dictionary of Contemporary English. In *Proceedings of the 25th Annual Meeting of the Association for Computational Linguistics*, Stanford, California (to appear).

[6] Briscoe, Ted (1986). *Tools projects grammar formalism and related issues*. Alvey Grammar Project Working Paper: Department of Linguistics, University of Lancaster: England.

[7] Briscoe, Ted; Craig, Ian; and Grover, Claire (1986). The use of the LOB Corpus in the development of a phrase-structure grammar of English. In *Proceedings of the Seventh International Conference on English Language Research on Computational Corpora (ICAME)*, Amsterdam, The Netherlands.

[8] Carroll, John (1986). *Grammar development environment - V 1.09. User Documentation*: University of Cambridge Computer Laboratory: Cambridge, England.

[9] Chung, P.W.H. (Ed); Bowen, D.; Byrd, L.; Pereira, F.; Pereira, L.; Rae, R.; and Warre, D. (1985). *Edinburgh Prolog: the new implementation (NIP) user's manual*. University of Edinburgh AI Applications Institute, Edinburgh, Scotland.

[10] Evans, Roger (1985). ProGram - a development tool for GPSG grammars. *Linguistics* 23 (2), 313-243.

[11] Garside, Roger and Leech, Geoffrey (1982). Grammatical tagging of the LOB corpus: general survey. In Johansson, S., Ed. *Computer Corpora in English Language Research*. Norwegian Computing Centre for the Humanities, Bergen, Norway.

[12] Gawron, Mark; King, Jonathan; Lamping, John; Loebner, Egon; Paulson, Anne; Pullum, Geoffrey; Sag, Ivan; and Wasow, Thomas (1982). The GPSG linguistics system. In *Proceedings of the 20th Annual Meeting of the Association for Computational Linguistics*, Toronto, Ontario.

[13] Gazdar, Gerald (1982). Phrase Structure Grammar. In Jacobson, P. and Pullum, G. Eds., *The nature of syntactic representation*, Dordrecht: D. Reidel.

[14] Gazdar, Gerald and Pullum, Geoffrey (1982). Generalized Phrase Structure Grammar: a theoretical synopsis. University Linguistics Club, Bloomington, Indiana.

[15] Gazdar, Gerald (1984). Recent computer implementations of phrase structure grammars. *Computational Linguistics* 10 (3-4), 212-214.

[16] Gazdar, Gerald; Klein, Ewan; Pullum, Geoffrey K.; and Sag, Ivan A. (1985). *Generalized phrase structure grammar*. Oxford: Blackwell and Cambridge: Harvard University Press.

[17] Grover, Claire (1986). The analysis of NP specifiers in English. Paper presented at the *Autumn Meeting of the Linguistic Association of Great Britain*. Edinburgh University, Edinburgh, Scotland.

[18] Kaplan, Ronald (1986). Three seductions of computational psycholinguistics. In Whitelock et al.

[19] Karttunen, Lauri and Kay, Martin (1985). Structure sharing with binary trees. In *Proceedings of the 23rd Annual Meeting of the Association for Computational Linguistics*, Chicago, Illinois.

[20] Kilbury, James (1984). A modification of the Earley-Shieber algorithm for direct parsing of ID/LP grammars. Project KIT Technical Report, Technische UniversitHat, Berlin.

[21] Kilbury, James (1986). Category cooccurence restrictions and the elimination of metarules. In this volume. Also in *Proceedings of the 11th International Conference on Computational Linguistics*, Bonn, Germany.

[22] Koskenniemi, Kimmo (1983). Two-level model for morphological analysis. In *Proceedings of the Eighth International Joint Conference on Artificial Intelligence.* Karlsruhe, Germany.
[23] Koskenniemi, Kimmo (1983). *Two-level morphology: a general computational model for word recognition and production.* Publication No. 11: University of Helsinki: Finland.
[24] Pereira, Fernando and Warren, David (1980). Definite clause grammars for language analysis - a survey of the formalism and a comparison with augmented transition networks. In *Artificial Intelligence,* vol.13: 231-278.
[25] Pereira, Fernando (1985). A structure-sharing representation for unification-based grammar fornalisms. In *Proceedings of the 23rd Annual Meeting of the Association for Computational Linguistics,* Chicago, Illinois.
[26] Phillips, John and Thompson, Henry (1985). GPSGP - a parser for generalised phrase structure grammars. *Linguistics* 23 (2), 245-261.
[27] Phillips, John and Thompson, Henry (1986a) A parser for generalised phrase structure grammars. To apper in Klein, E. and Haddock, N., Eds. *Edinburgh Working Papers in Cognitive Science,* University of Edinburgh: Edinburgh, Scotland.
[28] Phillips, John and Thompson, Henry (1986b). A parser and an appropriate computational representation for GPSG. To be presented at the *Autumn Meeting of the Linguistics Association of Great Britain,* University of Edinburgh, Edinburgh, Scotland.
[29] Procter, Paul (1978). *Longman dictionary of contemporary English.* Longman Group Limited, Harlow and London, England.
[30] Russell, Graham; Pulman, Steve; Ritchie, Graeme; and Black, Alan A Dictionary and Morphological Analyser for English. In *Proceedings of the Eleventh International Congress on Computational Linguistics,* Bonn, Germany.
[31] Shieber, Stuart (1984a). Direct parsing of ID/LP grammars. *Linguistics and Philosophy,* 7, 135-154.
[32] Shieber, Stuart (1984b). The design of a computer language for linguistic information. In *Proceedings of the Tenth International Conference on Computational Linguistics.* Stanford University, Stanford, California.
[33] Shieber, Stuart (1985). Criteria for designing computer facilities for linguistic analysis. *Linguistics* 23 (2), 189-211.
[34] Shieber, Stuart (1986a). Separating linguistic analyses from linguistic theories. In Whitelock et al.; revised version in this volume.
[35] Shieber, Stuart (1986b). A simple reconstruction of GPSG. In *Proceedings of the 11th International Conference on Computational Linguistics,* Bonn, Germany.
[36] Thompson, Henry (1981). Chart parsing and rule schemata in PSG. In *Proceedings of the 19th Annual meeting of the Association for Computational Linguistics,* Stanford, CA.
[37] Thompson, Henry (1983). A flexible, modular chart parsing system. In *Proceedings of the National Conference on Artificial Intelligence,* Washington, D.C.
[38] Thompson, Henry (1982). Handling metarules in a parser for GPSG. In Barlow, M.; Flickinger, D.; and Sag, I., Eds. *Developments in Generalised Phrase Structure Grammar: Stanford Working Papers in Grammatical Theory, Volume 2,* Indiana University Linguistics Club: Bloomington, Indiana.
[39] Thompson, Henry (1985). Implementation: distraction or contribution. In Whitelock et al.

[40] Whitelock, P.; Somers, H.; Bennett, P.; Johnson, R.; and Wood, M.M., Eds. (1986). *Proceedings of Alvey/ICL Workshop on Linguistic Theory and Computer Applications.* Transcripts available as a CCL/UMIST report No. 86/2: Centre for Computational Linguistics, University of Manchester Institute of Science and Technology, Manchester, England.

JÖRG KINDERMANN
JUSTUS MEIER
FAKULTÄT FÜR LINGUISTIK UND LITERATURWISSENSCHAFT
UNIVERSITÄT BIELEFELD

AN EXTENSION OF LR-PARSING
FOR LEXICAL FUNCTIONAL GRAMMAR

1. INTRODUCTION

Syntactic parsing is a well investigated domain in Computational Linguistics. Efficient Algorithms for context free grammars such as LR Parsing (for deterministic grammars) or Earley's Algorithm were developed more than a decade ago. But only very recently one of them, Earley's algorithm, has been applied to Lexical Functional Grammar (Block/Haugeneder 1986). In this paper we show an alternative approach using methods of LR parsing.

We think that for a natural language syntactic parser (an LFG parser in particular) the following criteria (among others) are important:

- Efficiency of the parsing procedures: This includes the degree of determinism of decisions taken by the parser as well as its requirements of computing time and storage space with respect to the length of a given input.

- Restrictions imposed on the grammar: A relevant topic here is the ability of the parser to process certain types of grammar rules (i.e. left-recursive). Equally important are restrictions on the ordering of grammar rules.

- A topic which is relevant in particular for Lexical Functional Grammar (LFG) is the treatment of unification by the parser.

- debugging facilities: A good working environment for the development of natural language grammars is of great importance in any experimental system containing a parser.

In the following we will show how these criteria are met by an LR parser which is extended to handle LFG rules. (By the terms "LR parser" and "LR algorithm" we refer throughout this paper to any parser using a parsing table computed by any LR(k), SLR(k) or LALR(k) algorithm as defined e.g. in Aho/Ullman(1972). Our implementation of Tomita's Parser uses the SLR(1) algorithm.)

2. LR PARSING

2.1 Chart parsing and deterministic parsing

In order to avoid backtracking in context free parsing one has two choices: chart parsing and deterministic parsing.

For chart parsing one can use Earley's algorithm. Supplied with a grammar and an input string it produces all parses of the string. It accepts any CFG. The price you pay for keeping track of all possibilities in the chart is that you must store many partial analyses which will not contribute to the output structure. J. Kilbury (1984), J. Dörre and S. Momma (1985) modified Earley's algorithm so as to produce a smaller number of useless partial structures.

But one may also turn to deterministic parsing, which for our purposes can be characterized by the property that no useless structures are produced. The LR algorithm generates such a deterministic parser for a given grammar.

It is true that the LR algorithm produces a deterministic parser only for deterministic languages. But one can apply it to a non-deterministic grammar and still retain the deterministic property that useless pieces of structure are never built up.

2.2 The LR parsing strategy

An LR parser consists of a shift-reduce parser with a push-down stack and lookahead facility as well as a parsing table. The general strategy of the parser is to shift every symbol unless it is definitely told to do a reduction. It is the parsing table which tells the parser when to reduce. The LR algorithm computes the parsing table for a given grammar. To find out when to reduce one needs to know first what follows the current input symbol, and second what has already been parsed, i.e. the left context of the current symbol.

The first task is accomplished by using a lookahead of one symbol. (Because of the definitional property of deterministic languages one symbol is sufficient.)

The left context is coded by nodes in the "goto graph", each node representing a set of "viable prefixes" of the language. A viable prefix is a string of grammar symbols which is at most so long that it can be reduced, but never longer. The viable prefixes thus represent all possible strings which may be the left context of an input symbol.

There is now a simple test to determine whether a reduction should be performed or not: add the lookahead symbol to the current viable prefix. If the outcome is again a viable prefix, we shift the symbol. If it is not, the old prefix must be reduced.

We make sure that the parser never leaves the world of viable prefixes by letting it take the nodes of the goto graph as internal states. For every state there is a row in the parsing table with an entry for every possible lookahead symbol. (See for example figure 1 below: Take the entry "sh3" in the row for state 7. This tells us to shift the lookahead symbol "DET" and change the state of the parser into "state3". The entry for "$" in the same row tells us to perform a reduction by rule (5) if the end of the input string has been reached.)

This therefore means that for a string which is not a sentence of the language the parser is able to announce an error even before shifting the symbol that makes it a non-sentence.

2.3 Applications of LR parsing

With an LR parser we have a very simple parsing mechanism strictly separated from the data structure which gives the parser access to the grammar. The grammar, however, has influence only on the parsing table. It never intervenes in the parsing process. The parsing strategy imposes no restrictions on the grammar, we can therefore parse any CFG.

The parsing table provides automatic detection of ambiguities and constructs that are difficult to parse. Thus it makes clear to the grammar writer what rules are responsible for the difficulties and what might be changed in the grammar.

On the other hand, instead of changing the grammar one can modify the parsing table, should the grammar contain an ambiguity concerning the associativity of an operator which is understood to be solved by a rule external to the grammar, e.g. "associate to the left". The parsing table is the place to code such external parsing rules. Pereira (1985) used the table to formulate preferences used in natural language processing such as Minimal Attachment and Right Association. Such rules are "higher" than grammar rules but are still independent of the parsing strategy which the parser follows. They can therefore be stated in a declarative way in the parsing table.

It can be easier to remove double entries from a small parsing table for an ambiguous grammar than to work with a larger table for an unambiguous one.

Of course most grammars for natural languages will contain ambiguities which may not be removed for linguistic reasons. But even these grammars may be so close to deterministic grammars that it would be more efficient to parse them deterministically as far as possible than to use Earley's algorithm.

3. EXTENSION OF AN LR PARSER FOR CONTEXT FREE GRAMMARS.

Multiple entries in the parsing table can in principle be treated in one of two ways:

(a) by using backtracking: Note that in this case backtracking is not used to undo wrong reductions but only to obtain all parses in the case of global ambiguity. Thus a table-driven backtracking parser would still be more efficient than a simple non-deterministic shift-reduce parser. Wrong decisions would also not occur during a particular parse. Nevertheless, the backtracking parser would need exponential time to parse ambiguous inputs. It would therefore be significantly less efficient than a chart parser using Earley's algorithm.

(b) by simulating parallel processing: A first approach to this could be to represent ambiguities in a list of stacks which are reduced in parallel. But this would still be exponential in time and space. The problem here is to interconnect different parses of ambiguous input to make their results available to all other paths. Such an interconnection would guarantee that each reduction is done only once in the same context. Tomita (1985) shows that the order of complexity for processing ambiguous input can be reduced to polynomial. (The parser, however, only constructs simple phrase structure representations as a parsing result. This is considerably different from the situation with LFG as is pointed out in section 4.)

3.1 Parsing with a graph-structured stack.

In the following we will show our re-implementation of the parser, which is extended to construct LFG representations. We will proceed using an example to illustrate the explanations. Starting with a simple context free grammar, which, however, is non-LR, a parsing table can be generated using standard LR-techniques. The grammar and the corresponding table of parsing actions and "goto" relations is shown in figure 1.

A sample grammar:

(1) s   --> np vp
(2) np --> det n
(3) np --> np pp
(4) pp --> p np
(5) vp --> v
(6) vp --> v np
(7) vp --> v np pp

The corresponding parsing table:

| | Actions ||||| Goto ||||
	det	n	p	v	$	s	np	vp	pp
state0	sh3					1	2		
state1					acc				
state2			sh6	sh7				5	4
state3		sh8							
state4			re3	re3	re3				
state5					re1				
state6	sh3						9		
state7	sh3				re5		10		
state8			re2	re2	re2				
state9			re4	re4	re4				4
			sh6						
state10			sh6		re6				11
state11			re3	re3	re7				
					re3				

figure 1

Note that the states 9 and 11 show multiple entries which represent a shift-reduce conflict for state 9 and a reduce-reduce conflict for state 11, respectively.

The parser uses a stack which is an alternating sequence of state

AN EXTENSION OF LR-PARSING

numbers and constituent representations as is shown in figure 2. (The top of the stack is on the right.) This figure shows a snapshot of the stack when processing the input

The girl saw the baby with the telescope in the park.

The constituent representations are actually phrase structure trees, which we have substituted by words for better readability. The state numbers correspond to rows in the parsing table. The parser is said to be "in state n" if the number n is on top of the stack.

|0|——NP—|2|—V—|7|——NP——|10|——P—|6|——DET—|3|——N——|8|
     the girl   saw   the baby   with   the   telescope

figure 2

The next word to be read is "in", which is a preposition. The parser proceeds in the following steps:

- Determine the next action: The parser currently is in state 8. This state has an entry in the parsing table which says that the next action should be to reduce the stack by rule 2.

- Perform the next action: The reduction is executed as follows: The constituents N and DET are popped off the stack together with the corresponding states 8 and 3. The reduction results in the construction of an NP.

- Determine the next state: The parser now is in state 6. The next state (i.e. state 9) is determined by the entry of state 6 in the goto table. Eventually the new NP constituent and the new state number are pushed onto the stack, which is then shown in figure 3.

|0|—— NP——|2|— V——|7|—— NP ——|10|—— P ——|6|—— NP ————|9|
     the girl   saw   the baby   with   the
                                                                               telescope

figure 3

The next word to be read is still "in". This time a shift-reduce conflict occurs: the entries of state 9 are "reduce by rule 4" and, alternatively, "shift and move to state 6".

The naive way to simulate parallel processing of alternative entries in the parsing table would be to copy the stack every time an ambiguity is encountered. This is shown for our example in figure 4.

|0|——NP——|2|—V—|7|——NP——|10|——P——|6|——NP——|9|——P——|6|
     the girl   saw   the baby   with   the   in
                                                             telescope

|0|—— NP——|2|—V—|7|————————— NP ————————|10|————————————P ————|6|
     the girl   saw   the baby with   in
                                  the telescope

figure 4

The stacks must be synchronized with respect to shift operations. This means that the execution of shifts must be delayed until every other stack has been reduced as far as possible (i.e. the table entries only show shift actions for every top-of-stack).

This treatment of ambiguous input is very ineffective because the same reductions have to be applied several times. Tomita's first improvement in space requirements is to split only relevant portions of the stack: those parts which are not affected by the current parsing action need only be represented once. Prolog provides this improvement for free via the structure sharing property. We now do not have a list of independent stacks but a tree of stacks as shown in figure 5

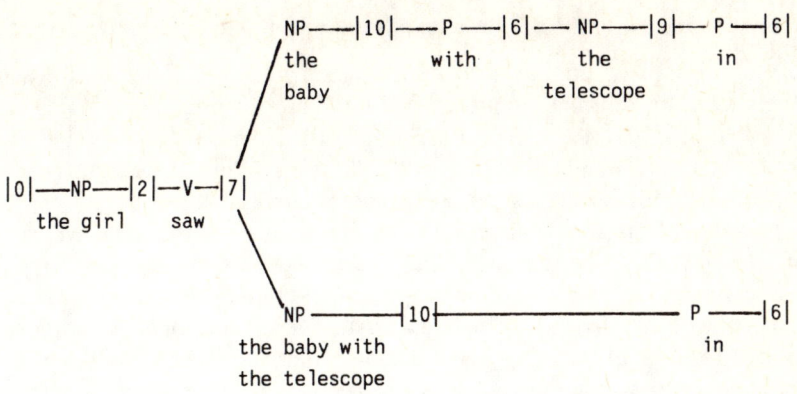

figure 5

Tomita's second improvement is to also combine identical top portions of stacks (see figure 6). In this version the list of stacks has been transformed into a directed acyclic graph. This combination technique ensures that every reduction is done only once in the same context. Thus the parsing times are polynomial for ambiguous input.

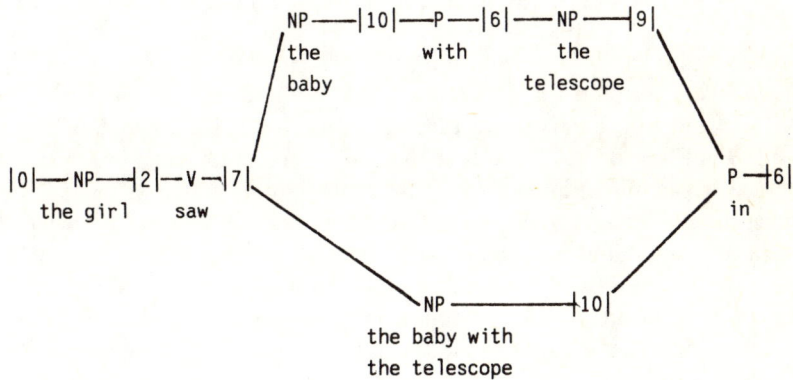

figure 6

3.2 Parsing of unknown words.

Our re-implementation of Tomita's parser improves the robustness of the system by allowing the processing of unknown words in the input. It is possible to infer categories of unknown words from the parsing table. Let us for example assume that the word following "in" in our example cannot be found in the lexikon. Since the parser is currently in state 6, it can be determined from the parsing table that the category of the unknown word must be "DET". The reason for this is that there exists only one entry in the column "DET" for state 6. In general the table may offer more than one choice (take for example state 2). Alternatives may again be explored either in parallel or using backtracking. Guessing is not limited to the occurrence of a single unknown word. In principle it is possible to parse a string consisting exclusively of unknown words. This would, however, result in a high number of ambiguous solutions for any reasonably complex grammar.

4. CONSTRUCTION OF F-STRUCTURES.

So far this paper has described a re-implementation of Tomita's parser, which constructs simple phrase structure representations. We adapted our implementation to the processing of LFG rules. Kaplan/Bresnan 1982 should be consulted for details on LFG. With respect to parsing, LFG differs from an ordinary context free grammar in the following details:

LFG consists of a structural context free part and a functional part. A phrase structure grammar assigns a tree representation called the constituent structure (c-structure) to a sentence. The phrase structure rules are annotated with functional equation schemata. For a given c-structure these provide a system of functional equations which has a common solution (if the sentence in question is well-formed). This solution in turn is known as the functional structure (f-structure) of the sentence. The functional equations are solved by unification. There is an important distinction with respect to the role of functional schemata:

- Defining equations augment a given f-structure with a new feature.

- Constraining equations pose restrictions on expected features and the range of their values. These features have to be present in the final f-structure.

- Existential constraints are non-equational schemata which postulate the occurrence of a particular feature with an arbitrary value.

Defining equations may thus be processed when the c-structure representation is constructed. This means that the parser constructs c-structure and f-structure in parallel. Constraining equations and constraints are furthermore used to check well-formedness. They thus apply only after the processing of the defining equations.

The relations between sentence, c-structure and f-structure are non-trivial. The phrase structure grammar usually has generative overcapacity with respect to the natural language fragment to be described. Ungrammatical strings which are generated by the grammar are ruled out by special conditions of uniqueness, completeness and coherence imposed on the f-structure part of the representation. On the other hand, theoretical investigations (cf., e.g., Kaplan/Bresnan 1982) show that the use of functional schemata in the grammar leads to at least context sensitive generative power. This means that for certain grammars it will be impossible to parse a given input in polynomial time. Nevertheless, Tomita's parser would be significantly more efficient than backtracking parsers even in this case.

To explain the adaptation of Tomita's parser to the processing of LFGs we begin with an introduction of our representation of f-structures and the implementation of f-structure unification. Figure 7 shows the f-structure for the sentence "The girl sleeps."

$$\begin{bmatrix} \text{SUBJ} & \begin{bmatrix} \text{SPEC} & \text{THE} \\ \text{NUM} & \text{SG} \\ \text{PRED} & \text{'GIRL'} \end{bmatrix} \\ \\ \text{TENSE} & \text{PRESENT} \\ \\ \text{PRED} & \text{'SLEEP<(\uparrow SUBJ)>'} \end{bmatrix}$$

figure 7

F-structures consist of sets of so called "attribute-value pairs". The attribute names (which are arbitrary in principle) are uniquely associated with values which can be atoms, f-structures or sets of f-structures. F-structures are represented as lists in Prolog (see figure 8).

```
[subj=[spec=the,
       num=sg,
       pred=girl|_],
 tense=present,
 pred=sleep([subj])|_]
```

figure 8

The tail variables of the lists are used for unification of f-structures. Unifying two f-structures means to insert attribute-value pairs which are unique to one f-structure into the other and also to check values of common attributes for equality or to unify sub-f-structures of common attributes, respectively. The tail variables of Prolog representations will be instantiated to those new attribute-value pairs during unification.

Unification of f-structures is furthermore implemented by the predicate "merge" (after a proposal in Eisele 1984). The Prolog code and an example is shown in figure 9.

del(F,[F|X],X):-!.
del(F,[E|X],[E|Y]):-del(F,X,Y).

merge(X,X):-!.
merge([A=V1|R1],F2):-del(A=V2,F2,R2),
                    merge(V1,V2),
                    merge(R1,R2).

example:
merge([subj=[spec=the,num=sg,pred=girl|R_Subj1]|R_F1],
     [tense=present,
      pred=sleep([subj]),
      subj=[num=sg|R_Subj2]|R_F2]).

R_Subj1 = _G28
R_F1 = [tense = present,pred = sleep([subj])|_G37]
R_Subj2 = [spec = the,pred = girl|_G28]
R_F2 = _G37

figure 9

This implementation of unification allows for incremental construction of f-structures. Thus for every reduction a unification of the f-structures of the constituents which are involved yields the f-structure of the new constituent.

We will now show in two steps how a rule given in LFG notation can be transformed into a data structure which the parser can use. In the first step we concentrate on a simple context free rule to explain the rule format of the parser. Figure 10 shows a context free rule and its Prolog equivalent.

CFG rule:

S ->   NP   VP   /* CFG rule */

Parser reduction rule:

```
reduce1([_,[vp|VP],_,
    [np|NP]|Rest_Stack],               /* stack before reduction */
    [Newstate,[[[s,[np|NP],
    [vp|VP]],Rest_Stack]]]):-          /* after reduction */
    get_goto(Y,s,Newstate).            /* table lookup */
```

figure 10

The first argument of the predicate "reduce1" represents the stack to be reduced. Note that because of the properties of the Prolog list representation the constituents appear in reverse order. The second argument of "reduce1" represents the stack after reduction. On top of the stack appears the new phrase structure representation together with the new top state (looked up in the parsing table by the predicate "get_goto"). The variable "Rest_Stack" is instantiated to the bottom part of the stack, which is not affected by the reduction. This part is thus copied unchanged.

The simultaneous construction of f-structures can furthermore be integrated into the parser in a modular way. Nothing concerning the computation of the parsing table and the manipulation of the graph-structured stack would therefore need to be changed. In fact, only the format of grammar rules would have to be changed slightly to handle the construction of f-structures. The identification of bottom parts of the stacks must be kept apart from unification of f-structures. Thus only the atoms of f-structures may be shared in the graph-structured stack representation but not the tail variables. This separation can be achieved by renaming the tail variables of involved f-structures before every reduction.

Figure 11 shows a typical LFG rule and its transformation into the format required by the parser.

LFG rule:

$$S \rightarrow \quad NP \quad\quad VP \qquad \text{/* CFG rule */}$$
$$(\uparrow SUBJ) = \downarrow \quad \uparrow = \downarrow \quad \text{/* f-schemata */}$$
$$(\uparrow TENSE)$$

An Extension Of LR-Parsing

Parser reduction rule:

```
reduce1([_,[vp,VP],_,
    [np,NP]|Rest_Stack],             /* stack before reduction*/
    [Newstate,[[[s,RVP],Rest_Stack]]]):-  /* after reduction */
  rename_vars(VP,RVP),               /* renaming of variables */
  rename_vars(NP,RNP),
  merge(RVP,[subj=RNP,tense=_|_]),   /* unification */
  get_goto(Y,s,Newstate).            /* table lookup */
```

figure 11

This is not very different from a simple CFG rule. The new constituent representation is not a phrase structure tree but an f-structure representation, i.e. the value of the variable "RVP". To obtain this representation the variables of the affected f-structures first have to be renamed (by the predicate "rename_vars") and then to be unified (by "merge").

The example shows the modular integration of the treatment of defining f- equations into the parser. Inconsistent f-structures can be excluded from further processing as soon as they are detected during the incremental construction of f-structures. The checking of constraints, however, has to be delayed until all of the input has been processed. Thus this check does not affect the design of the parser.

There are now some notational conventions for writing LFG rules which have to be treated in a special way. In particular they are the following:

- The Kleene-star operator "*" indicates that the rule element may be left out or repeated any number of times. A rule showing the Kleene-star has to be rewritten before the parsing table can be computed: The rule

    A -> B C* D

has to be transformed into the set of rules

    A   -> B A_1
    A_1 -> C A_1
    A_1 -> D

The functional schemata which are attached to the rule elements B, C and D remain unchanged. Every occurrence of the new symbol A_1 on the right side of one of the rules is annotated with the trivial equation $f = v$.

- Optional elements of a rule are indicated by the brackets "[" and "]". These rules also have to be rewritten, i.e.: the rule

   A -> B [C] D

has to be transformed into the set of rules

   A -> B D
   A -> B C D

- Disjunctions of sets of functional schemata are represented by the following notation:

   A -> B {/ f1 f2 / f3 f4 f5 /} C f6

In this example the rule element B is annotated with the schemata f1 and f2 or, alternatively, with the schemata f3, f4 and f5. The use of braces with functional schemata results in different versions of rules which, however, show the same context free structure. We think that it is not a good idea to duplicate the rules according to possible combinations of f-schemata. This strategy would blow up the parsing table unnecessarily.

We represent disjunctions of f-schemata by including all possibilities stemming from the disjunction into one parser rule. The rule above would therefore be transformed into the following

```
reduceN(Stack,Newstacks):-
    reduceNa(Stack,N1),
    reduceNb(Stack,N2),
    append(N1,N2,Newstacks).
```

where the alternatives "reduceNa" and "reduceNb" represent the disjunction of f-schemata in the LFG rule. If unification in one of the alternatives fails, this alternative will then produce an empty list as its result.

Finally it should be pointed out that providing debugging facilities is important if the parser is to be integrated into an experimental system for the development of Lexical Functional grammars. The parser should not only announce the failure of the analysis of a particular sentence but also provide good hints as to what went wrong. It is also important to be able to reconstruct the way in which a particular f-structure was obtained. For this reason the parser should provide some kind of derivation history, i.e. it should be possible to find out which grammar rules have contributed to the solution. Both tasks are difficult to achieve with a top down backtracking parser. With this type of parser, however, failures of particular rules occur in the course of almost every analysis, even an eventually sucessful one. Failure is nothing unusual because it is the combination of (local) failure and backtracking that is used to determine the right analysis. This property makes it very difficult both to find the crucial point at which the whole analysis of an ungrammatical input fails and to record the history of derivation in case of a grammatical input.

To provide debugging information seems easier with our LR style algorithm: the different alternatives of input analysis are processed deterministically. Thus failure of a grammar rule is essential in any case because it means failure of the whole alternative. Furthermore the history of one analysis only contains relevant rules because of the deterministic procedure. A further advantage comes from the parallel processing: one gets all possible analyses at one go.

The parsing table also turns out to be useful with respect to the grammar under development. The table provides insight into the properties of the grammar because it contains information about the ambiguities of the grammar rules in readable form. This information could otherwise only be retrieved by inspection of the rules and would therefore have to be confirmed by testing a great number of input strings with the parser.

5. CONCLUSION.

With respect to the criteria listed in the introduction the parser can be characterized as follows:

- The parser shows a high degree of determinism. No useless reductions are performed. The complexity with respect to input length is comparable to the complexity of Earley's algorithm.

- There are no limitations on the form and ordering of CFG rules. In particular, left and right recursion can be treated. The special notations used in LFG rules can be transformed into the format required by the parser.

- The incremental construction of f-structures supports effective treatment of ambiguities because inconsistent paths are detected and eliminated as soon as possible.

- Augmentation of the parser by specific debugging facilities is easier than with top down backtracking parsers.

6. REFERENCES.

Aho, A.V./Ullman, J.D.: *The Theory of Parsing, Translation and Compiling*, Prentice Hall 1972

Block, U./ Haugeneder, H.: "*An Efficiency Oriented LFG-Based Parsing System.*", 1986 (in this volume)

Bresnan, J./Kaplan, R.M.: "Lexical-Functional Grammar: A formal system for grammatical representation.", in: Bresnan, J.(ed): *The Mental representation of grammatical relations*, MIT Press 1982

Dörre, J./Momma, S.: *Modifikationen des Earley-Algorithmus und ihre Verwendung für ID/LP-Grammatiken*, ms Uni Stuttgart 1985

Earley, J.: "*An Efficient Context-Free Parsing Algorithm*", CACM 13 (1970), 94-102

Eisele, A.: A Lexical Functional Grammar System in *Prolog*, ms Uni Stuttgart 1984

Kilbury, J.: *Earley-basierte Algorithmen für direktes Parsing mit ID/LP- Grammatiken*, TU Berlin, KIT 16, 1984

Pereira, F.C.N.: "A new characterization of attachment preferences", in: Dowty, D.R./Karttunen, L./Zwicky, A.M. (eds): *Natural language parsing*, CUP 1985, 279 - 306

Tomita, M.: "An Efficient Context-free Parsing Algorithm For Natural Languages", in: *IJCAI* 1985, 756-764

HANS-ULRICH BLOCK, HANS HAUGENEDER
SIEMENS AG, ZT ZTI INF
MÜNCHEN, W. GERMANY

AN EFFICIENCY-ORIENTED LFG PARSER

1. INTRODUCTION

This paper describes work with the aim of the development of an LFG-based parser and grammar development system, which is to be applied as syntactic analysis component in a natural language consulting system under development. The implementation of the parser and the grammar development environment has been performed in Interlisp-D on a Lisp machine. The parser covers the various types of equations proposed in LFG (as described in Kaplan/Bresnan 82); the grammar development environment enables the grammar writer to specify the linguistic knowledge sources like grammar and lexicon in a descriptive way, where the specification format is very near the standard notational conventions used in LFG.

When we started to design and implement the parser on the basis of the theoretical framework of LFG, we identified three areas, which contribute in a very critical way to the overall performance of the parser. These are
- the way long-distance dependencies are handled
- the way the parser deals with the problem of representing and computing the f-structures, i.e. the actual implementation of the merging algorithm
- the way in which c-structural analysis and f-structure construction interact.

In the following section we will describe our approaches to the first two problems, namely the handling of long-distance dependencies and the specifics of our merging algorithm. Our approach to the third topic, which can be roughly characterized as incremental construction of c-structure and f-structure will not be under discussion here. It is described in Block/Hunze 86, where the interested reader can find details on it.

2. A C-STRUCTURAL TREATMENT OF LONG-DISTANCE DEPENDENCIES

2.1 Motivation

Since our way of parsing long-distance dependencies tries to combine features that have their origin in two rather opposite theories, LFG and GB, we give a short characterisation of the two theories' approaches to the description of these phenomena. Therein the reader is assumed to have some acquaintance with these two theories.

LFG in the course of its development has undergone a major change concerning the treatment long-distance dependencies, which roughly speaking can be seen as a drastic shift from an at least partly c-structural approach, as proposed in Kaplan/Bresnan 82 (hence LFG-82) to a totally f-structural approach based on the concept of functional uncertainty (Kaplan/Zaenen 85 and Kaplan/Zaenen 86). Since the older version of LFG's treatment of long-distance phenomena was the starting point of our work we will be exclusively refering to it, not assuming that anything said about it will hold for the new approach as well.

The aim of the analysis of long-distance dependencies in LFG-82 is to have the f-structural pendants of the two positions between this dependency holds (namely its surface position and its "originating" position) play the two f-structural roles associated with these two simultaneously. This is manifested in f-structures is the common value of different attributes (as illustrated in figure 1).

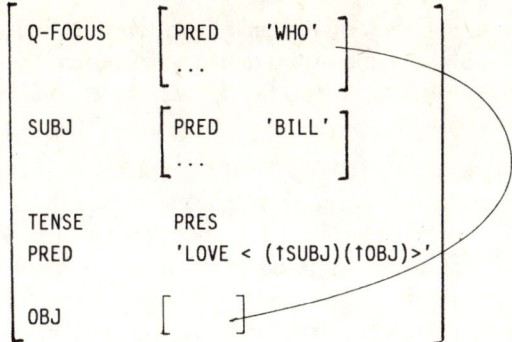

figure 1

In order to come up with f-structures of that type the following assumptions were made in LFG-82 (for a more detailed but still rather compact exposition see Block/Haugeneder 86):

1. The c-structural description of long-distance constructions represents the lexically filled surface position of the displaced constituent as well as its lexically empty "originating" position, assuming c-structures like the following:

(1) [S'[NP who][S does he love [NP e]S]S']

This is achieved by augmenting the phrase structure part of the grammar by empty productions for phrasal categories.

2. In addition to the immediate domination metavariables the equation association formalism is enriched by the bounded domination metavariables that allow to identify the f-structures associated with phrase structure nodes not standing in the relation of immediate domination, i.e. linearly and structurally far apart.

3. In order to capture the linguistic constraints limiting the identification allowed by the formalism introduced in 2., so-called root nodes and bounding nodes were introduced, the former defining the domain, where the originating position of a displaced constituent has to be, the latter defining islands which exclude its

constituents from long-distance relationships outside of it. Together with a general bounding convention these concepts enable the grammar writer to express these constraints in the grammar.

In the framework of GB (Chomsky 81) long-distance-phenomena are handled by the general transformation "move α", which in the case of wh-movement moves a wh-phrase out of its position into the S'-dominated COMP-Position leaving a coindexed trace in its original D-structure position. The applicability of this transformation is constrained by global bounding categories and the principle of subjacency, which limits wh-movement by the occurence of nodes of these bounding categories, roughly saying that no movement transformation may cross two or more bounding nodes. By the assumption of a cyclic application of wh-movement this local effect of subjacency may be overcome globally by moving constituents over pairs of bounding category nodes via intermediate COMP-positions.

Leaving aside reflections on the possible contribution of the two theories to the explication of principles of universal grammar and neglecting the question what the impact of the two theories for language acquisition and learnability might be, the main differences between them are the following:

1. LFG-82 assumes bounding nodes to constrain the antecedent-trace relation; by the assumption of bounding categories GB aims towards a greater generalisation, since it is not allowed for two nodes with identical categories to have different characteristics concerning their bounding properties.

2. In GB (i.e. in the version of it exemplified by Chomsky 81) the principle of subjacency together with the assumption of the suitable bounding categories explains the difference in (un-)grammaticality of sentences (2) and (3) respectively:

   (2) *[S' who [S do you believe [NP the claim
        [S' that John loves]NP]S]S']

   (3) [S'who do you think that [S John loves]S']

In LFG-82 this difference in grammaticality is expressed by the identity of the rootnode and bounding node in the corresponding grammar rule. The root node being by definition a sister of the displaced constituent defines the subtree where the phrases' originating position has to be found. The fact that crossing of bounding nodes is allowed, if they are characterized as root nodes as well and that the occurence of a further bounding node constitutes an inaccessible domain of the tree, evoques the subjacency effect.

3. Whereas GB accounts for the grammaticality of sentences like "who do you claim that Pat saw" by cyclic COMP-to-COMP movement (4), LFG-82

(4) [S'who$_1$ [S do you claim [S't$_1$ that [S Pat saw t$_1$]S']S]S']

assumes an additional grammar rule which contains a linking schema associated with the deepest embedded S-phrase which prevents the bounding convention from being applied inadequately. (See Kaplan/Bresnan 82, 253 for details!)

4. A final rather fundamental difference can be seen if one compares the grammar modules long-distance movement is treated in. GB's strict constitutional approach is part of the grammar's movement-transformation module and operates on nothing but positions.

In LFG-82 the handling of long-distance-phenomena is distributed over the c-structure part of the grammar and the variable instantiation mechanism especially for bounded domination metavariables. Thus, although being introduced at c-structure level it effectively does not operate on phrases but on the descriptions associated with functional variables.

When designing our parser we decided to blend the two theories with respect to the differences summarized before in the following way:

- We adapt the more flexible LFG-82 view of assuming rule-specific bounding nodes instead of global bounding categories. This on the one hand gives the grammar writer more freedom to deal with constructions that withstand a grammatical description by means of global bounding categories (see Kaplan/Bresnan 82, 245f). On the other hand one can always express bounding categories in terms of bounding nodes by replacing each occurence of a bounding category on the right hand side of a production by a bounding node marker.

- We consider subjacency as an epiphenomenon of the fact, that bounding nodes are strict boundaries for movement, which only may be passed, if the bounding node is marked as a root node, too.

- We prefer the principle of cyclicity over additional grammar rules.

- We treat long-distance phenomena strictly configurationally in the sense that the identification of a displaced constituent with its originating position is described totally in terms of c-structure.

- On the level of f-structure we want a representation of long-distance dependencies just along the lines LFG proposes, namely the sharing of a common f-structure by the grammatical functions that are associated with the "moved" constituent's actual and "originating" position.

With these aims in mind we developed an approach, in which the core parsing mechanism is able to transport displaced elements until they can be consumed at suitable positions, if the grammatical description marks a constituent as appearing in a displaced position.

The suitability of the consuming position thereby is restricted by several constraints. Firstly only such positions can come into account where the parser expects a phrase of the same category as the one being transported. Secondly the mechanism must be sensible to certain linguistic constraints such as bounding and root nodes as specified in the grammar rules.

This approach has the advantage that one can do without empty productions in the grammar, that tend to lead to an enormous amount of spurious phrase structure trees. Furthermore in our approach the processing overhead of propagating moved constituents through the parser's states just shows up in the case, when a constituent acutally has been found in a displaced position.

A further central feature of the approach just described is that it deals with long-distance dependencies in a way that assumes the displaced element occurs before its originating position in terms of parsing direction. Since the parser does its work from left to right the parser's inherent structure predicts that there are no rightward long-distance dependencies.

On the grammar specification level we have augmented the format for phrase structure rules by anotating the phrasal categories on the right hand side by a marker (↑) indicating, that the constituent has to be moved or by the markers (r,b) designating nodes and root nodes and/or bounding nodes. So a grammar rule describing a long-distance construction typically looks like the following production,

(5) XP --> .. YP/↑ .. ZP/r ..

(which reads as: XP expands to an YP, which has to be moved and a ZP which constitutes the root node for the moved YP with possibly further (non)terminal symbols at the ". ."-marked positions).

At the grammar rule level bounding nodes are specified in a similiar fashion:

(6) XP --> .. YP/b ..

(This reads: XP expands among other things to an YP, which is a bounding node.)

2.2 The Parser

Our parser is based on Earley's (1970) algorithm augmented by a mechanism for treating long-distance phenomena according to the above mentioned principles. The basic context-free parser operates on two ordered sets of states that correspond to the state sets s_i and s_{i+1} in the Earley-algorithm to the end of which constantly new states which are still to be worked on are added. A state is a quintupel (<tree> <left> <right> <dot> <pred.-list>), where

- <tree> (abbreviated as <tr> in the sample traces in 2.3) the current parsetree of that path,

- <left> and <right> (abbreviated as <l,r>) are pointers to the input string the constituent begins with and the input string that immediately follows the constituent respectively,

- <dot> marks the current position in the right side of the cf grammar rule and

- <pred.-list> (abbreviated as <plst>) is a set of pointers to all preceeding states who's treenodes might become the mother of current states' tree.

A treenode is a complex data structure that contains the node's label (i.e. its syntactic category), a list of its daughters and a pointer to the F-structure attached to it.

The basic operations are *predict*, *scan* and *complete* which are close to the definition in Earley (1970). For the construction of the c-structure these operations are augmented in the following way: *predict* creates an empty treenode labeled with the predicted category, *scan* attaches the next input word as the rightmost daughter to the state's <tree>, and *complete* attaches the state's <tree> as the rightmost daughter to all treenodes in the states of the current state's <pred.-list>.

For the treatment of movement phenomena <dot> is expanded to the complex data-structure of the type (<syn. cat.> <equations> <slash>) where <slash> is a flag containing information on constituents to be moved. If <slash> is empty no movement is performed. If <slash> is set the node which is associated to the <dot> will be moved rightward.

A state is augmented by three additional components, namely <pending> and <consumed> <to-be-moved> that are used for the bookkeeping of moved nodes.

<pending> (abbreviated as <pd>) is a pushdown stack of the nodes that are moved. Each time a node is declared in the grammar to be moved it is pushed onto the <pending> of the state being developed. The nodes in <pending> are then propagated to the subsequent paths.

<consumed> (abbreviated as <cd>) is the list of all traces consumed in a subtree. That is whenever a constituent on <pending> is used to satisfy the corresponding prediction of some state (i.e. being used as if it was the current element in the input at some state) it is popped from <pending> and pushed on <consumed>. Furthermore <consumed> is used to control the attachment of phrases to their mother nodes by the completer, allowing phrases dominated by a root node with consumed subphrases in them to be attached only if that phrase is also in <pending> in the mother state.

<to-be-moved> (abbreviated as <tbm>) is used to transport a displaced constituent to its corresponding root-node, where after being pushed onto <pending> it can be consumed as a missing constituent.

2.3 Some Examples

In this section we will present some examples in the form of partial, commented traces, giving a more detailed description of the parser when processing constructions with long-distance dependencies.

The snapshot of the parser's states in (8) shows the relevant subset of states induced by the attachment of an wh-NP by a grammar rule like (9) whilst parsing the embedded wh-clause of a sentence like the one in (7).

(7) (I don't know)$_1$ who$_2$ he$_3$ loves$_4$?

(8)

<tr>	<l,r>	<dot>	<plst>	<pg>	<cd>	<tbm>	
[S']	(1,1)	.NP	..	NIL	NIL	NIL	(1)

..

[NP$_{who}$]

| | (1,2) | EOR | (1) | NIL | NIL | NIL | (2) |

[S' [NP$_{who}$]]

| | (1,2) | .S | NIL | NIL | NIL | NP$_{who}$ | (3) |

(* the parsed wh-NP "who" is moved to its root-node)

| [S] | (2,2) | .NP | (3) | (NP$_{who}$) | NIL | NIL | (4) |

(* in order to be available for consumation it is pushed on <pending>)

..

[S [NP$_{he}$]]

    (2,3) .VP   (3)   (NP$_{who}$)   NIL   NIL   (5)

..

[VP [V$_{love}$]]

    (2,4) .NP   (5)   (NP$_{who}$)   NIL   NIL   (6)

[NP] (4,4) .PN   (6)   (NP$_{who}$)   NIL   NIL   (7)

[VP [V$_{love}$] [NP$_{who}$]]

    (3,4) EOR   (5)   NIL   (NP$_{who}$)   NIL   (8)

(* the moved NP is consumed as direct object of "love")

..

[S [NP$_{he}$] [VP [V$_{love}$] [NP$_{who}$]]]

    (2,4) EOR   (3)   NIL   (NP$_{who}$)   NIL   (9)

[S' [NP$_{who}$]] [S [NP$_{he}$] [VP [V$_{love}$] [NP$_{who}$]]]]

    (1,4) EOR   NIL   NIL   NIL   NIL   (10)

(* after completing a state with a root-node category predicted, the moved NP is taken out of <consumed>, meaning that the structure, where it has to be consumed is closed and the movement is performed completely)

(9) S'   NP/ ↑   S/r
            (↑ Q-FOC) = ↓   ↑ = ↓

In order to see the working of our mechanism in the case of a cyclic movement a look at the following examples shows its features. Thus in an example like (10)

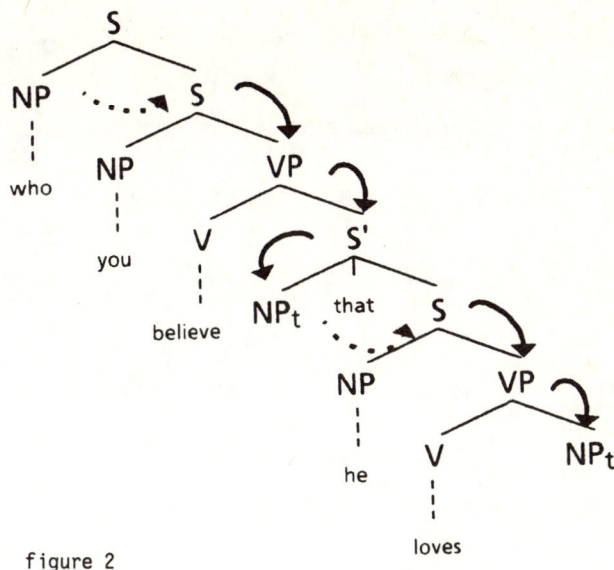

figure 2

(10) Who do you believe$_1$ that$_2$ he$_3$ knows$_4$

the moved wh-NP is transported into the embedded sentence via landing at a S'-initial optional NP-position, from where it is moved in turn.

(11) S' ->   (NP/↑) S/rb

With a grammar rule like (11) the wh-NP who is first moved form its matrix-sentence initial position and consumed at the embedded sentences' NP-position, from where it is moved again as shown in Figure 2 (where the dashed arrows indicate the propagation into the next embedded cycle).

The treatment of the three critical components <pending>, <consumed> and <to-be-moved> in such a case of cyclic movement is shown in the following partial trace.

(12)

```
          <tr> <l,r><dot>   <plst><pg>      <cd>       <tbm>
```

[VP [V_believe]]
```
         (1,1)  .S'     ..    (NP_who)   NIL       NIL      (1)
```

(* when the embedded sentence is predicted the moved constituent is already pending)

```
[S'] (1,1) .NP ↑   (1)    (NP_who)   NIL       NIL      (2)
..
```

[S' [NP_who]]
```
         (1,1) .COMP  NIL   NIL      (NP_who)  NP_who   (3)
```

(* the moved constituent is consumed and moved in turn by putting it on <to-be-moved>)

[S' [NP_who that]]
```
         (1,2) .S/r   (1)    NIL      (NP_who)  NP_who   (4)
[S]      (2,2) .NP    (4)   (NP_who)  NIL       NIL      (5)
```

(* in order to be available for consumation it is pushed on <pending>)

```
..
```

[VP [V_love] [NP_who]]
```
         (3,4) EOR    (5)    NIL      (NP_who)  NIL      (6)
```

(* the moved NP is consumed as direct object of "love")

[S [NP_john] [VP [V_love] [NP_who]]]
```
         (2,4) EOR    (3)    NIL      (NP_who)  NIL      (7)
```
[S' [NP_who that] [S [NP_john] [VP [V_love] [NP_who]]]]
```
         (1,4) EOR    (1)    NIL      (NP_who)  NIL      (8)
```
[VP [V_believe] [S' [NP_who that] [S [NP_john] [VP [V_love] [NP_who]]]]]
```
         (...,4) EOR  ..     NIL      (NP_who)  NIL      (9)
```

(* the moved wh-NP is still on <consumed>, waiting to be discarded when the state predicting its originating root-node category is completed)

The organisation of the list of <pending> nodes as a pushdown-stack rather than a queue mirrors the property of long-distance movement to be nested. The parser will therefore account for the ungrammatical trace bindings in (13).

(13) *Which sonata$_i$ is this violin$_j$ easy to play t$_i$ on t$_j$

Though the sentence will finally be parsed, it will have, as predicted, the semantically deviant nested binding of the traces: *to play the violin on which sonata*.

The mechanism presented so far does not cover the treatment of bounding nodes, as there are no bounding restrictions on the way how the constituents on <pending> are transported and/or consumed. Without imposing any further restrictions on our mechanism, it is possible to move a constituent into a subtree dominated by a bounding node.

To prevent this a new empty <pending> is used in every state that is a consequence of the prediction of a bounding node category. Thus any moved constituent which is possibly on <pending> at such a state of the analysis is not available during the parsing of the bounded node category dominated substructure. When, however, this substructure is parsed completely and attached to its mother structure by the completer the old (i.e. the mother's state) <pending> is used and propagated in the subsequent states.

Thus in an example like (14) if at some state the bounding node category S (S/b) is predicted all the successive states (as for example state$_j$) have a new empty <pending>.

(14) *What does he[$_{VP}$ wonder [$_{S'}$ whether
　　　[$_S$ she wants [$_{NP}$ e]]$_S$]$_{S'}$]$_{VP}$

(15) ....$_1$whether$_2$she$_3$wants$_4$

```
<tr>  <l,r>  <dot>  <plst><pg>      <cd>   <tbm>
```

[S' [V wonder]]

```
          (1,1) .S/b    ..    (NP_what)   NIL    NIL    (i)
```

(* when the bounding node category is predicted "what" is pending; it will not be propagated to those subsequent states that expand the bounding node doinated substructure)

```
[S]   (1,1) .NP     ..    NIL         NIL    NIL    (j)
```

[S she wants]

```
      (2,4) .EOR    ..    NIL         NIL    NIL    (k)
```

[S' whether] [S she wants]]

```
      (1,4) .EOR    (i)   (NP_what)   NIL    NIL    (l)
```

(* after the completion of the S/r-structure the old <pending> is activated again, making "what" acessible again)

[S' what .. ..wants]

```
      (..,4) .EOR NIL  (NP_what)      NIL    NIL    (m)
```

In our example the parser will come to state l after completing state i and finally (via some more completer operations) to state m. State m finally represents a configuration that says that (15) will not be parsed due to the fact that <pending> is not empty while the complete input is analysed with no predictions left.

3. UNIFICATION ON SHARED STRUCTURES

In this chapter we will first present a simple merge-algorithm that works on shared structures. We will then show its deficiencies and discuss possible refinements.

The LFG-Merge-Algorithm as proposed in Kaplan/Bresnan 1982 is not defined on shared structures. Therefore, a parser that has a direct implementation of that algorithm as component, has to copy the f-structures before they are merged. Typically then, a parser that follows this line spends a lot of time in copying f-structures. In a first prototype of our grammar tool we followed this line and were rather disappointed about the results. We therefore decided to try some alternative merging algorithms, especially those that operate on shared structures.

EFFICIENCY-ORIENTED LFG-PARSER 163

The representation of an f-structure that supports the sharing of substructures consists in two components: 1) a variable that represents the f-structure and 2) a binding environment that contains the values of the variables.

Let $\uparrow$ and $\downarrow$ denote the f-structure of some mother and some daughter node respectively. Variables begin with a question mark. Without any equations applied a typical situation might be the one in (16), where the mother node has a variable as its f-structure, but this variable doesn't have any value, the environment being empty.

(16) F-structure   Environment

   $\uparrow$ = ?01

After evaluation of the equation in (17) the corresponding bindings are made. The representation corresponds to the f-structure $\uparrow = [a1 = v1]$.

(17) merge(locate($\uparrow$,a1),v1)   [($\uparrow$ a1) = v1]

   F-structure   Environment

   $\uparrow$ = ?01   ?02 . v1
                            ?01 . (a1 = ?02)

Now suppose that the equation in (18) is applied to the f-structure in (17). The following binding results. Notice that ?01 is now bound twice. But as the environment is organized as a stack only the topmost binding can be accessed. The representation corresponds to the f-structure $\uparrow = [a1 = v1, a2 = v2]$.

(18) merge(locate($\uparrow$,a2),v2)   [($\uparrow$ a2) = v2]

   F-structure   Environment

   $\uparrow$ = ?01   ?03 . v2
                            ?01 . (a2 = ?03, a1 = ?02)
                            ?02 . v1
                            ?01 . (a1 = ?02)

The next two snapshots show how two attributes can share their value.

In (19) the two f-structures ↑=[a1=v1, a2=v2, a3=$\_{-1}$] and ↓=[a1=$\_{-1}$] after evaluation of the corresponding equation are represented. The placeholder $\_{-1}$ is represented by the unbound variable ?07 that ?06 and ?05 have as their value.

(19) merge(locate(↑,a3),locate(↓,a1))   [(↑ a3) = (↓ a1)]

    F-structure   Environment

    ↑ = ?01   ?06 . ?07
    ↓ = ?04   ?05 . ?07
                                ?01 . (a3 = ?05, a2 = ?03, a1 = ?02)
                                ?03 . v2
                                ?01 . (a2 = ?03, a1 = ?02)
                                ?02 . v1
                                ?01 . (a1 = ?02)

In (20) you can see how the value of a sharing variable is accessed by both holders of that shared variable in following the bindings ?05 - ?07 - v3 and ?06 - ?07 - v3. The situation expresses the f-structures ↑=[a1=v1, a2=v2, a3=v3] and ↓=[a1=v3].

(20) merge(locate(↑,a3),v3)   [(↑ a3) = v3]

    F-Structure   Environment

    ↑ = ?01   ?07 . v3
    ↓ = ?04   ?06 . ?07
                                ?05 . ?07
                                ?04 . (a1 = ?06)
                                ?01 . (a3 = ?05, a2 = ?03, a1 = ?02)
                                ?03 . v2
                                ?01 . (a2 = ?03, a1 = ?02)
                                ?02 . v1
                                ?01 . (a1 = ?02)

In an appraoch exemplified by the preceeding examples the variables are managed by the following access and setting functions:

(I) ImmediateValue(var,env)
   return Value(Var,env)!

(II) Value(var,env)
   return the value of the *first* occurrence of var in env
   (Like (CDR (ASSOC var env)) in LISP)!

(III) UltimateVariable(var)
   let x be ImmediateValue(var,environment)!
   if Variable(x)
     then return UltimateVariable(x)
     else return(var)!

(IV) UltimateValue(var)
   let x be UltimateVariable(var)!
   let y be ImmediateValue(x,environment)!
   if y] NIL
     then return y
     else return x!

(V) Bind(var,val)
   set environment to var . val + environment!
   (SETQ environment (CONS (CONS var val) environment))

The function ImmediateValue is used here only to facilitate the comparison with the next version described below. Here it is identical to Value. UltimateVariable returns the last variable in a variable chain. UltimateVariable (?05) would yield ?07 in the environment of (20). UltimateValue returns the last value of a variable in a variable chain. In the context of (20) UltimateValue(?05) yields v3.

The following example shows how two environments are joined in a Completer-operation. Suppose that the upnode and the downnode are characterized by the F-structures in (21) represented internally as in (22):

(21) $\uparrow$ = [agr = [prs = 3prs,num = sg],subj = [case = nom,gen = mask,
         agr = [prs = 3prs,num = sg]]]

$\downarrow$ = [agr = [prs = 3prs,num = sg],pred = tanzen]

(22) upnode.FS = ?07

    upnode.env = ?07 . (agr = ?02, subj = ?01)
                  ?07 . (subj = ?01)
                  ?06. nom
                  ?01. (case = ?06, gen = ?05, agr = ?02)
                  ?05. mask
                  ?01. (gen = ?05, agr = ?02)
                  ?04. 3prs
                  ?02 . (prs = ?04, num = ?03)
                  ?03 . sg
                  ?02 . (num = ?03)
                  ?01 . (agr = ?02)

    downnode.FS = ?34

    downnode.env = ?38. 3prs
                      ?36. (prs = ?38, num = ?37)
                      ?37. sg
                      ?36. (num = ?37)
                      ?34. (agr = ?36, pred = ?35)
                      ?35. tanzen
                      ?34. (pred = ?35)

Now, before a set of functional equations is to be evaluated in xa mother and a daughter node, the f-structure variable of the mother and daughter are set up and the environment is constructed in the following way:

    a) if the f-structure of the mother = nil then set it to a new variable!

    b) Set environment to the "Append" of the environment of the mother and daughter!

Thereafter the equation set is evaluated!
(23) and (24) show the environment before and after evaluation of the equation "↑ = ↓".

(23)   ?07 . (agr = ?02, subj = ?01)
                         ?07 . (subj = ?01)
                         ?06. nom
                         ?01. (case = ?06, gen = ?04, agr = ?02)
                         ?05. mask
                         ?01. (gen = ?05, agr = ?02)
                         ?04. 3prs
                         ?02 . (prs = ?04, num = ?03)
                         ?03 . sg
                         ?02 . (num = ?03)
                         ?01 . (agr = ?02)
                         ?38. 3prs
                         ?36. (prs = ?38, num = ?37)
                         ?37. sg
                         ?36. (num = ?37)
                         ?34. (agr = ?36, pred = ?35)
                         ?35. tanzen
                         ?34. (pred = ?35)

(24)   ?07. (pred = ?35, agr = ?02, subj = ?01)
                         ?07 . (agr = ?02, subj = ?01)
                         ?07 . (subj = ?01)
                         ?06. nom
                         ?01. (case = ?06, gen = ?04, agr = ?02)
                         ?05. mask
                         ?01. (gen = ?05, agr = ?02)
                         ?04. 3prs
                         ?02 . (prs = ?04, num = ?03)
                         ?03 . sg
                         ?02 . (num = ?03)
                         ?01 . (agr = ?02)
                         ?38. 3prs
                         ?36. (prs = ?38, num = ?37)
                         ?37. sg
                         ?36. (num = ?37)
                         ?34. (agr = ?36, pred = ?35)
                         ?35. tanzen
                         ?34. (pred = ?35)

To see how the structure sharing works, let us suppose the grammar rule (25) and the sentences in (26).

(25) VP --> (NP)   (NP)   V
         (↑ io) = ↓   (↑ do) = ↓
         (↓ case) = dat (↓ case) = akk

(26) a. (weil) Peter Maria kennt
    b. (weil) Peter Maria ein Buch schenkt

At the time the parser is attaching the NP *Maria* this NP can either receive dative or accusativ case. It is shared by the two different parsing states in (27):

(27) a. (VP (NP *Maria*)),3,4,.NP
    b. (VP (NP *Maria*)),3,4,.V

Suppose that the f-structure variables of the daughter NP and the two VPs in (27) are respectively ?01, ?02 and ?03. The the following variable binding could occur. For the sake of clarity, shared structures are underlined:

(28)   a. ?06. dat
              ?01. (case = ?06, pred = ?05, gen = ?04)
              ?02 . (io = ?01)
              ?05 . 'Maria
              ?01 . (pred = ?05, gen = ?04)
              ?04 . fem
              ?01 . (gen = ?04)

              b. ?07. akk
              ?01. (case = ?07, pred = ?05, gen = ?04)
              ?02 . (do = ?01)
              ?05 . 'Maria
              ?01 . (pred = ?05, gen = ?04)
              ?04 . fem
              ?01 . (gen = ?04)

Though it is obvious that with the described algorithm it is not necessary to copy the whole f-structure before merging and that a considerable amount of the structure can be shared, the algorithm is deficient in two ways: Firstly, the environment rather often becomes very large. As in the completer at least one environment has to be copied, in some way one has get rid of copying f-structures for the price of copying environments. Furthermore the number of tests to perform to access the Value of a variable may become very big. Consider for example the number of tests to perform to get the value of variable ?34 in (24) above. And finally, in variable chains, the function ImmediateValue may have to be performed several times.

Some criticism of this approach by Martin Kay in response to our talk led us to look for another structure sharing method that would lack this disadvantage. (We did not however implement algorithm he proposed (Kay/Kartunnen 1985)).

In our second approach we think of the parsing process as a walk through a set of states. Each time before a set of functional equations is evaluated - that is in every scanner and completer operation - a new statenumber is generated and associated to the new node by pushing it onto the environment list of the previous node(s). For example, starting a parsing process with three scanner operations would lead to three states characterized by the three environments (1), (2 1) and (3 2 1). If each of the first three scanner operations leads to a two way ambiguity, this results in states characterized by the following environments: (1), (2); (3 1), (4 1); (5 2), (6 2); (7 3 1), (8 3 1), (9 4 1), (10 4 1), (11 5 2), (12 5 2), (13 6 2), (14 6 2). We could then - theoretically but not practically - store the value of a variable in a two-dimensional field varValue, where one dimension is indexed by variable number, the other by state number. Then, the value of a variable i in a given environment $(s_1, ..., s_m)$, is given by varValue(i,s_k), where

$k = \min \{1 \leq j \leq m \mid \text{varValue}(i,s_j) \neq \text{NIL}\}$.

In practice it is neither feasible nor necessary to have a huge array of variables and values. We decided to use a one-dimensional array indexed by variable number, the value of each cell being an association list, where state numbers are associated to values. (29) to (32) give snapshots of the same state configurations as in (17) to (20) above.

(29) merge(locate(↑,a1),v1)

F-structure	VarValue	Environment
↑ = ?01	?02: (1 . v1) ?01: (1 . (a1 = ?02))	(1)

(30) merge(locate(↑,a2),v2)

F-structure	VarValue	Environment
↑ = ?01	?03: (2 . v2) ?02: (1 . v1) ?01: (2 . (a2 = ?03, a1 = ?02) 1 . (a1 = ?02))	(2 1)

(31) merge(locate(↑,a3),locate(↓,a1))

F-structure	VarValue	Environment

↑ = ?01
↓ = ?04
	?06: (3 . ?07)
	?05: (3 . ?07)
	?04: (3 . (a1 = ?06))
	?03: (2 . v2)
	?02: (1 . v1)
	?01: (3 . (a3 = ?05, a2 = ?03,
	        a1 = ?02)
	     2 . (a2 = ?03, a1 = ?02)
	     1 . (a1 = ?02))
		(3 2 1)

(32) merge(locate(↑,a3),v3)

F-structure	VarValue	Environment
↑ = ?01	07: (4 . v3)	(4 3 2 1)
↓ = ?04	06: (3 . ?07)	
	05: (3 . ?07)	
	04: (3 . (a1 = ?06))	
	03: (2 . v2)	
	02: (1 . v1)	
	01: (3 . (a3 = ?05, a2 = ?03, a1 = ?02)	
	2 . (a2 = ?03, a1 = ?02)	
	1 . (a1 = ?02))	

Only two of the variable management functions defined in (I) and (V) have to be changed in a suitable way. ImmediateValue has to find the first state in the env where a value is defined for var. Bind has to update the environment correspondingly.

(I') ImmediateValue(var,env)
    for state in env do
      let val be Value(state,varValue[var])!
      if val then return val!
    end

(V') Bind(var,val,env)
    set state to the first element of env!
    set varValue[var] to state . val + varValue[var]!

As in the first approach the environments of the upnode and the downnode have to be appended in a completer operation, furthermore a new state number has to be generated and pushed onto the environment in the following manner:

If the f-structure of the mother = nil
    then set it to a-new-variable!

Set environment to
   Cons(a-new-statenumber, Append(env-of-upnode, env-of-downnode))!

Eval the f-equations of the corresponding rule position!

(33) to (34) show the corresponding configurations of the Completer operation in (23) to (24) above.

(33) upnode.FS = ?07
   upnode.env = (3 2 1)

   downnode.FS = ?34
   downnode.env = (16)

   environment: (17 3 2 1 16)

(34) varValue before evaluation of "↑ = ↓"

```
01: (1. (case = ?06, gen = ?05, agr = ?02),
     1. (gen = ?05, agr = ?02),
     1. (agr = ?02))
02: (1. (prs = ?04, num = ?03),
     1. (num = ?03))
03: (1. sg)
04: (1. 3prs)
05: (1. mask)
06: (1. nom)
07: (3. (agr = ?02, subj = ?01),
     3. (subj = ?01))
08: ...
09: ...
34: (16. (agr = ?36, pred = ?35),
     16. (pred = ?35))
35: (16. tanzen)
36: (16. (prs = ?38, num = ?37),
     16. (num = ?37))
37: (16. sg)
37: (16. 3prs)
```

(35) varValue after evaluation of "↑ = ↓"

```
01: (1. (case = ?06, gen = ?05, agr = ?02),
     1. (gen = ?05, agr = ?02),
     1. (agr = ?02))
02: (1. (prs = ?04, num = ?03),
     1. (num = ?03))
03: (1. sg)
04: (1. 3prs)
05: (1. mask)
06: (1. nom)
07: (17. (pred = ?35, agr = ?02, subj = ?01)
     3. (agr = ?02, subj = ?01),
     3. (subj = ?01))
08: ...
09: ...
34: (16. (agr = ?36, pred = ?35),
     16. (pred = ?35))
35: (16. tanzen)
36: (16. (prs = ?38, num = ?37),
     16. (num = ?37))
37: (16. sg)
37: (16. 3prs)
```

One of the main differences in efficiency between the two approaches can be seen in the following worst case assumptions for a single variable value access in non-ambigous grammars. The worst case always happens if a variable is not bound in a given state k. The new algorithm is superior by a factor of V, where V is the sum of variable bindings in all the states the parser has constructed so far:

(36) without ambiguity

old algorithm:

$$\sum_{i=1}^{k} V_i \quad V_i = \text{number of variable bindings in state}_i$$

new algorithm:

$$\sum_{i=1}^{k} 1 = k$$

In ambigous grammars the result is not as favourite for the new algorithm as in non-ambigous grammars. The worst case for a single variable access is computed in the following way.

(37) with amibguity

old algorithm: as in (36)

new algorithm:

$$\sum_{i=1}^{k} a = k.a, \quad a = |\{s_j \mid s_j \neq s_i \text{ and x has a value in } s_j\}|$$

Informally speaking, a is the length of the association list in varValue(x). If, for example, we have an environment as in (38) and a varValue cell as in (39), a = 7.

(38) (15 5 3 7 2)

(39) x: (14 . v2,
         13 . v3,
         10 . v3,
         06 . v4,
         04 . v1,
         03 . v9,
         01 . v6)

For binary grammars k is computed as $2l - 2$, where l is the length of the input string.

4. CONCLUSION

The measures taken in the design and implementation of our LFG parser have altogether lead to a considerable increase of the overall performance, to which our specfic merge algorithm has contributed as well as our solution to the problem of handling long-distance dependencies. The two techniques presented here together with other efforts aimed towards higher performance are, however, not to be seen as a final, static stage of development; we would rather regard it as necessary steps towards the aim of creating an LFG-based parser with performance characteristics, that makes such a system applicable to large scale applications,in the sense of processing large amount of (language) data with grammars of comprehensive coverage.

ACKNOWLEDGEMENTS

We are gratefully indebted to our colleague Rudolf Hunze who discussed many of the topics adressed in this paper with us.

The work described here is partly sponsored by the Federal Ministry of Research and Technology (BMFT) in the WISBER-project.

LITERATURE

Hans-Ulrich Block, Rudolf Hunze (1986), Incremental Construction of C- and F-structure in a LFG-Parser. In: *Proceedings of COLING* 86, 490-493

Hans-Ulrich Block, Hans Haugeneder (1986), The Treatment of Movement-Rules in a LFG-Parser. In: *Proceedings of COLING* 86, 482-486

Noam Chomsky (1981), *Lectures on Government and Binding*. Dordrecht: Foris

Jay Earley (1970), *An Efficient Context free Parsing Algorithm*, CACM 6(8), 541-545

Ronald M. Kaplan, Joan W. Bresnan (1982), Lexical-Functional Grammar: A Formal System für Grammatical Representation. In: Joan W. Bresnan (ed): *The Mental Representation of Grammatical Relations*, Cambridge/Mass.

Ronald M. Kaplan, Annie Zaenen (1985), *Grammatical Functions and Long-Distance Dependencies*. ms. Xerox-PARC

Ronald M. Kaplan, Annie Zaenen (1986), *Functional Uncertainty in LFG*. unpublished ms., Stanford

Lauri Kartunnen, Martin Kay (1985), Structure Sharing with Binary Trees. In: *Proceedings of 23rd Meeting of the ACL* 1985, 133-136A

ERIC WEHRLI

U.C.L.A.

PARSING WITH A GB-GRAMMAR

1. INTRODUCTION

Over the last few years, research in theoretical linguistics has been marked by a significant change of perspective with regard to the conception of natural language grammars. Often characterized as a shift in focus from a conception of grammar as a set of rules to a conception of grammars as a set of interactive principles of well-formedness and parameters (in short *rule-based* vs. *principle-based grammars*), this change has been primarily triggered by the search for a more explanatory theory. It took place gradually, extending from the first attempts to reduce the excessive generative power of the transformational component of generative grammars, in the early '70s, to the more recent developments affecting the phrase-structure component of the grammar[1].

In connection with these theoretical developments, there has been an emergence of a new breed of natural language parsers, dubbed *principle-based parsers*, which are, to various degrees, based on - or influenced by - grammars of principles[2]. These parsers differ from the more traditional rule-based ones in many interesting ways, and seem -- at least in principle -- to be somewhat better equipped to cope with some of the basic

---

[1] See Chomsky (1986) for an enlightening discussion of the various theoretical underpinnings of this shift, as well as for a historical overview of these developments. Chomsky (1981) and Stowell (1981) discuss various cases of redundancy between phrase-structure rules and other components of a principle-based grammar and suggest ways of eliminating the phrase-structure rule component of the grammar altogether.

[2] cf. Wehrli (1983, 1984), Barton (1984), Berwick and Weinberg (1984, 1985), Abney and Cole (1985), Sharp (1985), Kuhns (1985), Kashket (1986), Stabler (1986), Thiersh and Kolb (1986).

challenges of natural language parsing.

In this paper, we would like to address several issues related to the reliance of natural language parsers on grammars of principles, restricted here to the Government and Binding model (henceforth GB). First, we will try to clarify somewhat what is meant by principle-based parsing and show how this new approach contrasts with the more traditional view of parsing. Specifically, it will first be shown that what distinguishes both approaches relates to particular views of language and grammar. On the one hand the rule-based approach focuses on the notion of language in its formal-language theoretic sense of a set of sentences generated by the grammar, while a principle-based grammar, on the other hand, focuses on the notion of grammar as the internalized knowledge that a native speaker has of his language. Choice of a particular theoretical approach leads to certain preferences or natural tendencies with regard to the architecture of the parser, choice of parsing strategies, specification of relevant levels of representation, and so on. Thus, generally speaking, rule-based systems tend to favor uniformity, while principle-based systems seem to favor modularity. To illustrate how a principle-based parser assigns a syntactic representation to a sentence, a concrete example of a parser based on a GB-theory will be presented and some of its features discussed in some detail. Finally, in the last section of this paper, we shall argue that, although they may be much harder to implement, modular principle-based parsers present definite advantages over non-modular rule-based parsers in dealing with some of the intricacies of natural language, such as ambiguity and word-order flexibility.

2. RULE-BASED VS. PRINCIPLE-BASED

Natural language parsers have been traditionally based on phrase-structure grammars, usually with some augmentations to handle phenomena known to be outside the scope of this grammar formalism (*e.g.* long-distance dependencies). Essentially, these models, which we shall refer to as **rule-based models**, assume a view of the grammar as a uniform set of rules focusing primarily on structural properties of the surface structure representations of sentences, *i.e.* dominance and precedence relations between constituents. Although its well-known mathematical and computational properties, as well as the availability of several efficient parsing algorithms make phrase-structure grammar (and more specifically context-free grammar) an understandably popular model for natural-language parsing, it presents various limitations of the types discussed in section 4, which cast serious doubts about its adequacy as a computational model for natural language parsing[3].

In contrast to rule-based parsers, principle-based parsers are not guided by grammar rules specifying the structural properties of surface representations, but rather by the more abstract principles which underly these rules. As we shall see, such parsers exploit to a considerable degree lexical properties of heads of constituents, mostly predicates, using Case-assigning properties, thematic-role assigning properties, *etc.* rather than strict obedience to precedence and dominance relations to guide the parser's steps.

To a large extent, the differences between parsers based on Governement and Binding theory (henceforth GB-parsers) and rule-based parsers reflect quite directly the contrast between the grammatical theories that such parsers assume. As pointed out by Chomsky (1986), this contrast goes back to the basic conception of language and grammars, opposing on the one hand the structuralist/behaviorist view of language as a collection of linguistic forms (sentences) related to some meaning and the generativist/mentalist view focusing on knowledge. According to the former, the grammar of a language is viewed as a set of rules specifying the various grammatical constructions of this language. In a sense, this set of rules -- phrase-structure rules, transformations, *etc.* -- determines the set of well-formed sentences in the language. This conception of grammars, which incidentally was quite popular among pre-GB generative linguists, coincides with the one of the theory of formal languages, according to which, a grammar G defines the language G(L) as the set of all and only the sentences that can be generated by G. The development of generative grammar, which eventually led to the current Government

---

[3] The prominent role played by phrase-structure grammar theory within the field of computational linguistics can, to a large extent, be attributed to the spectacular success of this model with artificial languages and to a certain degree also to the fact that the overwhelming majority of work on natural language parsing has been centered on English. One can speculate that if more work on parsing had focused on Finnish or Warlpiri rather than English, the limitations of context-free grammars and algorithms as models for natural language would have been more conspicuous.

and Binding model, gradually shifted from the formal-language theoretic views of language and grammar to a rather different view which focuses on the notion of knowledge in the sense of what a person knows when he is said to know a language. A principle-based grammar does not define a language, but rather singles out certain structures as violating some basic well-formedness conditions: it assigns any input sentence some representation (complete or not), marking the ones which do not satisfy whatever universal and/or language-specific conditions the grammar specifies. Whereas the notion of language -- in the sense of a collection of sentences generated by a grammar -- is a central one, perhaps the most important one, for traditional models, it only plays, at best, a rather marginal role in a framework like government and binding, which focuses primarily on the notion of grammar, viewed as the internalized knowledge that a native speaker has of its language. In fact, for Chomsky, language, in its traditional sense, can be regarded merely as an ephiphenomenon:

> "The system of knowledge attained -- the I-language -- assigns a status to every relevant physical event, say, every sound wave. Some are sentences with a definite meaning (literal, figurative, or whatever). Some are intelligible with, perhaps, a definite meaning, but are ill-formed in one way or another ("the child seems sleeping"; "to whom did you wonder what to give?" in some dialects; "who do you wonder to whom gave the book?" in all dialects). Some are well formed but unintelligible. Some are assigned a phonetic representation but no more; they are identified as possible sentences of some language, but not mine. Some are mere noise. There are many possibilities. Different I-languages will assign status differently in each of these and other categories. The notion of E-language has no place in this picture." Chomsky (1986: 26)

In practice, these two radically different conceptions of language lead to a rather different characterization of natural language grammars and parsing. The following list points out some of the differences that are directly relevant for parsing. At the ouset, it should be stressed that these characteristics do not represent logical necessities, but rather seem to correspond to natural choices and tendencies.

Rule-based grammars focus on structural properties. Since phrase structure rules encode precedence and dominance relations which directly determine the structural properties of phrases, grammars based on such rules tend to be biased towards structural properties. In contrast, a principle-based grammar focuses on more abstract properties such as thematic relations, case relations, binding properties, *etc.*[4]

Rules tend to be construction-specific, whereas principles tend to characterize more abstract, construction independent properties of the language. For instance, rule-based grammars typically contain rules to derive specific constructions such as passive, interrogative, causative, topicalization, extraposition, cliticization, *etc.*

Rule-based grammars tend to be language specific. This is a consequence of the focus on properties of surface structures. Since languages vary a great deal in terms of their surface structures, the (rule-based) grammars which generate them will necessarilly be quite from one another. On the other hand, systems relying on more abstract properties of languages are in a better position to express general properties of NL, *i.e.* properties that hold crosslinguistically.

The distinctions between rule-based and principle-based grammars carry over to the parsers based on such grammars. Hence, rule-based parsers tend to focus primarily on properties of surface structure representations, they tend to be language specific, and so on. Again, the important characteristic of these rule-based models is that they assume a view of the grammar as a uniform set of rules focusing primarily on structural properties of surface structure representations of sentences. On the other hand, a principle-based grammar, according to which syntactic representations are the product of the interaction of several distinct and largely autonomous components leads to a very different picture of the parser.

Perhaps the most significant difference between the notions of syntactic

---

[4] This is not to say that structural properties are not important. In fact, binding theory, case theory, among others rely in some fundamental way on structural notions such as c-command or government.

parser as a rule-based vs. principle-based system has to do with the contrast between uniformity and modularity. The fact that the grammar consists of a uniform set of rules greatly encourages the use of a uniform parsing algorithm, as well as of uniform representations. This point is made quite explicitely by Crain and Fodor:

> "(...) we can picture parsing as in general a quite straightforward business, based on a grammar containing rules of a type that can be applied directly to word strings by fairly efficient algorithms. (...) It is argued in J.D.Fodor (1983) that all syntactic constraints in a GPSG grammar apply to the metarules, so that the derived syntactic component does not itself contain any constraints or filters. Thus the syntactic component that the parser refers to *is completely uniform* [my emphasis, EW]; it consists solely of CFPS rules."
>
> Crain and Fodor (1985:98-99)

In other words, homogeneity of the grammar leads to uniformity of both processing and representation. Whatever algorithm is used to match a sentence against the rules of the grammar is used uniformly, making in principle no distinction among rules or, a fortiori, among parts of rules. In such models, the logico-semantic nature of the relationship between constituents cannot easily be taken into account[5] and, therefore, specifiers, complements, operators, adjuncts are all parsed in a uniform fashion.

Another standard problem with rule-based parsers, also related to their lack of modularity, has to do with duplication of constituents (structure). Given the fact that nothing prevents the parser from accessing the whole range of linguistic information provided by the grammar and by the lexicon, and since the syntactic/semantic features are often used to decide what rule should or should not apply, there is a strong tendency to multiply constituents which only differ in terms of some of their features. To give a concrete and banal example, a verb with dual subcategorization might be considered as two distinct elements, satisfying slightly different sets of rules. Such duplication naturally leads to a rapid proliferation of

---

[5] For instance, a definition of VP in terms of the phrase-structure rule VP ---> (Aux) V (NP) under-emphasizes the fact that the relation between Aux and V is qualitatively different from the relation between V and NP.

structures that the parser must consider. We will argue that this is an undesirable feature, which is largely responsible for the well-known inadequacy of current parsers to cope in a satisfactory manner with the problem of ambiguity in natural language. We shall return to this point in section 4.2.

3. PRINCIPLE-BASED PARSING

3.1 The realization problem

The answer to the question "what is a parser which realizes grammar G", is relatively straightforward when G is a rule-based grammar, say a context-free (CF) grammar. Numerous algorithms have been developed which match a sentence against a CF-grammar. Quite literally these procedures execute the rules of the grammar, attempting to find a possible derivation for an input sentence[6]. Such a direct use of grammar rules by the parser is made possible by the fact that this type of grammars defines well-formed derivations. A phrase-structure grammar rule defines a possible step in the derivation of a constituent and, therefore, can be directly executed by the parser.

Because a principle-based grammar does not primarily rely on derivational rules, but rather on abstract well-formedness conditions and principles, the relationship between a principle-based grammar and a parser which realizes it is naturally less direct and hence less obvious than in the case of a rule-based system. The issue of "what counts as a gb-parser" is, therefore, a non-trivial one and likely to be a controversial one. Following Berwick and Weinberg (1985), we can consider two informal criteria, one external, stating the so-called condition of input/output, the other internal, requiring some direct correspondence between the organization of the grammar and the internal states of the parser.

> condition of input/output, *i.e.* the parser must assign to an input sentence the structure(s) that a GB grammar would assign. In

---

[6] For instance, a bottom up algorithm tries to reconstruct a rightmost derivation (in reverse), while a top-down algorithm builds up leftmost derivations for the sentence.

other words, the parser must return for a given sentence the set of S-structures (possibly LFs or PFs) as specified by GB grammars.

the internal organization of the parser must reflect (in some direct fashion) the organization of the grammar. For instance, the parser must have specific components (modules, procedures) which perform the computational equivalent of the declarative principles of the grammar. Also, the parser's actions should be directed by general rules (as opposed to construction-specific rules).

Clearly, both conditions are necessary. By itself, the first condition is obviously not sufficient to characterize a GB-parser, since one could very well design a purely rule-based parser (for instance using an ATN grammar, or a definite clause grammar) which would assign enriched surface structures to input sentences.

3.2 An example

As a concrete example of a GB-parser, consider the parser for French described in Wehrli (1983, 1984)[7]. This parser takes as input sentences from a subset of French and assigns them a set (possibly empty) of S-structures, as in the following examples:

(1) a. Jean a donné un livre à Marie.
'Jean has given a book to Marie'
b. $[_S[_{NP}Jean[_{VP}a\ donné\ [_{NP}un\ livre[_{PP}\ à\ [_{NP}Marie]]]]$

(2) a. quel livre avez-vous promis de lui donner?
'what book have you promised to give him'
b. $[_{S'}[_{COMP}[_{NP}quel\ livre]_i]\ [_S[_{NP}e]_j\ [_{VP}avez\text{-}\ [_{CLI}vous_j]$ promis $[_{S'}de\ [_S[_{NP}e]_j\ [_{VP}[_{CLI}lui_k]\ donner\ [_{NP}e]_i$ $[_{PP}e]_k]]]]]]$

---

[7] This parser has undergone major revisions and expansions. As a result, some of the features described here may be different from the ones presented in previous descriptions of this parser.

(3) a. la lettre a été envoyée hier.
   'the letter was sent yesterday'
   b. [$_S$[$_{NP}$la lettre]$_i$[$_{VP}$a été envoyée [$_{NP}$e]$_i$hier]]

Structures (1b)-(3b) are the actual outputs that the parser returns, given the *a* sentences. They correspond to (slightly simplified) S-structure representations of a GB-grammar in the sense that they encode the kind of structural relations which are specified by this theory. For instance, *wh-*phrases in COMP bind empty categories (*i.e.* [$_{NP}$e]) in A-positions[8], a relation expressed by coindexing in (2b). Thus, the index *i* associated with the phrase *quel livre* ('what book') is also assigned to the empty category adjacent to the verb *donner* ('give'). Similarly, the subject clitic *vous* in the matrix clause is coindexed with the empty subject position and the indirect object clitic *lui* in the embedded clause is coindexed with an empty prepositional phrase in indirect object position. These three cases of coindexing correspond to cases of A-bar-binding (*c.f.* section 3.3.3). Notice that coindexing also expresses the so-called control relation -- *i.e.* the subject of the infinitival verb *donner* is controlled by the subject of the matrix verb *promettre* ('promise') -- as well as cases of A-binding such as cases of "preposed subjects" (*e.g.* subject of passive or raising verbs), as in example (3). This parser clearly satisfies the condition of input/output. In the following sections, we will show that it also satisfies the second criterion.

In accordance with GB-theory, the parser is not based on construction specific rules. While it can handle passive, interrogative, and relative constructions (among many others), as well as more language specific constructions such as causative and clitic constructions, this parser does not include construction specific rules for those constructions. That is, it does not rely on a passive rule or on a relativization rule to parse those sentences. The way it does it clearly corresponds to the spirit of GB-theory. For example, the passive construction as in example (3) results from the interaction of morphological processes and syntactic processes. Roughly, it is assumed that the presence of passive morphology associated with a verb leads to a modification of the argument structure of this verb

---

[8] Roughly, D-structure argument positions, *i.e.* subject position or complement positions. Other possible S-structure positions for arguments are called A-bar-positions and include COMP and clitic positions.

as well as to a modification of its case-assignment properties. That is, (*i*) the external argument of the verb is internalized (*cf*.Williams 1981) and (*ii*) case-assignment to the direct object is suppressed. This double modification triggers the movement of the direct object to the subject position. As a result, the D-structure direct object of a passive sentence occurs in the subject position at S-structure. From a parsing viewpoint, the task of the parser, given a passive sentence as input, concerns the recovery of the chain linking the subject NP to its trace, an empty NP in direct object position.

Turning now to another, perhaps more striking, example of constructions handled by this parser without relying on construction-specific rules, *wh*-interrogatives, relatives as well as *tough*-movement constructions are all handled by the same binding procedure -- the parser's counterpart to the *wh*-movement rule of the grammar. The fact that the same procedure handles constructions which can differ rather drastically in terms of their surface structures clearly illustrates a crucial advantage of parsers based on relatively abstract mecanisms. The generality of the A-bar-binding process is further attested by the fact that a parametrized version of it handles the clitic constructions, as we will show in section 3.3.3.

3.3 Organization of the parser

The parser has a modular organization. It consists of several interacting components corresponding to some of the modules of a GB-grammar. Some of these components build representations, while others function as well-formedness conditions on these representations, filtering out the ill-formed representations. In this paper, we will only be concerned with the three main components, which are listed below and will be further discussed in subsequent sections:

- the X-bar-component
- the θ-component
- the binding component

3.3.1 The X-bar-component

This component builds up structures in accordance with the principles of X-bar-theory. Essentially, it creates a phrasal category on the basis of a lexical head (*e.g.* Adj, N, V) to which it then attaches the specifier. For example, given an input sentence such as (4), the X-bar-component creates two phrases [$_{NP}$tous les enfants] and [$_{VP}$sont partis].

(4) tous les enfants sont partis.
    'all the kids have left'

The first constituent is triggered by the head noun *enfant* ('kid'), the second one by the verb *partir* ('leave'). In the first case, the specifier consists of a quantifier followed by the definite article. In the second case, the specifier consists only of an auxiliary verb[9].

As pointed out by Wehrli (1984), specifiers and complements appear to have very distinct properties. For instance, nouns, verbs and adjectives have different and non-intersecting sets of specifiers. The set of possible specifiers for nouns includes the various determiners, quantifiers, *etc*. The set of specifiers for verbs includes auxiliaries, modals, verbal clitics, and so on. For the adjectives, we have some adverbial modifiers. Notice that the same property does not hold of complements. In fact, nouns, verbs and adjectives take their complements from the same set of constituents, namely NPs, PPs and Ss, a property responsible for many difficult cases of ambiguities. Also, complements but not specifiers are always maximal projections (X^{max}). Another well-known difference between specifiers and complements, which is of importance for processing, has to do with word-order. In languages with relatively fixed word-order, it is usually the case that the order of specifiers is stricter (often absolute) whereas the order of complements, adjuncts, and so on allows for some flexibility.

The distinction between specifiers and complements is directly exploited by the parser, which handles them in a very different fashion. Specifiers are parsed deterministically by means of a procedure which, triggered by the presence of a lexical head, searches for the largest well-formed sequence of specifiers and attaches it to the phrasal category dominating

---

[9] The reader may wonder how the parser actually finds a lexical head which will trigger the structure building process. In the implementation discussed in Wehrli (1983, 1984), the search for lexical heads is determined by a right to left search of the input sentence. A more realistic strategy has been adopted in a revised version (under development) according to which, creation of a phrase is done in a left-to-right manner, triggered by the presence of a specifier or of a head. This new strategy directly exploits the specificity of the specifiers described below.

the lexical head. Complements, on the other hand, cannot be parsed deterministically, given the systematic ambiguity of X^{max} attachment. Rather, the parser assumes a (pseudo-) parallel processing strategy and attempts to combine a newly created maximal projection, X^{max}, with all the Y^{max} constituents which might license it, or be licensed by it. In other words, when the parser encounters an X^{max}, it determines which constituents could license this X^{max}. In French, as in English, an X^{max} constituent can be licensed by a preceding VP, NP or AP. In addition, we assume that an NP constituent can be licensed by a right-adjacent VP.

3.3.2 The θ component

One well-formedness condition that is integrated in this parser is Chomsky's θ-criterion, according to which NP chains must be θ-marked. In more traditional terms, this means that any lexical NP must be assigned a thematic role. The grammar on which this parser is based specifies three different ways in which an NP can receive a θ-role:

direct θ-marking
> This is the unmarked case. NPs in A-positions are θ-marked by a predicate governing them just in case this predicate is lexically marked as a θ-assigner for this position. For example, a transitive verb such as *kiss* is lexically marked as assigning a thematic role to its direct object. This θ-feature is directly assigned to an NP occuring in the direct object position of this verb.

indirect θ-marking
> There are several constructions in French or English in which some surface structure NPs are not in A-positions, and hence cannot be directly θ-marked. A typical example is provided by the *wh*-construction as illustrated in (5)

(5) quels livres Jean a-t-il acheté?
    'what books has Jean bought'

To satisfy the θ-criterion, these NPs must be related to some θ-marked NP position. In this parser, this relation is established by the binding component described below.

inherent θ-marking
Some constituents, which normally must be θ-marked in one of the two ways just described, may not have to undergo θ-marking, provided that they are inherently θ-marked. In this parser, two such cases are considered:

idiomatic phrases
(6) a. Jean a fait peur à son ami.
    'Jean frightened his friend'
  b. le vieillard a finalement cassé sa pipe.
    'the old man finally kicked the bucket'
  c. ils s'en sont allés.
    'they went away'
  d. [$_S$[$_{NP}$e]$_i$ [$_{VP}$[$_{CLI}$ils$_i$ s' en] sont allés]]

In example (6a), the NP *peur* ('fear') is part of the idiomatic expression *faire peur* ('to frighten'). Similarly, in (6b), the direct object NP *sa pipe* ('his pipe') is part of the idiomatic expression *casser sa pipe* ('to kick the bucket'). As such, they are not considered arguments of the predicate, and therefore are not θ-marked by it in the normal fashion. More striking, perhaps, is example (6c), which involves the clitic pronouns *se* and *en* in the idiomatic expression *s'en aller* ('to go away'). Since these clitics are not arguments, they do not have to be linked to a postverbal argument position, and, hence, they do not form A-bar-chains. In this case, the parser will assign the structure (6d), with no empty categories in postverbal positions.

adverbial NPs
A small class of NPs, in French, can be used adverbially[10]
(7) a. Jean est parti hier soir.
    'Jean left last night'
  b. la dernière fois, ils ont tout cassé.
    'the last time, they broke everything'

---

[10] *cf.* Larson (1985) presents an analysis of similar facts in English based on the idea that certain NPs can be inherently case-marked and θ-marked, *i.e.* specifically, they can receive case and θ-roles through the lexical properties of their own heads.

c. il a toujours une gueule de bois le premier jour de l'année.
'he always has a hangover on New Year's day'

The NPs *hier soir*, *la dernière fois* and *le premier jour de l'année* ('last night', 'last time', 'the first day of the year') are used as adverbs in (7). As such, and following Larson (1985), we assume that they are inherently θ-marked and, therefore, can occur in non-θ positions.

When the parser encounters an NP and attempts to combine it with the left-context (*i.e.* the structure built so far), the range of possible attachments is indirectly constrained by the θ-component, in the sense that those attachments which fail to satisfy the θ-criterion will be rejected. The θ-procedure first examines the lexical θ-marking features of the relevant predicate and then verifies if these features are still available, *i.e.* if they have not already been assigned to some other constituents. θ-assignment is formulated in terms of grammatical functions, that is, predicates are lexically marked as assigning θ-roles to their subject and/or to their direct object, and so on. In a language such as French, the grammatical functions are determined configurationally in the usual manner -- *i.e.* the subject is the most prominent NP dominated by S, the direct object, the most prominent NP dominated by VP.

3.3.3 The binding component

In the previous section we saw that the θ-criterion acts, in part, as a well-formedness condition on syntactic structures, requiring that arguments (*i.e.* NPs) be θ-marked. While this requirement is directly satisfied by NPs occuring in θ-marked A-positions or by NPs eligible for inherent θ-marking, other NPs can still satisfy the θ-criterion by virtue of binding an empty θ-marked position, which which it forms a chain[11]. In this parser, it is the binding component which is responsible for the creation of these chains, or, to put it in more traditional terms, for undoing movement transformations[12]. Specifically the binding component

---

[11] Informally, a chain can be defined as "a sequence of co-indexed positions such that each of them (but the last) is the closest antecedent of the following one" *cf.* Rizzi (1986:66).

[12] The binding component implemented in this parser is more limited than Chomsky's

(or procedure) handles three types of cases: (*i*) NPs in non θ-marked A-positions, as in the case of the subject of a passive clause, (*ii*) *wh*-elements in COMP, *e.g. wh*-interrogatives, relatives and *tough*-movement constructions, and (*iii*) clitic pronouns attached to a verb. In transformational terms, these three cases correspond respectively to NP-movement, *wh*-movement and clitic placement.

In the three cases, the binding procedure is triggered, in part, by the presence of an argument which cannot be directly θ-marked (*cf.* footnote 14 for *wh*-adjuncts). The procedure examines the structure, looking for an appropriate gap in which an empty NP could be inserted. Although the same procedure is used in the three cases, its scope is clearly different, being clause-bounded in cases (*i*) and (*iii*) but not in (*ii*).

Consider the following examples:

(8) a. l'événement dont vous connaissez la cause.
   'the event whose cause you know'
   b. $[_{NP}[_{NP}\text{l'événement}]_i\ [_{S'}[_{COMP}\ [_{NP}\text{dont}]_i]\ [_S[_{NP}e]_j$
      $[_{VP}[_{CLI}\text{vous}_j]\ \text{connaissez}\ [_{NP}\text{la cause}\ [_{PP}e]_i]]]]]$

(9) a. le livre dont vous avez parlé.
   'the book you talked about'
   b. $[_{NP}[_{NP}\text{le livre}]_i\ [_{S'}[_{COMP}[_{NP}\text{dont}]_i]\ [_S[_{NP}e]_j$
      $[_{VP}[_{CLI}\text{vous}_j]\text{avez parlé}\ [_{PP}e]_i]]]]$

(10) a. vous en connaissez la cause.
    'you know the cause of it'
    b. $[_S[_{NP}e]_i\ [_{VP}[_{CLI}\text{vous}_i\ \text{en}_j]\ \text{connaissez}\ [_{NP}\text{la cause}\ [_{PP}e]_j]]]$

(11) a. vous en avez parlé.
    'you talked about it'
    b. $[_S[_{NP}e]_i\ [_{VP}[_{CLI}\text{vous}_i\ \text{en}_j]\ \text{avez parlé}\ [_{PP}e]_j]]$

Examples (8) and (9) illustrate two different ways to interpret the relative pronoun *dont*. In the first example, it is interpreted as a

---

(1981) binding theory, roughly speaking limited to the cases of A- and A-bar-binding of traces.

complement of the direct object *la cause*, while in the second example it is interpreted as a complement of the verb *parler*. The choice between the two options is made on the basis of the lexical properties of the verb. The next two examples, (10) and (11), show that the same options are also available to the clitic *en*, emphasizing the rather striking parallelism between some cases of *wh*-binding and some cases of clitic binding.

3.4 A full parse

The best way to see how the various components of this parser interact in the process of assigning a syntactic representation to a given input sentence is to trace the parser step by step. Consider the following example:

(12) quel livre est-ce que Jean a fait acheter à Paul?
 'what book has Jean made Paul buy'

First of all, the X-bar component creates the following constituents, as described in section 3.3.1:

(13) [$_{NP}$quel livre]
 [$_{NP}$Jean]
 [$_{VP}$a fait acheter]
 [$_{PP}$à Paul]

Considering the four constituents of (13) in a left-to-right order, the parser will reach the VP constituent and project a S constituent headed by VP. The NP on the left of this new constituent is then attached as subject of the clause. Attachment of an argument (*i.e.* NP) to the structure triggers the θ-component. The θ-component has access to the lexical information associated with the head of the constituent, specifically to its θ-marking features. If the argument is attached to the structure in a A-position, it is θ-marked if and only if the head of the constituent is lexically-marked to θ-mark this position. Notice, incidentally, that once a θ-role has been used, it is no longer available, *i.e.* a particular θ-role cannot be used more than once.

Returning to our example, the subject NP *Jean* is directly θ-marked by the complex verb *faire acheter*. The S node can now be projected to S'. If a complementizer -- or a *wh*-phrase, as in this example -- immediately precedes S, it is attached to the COMP position of the S'[13]. If the COMP node contains an NP, as in (13), the θ-component is invoked. Since COMP is an A-bar-position, there is no possible direct θ-marking for this argument. Failure to license an argument by direct θ-marking triggers the binding component[14]. The binding component examines the predicate of the sentence -- the complex verb *faire acheter*. Since this verb can have a transitive reading, a θ-marked empty NP constituent is inserted in the direct object position, bound by the *wh*-constituent. Finally, the PP constituent *à Paul* is attached as prepositional complement and is directly licensed, given that it is in an A-position and that it is governed by a verb which θ-marked its direct object. The structure is now complete. The θ-component checks if all the θ-marking features of the predicate have been assigned. Since this is the case, the parser accepts the input sentence and outputs its syntactic structure, illustrated in (14):

(14) $[_{S'}[_{COMP}[_{NP}\text{quel livre}]_i]\,[_S\text{est-ce que}[_{NP}\text{Jean}]\,[_{VP}\text{a fait acheter}\,[_{NP}e]_i\,[_{PP}\text{à}\,[_{NP}\text{Paul}]]]]]$

3.5 Overgeneration

It follows from the modular architecture of the parser, that the structure-building modules (X-bar) and the binding module and the θ-module are not only represented separately but also apply separately. This, along with the non-determinism of the parser[15] leads to cases of overgeneration, *i.e.* the parser creates some ill-formed structures along with well-formed ones. For instance, given sentences such as (15), the parser would create in all three cases an S-constituent.

---

[13] In the case of a root clause, as in our example, projection to S' is actually made contingent on the presence of a complementizer, to avoid building unnecessary structures.

[14] More precisely, what triggers the binding component is the failure to license a COMP constituent. This can happen when COMP contains an argument, as in our example, but it can also happen when COMP contains an adjunct -- *e.g. at what time are they coming?, where are they going?*

[15] Recall that the only deterministic module in the one responsible for the attachment of specifiers.

(15) a. *Jean embrasse.
'Jean kisses'

b. *à qui est-ce que Jean rencontre Marie.
'to whom does Jean meet Marie'

c. *Jean pense les chats.
'Jean think the cats

d. *Jean le lit le livre.
'Jean it reads the book'

These structures, however, are ruled out by the well-formedness constraints. In (15a), an argument is missing, which causes the sentence to be rejected by the θ-component. Sentence (15b) has too many arguments. The verb *rencontre* ('to meet') can only case-mark two arguments (*Jean* and *Marie*). The binding component will not be able to find a gap for the *wh*-phrase. Since the *wh*-pharse is not licensed, the sentence is rejected. In example (15c), the direct object *les chats* ('the cats') cannot be licensed since the verb is intransitive. Here again, the sentence is rejected by the θ-component. Finally, in (15d), the clitic *le* and the direct object *le livre* are competing for the direct object position and its related θ-role. Once the direct object has been directly θ-marked, the predicate has no longer any available θ-role for the clitic and its trace and the sentence is rejected as ill-formed.

4. TWO ARGUMENTS FOR PRINCIPLE-BASED PARSERS

As we have already pointed out, what the contrast between rule-based and principle-based systems reflects is essentially a difference of points of view. We have also suggested that the adoption of a principle-based approach opens new perspectives about the way the parser is organized and how it functions. In this section, we would like to briefly consider two well-known problems for natural language parsers, -- *i.e.* languages with relatively flexible word-order and ambiguity -- and suggest that a modular, principle-based approach seems more likely to come up with a satisfactory solution to these problems than the traditional rule-based approach.

4.1 Constituent-order flexibility

A great deal of the syntactic structures of English and other so-called "configurational languages" is encoded in the linear order of words, and the organization of continuous words into constituents. In languages with freer word (and constituent) order, however, much more information about syntactic structure is carried directly by the inflectional properties of particular words. Manifestly, word order in languages like Latin, Finnish, Japanese or Russian is not completely free, since it is determined by factors of discourse organization, as well as being subject to at least some purely syntactic constraints[16]. Obviously, a characterization of languages with relatively free-word order in terms of rules specifying dominance and precedence relations turns out to be rather problematic in the sense that it will be necessary to multiply the number of rules in order to represent all the possible orders of surface structure constituents. Since in such models the range of possible constituent structures is defined by the phrase-structure rules, *i.e.* each rule determines a particular structure, grammars for languages displaying a fair amount of flexibility with regard to constituent order require a very large number of rules to account for all the possibilities. To illustrate this point, consider the hypothetical case of a language in which the constituents of the verb phrase can occur in any order. The grammar of this language would require the following rules to express all the possible permutations of V NP, V PP and V NP PP:

(16)   VP ---> V NP
          VP ---> V PP
          VP ---> NP V
          VP ---> PP V
          VP ---> V NP PP
          VP ---> V PP NP
          VP ---> PP V NP
          VP ---> NP V PP
          VP ---> PP NP V
          VP ---> NP PP V

The resulting multiplication of grammar rules has a negative effect not

---

[16] For a review of some of the problems involved in Finnish, see Karttunen and Kay (1985), and in Warlpiri see Kashket (1986).

only from a theoretical linguistics standpoint -- obvious generalizations are missed -- but also from a computational standpoint, since the size of the grammar is an important factor determining the efficiency of the parser.

Whereas traditional rule-based approaches seem irrevocably bound to strategies that rely crucially on idiosyncratic properties of surface constituent order, we have shown in the previous section how a principle-based approach can be constructed to function in a large part at a more abstract level of organizational structure. That is, principle-based parsers are not guided by rules specifying the structural properties of surface representations, but rather by the more abstract principles which underly these rules. As we pointed out, such parsers exploit to a considerable degree lexical properties of head of constituents, mostly predicates, θ-role assigning properties, *etc*, rather than strict obedience to precedence and dominance relations to guide the parser's steps. So, for instance, a slightly modified version of the parser described in section 3 could presumably handle a language with the word-order flexibility expressed by the rules (16). Recall that with regard to complement attachment, this parser essentially considers pairs of constituents and attempts to combine them, to form larger constituents. Whether or not attachment is possible depends on various parameters, such as, lexical properties of the heads of the constituents. To handle our example, the parser would have to consider the following four cases: NP VP, PP VP, VP NP, VP PP. Just like in French, whether the pair VP PP can be combined into a single constituent depends on the properties of both constituents. It is expected that in a language with relatively free word-order, inflectional information will play an important role with regard to the recovery of grammatical functions such as subject, object, *etc.*, which are relevant for θ-assignment. Assuming this, the crucial difference between French and our hypothetical language would be in the way they realize grammatical functions. Although, obviously, much more needs to be said about parsing languages with relatively free constituent order, it appears that a GB-parser might be able to parse such languages without relying on an exhaustive enumeration of possible surface structures[17].

Summarizing, an advantage that GB-parsers might have over rule-based

---

[17] Cf. Kahsket (1986) for a description of an experimental GB-parser for Warlpiri.

parsers in application to other languages -- and in particular languages with relatively free surface constituent order -- is that whereas the surface order of constituents differs significantly from one language to the next, is it to be expected that lexical properties associated with case and thematic structure should hold relatively constant. For instance, under the reasonable assumption that θ-roles are assigned by predicates to constituents which bear a particular grammatical function, parsers for strictly configurational languages and parsers for languages exhibiting more flexibility with regard to word-order would only differ minimally, *i.e.*, they would essentially differ in the way they assign grammatical functions. In some languages, grammatical functions are defined configurationally, while in others, they are defined to various degrees by morphological case marking. The important fact is that under this view, the grammars of both languages are essentially the same, modulo the realization of grammatical functions.

4.2 Handling ambiguities

An important factor of inefficiency and inadequacy of current natural language parsers comes from the way they handle ambiguities. Consider, for instance, the case of lexical ambiguity: most lexical items, and in particular frequently used verbs, nouns and adjectives, allow for more than one reading. These readings may differ in terms of their subcategorization features, selectional features, or other syntactic and/or semantic properties, not to mention features such as tense, modality, case, number, possibility of idiomatic readings, and so on. For instance, English verbs such as *get*, *have* and *go*, or French *faire*, *aller* and *mettre* can easily be associated with a dozen different readings -- in fact a lot more if one considers all the idiomatic expressions based on these verbs.

The way current parsers usually deal with this problem is simply to consider each reading of such words as an independent element that has to be taken into account[18]. So, for instance, when the word *leave* is

---

[18] This is, of course, not the case for deterministic parsers, such as Marcus (1980), Berwick and Weinberg (1985), Milne (1986), *etc*. Those parsers, by definition, cannot consider more than one possible structure and must, therefore, resolve lexical ambiguity "on the spot", based on the immediate context. See Wehrli (in preparation) for a detailed discussion of the problem of ambiguity for deterministic parsing.

encountered, both the transitive and the intransitive readings of this verb will be considered, as if they were independent words. Even though further context is likely to be compatible with only one of the readings, which will make it possible to discard the other reading, this way of handling the problem of lexical ambiguity leads to a large amount of duplication of partial structures and unnecessary computations. Thus, to go back to our example of the verbs *go* or *get*, depending on the particular choice of parsing strategy, the parser might indeed build as many phrase-structure representations as there are readings of these verbs. Furthermore, in configurations where the verb is preceded by some specifiers (*e.g.* auxiliairies), attachment of the specifiers to the verb could be repeated for each structure considered.

This problem is not restricted to cases of lexical ambiguities but concerns higher-level ambiguities as well -- *i.e.* attachment ambiguities, θ-assignment ambiguities, referential ambiguities, *etc.*-- and the parser's answer is likely to be a multiplication of structures, leading to a large amount of duplication. In all these cases, it appears that traditional parsers are not well-equipped to cope with this fundamental problem.

A partial solution to this problem lies with the concept of structure-sharing, *i.e.* the idea that a particular element could be simultaneously part of more than one structure, avoiding costly duplications[19]. This, for instance, can be achieved by using complex data structures such as Martin Kay's (1980) "chart", a kind of well-formed substring table. Chart parsers never compute a constituent more than once. When a particular constituent has been recognized, it is entered in the chart and becomes available to alternative analyses without having to be recomputed again and again.

However, as pointed out by Winograd (1983), among others, while this technique lends itself nicely to CF-parsing, its use (and its benefits) are much less evident when the constituents manipulated by the parser are no longer strictly identified by their categorial symbol (as in CF-parsing) but are treated as complex bundles of features. For one thing, as the descriptive complexity of linguistic units increases, so does their specificity. This, in turn, decreases the possibility of coalescence given the

---

[19] For a discussion of the advantages of structure-sharing for parsing theory see Earley (1970), Kay (1977), Kuno (1965), Winograd (1983).

fact that the coalescence of constituents presupposes their identity.

Because non-modular parsers tend to focus on a single level of representation, they build linguistic representations which are maximally detailed, in the sense that they contain all the features available in the system. For the reasons mentioned earlier, the specificity of these representations seriously limits the use of structure-sharing techniques for such parsers. On the other hand, parsers based on a modular organization appear to be in a much better position to exploit the advantages of structure-sharing, and thus might be in a much better position to handle the ambiguity problem. Modular parsers do not consider just one level of representation but several distinct levels, each one of them focusing on some limited subset of grammatical properties. Assume (*i*) that each module determines a particular level of representation and (*ii*) that a particular module can only "see" the features which are relevant for its task. Given these two rather natural assumptions, the level of representation computed by a particular module would be rather unspecific, maximizing the opportunities for structure-sharing.

To further illustrate this point, suppose that constituents which only differ in terms of features which are not relevant for a particular module are indistinguishable for this module and, therefore, are considered a single element. Take, for instance, the module handling the attachment of specifiers to heads *cf.* section 3.3.1. If, as is usually the case, auxiliary selection does not depend on the choice of particular subcategorization features of the head verb, the module which parses the specifier system of the verb will not be sensitive to the various readings of this verb which differ in terms of subcategorization features and/or semantic features. Hence, all those readings will be treated as a single element to which the auxiliaries will be attached.

The same point can be made for other modules of the syntax. Consider, for instance, ambiguities related to thematic assignment, as in the following sentence:

(17) Jean a fait porter les livres aux enfants.
  'Jean made the kids carry the books'
  'Jean made someone carry the books to the kids'

Sentence (17) is ambiguous. Under one reading, the PP constituent *aux enfants* is construed as the agent of the action of carrying the books, but another reading is available, in which it is interpreted as the recipient of the action. However, there is no particular reason to assume that this sentence should receive more than one syntactic structure. In other words, we shall argue that the same structure accomodates the two readings, which can only be distinguished at the level of thematic representation.

The same situation arises in many other cases, and is not limited to the syntactic component. Take for instance the very common case of semantically ambiguous words such as the English nouns *bank* or *pen*. To the extent to which the lexical readings of these words share all syntactic features, the fact that these words are ambiguous should not concern the syntactic modules of the parser, for which there is a single noun *bank* and a single noun *pen*. The fact that these nouns can receive various interpretations is a matter of semantic and pragmatic interpretation that should not concern syntactic processing.

REFERENCES

Abney, S. and J. Cole (1985). "A government-binding parser," *Proceedings of the North Eastern Linguistic Society* XVI.

Barton, G. E. Jr.(1984). "Toward a principle-based parser," *A.I. Memo* **788**, MIT AI Lab.

Berwick, R. and A. Weinberg (1984). *The Grammatical Basis of Linguistic Performance: Language Use and Acquisition*, MIT Press.

Borer, H., ed. (1986). *The Syntax of Pronominal Clitics. Syntax and Semantics*, vol.19, Academic Press.

Chomsky, N. (1981). *Lectures on Government and Binding*, Foris Publications.

Chomsky, N. (1982). *Some Concepts and Consequences in the Theory of Government and Binding*, MIT Press.

Chomsky, N. (1986). *Knowledge of Language: Its Origin, Nature and Use*, Praeger Publishers, New York.

Crain, S. and J. D. Fodor (1985). "How can grammars help parsers?" in Dowty *et al.* (1985), 94-128.

Dowty, D., L. Karttunen and A. Zwicky, eds. (1985). *Natural Language Parsing: Psychological, Computational and Theoretical Perspectives*, Cambridge University Press.

Earley, J. (1970). "An efficient context-free parsing algorithm," Communications of the Association for Computing Machinery **13**:2 94-102.

Fodor, J.D. (1983). "Phrase structure parsing and the island constraints," *Linguistics and Philosophy* **6** 163:223.

Karttunen, L. and M. Kay (1985). "Parsing in a free word order language," in Dowty *et al.* (1985).

Kashket, M.B. (1986). "Parsing a free-word order language: Warlpiri," *Proceedings of the 24th ACL Conference*, 60-66.

Kay, M. (1977). "Morphological and syntactic analysis" in A. Zampolli (ed.) *Syntactic Structures Processing*, North Holland.
Kay, M. (1980). "Algorithm schemata and data structures in syntactic processing" CSL-80-12 Xerox Palo Alto Research Center.
Kuhns, R.J. (1986). "A PROLOG implementation of government-binding theory," *COLING*.
Kuno, S. (1965). "The predictive analyzer and a path elimination technique." *Communications of the ACM* **8** 453-462.
Larson, R.K. (1985). "Bare-NP adverbs," *Linguistic Inquiry* **16:4** 595-621.
Marcus, M. (1980). *A Theory of Syntactic Recognition for Natural Language*, MIT Press.
Milne, R. (1986) "Resolving lexical ambiguity in a deterministic parser," *Computational Linguistics* 12.1. pp. 1-12.
Rizzi, L. (1986). "On chain formation," in H. Borer (ed).
Sharp, R. (1985). *A Model of Grammar Based on Principles of Government and Binding*, M.S. Thesis, The University of British Columbia.
Stabler, E.P. (1986). "Restricting logic grammars with Government-Binding theory", mimeo, Quintus Computers Systems.
Stowell, T. (1981). *Origins of Phrase Structure*, Ph.D. Dissertation, MIT.
Stowell, T. (1982). "A formal theory of configurational phenomena," in J. Pustejovsky and P. Sells *Proceedings of the XIIth conference of the North Eastern Linguistic Society*, 235-257.
Thiersh, C. and H-P. Kolb (1986). "Strict X-bar parsing: prolegomena to a government and binding parser", paper presented at the GLOW meeting, Barcelona-Girona.
Wehrli, E. (1983). "A modular parser for French," in *Proceedings of the Eighth International Joint Conference on Artificial Intelligence*, William Kaufmann, 686-689.
Wehrli, E. (1984). "A Government-Binding parser for French," Working Paper No 48, Institut pour les Etudes Sémantiques et Cognitives, Université de Genève.
Wehrli, E. (in preparation). "Deterministic parsing: a critical evaluation".
Williams, E. (1981). "Argument structure and morphology," *The Linguistic Review* **1:1** 81-114.
Winograd, T. (1983). *Language as a Cognitive Process*, Addison Wesley.

HENK ZEEVAT

CENTRE FOR COGNITIVE SCIENCE

UNIVERSITY OF EDINBURGH

EDINBURGH, SCOTLAND

COMBINING CATEGORIAL GRAMMAR AND UNIFICATION

ABSTRACT

This paper discusses a combination of ideas from categorial grammar, unification based linguistic formalisms and discourse representation theory. The resulting formalism, dubbed U(nification) C(ategorial) G(rammar) is introduced and applied to a number of linguistic problems, among which Dutch infinitival complements. Thereby it is illustrated in what way the addition of unification to categorial grammar increases its expressive power.*

1. UNIFICATION CATEGORIAL GRAMMAR

Unification categorial grammar (UCG) is a version of categorial grammar in which several insights from Head-driven Phrase Structure

---

* The work on UCG reported here was carried out as part of ESPRIT Project 393 (ACORD), "The Construction and Interrogation of Knowledge Bases using Natural Language Text and Graphics". A more comprehensive account of UCG is given in *Problems of Dialogue Parsing*, ACORD deliverable T2.1, by Jo Calder, Ewan Klein, Marc Moens and Henk Zeevat, that will be available as an Edinburgh Working Paper in Cognitive Science. An introduction to UCG is forthcoming as: *An Introduction to Unification Categorial Grammar*, by Henk Zeevat, Ewan Klein and Jo Calder. That paper will share some introductory material with the present one. I am grateful to the following people for comments and criticism: Jo Calder, Einar Jowsey, Ewan Klein, Manfred Pinkal and Stuart Shieber. All errors are of course my own.

U. Reyle and C. Rohrer (eds.),
Natural Language Parsing and Linguistic Theories, 202–229.
© 1988 *by D. Reidel Publishing Company.*

Grammar and PATR-II have been incorporated.[1] It was developed as the groundwork for a English parsing system in which syntax and semantics are tightly integrated (we assume a version of Discourse Representation Theory) and in which a fairly large coverage is intended. This makes it necessary to formulate the grammar formalism with sufficient detail and precision to allow for computer implementation. In this paper the basic ideas are discussed and a comparison is carried out with phrase structure grammars and classical categorial grammar, by some linguistic examples, especially Dutch infinitival groups in subordinate clauses.

Classical categorial grammar is defined in terms of a notion of *category* and a rule of functional application. It is customary to start with two primitive categories: N (name) and S (sentence). The set of categories is then defined as:

(1) i. N and S are categories
    ii. If A and B are categories, then A/B is a category.

Functional application is the following rule:

(2) If E_1 is an expression of category A/B and E_2 is an expression of category B, then E_1E_2 (i.e. the concatenation of E_1 and E_2) is an expression of category A.

A particular categorial grammar is obtained by specifying a list of basic expressions together with their categories. The set of expressions that the grammar generates is the closure of the set of basic expressions under functional application.

For applications to natural language, various extensions of this scheme have been proposed.[2] UCG is just one of these extensions. The main departure[3] from categorial grammar is given by a more complex notion of

---

[1] (Flickinger, Pollard and Wasow 1985, Pollard 1985b, Proudian and Pollard 1985) and (Shieber 1986, Shieber et al. 1986) Recent work carried out at SRI within the PATR framework, in particular (Uszkoreit 1986)and (Karttunen 1986) has independently arrived at a similar integration of ideas from categorial grammar and unification grammar.

[2] For example, directional categories, Montague grammar (where a notion of syntactic rule subsumes functional application), and combinatory grammar (cf. Geach 1972, Lambek 1958, Lambek 1961, Montague 1973, Steedman 1985a, van Benthem 1986).

[3] In this paper we also assume bidirectionality. Other mechanisms may have to be added to deal with long distance dependencies, anaphora and conjunction.

category. We assign to each expression a number of representations. Most importantly, these are: (a) the way in which the expression is *phonologically* realised (its orthography, for our current purposes), (b) a *category* specification, and (c) a *semantic* representation. Following Pollard 1985b, a (complete or incomplete) list of such representations is called a *sign*.

The most interesting aspect of the use of a single sign for a linguistic expression instead of a number of associated representations, is that it allows one to have the same variables on several levels of the sign. In this way one can force a specification in the semantics to be the same as one in the category, or in the phonology, and one naturally arrives at a single process by which the phonology and the semantics are constructed.

In UCG, we employ three primitive categories: nouns (*noun*), sentences (*sent*) and noun phrases (*np*). These primitive categories admit further specification by features, so that we can distinguish finite and non-finite sentences, nominative and accusative NPs, and so on. Categories are now defined as follows:

(3) i. Any primitive category (together with a syntactic feature specification) is a category.
ii. If A is a category, and B is a sign, then A/B is a category.

In a category of the form A/B, we call B the *active* part of the category, and also of the sign as a whole in which A/B occurs as category. It will be observed that (3ii) is just the categorial analog of Pollard's (1985a) proposal for subcategorization, according to which phrasal heads are specified for a list of signs corresponding to their complements.

Within the grammar, we allow not just constant symbols like *sent* and *np*, but also variables, at each level of representation. Variables allow us to capture the notion of incomplete information, and a sign which contains variables can be further specified by unification. The unification of two representations (if defined) is a third representation which combines all the information in the first two, if that information is compatible. Confining our attention to atomic expressions, the situation can be summarized as follows: the unification of two variables is a variable, the unification of a variable and a constant is that constant, and the unification of two distinct constants always fails. We will presently see more complex illustrations of this simple idea.

Unification plays an important role in our use of signs.

Functional application in UCG splits into two separate operations that we call *instantiation* and *stripping*. It will be recalled that if a sign has category A/B, then B is said to be its active part. Instantiation is defined as follows:

(4) S_3 is the *instantiation* of S_1 with respect to S_2 if it results from S_1 by unifying S_1's active part with S_2.

Since unification can fail, there may be many signs with respect to which a given sign S_1 cannot be instantiated. The second notion, stripping, receives the definition in (5).

(5) Given a sign S_1 with category A/B, the result of *stripping* S_1 is the sign S_2 just like S_1 except that its phonology is the concatenation of S_1's and B's phonology, and its category is stripped down to A.

The rule of functional application now takes the following form:

(6) Let S_1 and S_2 be wellformed signs. Then stripping the instantiation of S_1 with respect to S_2 also results in a wellformed sign.

The set of wellformed expressions can be defined as the phonologies of the set of wellformed signs. These in turn can be defined as the closure of the lexicon under functional application.

To find out if S_1 can be applied as a functor to an argument sign S_2, all that we need to do is look at the actual definition of S_1's category, say A/C, and try to unify C with S_2. If unification is successful, then stripping the instantiated functor sign will give rise to a result sign S_1'; moreover, instantiation will have made S_1' more completely specified in various useful ways.

This, in essence, is the structure of UCG. We will complicate the picture by giving more content to the notions of semantics, features and linear order.

2. SIGNS, CATEGORIES, ORDER AND SEMANTICS

2.1. Signs

A UCG sign contains four major attributes: phonology (W), syntactic category (C), semantics (S) and order (O). These are presented either as a vertical list

  W
  C
  S
  O

or as a sequence separated by colons:

  W:C:S:O

(7) illustrates a typical case, the lexical entry for the verb visit:

(7) visit
  sent[fin]/W_1:np:x:pre/W_2:np:y:post
  [e]VISIT(e, x, y)
  O

This is a sign whose phonology attribute is the string visit, whose syntactic category is *sent[fin]/W1:np:x:pre/W2:np:y:post*, whose semantics is *[e]VISIT(e, x, y)*, and whose order is the unspecified variable *O*. The significance of these attributes will be explained shortly. However, some further comment on the complex category may be helpful at this point. It has the form *A/S/S'* (i.e. *(A/S)/S'*, assuming association to the left), where *S* and *S'* are themselves signs. Thus, the active part of the category is a sign whose phonology is the variable W_2, whose category is *np*, whose semantics is the individual variable *y*, and whose order is *post*.

In order to simplify notation, we feel free to omit unspecified attributes from the description of the sign (unless the variable occurrence in question is cross-identified with some other occurrence elsewhere in the sign). In practice, this does not seem to lead to difficulties. Thus, the example above can be reduced slightly as follows:

(8) visit
    sent[fin]/np:x:pre/np:y:post
    [e]VISIT(e, x, y)

2.2. Categories

We pointed out earlier that our grammar employs the primitive categories *sent*, *np* and *noun*. The first two of these can carry additional feature specifications. These are drawn from the following list inspired by Gazdar et al. 1985.

	Features	*Morphology*
on *sent* :		
	FIN	finite verb form
	CFIN	complementized finite verbal element
	BSE	base verb form (i.e. a bare infinitive)
	CBSE	complementized base verb form
	INF	infinitive verb form
	PRP	present participle
	PSP	past participle
	PAS	passive participle
on *np* :		
	NOM	nominative
	OBJ	objective

Having features on these two primitive categories allows for an extra variable, so that

    sent

can be read as

    sent[F]

where F stands for an arbitrary feature.

The main motivation for defining complex categories as C/Sign is that it yields a very simple notion of functional application, while simultaneously allowing information from the argument sign to flow to the sign that results from application. This is made possible by sharing variables between the sign and the active part of its category. The information that is transmitted can involve semantics, features, order or even the syntactic category of the argument expression.

Information flows whenever unification occurs, and since unification is commutative, the flow can go in either direction. We illustrate with a simple example. (9) is a lexical entry for the verb *dance*.

(9) dances
    sent[fin]/np[nom]:x:pre
    [e]DANCE(e, x)

(10) is plausible as a lexical entry for a proper name (though in fact we adopt a slightly different treatment, to be discussed below):

(10) harry
    np
    HARRY

Now suppose we try to unify the active sign

(11) np[nom]:x:pre

with (10). In order to see what is going on more clearly, let's use a uniform format which includes all the variables:

(10') harry
    np
    HARRY
    0

(11') W
    np[nom]
    x
    pre

What results from unification of these two is the sign (12).

(12) harry
   np[nom]
   HARRY
   pre

The value for phonology is contributed by (10'), as is the semantics, *HARRY*, while a further specification of *np* is contributed by (11'), as is a value for the order attribute. As a result, we obtain the following instantiation of (9):

(13) dances
   sent[fin]/harry:np[nom]:HARRY:pre
   [e]DANCE(e, HARRY)

Notice that as a side-effect of instantiation, the semantics has been further specified. It can now be interpreted as saying that there is an event e in which Harry -- not some anonymous x -- dances.

The argument sign is now marked by the order declaration *pre*, meaning that functional application only succeeds if *Harry* comes after *dances* in the phonology after functional application. The role of the order attribute will be explicated in the next section.

Now that we have instantiated (13), it can be stripped, yielding (14) as a result.

(14) dances harry
   sent[fin]
   [e]DANCE(e, HARRY)

The most spectacular changes that instantiation can induce are to be found when unification specifies the result category in the functor sign. For well-known semantic reasons, we follow Montague 1973 and others in assigning noun phrases a type-raised category. Our notion of type-raising is slightly more general than usual, since we allow category variables (cf. section 3 and 4). Thus, our lexical entry for *Harry* looks like (15) (rather than (10)):

(15) Harry
   C/(C/np:HARRY:O):S:O
   S

The active sign

> (C/np:HARRY:O):S:O

contains a complex category C/np:HARRY:O. This can be unified with the sign for *dance* we gave above, yielding (16).

(16) dances
>   sent[fin]/np[nom]:HARRY:pre
>   DANCE(e, HARRY)
>   pre

That is, C has been unified with *sent[fin]*, O with *pre*, S with *[e]DANCE(e, HARRY)*, and the (omitted) phonology variable with *dances*. Note that all the changes we obtained in instantiating (13) with respect to (10) occur here as well. Our original expression (15) has been transformed into (17) as a result of the unification.

(17) Harry
>   sent[fin]/(dances:sent[fin]/np[nom]:HARRY:pre:[e]DANCE(e, HARRY):pre)
>   [e]DANCE(e, HARRY)

Functional application can now yield (18).

(18) Harry dances
>   sent[fin]
>   [e]DANCE(e, HARRY)

Note that this time *dances*, whose sign is marked for order *pre*, is indeed preceded by its functor in the phonology of the result sign.

2.3. Order

For the time being, we adopt the restriction that only adjacent constituents can combine grammatically, and that the only order specifications are *post* and *pre*. *Post* says, on a sign: "if I am an argument in a functional application, my functor follows me". *Pre* says: "if I am an argument in a functional application, my functor precedes me".

Functional application is realized by two rules in our current system, depending on the order of functor and argument. The easiest way to understand them is probably to look first at their non-unification categorial equivalents. R1' allows a functor to apply to a constituent of category B to its right, while R2' allows application to a constituent B to the left:

(19) R1': A -> A/B B
     R2': A -> B A\B

(20) is a formulation which assumes that unification tests for the appropriate order specifications on the arguments themselves.

(20) R1: $W_1 W_2$:C:S -> W_1:C/(W_2:C_1:S_1:pre):S W_2:C_1:S_1:pre
     R2: $W_2 W_1$:C:S -> W_2:C_1:S_1:post W_1:C/(W_2:C_1:S_1:post):S

Let us look at the interpretation of the first rule: if a functor sign with phonology W_1, category *C/X* and semantics *S* precedes an argument sign *E* with phonology W_2, and order *pre*, and if *E* is successfully unified with *X*, then the result is a sign with phonology $W_1 W_2$, category *C* and semantics *S*, where *C* and *S* may have been altered as a result of unifying *X* with *E*. Exactly the same thing happens with R2, except that the order of functor and argument is reversed. In essence this is bidirectional categorial grammar. The only difference is that when the order is unspecified both forward and backward application to another sign are allowed.

2.4. Semantics

It is not the aim of this paper to discuss the semantics in depth. This section only contains what is necessary to read the semantic representations and their construction. The representation language is closely related, in its interpretation, to D(iscourse) R(epresentation) T(heory) (Kamp 1981, Heim 1982). DRT style languages form a good basis for pronoun resolution, have quantification over cases and do without explicit quantifiers, while retaining the full expressive power of first order logic.

Compared with the standard syntax for DRT (see Kamp 1981) there is one difference: every formula is provided with a special variable called its index. Intuitively the values of this variable are the thing described or postulated by the expression, and since variables may be sorted one may express sortal information about the kind of entity the expression describes. Technically, they are best thought of as the analogies of *discourse referents*: the discourse referents of a given expression are its index, together with, if the formula is a conjunction, the discourse referents of its conjuncts[4]. The syntax of the semantical representations is relatively simple. One assumes a set of of predicates with a fixed arity and an indication on the kind of arguments that can fill a certain argument place. As *terms* we allow (sorted) variables, constants and formula's. The set of formula's can now be defined as follows:

1. If x is a variable, P is a predicate of arity n and $t_1,...,t_{n-1}$ are terms of kind prescribed by P then
$$P(x,t_1,...,t_{n-1})$$
is an (*atomic*) formula with index x.

2. If x is a variable and A and B are formula's then
$$[x][A,B]$$
is a (*conjunctive*) formula.

3. If x is a variable and A and B are formula's then
$$[x][A=>B]$$
is an (*implicative*) formula.

4. | is a formula (the *absurdum*).

It is easier to translate the formula's into predicate logic than to give a model theoretic definition. The following definition gives equivalents A' in predicate logic[5] for formula's A from the language specified above using an intermediate translation A".

0. If A is a formula with discourse referents $x_1,...,x_n$ A' = $\exists x_1,...,x_n$ A"

---

[4] This can be expressed in a simple recursive definition of the set DR(A), the set of discourse referents of a formula A:

$$DR([a]A) = \{a\} \text{ if A is not a conjunction}$$
$$DR([a][A,B] = \{a\} \cup DR(A) \cup DR(B)$$

[5] This translation is only intended for the extensional fragment. When a formula occurs as a term in an atomic formula, its occurrence is intensional.

1. If A is an atomic formula or | A" = A

2. If A is a conjunction [x][B,C] A" = B" & C"

3. If A is an implication [x][B = >C] and $x_1,...,x_n$ are
   B's discourse referents and $y_1,...,y_k$ C's, then
   A" = $\forall x_1,...,x_n(B" => \exists y_1,...,y_k C")$

In this paper sorts are indicated by reserved variable letters. The following schema gives a relation between certain variables and sorts.

(21)   object variables $x, y, z, x_1, x_2, x_3, ...$
       mass variables $m, m_1, ...$
       event variables $e, e_1, e_2, e_3, ...$
       state variables $s, t, s_1, s_2, s_3, ...$
       unsorted variables $a, b, c, a_1, a_2, a_3, ...$

Furthermore, for each of the above sorts, and for others not listed, we assume that we can write labeled declarations as in (22).

(22) state(a)
      plural(a)
      female(x)
      singular(a)

The rest of this section will be devoted to some examples of repesentations of natural language sentences in the formalism.

(23) John visits Mary
      VISIT(e,JOHN,MARY]

The translation states that there is an event of John visiting Mary. In the next example, the event variable, introduced as the index of the translation of the verb, is passed over in three steps to become the index of the whole formula.

(24) A burglar breaks into a flat.
      [e][BURGLAR(x),[e][FLAT(y),[e][INTO(e,y),BREAK(e,x)]]

That this not the general pattern, can be seen in the following example. The quantification, introduced by *every student* makes it impossible to regard the sentence as reporting a single event. So it must become either a multiplicity of events or a state. For simplicity we assume the latter.

(25) Some boy hits every student
[s][BOY(x),[s][STUDENT(y) = > HIT(e,x,y)]]

In complex sentences as in (26) an advantage of having indexed conjunctions emerges. The temporal modifier *when Harry comes* in itself introduces an event that is distinct from the one reported in the main clause. But we can still catch the fact (and temporal resolution is influenced by the distinction between main and subordinate clauses) by having the index introduced by the main clause *everybody leaves* appear as the index of the whole formula.

(26) When Harry comes in, everybody leaves.
[s][COMEIN(e',HARRY),[s][AT(s,e'),[s][HUMAN(x)
= >LEAVE(e,x)]]]

The last two examples illustrate negation and intensional contexts (in the second example *his* is ignored). Notice that negation, like quantification, sets up a new index.

(27) Nobody walks in the park
HUMAN(x),[e][PARK(y),[e][IN(e,y),WALK(e,x)]]]= > [ ]

John believes a burglar to break into his flat
[s][BURGLAR(x),BELIEVE(s,JOHN,[e][FLAT(y),[e][INTO
(e,y), BREAK(e,x)]])

3. VARIABLE CATEGORIES

We introduced variable categories originally to deal with a simple problem that arise in Montague grammar. If one is dealing with type raised NPs, their category must become of the form A/B where B is the category of the thing that would normally look for an NP. But there are many such categories: intransitive, transitive and ditransitive verbs and prepositions are the most common ones. If one does not have variable categories the only strategy is the one Montague adopts: select a good representative (in his case intransitive verbs of category s/np) and deal with the other cases by means of meaning postulates[6]. The only alternative would be to make NPs highly ambiguous and put them in all four categories in (28).

(28) s/(s/np)
 (s/np)/(s/np/np)
 (s/np/np)/(s/np/np/np)
 ((s/np)/(s/np))/(((s/np)/(s/np))/np)

But this alternative is unattractive, since the ambiguity would promulgate to other categories.

In a unification framework it is more interesting to see if it is possible to deal with NPs in a uniform way by assigning them the category in (29).

(29) X/(X/np)

Here X is a variable ranging over categories. So (29) subsumes all four cases in (28), and any other case that may crop up as well.

Let me give one example that brings out this use of variables in the category specification of NPs.

(30) Every student's bike has a lock

The lexical specifications for the words in (30) are given in (31).

(31) student
 noun
 STUDENT(x)

 bike
 noun
 BIKE(x)

---

[6] These so called extensionalisation meaning postulates are, by restrictions on their scope, also used to distinguish between extensional and intensional NP positions. The only position that (but this has been challenged) does not have intensional readings is the subject position, and therefore s/np is the proper choice. It seems however, that a lexical treatment of intensional NPs is feasible, as soon as meaning postulates are no longer needed for NP attachment.

lock
noun
LOCK(x)

has
sent[fin]/np[nom]:x:pre/np[obj]:y:post
HAVE(s,x,y)

a
X/(X/np:x:O):[a]A:O/noun:[b]B:pre
[a][[b]B,[a]A]

every
X/(X/np:x:O):[a]A:O/noun:[b]B:pre
[s][[b]B => [a]A]

's
X/(X/np:x:O):[a]A:O/noun:[b]B:pre/np:c:pre
[a][[b][POSSESS(b,c),[b]B],[a]A]

Notice that the genitive connector transforms an NP into a determiner with exactly the same category as *a* and *every*. By forward application *a* and *lock* combine straightforwardly into the NP sign (32).

(32) a lock
X/(X/np:x:O):[a]A:O
[a][LOCK(x),[a]A]

For the combination with *has* X must unify with the whole remaining category of has:

sent[fin]/np[nom]:x:pre

and the order variable O with the specification *post*. This leads to the result (33).

(33) has a lock
sent[fin]/np[nom]:x:pre
[s][LOCK(y),HAVE(s,x,y)]

In the same way as *a lock* (33), (34) is formed.

(34) every student
X/(X/np:x:O):[a]A:O
[s][STUDENT(x) => [a]A]

In combining with the genitive marker 's the variable X must now unifiy with the whole remaining category (35).

(35) Y/(Y/np:x:O):[a]A:O/noun:[b]B:pre

and the order variable O with *pre*. In this way the sign (36) results.

(36) every student's
Y/(Y/np:x:O):[a]A:O/noun:[b]B:pre
[s][student(x) => [a][[b][possess(b,x),[b]B],[a]A]

Combining this with the noun *bike* leads again to an NP: (37).

(37) every student's bike
Y/(Y/np:x:O):[a]A:O
[s][STUDENT(x) => [a][[z][POSSESS(z,x),BIKE(z)],[a]A]

To combine this with *has a bike* the variable Y must unify with the again different remainder of the category:

sent[fin]

so that the result is (38).

(38) every student's bike has a lock
sent[fin]
[s][STUDENT(x) => [s'][[z][POSSESS(z,x),BIKE(z)],
[LOCK(y),HAVE(s',z,y)]]]

In predicate logic the semantics would be rendered by (39).

(39) $\exists$s ($\forall$x (student(x) -> $\exists$s' $\exists$z $\exists$y (possess(z,x)
bike(z) & lock(y) & have(s',z,y))))

There are two other points where an appeal to variable categories is useful, or may be useful: modifiers and auxiliaries. Though some modifiers (e.g. adjectives) have a strong preference for a certain kind of expression to combine with, others, especially PPs, do not. One can combine PPs with verbs, nouns and sentences and on each of these occasions their contribution seems to be the same. So to give them a category like (s/np)/(s/np) seems misguided, since again special mechanism must be invoked to get them to combine with sentences. So two treatments seem to be available: one where they receive a category

$$X/X$$

and one where, like NPs, their arguments are subcategorised for a PP applying to them:

$$X/(X/pp)$$

There are some arguments against the first approach.

The first of these has to do with the fact that it is hard to give a characterisation of PP positions, so that one faces the choice between using a disjunction or heavy overgeneration.

The second objection falls outside the scope of this paper but is clear enough: it is impossible to have a notion of a PP-gap. That one must have such a notion for English can be seen from examples such as (40).

(40) When did you say that John will come

The reading where one queries the time of John's arrival, rather than the moment of talk about John's arrival is the one that is difficult to obtain without PP-gaps. It is hard to imagine a treatment that allows for PP-gaps without subcategorizing verbs and nouns for PPs. So for the moment we have adopted the second approach.

Another application of variables over categories are auxiliaries. In a slightly different organisation of the signs[7], it is also possible to treat auxiliaries as arbitrary premodifiers of non finite sentences with an arbitrary number of arguments. (At least one argument is required, since we do not want the auxiliary to occur before the subject). This would allow for a number of some scope ambiguities that are otherwise hard to

---

[7] This involves bringing the primitive categories to the surface of the sign, rather then having them as the final element of the category structure. This approach is the one current in HPSG and is also partially adopted in (Calder et al. 1986). The approach sketched in this paper is slightly simpler, and functions, as far as we have seen, well for English. The only point where the HPSG approach does have advantages is in the formulation of lexical rules. In our approach we often have to distinguish between verbs of a different arity in order to describe apparently uniform operations like passivisation or particle formation.

capture. For example, take (41).

(41) John did not give a girl a book

Making *did not* a premodifiers over infinite one two and three place verbs, leads to three possible ways in which the semantics may come out as illustrated in (42).

(42) [s][BOOK(x),GIRL(y),[s][GIVE(e,s,y,x) => |]]
[s][BOOK(x),[s][[e][GIRL(y),GIVE(e,s,y,x)] => |]]
[s][[e][BOOK(x),GIRL(y),GIVE(e,s,y,x)] => |]

(42) corresponds with the parse trees in (43).

(43) [John, [[[[did, not], give], [a, girl]], [a, book]]]
[John, [[[did, not], [give, [a, girl]]], [a, book]]]
[John, [[did not][[give a girl] a book]]]

All the uses of variables discussed in this section seem abbreviatory: they abbreviate a finite disjunction of possibilities, that could be spelled out completely if one wanted. The next chapter illustrates a less innocent use, that suggests that using variables in the category specifications leads to a system that is stronger than classical categorial grammar. Indeed, the variables there abbreviate infinite disjunctions that could never be spelled out completely.

4. DUTCH INFINITIVAL GROUPS IN UCG.

The framework described above whereby unification and variable categories are added to the classical formulation of categorial grammar has a considerable expressive power. As noted in Wittenburg 1986, one of its uses can be to increase the complexity of any given category (when one thinks of a variable category as having the same complexity as a primitive category) in a "reduction". E.g. it is possible to increase the length of a given instantiated category list by one, as in the following example:

$$(X/n)/X \;+\; s/n \;\to\; s/n/n$$
$$(X/n)/X \;+\; s/n/n \;\to\; s/n/n/n$$
$$(X/n)/X \;+\; s/n/n/n \;\to\; s/n/n/n/n$$
...

Allowing variables over categories in general, leads thereby to a potentially infinite set of categories. For a categorial grammar with infinitely many categories, the standard proof of equivalence with context free phrase structure grammars is not possible. Indeed, the following sketch of a treatment of cross serial dependencies in Dutch shows that the categorial grammar must be stronger than classical categorial grammars. Though Pullum and Gazdar 1982 have shown that, if one is only interested in string generation, they can be handled in a PSG framework, it is not the case that this is true if one is interested in obtaining either correct semantic representation for them, or the commonly accepted analysis tree as the generation tree. The present analysis conforms to both of those demands.[8] Since classical categorial grammar is equivalent to phrase structure grammar, it follows that the expressive power of UCG is stronger. One can in fact show that the indexed languages of Gazdar 1985 are within the expressive power of UCG; whether the reverse holds as well we do not know.

The crucial case are Dutch infinitivals in subordinate clauses as in the example (44) below.

(44) dat Jan Marie de kinderen bier ziet laten drinken

I do not claim that the treatment below is a unified treatment of all infinitives and infinitival complements in Dutch. It would be interesting to try to integrate this treatment with the description of other phenomena in Dutch grammar. Here however, we are just interested in showing the expressive possibilities of the UCG framework.

A verb like *laten* in Dutch in the finite main clause form has a categorisation like (45).

---

[8] Both of these demands are also met in the analysis in (Steedman 1985), who treats them in a combinatorial extension of categorial grammar. Shieber 1984 notes that where the Dutch nested construction is combined with case marking as in Swiss German, the analysis proposed by Gazdar and Pullum is also ruled out on syntactical grounds. The standard constituent tree is due to Ewan Klein, using a variety of syntactic constituency tests. It is quoted in Bresnan et al. 1982 which gives an LFG treatment of cross serial dependencies.

(45) laat
    sent[fin,mc]/
        np[nom]:x:pre/
        np[obj]:y:post/
        (sent[bse]/np:y):A:post
    LET(e,x,y,A)

Here *mc* and *sc* (which will be employed later) are features indicating occurrence in main or subordinate clauses. In the subordinate case, the finite forms take their arguments in a different order: all the non verbal arguments that would come after them in a main clause now precede them. Bare infinitives however may appear on both sides, and complementized infinitives and that-clauses retain their post verbal position. We can capture this succinctly by (1) reversing the *post* order specification to *pre* on non verbal arguments and (2) making the order slot uninstantiated for bare infinitives.

In this way one accounts for the two possible orders that are possible with respect to its complement infinitives, as in (46).

(46) dat Jan Marie zwemmen laat
     dat Jan Marie laat zwemmen

This changes the main clause sign for *laat* into the subordinate clause sign (47).

(47) laat
    sent[fin,sc]/
        np[nom]:x:pre/
        np[obj]:y:pre/
        (sent[bse]/np:y):A:O
    LET(e,x,y,A)

I assume that complement infinitives are functors taking verbs like *laten*, *helpen* or *zien* as their arguments. In this way they are rather like type raised proper names applying to a verb that is subcategorised for *np*. Accordingly, a verb like *zwemmen* obtains (48) as one of its categorisations.

(48) zwemmen
X/(X/(sent[bse]/np:x):SWIM(e,x):O):A:O
A

Together with *laat* this leads to (49) or (49) with phonology *zwemmen laat*.

(49) laat zwemmen
sent[fin,sc]/
np[nom]:x:pre/
np[obj]:y:pre
LET(e,x,y,SWIM(s,y))

For transitive (and similarly for ditransitive) infinitives we need to take care of the post verbal arguments, that in subordinate cases are filled in only after the infinitive has become the complement of another verb. This is achieved by adding them to the category of the other verb, so that after the infinitive has combined with a verb with active sign *sent[bse]/np:x* the new complex obtains, as the arguments it has to deal with first, the arguments of the infinitive. This is expressed by the category sepcifications in (50).

(50) drinken
X/np[obj]:y:pre/
(X/
(sent[bse]/np:x): DRINK(s,x,y)):A
A

geven
X/
np[obj]:y:pre/
np[obj]:z:pre/
(X/(sent[bse]/np:x): GIVE(s,x,y,z)):A
A

It is slightly more complicated to give a specification for bare infinitives in the case of verbs that are subcategorised for infinitive or subordinate clauses. If they have a complementiser (*te* or *dat*) they appear, as in main clauses, after the verb they are a complement of. Witness (51):

(51) a. dat Jan Piet laat beloven dat Marie zal komen
　　　b. dat Jan Piet beloven laat te komen
　　　c. dat Jan Piet laat beloven te komen
　　　d. dat Jan Piet beloven laat te komen

(51a) can be rendered as (52),

(52) that Jan lets Piet promise that Marie will come

and (51b-d) as (53).

(53) that Jan lets Piet promise to come

A bare infinitive argument on the other hand can either remain in post verbal position or can take pre verbal position in subordinate clauses. So one must give to the versions in (54) for the infinitival forms of *beloven* and *laten*.

(54) beloven
　　X/
　　　sent[cfin]:B:post/
　　　(X/(sent[bse]/np:x):PROMISE(s,x,B)):A
　　A

　　beloven
　　X/
　　　(sent[cbse]/np:x):B:post/
　　　(X/(sent[bse]/np:x):PROMISE(s,x,B)):A
　　A

　　laten
　　X/
　　　np[obj]:y:pre/
　　　(sent[bse]/np:y):B:post/
　　　(X/(sent[bse]/np:x):LET(s,x,y,B)):A
　　A

One can formulate a schematical operation on signs that takes the stemform of a verb and transforms it into the appropriate infinitive. This operation can be seen as a lexical rule, that completes the lexicon for a given language after the specification of certain basic forms.

(55) W
  sent/
    X/
      Y_1:post/
      .../
      Y_n:post
  S

$$\Rightarrow$$

W
  Z/
    Y_1:O_1/
    .../
    Y_n:O_n/
    (Z/(sent[bse]/X):S):T
  T

(here O_i is *post* if Y_i is a *sent[cfin,sc]* or a *sent[cbse]/np*, variable if it is sent[bse]/np and *pre* otherwise). Let's see how to derive cross serial dependencies with these lexical specifications. The derivation tree for (56) that we obtain is closely related to the standard one.

(56) (dat) Jan Marie de kinderen bier zag laten drinken

It has the following form:

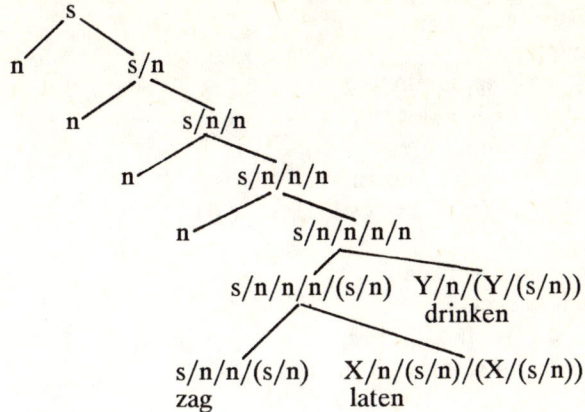

In (57), we give the full signs for the nodes on this tree.

(57) drinken
    X/
      np[obj]:y:pre/
      (X/(sent[bse]/np:x): DRINK(s,x,y):O):A:O
    A

    laten
    X/
      np[obj]:y:pre/
      (sent[bse]/np:y):B/(X/(sent[bse]/np:x):LET(s,x,y,B):O):A:O
    A

    zag
    sent[fin,sc]/
         np[nom]:x:pre/
         np[obj]:y:pre/
         (sent[bse]/np:y):A:pre or post
    [s][PAST(s),SEE(s,x,y,A)]

zag laten
sent[fin,sc]/
    np[nom]:x:pre/
    np[obj]:y:pre/
    np[obj]:z:pre/
    (sent[bse]/z):B:pre or post
[s][PAST(s),SEE(s,x,y,LET(s',y,z,B))]

zag laten drinken
sent[fin,sc]/
    np[nom]:x:pre/
    np[obj]:y:pre/
    np[obj]:z:pre/
    np[obj]:v:pre
[s][PAST(s),SEE(s,x,y,LET(s',y,z,DRINK(e,z,v)))]

bier zag laten drinken
sent[fin,sc]/
    np[nom]:x:pre/
    np[obj]:y:pre/
    np[obj]:z:pre
[s][PAST(s),SEE(s,x,y,LET(s',y,z,DRINK(e,z,BEER)))]

de kinderen bier zag laten drinken
sent[fin,sc]/
    np[nom]:x:pre/
    np[obj]:y:pre
[s][CHILD(X),PAST(s),SEE(s,x,y,LET(s',y,X,DRINK(e,X,BEER)))]

Marie de kinderen bier zag laten drinken
sent[fin,sc]/
        np[nom]:x:pre
[s][CHILD(X),PAST(s),SEE(s,x,MARIE,LET
(s',MARIE,X,DRINK (e,X,BEER)))]

Jan Marie de kinderen bier zag laten drinken
sent[fin,sc]
[s][CHILD(X),PAST(s),SEE(s,JAN,MARIE,LET
(s',MARIE,X,DRINK (e,X,BEER)))]

The present analysis allows the configurations in (58), but rules out the configuration in (59).

(58) (a) Jan Marie de kinderen bier zag laten drinken
     (b)? Jan Marie de kinderen bier laten zag drinken
     (c)? Jan Marie de kinderen bier drinken zag laten
     (d) Jan Marie de kinderen bier drinken laten zag
     (e)? Jan Marie de kinderen bier laten drinken zag

Dutch speakers seem to have a strong preference for (a) and, to a lesser degree, for (d), whereas the others are at best marginally acceptable. They tend to agree that (59) is out, but whether it is really worse than (58b,c and d) is unclear.

(59) * Jan Marie de kinderen bier zag drinken laten

One simple way to generate only the two sequences which seem to be preferred is to impose order on both the finite subordinate and the type raised infinitival form of verbs like *laten* and *zien*, which would force their infinitivalcomplements to follow them. This would generate the cross serial order. The other order could be generated by having a second version of the infinitives, where their types are not raised. A final choice for the analysis above or the alternative can only be made in the context of a more complete treatment of Dutch infinitives.

The possibility of treating cross serial dependencies in categorial grammar without invoking composition rules of various kinds confirms Hans Uszkoreit's conclusion that often unification can be used to obtain the effect of composition. It seems right to note that this does not hold for unbounded dependencies. It seems that unification categorial grammars have to rely on techniques developed in GPSG or LFG to obtain those as well, if some form of composition is not added to the system.

REFERENCES

van Benthem, J. 1986 Categorial Grammar. Chapter 8 in *Essays in Logical Semantics*. Dordrecht: D. Reidel.

Bresnan, J., Kaplan, R. M., Peters, S. and Zaenen, A. 1982 Cross-serial dependencies in Dutch. *Linguistic Inquiry*, 1313, 613-635.

Calder, J., Klein, E., Moens, M. and Zeevat, H. 1986 Problems of Dialogue Parsing. ACORD Deliverable T2.1, Centre for Cognitive Science, Edinburgh.

Davidson, D. 1967 The Logical Form of Action Sentences. In Rescher, N. (ed.) *The Logic of Decision and Action*. Pittsburgh: University of Pittsburgh Press.

Flickinger, D., Pollard, C. and Wasow, T. 1985 Structure-Sharing in Lexical Representation. In *Proceedings of the 23rd Annual Meeting of the Association for Computational Linguistics*, University of Chicago, Chicago, Illinois, July, 1985, pp262-267.

Gazdar, G. 1985 *Applicability of Indexed Grammars to Natural Languages*. Report No. CSLI-85-34, October, 1985.

Gazdar, G., Klein, E., Pullum, G. and Sag, I. 1985 *Generalized Phrase Structure Grammar*. London: Basil Blackwell.

Geach, P. T. 1972 A program for syntax. In Davidson, D. and Harman, G. (eds.) *Semantics of Natural Language*. Dordrecht: D. Reidel.

Heim, I. 1982 *The Semantics of Definite and Indefinite Noun Phrases*. PhD Thesis, University of Massachusetts. Distributed by Graduate Linguistics Student Association.

Kamp, H. 1981 A Theory of Truth and Semantic Representation. In Groenendijk, J. A. G., Janssen, T. M. V. and Stokhof, M. B. J. (eds.) *Formal Methods in the Study of Language*, Volume 136, pp277-322. Amsterdam: Mathematical Centre Tracts.

Karttunen, L. 1986 Radical Lexicalism. Paper presented at the Conference on Alternative Conceptions of Phrase Structure, July 1986, New York.

Lambek, J. 1958 The mathematics of sentence structure. *American Mathematical Monthly*, 6565, 154-170.

Lambek, J. 1961 On the calculus of syntactic types. In *Structure of language and its mathematical aspects*, Providence, Rhode Island, 1961, pp166- 178.

Montague, R. 1973 The proper treatment of quantification in ordinary english. In Hintikka, J., Moravcsik, J. M. E. and Suppes, P. (eds.) *Approaches to Natural Language*. Dordrecht: D. Reidel. Reprinted in R. H. Thomason (ed.) (1974), *Formal Philosophy: Selected Papers of Richard Montague*, pp247-270. Yale University Press: New Haven, Conn..

Pollard, C. J. 1985a Categorial Grammar and Phrase Structure Grammar: an excursion on the syntax-semantics frontier. In Oehrle, R. (eds.) *Categorial Grammars and Natural Language Structures*, 1985a.

Pollard, C. J. 1985b Lectures on HPSG. Unpublished lecture notes, CSLI, Stanford University.

Proudian, D. and Pollard, C. J. 1985 Parsing Head-driven Phrase Structure Grammar. In *Proceedings of the 23rd Annual Meeting of the Association for Computational Linguistics*, University of Chicago, Chicago, Illinois, 8-12 July, 1985, pp167-171.

Pullum, G. K. and Gazdar, G. 1982 Natural languages and context free languages. *Linguistics and Philosophy*, 44, 471-504.

Shieber, S., Uszkoreit, H., Pereira, F., Robinson, J. and Tyson, M. 1983 The Formalism and Implementation of PATR-II. In Grosz, B. and Stickel, M. E. (eds.) *Research on Interactive Acquisition and Use of Knowledge*, SRI International, Menlo Park, 1983, pp39-79.

Shieber, S. M. 1986 *An Introduction to Unification-based Approaches to Grammar*. Chicago, Illinois: The University of Chicago Press.

Shieber, S. M. 1984 Evidence against the context-freeness of natural language. *Linguistics and Philosophy*. In press.

Shieber, S. M., Pereira, F. C. N., Karttunen, L. and Kay, M. 1986 A Compilation of Papers on Unification-Based Grammar Formalisms Parts I and II. Report No. CSLI-86-48, CSLI, April, 1986.

Steedman, M. 1985 Combinators and grammars. In Oehrle, R. (eds.) *Categorial Grammars and Natural Language Structures*, 1985.

Steedman, M. 1985 Dependency and coordination in the grammar of Dutch and English. *Language*, 6161, 523-568.

Uszkoreit, H. 1986 Categorial Unification Grammars. In *Proceedings of the 11th International Conference on Computational Linguistics and the 24th Annual Meeting of the Association for Computational Linguistics*, Institut fuer Kommunikationsforschung und Phonetik, Bonn University, Bonn, 25-29 August, 1986, pp187-194.

Wittenburg, K. W. 1986 Natural Language Parsing with Combinatory Categorial Grammar in a Graph-Unification-Based Formalism. PhD Thesis, Department of Linguistics, University of Texas.

PETE J. WHITELOCK

DEPARTMENT OF ARTIFICIAL INTELLIGENCE

UNIVERSITY OF EDINBURGH*

A FEATURE-BASED

CATEGORIAL MORPHO-SYNTAX FOR JAPANESE

This paper describes an experiment to investigate the characterisation of Japanese morpho-syntax within a lexicalist framework. It forms part of a study into English and Japanese grammars from the parochial, contrastive and universal viewpoints, which is intended to support the implementation of machine translation systems between the two languages.**

0. BACKGROUND

As in many modern linguistic theories and grammar development software tools (see Shieber, 1986), the formalisms that we use for linguistic description are based on the notion of feature structures. A

---

* formerly of Centre for Computational Linguistics, University of Manchester, Institute of Science and Technology

** I would like to thank the following people: Natsuko Holden and George Jelinek for teaching me what Japanese I know, and Natsuko for acting as an ever-patient native informant; Brian Chandler for many discussions about Japanese; Rod Johnson, Harry Somers and Mary McGee Wood of UMIST for many discussions about language in general; Ewan Klein, Henk Zeevat and Jo Calder of Cognitive Science, Edinburgh for many discussions of Unification Categorial Grammars, and my anonymous referee for some immensely valuable and encouraging comments on the first draft of this paper. The opinions and mistakes remain, of course, purely my own responsibility.

Special thanks to George Jelinek, whose wonderfully explicit 'Japanese-English Grammar Dictionary' is the nearest thing to 'the native speaker on your desk' that any student of Japanese could wish for.

The work described herein was initially funded under The Alvey Programme in conjunction with International Computers Ltd.

feature structure is a set of feature specifications, where each feature specification is an <attribute-value> pair. Feature structures may be combined by the operation of unification, which offers a plausible realisation of a notion of obvious utility in a lexicalist linguistic description. It enables the building up of a description of a linguistic object by unifying information from various sources that represents the mutual constraints that words and their sentential environments put on each other.

The grammar of which the current work is intended to be a component is envisaged as monostratal but modular. Monostratality is relatively uncontroversial in modern feature-based linguistics, if it is taken to mean monotonic description of linguistic objects, projected from, i.e. subsumed by, the lexicon or syntax and directly interpreted. The main consequence of this assumption is the elimination of the terms 'transformation' and 'transformational cycle' from the vocabulary of linguistic description. Modularity, in the context of a unification grammar, I take to describe the use of disjoint sets of complex-valued features to represent levels of description. These levels might include morphosyntactic, discourse related, logico-thematic, and, crucial to Japanese, a level concerned with who is responsible for, and who or what is most affected by, the semantic content of a proposition. (For a similar idea, see the descriptions of 'actor' and 'undergoer' in RRG, Foley and van Valin, 1984.) Each level has its own well-formedness or felicity conditions, but each contributes to the interpretation of the utterance. Much of the substantive knowledge embodied in the grammar could be in the form of constraints on the possible relations between the different levels of description. This view of the organisation of a grammar I take to be compatible with that espoused by Halvorsen (1983), Fenstad et al. (1985), and Kaplan (1985).

The current work discusses the use in a morphosyntactic description of Japanese of the following components:

1. A set of lexical entries each of which describes a feature structure, i.e. a set of <attribute-value> pairs. The value of one attribute, corresponding to the phonology, is distinguished for the purposes of lookup. Other values may be feature structures. During parsing, these complex values will become unified with the feature structures associated with the lexical entries of surrounding words.

2. A set of templates which name commonly occurring feature structures, and thus allow lexical entries proper to be minimally redundant.

3. Two rules expressing how the feature structures of adjacent items may combine. These correspond to the rules of Backward Application and Forward Application of a Categorial Grammar. It will turn out that these two rules are used to build words from morphs and phrases from words respectively.

This description is interpreted in a shift-reduce fashion in Prolog, and can be applied in recognition, random generation and systematic generation modes. An earlier version of the grammar is used in the generation component of an English-Japanese Machine Translation system, (Whitelock et al.,1985).

The scope of the present study is strictly circumscribed from both sides, linguistically speaking. On the one hand, morphographemic phenomena are not treated with any degree of generality. On the other hand, there is no treatment of verb subcategorisation, and thus no attempt to build a semantic representation. The phenomena that are at the centre of the present study are inflectional and derivational morphology, and constituent and clause structure.

1. JAPANESE MORPHO-SYNTAX, A FEW INITIAL COMMENTS

1.1 General principles

Japanese morpho-syntax appears to be based on principles that give it significantly different systemic properties from English. By systemic, I mean the processes of lexicalisation and grammaticalisation that the language demonstrates. The relation of these processes to each other in the coding of meaning gives rise to systematic patterns of monolingual and interlingual ambiguity. A study of these systemic factors might form the basis of a linguistic theory of translation explicit enough to be useful in the mechanisation of that process.

Japanese is rigidly head final - verbs follow their arguments and modifiers, head nouns follow relative clauses, and (non-honorific) affixes, including adpositions, follow their lexical stems. Ordering of non-head, i.e. sister, constituents is relatively free, though there are ordering constraints on the interpretation of similarly marked constituents. In addition, there are unmarked orders based on the syntactic categories of sisters, but these are flexible under the influence of heavy constituents (to maintain the general left-branching pattern of the language) and discourse factors.

As a natural corollary of the free word order, constituents are case-marked, primarily according to a nominative-accusative system. The case marking system often receives attention, in particular its interaction with aspectual marking and the lexicalisation of event types (see Jacobsen,1982). In this paper, I will say little about case marking, indeed about the whole question of subcategorisation. The fact that Japanese demonstrates widespread null anaphora makes it impossible to give a purely morpho- syntactic characterisation of subcategorisation. This paper concentrates on the morpho-syntactic phenomena that derive from the type-theoretic properties of gross lexical classes and grammatical elements.

Japanese is a topic-prominent language, distinctively marking constituents as having referents in the current domain of discourse. Unlike English, constituents occupying central thematic roles topicalise freely. However, topicalisation can also occur with constituents whose role in a proposition is peripheral, even with those having no clear role, other than *about, as for, concerning*.

Topic marking and word order variations carry some of the same functional load that English determiners do, since explicit determination of noun(phrase)s is the marked case in Japanese. There is also some evidence (e.g. Kuno, 1973) that the head of a relative clause is interpreted as filling a thematic role in the clause according to similar principles to those that determine the topic's thematic role in a sentence. There are few constraints on the 'positions' from which nouns can be relativised.

1.2 Morphology and the structure of the lexicon

There appears to be a distinction in universal grammar between closed-class/grammatical morphs and open-class/lexical morphs. Of course, there are morphs whose status is unclear or intermediate, and I will discuss some Japanese examples below. However, the distinction is salient in Japanese.

In many languages, open-class morphs occur in many contexts with no visible affixation, but this is not true in Japanese. Except in compound nominals, lexical morphs are associated with obligatory, non-null, grammatical morphs. A Japanese sentence thus consists of a sequence of 'bunsetsu', that is, an open-class item, often in Chinese ideographic characters, followed by one or more closed-class items, almost invariably in Japanese syllabic characters. Morphology is basically agglutinative, with a few changes conditioned phonetically and otherwise arbitrarily (with respect to meaning), for instance by verb-conjugation.

The basis of the present morpho-syntactic description is that open-class items have simple categories, and that certain grammatical items map these into complex modifying categories, that is functions from sentences to sentences, or from nouns to nouns. Unlike in English, these two types of modifiers, which I call adverbials and adnominals respectively, are clearly distinguished in most cases. That is, most grammatical morphs fall into one or other, but not both, of the classes 'adverbialising' and 'adnominalising'.

1.3 Ambiguity types in English and Japanese

The rigidly head final property, the clear distinction between adnominal and adverbial elements, and the obligatoriness of bound morphs, means that certain of the systematic ambiguity types found in English do not arise in Japanese. These include:

a) noun-verb ambiguities arising from so-called null-affixation, as in *time flies*,

b) ambiguities of the sequence 'ing-form noun', as in *visiting relatives*,

c) ambiguities of attachment site between verb and noun, as in *put the block in the box on the table*.

However, ambiguities of constituent attachment to items of the same category are exacerbated by the free word order and null anaphora properties of the language.

2. LEXICAL REPRESENTATION

A dictionary entry gives the values for features corresponding to several different linguistic levels. The whole is termed a 'sign', in the terminology of Pollard(1985). **phon** is an atomic-valued feature used as the lookup key. **morpho_syntax** is a set of atomic-valued features, i.e. boolean or finitely enumerated. **subcat** is a feature with a value **set(X)**, where **X** is a set of signs. **cat** is a set of three sign-valued features, called **left**, **right** and **result**. A new sign may be constructed from a pair of signs if the values of their **phon** attributes are adjacent in the input string, and either

  a) the left sign unifies with the value **left** of the right sign, in which case the resulting sign is the value of the feature **result** of the right sign, or

  b) the right sign unifies with the value **right** of the left sign, in which case the resulting sign is the value of the feature **result** of the left sign.

In either case, the **phon** of the resulting sign is obtained by the concatenation of the **phon** values of the two signs. The two cases correspond to the rules of Backward Function Application and Forward Function Application respectively.

The novel aspect of this from the point of view of Categorial Grammar is that the morpho-syntactic features are independent of the sign-valued features. This means it is possible to characterise a sign in terms of a particular set of morpho-syntactic features regardless of its complex category as such. This increase in expressive power is exploited in the current grammar, where certain functors define their arguments in terms of morpho-syntactic features, and others define them in terms of their complex categories.

Note the use of sign-valued features **left** and **right**, rather than a single sign-valued feature **arg** and an atomic-valued feature **dir** with **left** and **right** as possible values. As Kartunnen(1986) points out, this can be used to introduce two-sided functors that combine either to the left or right but that put different constraints on their argument in the two cases. Although this potential appears superfluous for Japanese, the approach has been adopted for the sake of generality.

The null anaphora property of Japanese means that the rather intimate relation between syntactic type and subcategorisation frame that is usually employed for verbs in Categorial Grammars is less than ideal. The use of a feature **subcat**, which takes sets of signs as values, originates with Gunji(1986). Since I am not concerned in this paper with the details of verb subcategorisation, the only use made of this feature is to capture certain facts about intransitivization by reducing the set to a singleton (see section 4.6). However, I will sketch an outline of a mechanism that might be integrated with the account of phrase building given here.

All arguments of a verb are given the category adverbial, that is, functions from sentences to sentences. The rule that combines a modifier with what it modifies, forward application, stipulates that the modifying constituent (actually its non-recursive component, for implementation reasons), becomes a member of **subcat**. In the present account, **subcat** has as its initial value an uninstantiated variable. In a full account, I assume that the lexical entry for a verb will unify individual members of **subcat** with the values of logico-thematic features, either arg1, arg2 etc, or agent, patient etc., according to taste. Argument-adding affixes, such as causatives, will add further elements to the set. At some point, 'prior' to any modification (i.e. 'in the lexicon'), the members of **subcat** will be instantiated with the surface case of the constituent which will fill the associated argument position. This process, analogous to 'linking' in Farmer(1984), will induce an order on the members of **subcat**. Now, when each modifier is made a member of the set, it will unify with that element of the set which shares its case marking, and hence become the value of the appropriate argument feature, regardless of the relative order that the arguments appear in the sentence. Hence free argument order can be interpreted without any sort of scrambling rule. I also assume that some sort of operation can augment this set as required with elements corresponding to true modifiers such as temporals and locatives, which may appear in the surface string interspersed with arguments.

Note that the order in which constituents are unified with members of **subcat** is from the verb backwards. In combination with the order induced by 'linking', this fact can be exploited to account for several phenomena.

First, in the 'multiple subject' sentences described in Kuno (1973), it is the nominative constituent closest to the verb that fills the argument position. The other nominative constituents, ordered earlier in the sentence, will bind later, when the argument position marked nominative will already be filled, and will thus be interpreted as modifiers.

Secondly, topicalised constituents, marked with *wa*, are often ambiguous between nominative and accusative case. However, as they generally occur sentence initially, they will bind last, when other constituents that are unambiguously marked have already been bound. Thus local ambiguity will be kept to a minimum.

Thirdly, the resolution of null anaphors can be handled by continuing the process of binding argument slots, after all sentential constituents have been bound, backwards through the previous discourse.

3. IMPLEMENTATION ISSUES

In what follows, the procedure call **japply(F,A,V)** means that the feature structure **F** has the value **V** for attribute **A**. A definition of the structure of a sign (the procedure **featset**) is used to compile an extensional definition of this procedure, one clause per attribute. The graph unification implied by the description language is thus realised as the term unification of the Prolog interpreter.

The parser comprises two procedures. The first, **parse**, takes an input string and input stack and returns an output string and output stack. The termination condition is that the input string is empty and the input stack contains a single tensed structure. If this is not the case, **parse** looks up the first morph in the current input string, processes it, and calls itself recursively. In random generation mode, **parse** is called with a variable input string. In systematic generation mode, **parse** is called with succesively longer lists of variables, and if the first clause of **parse** is replaced by one without the condition, all constituents licensed by the grammar are generated.

```
% parse(String_in,String_out,Stack_in,Stack_out)

parse([],[],[F],[F]) :-
    japply(F,tensed,yes).

parse(S0,S,Stack0,Stack) :-
    lookup(S0,S1,F),
    do(Stack0,F,Stack1),
    parse(S1,S,Stack1,Stack).
```

The procedure **do** takes a stack and a feature structure and returns a stack. It has three clauses, namely forward application, backward application and shift. The conditions on shifting serve only to constrain random generation, and can be omitted in the other modes of use.

```
% do(Stack_in,Word,Stack_out)

do([F|Rest],A,Stack) :-            % forward application
    japply(F,right,A),
    japply(F,result,R),
    japply(A,phon,Pa),
    japply(F,phon,Pf),
    japply(R,phon,[Pf|Pa]),        % concatenate phonologies
    japply(F,self,S),              % copy the functor's non-recursive
    japply(IsoF,self,S),           % component, to prevent cyclic terms.
        japply(R,subcat,IsoF),     % IsoF becomes member of subcat set
    do(_,Rest,R,Stack).

do(2,[A|Rest],F,Stack) :-          % backward application
    japply(F,left,A),
    japply(F,result,R),
    japply(A,phon,Pa),
    japply(F,phon,Pf),
    japply(R,phon,[Pa|Pf]),        % concatenate phonologies
    do(_,Rest,R,Stack).

do(3,Stack,F,[F|Stack]) :-         % shift
    japply(F,left,[]),
    (Stack=[];Stack=[H|T],
    not japply(H,right,[])).
```

In parsing mode, the **lookup(String,Suffix,F)** procedure computes successively longer prefixes of the input string **String** non-deterministically and attempts to match these against dictionary entries. If successful, the functional description is evaluated and the resulting feature structure **F** returned, with the remainder of the input **Suffix**. The non-determinism of the string partition can become extremely computationally expensive with long input strings. Nevertheless, in a real text, the different character sets would reduce the problem considerably. For instance, a transition from syllabic to ideographic characters always indicates a morph boundary. In texts for children, written entirely in syllabic characters, this boundary is indicated by spaces. Introduction of a tree-structured dictionary would also alleviate the problem.

4. THE GRAMMAR

There are two principal classes of lexical items in Japanese, those that have a rich system of affixation, which are verbal in nature, and those that do not, which are nominal. Within each of these classes can be distinguished a minor sub-class which is adjectival, giving a total of four productive paradigms, as follows:

		Features	
		Noun	Adj
1. Nouns		+	−
2. Nominal Adjectives	(Na-nouns)	+	+
3. Verbal Adjectives	(I-verbs)	−	+
4. a) Verbs (consonant base)		−	−
b) Verbs (vowel base)		u	−

As shown, the true verbs can be subdivided according to whether their stem ends in a consonant or a vowel, which conditions the form of many affixes that they take. The isolated base of a vowel base verb also behaves as an infinitive, and is therefore undefined for the feature **noun**.

True adverbs, that is, those which are not morpho-syntactically derived from one of the other paradigms, are best treated as closed class items.

A further set of features is used to provide the fine-grained distinctions needed for the characterisation of morpho-syntactic processes. The most important of these is the boolean-valued feature **sent**. The major process of phrase building is defined principally in terms of the features **sent** and **noun**, as we shall see below.

Other features are as follows:

>**tense** - takes the values **past, pres** or **none**
>**tensed** - takes the value **no** if **tense** is **none, yes** otherwise
>**case** - takes various cases or **none** as value
>**base** - distinguishes various verb forms, or has the value   **none**

4.1 Types of lexical entry

The open-class words described above have two major properties. First, they license an unbounded number of arguments and/or modifiers - dependents in the sense of dependency grammar. That is, they have a set-valued feature **subcat**, all members of which will be interpreted in a similar fashion. Secondly, they are categorially inert. Thus their behaviour is given by the template:

```
template(lex,[subcat=set(_),left=[],right=[]]).
```

Grammatical elements share the property that they combine only to their left; the result of the combination inherits their morpho-syntactic features, and may not combine again to the left, giving the parse a canonical left-branching structure:

```
template(gram,[morpho_syntax=X, result/morpho_syntax=X,
               right=[],result/left=[]]).
```

Furthermore, apart from a small number of items which realise derivational morphological processes (including passive and causative suffixes), all grammatical items inherit the subcategorisation behaviour of the lexical stem with which they combine, thus:

```
template(infl, [@gram, left/subcat=X, result/subcat=X]).
```

The principal morpho-syntactic function of many of these grammatical elements is to build words into modifying phrases, that is, phrases that combine, always by forward application, with a constituent to give a constituent of the same type. Modifying phrases are characterised by the template:

```
template(mod,[right=X,result=X]).
```

We can distinguish two principal types of modifying phrase. Adnominals combine with a noun to their right to produce a noun, and adverbials combine with a sentence to their right to produce a sentence:

```
template(adv,[@mod,result=@sentence]).
template(adn,[@mod,result=@nominal]).
```

The templates **@nominal** and **@sentence** expand via other templates into the morpho-syntactic feature assignments:

```
template(nominal,[noun=yes,case=none,base=none,
  adj=no,sent=no,tensed=no,tense=none]).
template(sentence,[sent=yes,adj=no]).
```

The following sections describe how each of the major classes of words can be incorporated into an adnominal or adverbial phrase.

4.2 Cases

In Japanese, the role played by a noun-phrase in a proposition is determined by the postpositional particle or case which it carries. Hence case is the typical adverbialising morph. Case particles form a closed, very small set, - *ga, wo, ni, de, e, kara, to*. The behaviour of these particles is given by the template:

```
template(case,[@infl,left=@noun,result=@adv]).
```

In more standard categorial notation, this would be equivalent to giving case particles the category (S/S)\N. Note that the template @noun specifies **case = none**, preventing multiple casing, although noun phrases bearing certain cases may still have the feature specification **noun = yes**.

Each of the case particles has a range of functions, and no two of them have precisely the same distributional properties. To try and capture this diversity was too ambitious for the current study, as it is unclear what portion of the burden should fall on the semantic component. However, I have made a distinction between three groups, as follows.

```
jdict(ga,[@case,case=nom,noun=no,left/adj=no]).
jdict(ni,[@case,case=dat,noun=no]).
jdict(kara,[@case,case=abl,left/adj=no]).
```

Nominative (*ga*) and accusative (*wo*), i.e. the core cases, serve to adverbialise only true nouns and infinitives, and not nominal adjectives. Neither may they be followed by other elements such as *no* (see section 4.4), or the topic marker *wa* (whose use I do not discuss in this paper). I have chosen to describe this latter behaviour by failing to allow them to inherit the **noun=yes** specification.

Dative case (*ni*) has a vast range of uses, including the adverbialisation of nominal adjectives. A particle with similar distribution is the attributive *de*, though this is actually a form of the copula, and I have not tried to deal with it.

The peripheral cases - ablative (*kara*), allative (*e*), instrumental (*de*) and comitative (*to*) - may not follow nominal adjectives, but may be followed by *no* and *wa*.

4.3 Tenses

The adnominalising morph for verbs is tense. There is a two-way tense distinction, between past and non-past. Many authors have claimed that this is more accurately described as a distinction between perfective and imperfective aspect, but this consideration is irrelevant here. All tense morphs are (N/N)\V, or in our terms:

```
template(tense,[@infl,left=@notsent,result=@adn,@sentence]).
```

It is worth noting at this point the dual nature of a tensed verb. On the one hand it is a functor from nouns to nouns. Only by being tensed may verbal elements become noun modifiers, so that all manner of English phrases - participial clauses, adjective phrases, relative clauses and so on - translate into tensed clauses in Japanese. On the other hand, it has the morpho-syntactic properties of a sentence, so that it may be the argument of an adverbial. It is interesting to note that the point at which a tensed verb changes from behaving as an argument to behaving as a functor defines a major locus of non-determinism in the parsing process, and one that corresponds to a major type of ambiguity in Japanese.

Both true verbs and verbal adjectives may take either tense, though the morphs have a different form in the two cases. In the case of true verbs, the past tense morph follows a form of the verb that I call the gerund base, since it is also used for building the verbal gerund. The form of the gerund base for consonant base verbs depends on the particular consonant. Although this might be described more explanatorily in phonological terms, I have chosen to stipulate the form of the gerund base so that the form of the whole word can be obtained by simple concatenation of lexical entries. For details of this stipulation see the entries marked **@gerbuild** in the appendix. The actual entries for the various tense affixes are as follows:

```
jdict(ru, [@tense,tense=pres, left=@vowelbase]).
jdict(u, [@tense,tense=pres, left=@consbase]).
jdict(a, [@tense,tense=past, left=@gerbase]).
jdict(i, [@tense,tense=pres, left=@ivrbstem]).
jdict(katta, [@tense,tense=past, left=@ivrbstem]).
```

In summary therefore,

```
noun + case    ->   adverbial
verb + tense   ->   adnominal
```

In the following sections, this idea is extended to describe the modification of nouns and verbs by nouns and verbs respectively.

4.4 Adnominalisation with no and na

Diachronically, the adnominalising *no* is believed (Martin, 1975) to have developed from the sequence *ni aru*, that is, case marker + tensed form of copula, and it alternates synchronically, according to style, dialect and emphasis, with this and other similar sequences, - *de aru, ga aru, ni iru, ga iru*.

One typical adnominal use of *no* is as a possessive marker. This can be understood with reference to the following examples:

```
1. John ni   tomodati  ga   aru
   John DAT  friend    NOM  has/is
```

```
1a. John has a friend
```

1 demonstrates a case-marking pattern for possession that is widespread among human languages, with the possessor in the dative and the possessed in the nominative. Also widespread is the identity of this case-

marking with that of locative/existential sentences:

```
2. niwa    ni  ki   ga  aru
   garden  DAT tree NOM has/is
```

2a. there is a tree in the garden

Even English demonstrates traces of this identity, as in 3, the paraphrase of 2a,

3. the garden has a tree (in it)

By relativisation, 3 becomes:

```
4. niwa    ni  aru     ki
   garden  DAT is/has  tree
```

4a. the tree that is in the garden, the tree in the garden

no alternates with this sequence with little change in meaning, as in 5.

5. niwa no ki

6, the relativised equivalent of 1, is ungrammatical

6. * John ni aru tomodati

This may be due to it being supplanted by 7.

```
7. John ga motte    iru     tomodati
        acquire     STATIVE friend
```

7a. A/the friend that John has

Where possession is to be made explicit, the lexically full verb *motte iru*, (actually the stative, or perfective, of *motu*, acquire) with standard transitive case-marking, is exploited. Where possession is implicit, the fully grammaticalised form *no* is used:

```
8. John no tomodati
   John 's friend
```

Another adnominal use of *no* is illustrated by 9-11:

9. tomodati ga isya   de   aru
   friend   NOM doctor ATTR is

9a. (my) friend is a doctor

10. isya   de   aru tomodati
    doctor ATTR is friend

10a. (my) friend, who is a doctor

11. isya no tomodati

11a. (my) friend, the doctor

But since *no* neutralises the case distinction between *ni* and *de*, 11 is ambiguous between 11a and 11b.

11b. (my) doctor's friend

no can thus be considered as a grammaticalisation of the sequence of morphs - case marker, accounting for its noun-taking behaviour, followed by a semantically neutral predicating element, followed by a tense marker, accounting for its adnominal behaviour.

no can also be used to adnominalise an already cased nominal, particularly where the case is a locative of direction, as in 12 and 13.

12. tookyoo kara   no densya
    Tokyo   SOURCE   train

12a. the train from Tokyo

13. tookyoo e   no densya
    Tokyo   GOAL   train

13a. the train to Tokyo

There are alternative ways that this behaviour could be described. In the spirit of the rule-to-rule hypothesis, *no* could be treated as ambiguous between a form that incorporates case and a form that does not. However, I have chosen to allow semantically full postpositions to inherit the feature specification **noun=yes**. This gives *no* a single reading.

na serves the same adnominalising function over nominal adjectives that *no* does over true nouns.

Some nouns can take either, as in 14.

```
14. waduka   no/na  kane
    a little        money
```

These nouns can be left unspecified for the feature **adj**.

Some nouns which would normally take *no* can take *na* when they occur as adnominals of *no*, a quite distinct element meaning *the fact that*, as in 15.

```
15. gakusei  na  no
    student      fact

15a. the fact that he/she is a student
```

However, the current grammar does not license such an alternation.

The case incorporated in *na* is always attributive. When a *na*-taking element occurs in predicative position, it is cased by the attributive case particle *de*, as in 16, 17.

```
16. genki     na  kodomo
    health(y)     child

17. kodomo ga genki     de aru
    child      health(y)   is/has

17a. the child is healthy
```

The behaviour of *no* and *na* is given by the following template and lexical entries:

```
template(n_to_adn,[@infl,left/noun=yes,result=@adn]).
jdict(no,[@n_to_adn,left/adj=no]).
jdict(na,[@n_to_adn,left/adj=yes]).
```

4.5 Adverbialisation of verbs

There are several forms of true verbs that behave as adverbials. The infinitive is the base of a vowel base verb, and is formed by adding *i* to a consonant base verb. The gerund is formed by adding *e* to the gerund base. In what follows I will refer to this as the *te* form, Adjectival verbs form infinitives and gerunds by adding *ku* and *kute* respectively to their base. All these forms are used for the non-final verbs in a sequence of coordinated clauses, and all are used as participles with auxiliary verbs, particular auxiliaries selecting for particular forms. The *te* and *ku* forms are also used as manner adverbials

The most common use of the *te* form is probably in constructions such as 18.

```
18. John ga yonde iru
    John    read  be

18a. John is reading
```

The *V-te iru* construction marks progressive or perfective aspect, ambiguously or not according to the type of V. For instance, punctual verbs in this form can only receive perfective meaning. There is another aspect marking construct, less commonly used, that throws further light on *te*:

```
19. Mado    ga   shimete aru
    window  NOM  close

20. Mado    wo   shimete aru
    window  ACC  close

19/20a. The window has been closed
    or  Someone has closed the window
```

Native speakers differ in their judgements on the meaning relation between 19 and 20; the consensus seems to be that they are truth-conditionally equivalent, but that 19 is more a statement about the window, and 20 more about a certain state of affairs. This construction can only occur with transitive verbs, so the related sentence unmarked for this resultative aspect can only be 21.

21. Mado wo shimeru

21a. Someone closes/will close the window

We can account for the case marking by viewing the grammaticalisation of *te aru* as only partially complete. In 19, *aru* retains its lexical meaning of attributing a property to an object, (and consequently its valency of two). 19 could thus be paraphrased as 22.

22. The window has the property [such that someone] closed [it]

In 20, however, it appears that the grammaticalisation of *te aru* is further advanced. Here it is a function over a single argument, the proposition *mado wo shime*. Considering the data as a snapshot of an ongoing diachronic process offers some insight. It might be fruitful to compare this with the development of the periphrastic perfective aspect in Romance languages.

My referee made the observation that *shimete aru* could be viewed as a complex verb of the stative type, which would account for the nominative object that is associated with stativity of the verb in general. However, this does not explain why the same verb in 20, equally stative, should also license an accusative object. In addition, if it is assumed that all case assigning behaviour is lexically determined, then this would be the only example where a participle-auxiliary combination had to be entered in the lexicon. However, I leave it as an open question.

As mentioned above, another use of *te* is to mark coordinated clauses. The type of coordination implicated here is not logical coordination of propositions, but rather that of *and then*. The analysis of *te* as having a single morpho-syntactic type, i.e. adverbialising morph, entails that the coordinated clause is syntactically a daughter/dependent of the main clause verb. Thus 23:

23. utatte kaetta
     sing   go-home PAST

need not be viewed as syntactically ambiguous between the reading 23a,b.

23a. he sang and then went home

23b. he went home (in a) singing (manner)

but rather as underdetermined by syntax. Just as the absence of explicit case in the grammaticalised element *no* gives two readings to 11, so does the absence of explicit 'case' (manner or temporal precedence) in *te*.

As with non-core cases, *te* may be followed be the particles *wa* and *no*, and therefore must include the specification **noun=yes**. However, it is only a slight over-simplification to say that it cannot be followed by true cases, and therefore includes the specification **case=dummy**. The *i*-form, in contrast, can be followed by any case, and so must be **case=none**. A few infinitives are homophonous and cognate with forms that must be entered independently in the lexicon because of their non-productively derived semantics; however, no non-finite verb form with productive semantics can be the argument of an adnominal. This behaviour is accounted for by giving these forms values of **base** other than **none**, as follows:

    template(v_to_adv,[@infl,sent=yes,@untensed,adj=no,result=@adv]).
    jdict(i,[@v_to_adv,left=@consbase,noun=yes,case=none,base=cinf]).
    jdict(e,[@v_to_adv,left=@gerbase,noun=yes,case=dummy,base=ing]).
    jdict(ku,[@v_to_adv,left=@ivrbstem,noun=no,case=dummy,base=ku])
    jdict(kute,[@v_to_adv,left=@ivrbstem,noun=yes,case=dummy,base=ing]).

Another non-finite verb form is the conditional, which has no noun-like behaviour:

    template(conditional,[@v_to_adv,noun=no]).
    jdict(eba,[@conditional,left=@consbase]).
    jdict(reba,[@conditional,@onvbase]).
    jdict(kereba,[@conditional,left=@ivrbstem]).

4.6 Other adverbialising elements

The adverbial forms of verbs described in the preceding section are constructed by replacing tense on a tenseable stem. This restricts their usage to those constructions where the location in time of the proposition so-marked is unimportant or inferrable.

There are two common types of propositional construction which do not fulfil this restriction, namely subordination/coordination and sentential complements. Japanese has two classes of elements for dealing with these.

Subordinating/coordinating particles are a set of closed class items that map tensed elements directly into adverbial elements, i.e.

```
template(subconj,[@infl,left/tensed=yes,
                  left=@sentence,result=@adv]).
```

Items of this type include *ga* (but), *kara* (because), *si* (and), *yori* (rather than). A very few may follow only a particular tense, e.g. *to* (if, whenever), which may follow only non-past forms, and *ra* (if), which may follow only past tense forms.

```
jdict(si,[phon=si,@subconj]).
jdict(to,[phon=to,@subconj,left/tense=pres]).
jdict(ra,[phon=ra,@subconj,left/tense=past]).
```

Sentential complements are adverbialised indirectly with the help of open-class words that have become grammaticalised. Such words appear as perfectly normal members of open-classes with respect to their sentential environment rightwards. To the left, though, they require a single constituent of the type that would modify them if they remained lexical. Some of these words may still retain a full lexical reading. Thus 2 is ambiguous between readings 24a,b.

24. john ga mary ni itta   koto
                       tell PAST

24a. what john told mary (*koto* is lexical, meaning *the content of*)

24b. that john told mary (*koto* is grammatical, a complementiser)

If it has two arguments, as in 25, *koto* is unambiguously lexical - 25b is not a possible translation.

25. john ga mary ni itta   iya   na koto
                            disgusting

25a. the disgusting thing/fact that john told mary

25b. the disgustingness of john having told mary

To describe this behaviour, I assume that a process akin to type raising has taken place in the lexicon in the course of diachronic development, in conjunction with intransitivisation, thus:

```
template(type_raise,[morpho_syntax=[],right=[],
            result/left=[],left=X,result/subcat=set([X])]).
template(gram_noun,[@type_raise,left=@adn,result=@nominal]).
jdict(koto,[@gram_noun]).
```

Another of these grammaticalised morphs is *no*, as mentioned above. This is believed to be diachronically derived from *mono* (also grammaticalised). Hence its homophony with the adnominaliser *no* appears accidental, and not an indication of extra-categorical status, as Marcus (1985) believes. The two have definite, but distinguishable, categorial status, viz. *no* (=*ni aru*) is a function from nouns to adnominals, and *no* (=*mono*) is a function from adnominals to nouns.

This morph can be used as an indefinite pronoun, as in 26, 27:

```
26. muzukasi     moindai
    difficult    PRES     problem

27. muzukasi   i     no
    difficult  PRES  one
```

When the two different *nos* occur together, they are usually merged, as in 28, 29.

```
28. watasi     no      hon
    I          GEN     book

28a. my book

29. watasi     no      no
    I          GEN     one

29a. my one
     = watasi   no
       mine
```

This merging would appear to be predictable from a simple euphonic principle of the form 'two homophonous grammatical items with composable types may be composed to give a single instance'. If *no* were extra-categorial, how could we understand sentences like 30:

```
30. anata no boosi wa takai     ga, watasi no no wa yasui
    you       hat     expensive but I                cheap
```

```
30a. Your hat is expensive, but mine is cheap
```

This example, from Oomi dialect, is given by Matusita (1961). Other authors (e.g. Yuzawa, 1953, Martin 1975) have commented on the possibility of multiple *nos*, and all examples appear to be compatible with the type assignments given above.

4.7 Verb inflection

Japanese has productive verbal affixes for causative, passive, desiderative and negative. Causative and passive are functors over true verbs of either type into vowel base verbs. Note that the true Japanese passive is a morph that adds an argument to a verb's subcategorisation frame, unlike in English. The template for these affixes shows how this effect might be achieved, if a treatment of subcategorisation were included.

```
template(arity_change,[@gram,left/subcat=set(X),
              result/subcat=set([_|X]), result=@itidanstem]).
template(passive,[@arity_change]).
template(causative,[@arity_change]).

jdict(rare,[@onvbase,@passive]).
jdict(are,[left=@consbase,@passive]).
jdict(sase,[@onvbase,@causative]).
jdict(ase,[left=@consbase,@causative]).
```

Negative is a functor from any verb into a verbal adjective, and desiderative is a functor from true verbs only into verbal adjectives, so that following tense morphs are those appropriate for i-verbs, as in 37, 38,

```
37. ik  ana  katta
    go  NOT  PAST
```

37a. (He) didn't go

38. ik   ita   katta
    go   WANT   PAST

38a. (He) wanted to go

template(desiderative,[@infl,@ivrbstem]).

jdict(ta,[onvbase,@desiderative]).
jdict(ita,[left=@consbase,@desiderative]).

template(negative,[@infl,@ivrbstem]).

jdict(na,[onvbase,@negative]).
jdict(ana,[left=@consbase,@negative]).
jdict(kuna,[phon=kuna,left=@ivrbstem,@negative]).

4.8 Derivational morphology

There are several morphs that map between major categories. These include *sa*, which maps members of either adjectival paradigm to nouns, and *teki*, which maps true nouns into adjectival nouns. This sort of behaviour is easily described in a categorial grammar, as follows:

jdict(sa,[@gram,left/adj=yes,left/subcat=set([]),result=@nounstem]).
jdict(teki,[@gram,left=@nounstem,left/subcat=set([]),
            result=@nadjstem]).

5. CONCLUSION

This paper has described the use of a combination of techniques from unification and categorial grammars to describe various aspects of the morphology and syntax of Japanese. A description of the morphosyntactic behaviour of most of the major word and morph types of the language has been developed and tested computationally.

The most striking result to emerge from the present study is the ease with which the morpho-syntactic behaviour of a diversity of lexical items can be subsumed under the two combination rules of a simple categorial grammar. Word building, including derivational morphology, is naturally handled by backward application alone; forward application suffices to describe the construction of phrases, both noun phrases and sentences, including the scrambling facts.

A novel aspect of the present study, made possible by the unification framework, is the dual nature of certain phrases, representing their different behaviour as functors and as arguments, and allowing us to dispense with the unary rules used in categorial treatments of English syntax to convert relative clauses into noun modifiers. The use of binary syntactic rules only promises efficiency in parsing, and appears to do little violence to the phrase structure of Japanese.

Another interesting aspect is how the categorial viewpoint provides a natural characterisation of what appears to be a common diachronic process - the grammaticalisation of particular lexical items - as an operation of type-raising in the lexicon.

Obviously the grammar described herein overgenerates wildly, because of the lack of subcategorisation information. However, the representation produced by the parser seems more suitable as a basis for defining such information than the uninterpreted surface string. It abstracts away from the surface order and defines a family of constituent structures licensed by general syntactic principles that can be narrowed down by information specific to individual lexical items.

That a linguistic description consists of independant modules need not imply a lack of compositionality, nor even a sequential application of the information from different modules. Nevertheless, in the development of a large grammar, such a description obviates the problem of not being able to say anything about a text until one can say everything.

REFERENCES:

Farmer, A. K. 1984, *'Modularity in Syntax: A Study of Japanese and English'*, MIT Press, Cambridge, Mass.

Fenstad, J. E., P.-K. Halvorsen, T. Langholm and J. van Bentham 1985, *'Equations, Schemata and Situations: A framework for linguistic semantics'*, Center for the Study of Language and Information, Stanford University.

Foley, W. A. and R. D. van Valin 1984, *'Functional syntax and universal grammar'*, Cambridge University Press, Cambridge.
Gunji, T. 1986, *'Subcategorisation and Word Order'*, paper presented at the International Symposium on Language and Artificial Intelligence, Kyoto, March 1986.
Halvorsen, P.-K. 1983, 'Semantics for Lexical-Functional Grammar', *Linguistic Inquiry*, 14.
Jacobsen, W. 1982, *'Transitivity in the Japanese Verbal System'*, Indiana University Linguistics Club.
Kaplan, R. 1985, 'Three seductions of computational psycho-linguistics', in Whitelock et al. (eds.) 1985.
Kartunnen, L. 1986, 'Radical Lexicalism', CSLI-86-68, Center for the Study of Language and Information, Stanford University, California
Kuno, S. 1973, *'The Structure of the Japanese Language'*, MIT Press, Cambridge, Mass.
Marcus, M. 1985, 'Deterministic Parsing and Description Theory', in Whitelock et al. (eds.) 1985.
Martin, S. 1975, *'A Reference Grammar of Japanese'*, Yale University Press.
Matusita, D., 1961, *'Hyoojun Nihon Koogohoo'*, Hakuteisya, Tokyo.
Pollard, C. 1985, *'Lectures on HPSG'*, unpublished manuscript, Center for the Study of Language and Information, Stanford University, California.
Shieber, S. 1986, *'An Introduction to Unification-Based Approaches to Grammar'*, CSLI Lecture Notes, Centre for the Study of Language and Information, Stanford University, California.
Whitelock, P., H. Somers, P. Bennett, R. Johnson, M. M. Wood (eds.) 1985, 'Alvey/ICL Workshop on Linguistic Theory and Computer Applications (UMIST, September 1985) Transcripts of Presentations and Discussions', CCL Report 86/2, also to be published by Academic Press.
Whitelock, P. J., M. M. Wood, B. J.Chandler, N. Holden, H. J. Horsfall 1985, 'Strategies for Interactive Machine Translation:the experience and implications of the UMIST Japanese project', *Proceedings of the International Conference on Computational Linguistics* (COLING), Bonn, Aug, 1985.
Yuzawa, K. 1953, *Koogohoo Seisetu*, Meiji-syohin, Tokyo.

APPENDIX: A UNIFICATION CATEGORIAL LEXICON OF JAPANESE

Definitions of the structure of a sign

```
jfeatset(toplevel,[self,cat]).
jfeatset(cat,[left,right,result]).
jfeatset(self,[phon,gloss,morpho_syntax,subcat]).
jfeatset(morpho_syntax,[sent,tensed,tense,noun,adj,case,base]).
```

Lexical Templates

```
template(lex,[subcat=set(_),left=[],right=[]]).
template(gram,[morpho_syntax=X,result/morpho_syntax=X,subcat=[],
          right=[],result/left=[]]).
template(infl,[@gram,left/subcat=X,result/subcat=X]).
template(mod,[right=X,result=X]).
template(adv,[@mod,result=@sentence]).
template(adn,[@mod,result=@nominal]).
template(sentence,[sent=yes,adj=no]).
template(nominal,[@noun,adj=no,base=none,@notsent]).
template(minor,[@notsent,@notnoun,result/right=[]]).
template(notsent,[sent=no,@untensed]).
template(untensed,[tensed=no,tense=none]).
template(notnoun,[noun=no,case=none,adj=no]).
template(adj,[case=none,adj=yes]).
template(noun,[noun=yes,case=none]).
```

Stem and Gerund Building Morphs

```
template(onvbase,[left=@vowelbase,left/sent=no]).
template(oncbase,[left=@godanstem]).
template(stemcons,[@oncbase,@consbase]).
template(gerbuild,[@infl,@oncbase,@gerbase]).
template(consbase,[base=cons,@minor]).
```

```
template(gerbase,[base=gerund,@minor]).
template(vowelbase,[base=vowel,@untensed,case=none,adj=no]).

jdict(X,[phon=X,@stemcons,left/base=X,@infl]) :-
        member(X,[b,m,n,w,t,r,s,g,k]).
jdict(nd,[phon=nd,@gerbuild,left/base=X]) :-
        member(X,[b,m,n]).
jdict(tt,[phon=tt,@gerbuild,left/base=X]) :-
        member(X,[w,t,r]).
jdict(id,[phon=id,@gerbuild,left/base=g]).
jdict(it,[phon=it,@gerbuild,left/base=k]).
jdict(sit,[phon=sit,@gerbuild,left/base=s]).
jdict(t,[phon=t,@onvbase,@gerbase,@infl]).
```

Case assigning adverbialisers

```
template(case,[@infl,left=@noun,left=@untensed,@notsent,
        adj=no,base=none,result=@adv]).

jdict(ga,[phon=ga, @case, case=nom, noun=no,left/adj=no]).
jdict(wo,[phon=wo, @case, case=acc, noun=no,left/adj=no]).
jdict(ni,[phon=ni, @case, case=dat, noun=no]).
jdict(e,[phon=e, @case, case=all, noun=yes,left/adj=no]).
jdict(kara,[phon=kara, @case, case=abl, noun=yes,left/adj=no]).
jdict(de,[phon=de, @case, case=instr, noun=yes,left/adj=no]).
```

Tense assigning adnominalisers

```
template(tense,[@infl,left=@notsent,noun=no,base=none,@sentence,
        tensed=yes,result=@adn]).

jdict(ru,[phon=ru, @tense, tense=pres,left=@vowelbase]).
jdict(u,[phon=u, @tense, tense=pres,left=@consbase]).
jdict(a,[phon=a, @tense, tense=past,left=@gerbase]).
jdict(i,[phon=i, @tense, tense=pres,left=@ivrbstem]).
jdict(katta,[phon=katta, @tense, tense=past,left=@ivrbstem]).
```

Other Adnominalisers

template(n_to_adn,[@infl,base=none,left/noun=yes,result=@adn,
        @notnoun,@notsent]).

jdict(no,[phon=no,@n_to_adn,left/adj=no]).
jdict(na,[phon=na,@n_to_adn,left/adj=yes]).

Other Adverbialisers

template(v_to_adv,[@infl,@untensed,adj=no,result=@adv]).

jdict(i,[phon=i,@v_to_adv,left=@consbase,case=none,base=cinf]).
jdict(e,[phon=e,@v_to_adv,left=@gerbase,case=dummy,base=none]).
jdict(ku,[phon=ku,@v_to_adv,left=@ivrbstem,noun=no,case=none,
        sent=yes]).
jdict(kute,[phon=kute,@v_to_adv,left=@ivrbstem,case=dummy,sent=
        yes]).

template(conditional,[@v_to_adv,noun=no,sent=yes]).

jdict(eba,[phon=eba,@conditional,left=@consbase]).
jdict(reba,[phon=reba,@conditional,@onvbase]).
jdict(kereba,[phon=kereba,@conditional,left=@ivrbstem]).

Subordinating Adverbialisers

template(subconj,[@infl,@minor,left/tensed=yes,left=@sentence,
        result=@adv]).

jdict(si,[phon=si,@subconj]).
jdict(ga,[phon=ga,@subconj]).
jdict(to,[phon=to,@subconj,left/tense=pres]).
jdict(ra,[phon=ra,@subconj,left/tense=past]).

Non-final Verb Morphs

```
template(arity_change,[@gram,left/subcat=set(X),
         result/subcat=set([_|X]),result=@itidanstem]).
template(passive,[@arity_change]).
template(causative,[@arity_change]).

jdict(rare,[phon=rare,@onvbase,@passive]).
jdict(are,[phon=are,left=@consbase,@passive]).
jdict(sase,[phon=sase,@onvbase,@causative]).
jdict(ase,[phon=ase,left=@consbase,@causative]).

template(desiderative,[@infl,@ivrbstem]).

jdict(ta,[phon=ta,@onvbase,@desiderative]).
jdict(ita,[phon=ita,left=@consbase,@desiderative]).

template(negative,[@infl,@ivrbstem]).

jdict(na,[phon=na,@onvbase,@negative]).
jdict(ana,[phon=ana,left=@consbase,@negative]).
jdict(kuna,[phon=kuna,left=@ivrbstem,@negative]).
```

Derivational morphology

```
jdict(sa,[phon=sa,@gram,left/base=none,left/adj=yes,
         left/subcat=set([]),result=@nounstem,right=[]]).
jdict(teki,[phon=teki,@gram,left=@nounstem,left/subcat=set([]),
         result=@nadjstem]).
```

Grammaticalised Nominals

```
template(type_raise,[morpho_syntax=[],right=[],
         result/left=[],left=X,result/subcat=set([X])]).
template(gram_noun,[@type_raise,left=@adn,result=@nominal]).
template(gram_nadj,[@type_raise,left=@adn,result=@nadjstem]).
```

```
jdict(koto,[phon=koto,@gram_noun]).
jdict(no,[phon=no,@gram_noun]).
jdict(hoo,[phon=hoo,@gram_noun]).
jdict(tumori,[phon=tumori,@gram_noun]).

jdict(yoo,[phon=yoo,@gram_nadj]).
```

Open-class Words

```
template(nounstem,[@nominal,@lex]).
template(nadjstem,[@noun,@adj,base=none,@notsent,@lex]).
template(ivrbstem,[noun=no,@adj,base=none,@notsent,@lex]).
template(godanstem,[@notsent,@notnoun,@lex]).
template(itidanstem,[@vowelbase,@adv,subcat=set(_),left=[]]).

jdict(kono,[phon=kono,@adn,@notnoun,@notsent,left=[]]).
```

True Verbs

```
jdict(a,[phon=a,gloss=be,@godanstem,base=r]).
jdict(i,[phon=i,gloss=be,@itidanstem]).
jdict(ka,[phon=ka,gloss=write,@godanstem,base=k]).
jdict(kae,[phon=kae,gloss=go_home,@itidanstem]).
jdict(mo,[phon=mo,gloss=possess,@godanstem,base=t]).
jdict(modo,[phon=modo,gloss=return_trans,@godanstem,base=s]).
jdict(na,[phon=na,gloss=become,@godanstem,base=r]).
jdict(shime,[phon=shime,gloss=close_trans,@itidanstem]).
jdict(sonae,[phon=sonae,gloss=provide,@itidanstem]).
jdict(tabe,[phon=tabe,gloss=eat,@itidanstem]).
jdict(yo,[phon=yo,gloss=read,@godanstem,base=m]).
```

Verbal Adjectives

```
jdict(subaya,[phon=subaya,gloss=quick,@ivrbstem]).
jdict(muzukasi,[phon=muzukasi,gloss=difficult,@ivrbstem]).
```

Nominal Adjectives

jdict(benri,[phon=benri,gloss=convenient,@nadjstem]).
jdict(rippa,[phon=rippa,gloss=splendid,@nadjstem]).
jdict(iya,[phon=iya,gloss=disgusting,@nadjstem]).
jdict(genki,[phon=genki,gloss=healthy,@nadjstem]).

True Nouns

jdict(densya,[phon=densya,gloss=train,@nounstem]).
jdict(gakusei,[phon=gakusei,gloss=student,@nounstem]).
jdict(isya,[phon=isya,gloss=doctor,@nounstem]).
jdict(ki,[phon=ki,gloss=tree,@nounstem]).
jdict(kodomo,[phon=kodomo,gloss=child,@nounstem]).
jdict(mado,[phon=mado,gloss=window,@nounstem]).
jdict(hon,[phon=hon,gloss=book,@nounstem]).
jdict(niwa,[phon=niwa,gloss=garden,@nounstem]).
jdict(tomodati,[phon=tomodati,gloss=friend,@nounstem]).
jdict(tookyoo,[phon=tookyoo,gloss=tokyo,@nounstem]).

jdict(waduka,[phon=waduka,gloss=a_little,@noun,@notsent,
        base=none]).

CHRISTOPH SCHWARZE

THE TREATMENT OF THE FRENCH
ADJECTIF DETACHE
IN LEXICAL FUNCTIONAL GRAMMAR

0. INTRODUCTION

In French*, an adjective phrase may occur as a part of the noun phrase (*adjectif épithète*), as a part of the verb phrase (*adjectif attribut*) and in a detached, apposition-like position (*adjectif détaché*[1]), as illustrated by the following examples:

(1) Soulagé par la fraicheur, il allait encore plus vite
 'Relieved by the coolness, he went still faster'

(2) La pluie s'est mise à tomber, vaporeuse et sournoise
 'The rain started to fall, steamy and sneaking'

As these examples show, the *adjectif détaché* (AD) has variable word-order. We will investigate how this variable word-order can be treated in

---

* I want to thank Annie Jaisser, who checked my French data. Jane Edwards was most helpful in editing the text which I have presented at the Friedenweiler conference. I am also grateful to Pavla Rulfová-Schlegel, who helped me to understand the Russian text of Bredelite 1981.

[1] I adopt the terminology from Grevisse 1964, § 212, remarque 4. The term which is employed to refer to the construction under discussion varies from author to author. Wartburg & Zumthor 1958: 267 call it *attribut prédicat du sujet and attribut prédicat de l'objet*; for Fischer & Hacquart 1959: 117 it is an *apposition*, and Chevalier e.a. 1964: 203 use the term *adjectif apposé*. - The diversity of the terminology is paralleled by a lack of agreement on the nature of this construction. Even on the purely descriptive level, this construction appears to be not very well known: none of the grammars I consulted gives a full account of the distribution of the *adjectif détaché*, and a grammar which is quite good as a whole, Judge & Healey 1983, does not even mention it at all.

Lexical Functional Grammar (LFG). We will first see what the descriptive facts are, and then discuss their treatment within the LFG framework.

Before doing so, two remarks will be in order. The first concerns the notion of adjective phrase: In this paper, no distinction will be made between those APs which have genuine adjectives as their heads and those the head of which is a participle. In fact, participles may be used as heads of AD constructions (see (1) vs. (2)), and they may be coordinated with adjectives in these constructions (see (18), below). Participles seem to be even more typical in ADs than genuine adjectives[2].

The second remark concerns a stylistic property of the AD: It can be observed that the APs which occur as ADs typically have a complex internal structure (due e.g. to the presence of an argument, as in (1), or to coordination, as in (2)) and a linear length following from this complexity. Unexpanded APs are not exluded (see (27) and (39) below) but not typical.

1. THE DESCRIPTIVE FACTS

1.1 Distribution and agreement

The AD is separated from its context by pauses or by commas. It has to agree in number and gender with one of the nouns or pronouns of the sentence. We call this noun or pronoun the agreement controller[3]. The

---

[2] Among 910 adjective phrases used as ADs in a corpus of literary texts (Nerval, Claudel e .a.) Glatigny 1966 counted only 190 which had genuine adjectives as their heads.

[3] There are cases, however, in which there is no overt agreement controller in the sentence. Glatigny 1966:271 quotes the following examples:

   i. Plongé dans une demi-somnolence, toute ma jeunesse repassait en mes souvenirs (Nerval)
      'Plunged into a doze, my whole youth passed through my memory again'

   ii. Vivant, la poussière a été ma part, et couché, la terre (Claudel)
       'Living, dust was my share, and lying, earth'

   iii. Rentrés à la maison, y a eu du grabuge (spoken French)
        '(when we) came back home, there was a row'

These occurrences may be explained as cases of an agreement *ad sensum* with a "logical

agreement controller is most typically the subject of the main clause, alternatively, it may be the object, an oblique or an adjunct.

1.1.1 Agreement between the AD and the subject

In the most frequent and typical cases, the agreement controller is the subject, more precisely, the noun which is the head of the subject noun-phrase, or the pronoun which is the subject. Let us see which positions the AD may have, when it is in agreement with the subject.

a. Before the subject:
   The AD may occur:
preceding the subject and immediately adjacent to it, with the verb phrase at the end:

  (3) Pleine d'énergie, elle se mit au travail
      'AD: full-FEM/SG of energy, subject: she VP: started to work'

preceding the subject but separated from it by an adjunct:

  (4) Seule, dans la hâte commune, la jeune femme avait le droit de garder la maison ou de venir dans le pré
      'AD: Alone-FEM/SG, adjunct: in the general haste, subject: the young woman VP: had the right to stay in the house or to come to the meadow'

preceding the subject but separated from it by the verb:

  (5) Près de lui, grande et souple, se tenait une jeune femme
      'adjunct: Close to him, AD: tall-FEM/SG and supple-SG, VP: stood subject: a young woman'

preceding the subject and immediately adjacent to it, the verb preceding both. In my corpus[4] I have no example for this position, but it is not

---

subject", and they seem to be restricted to sentences in which they may be semantically referred to the first person.

[4] The corpus I used contains the rare examples given in reference grammars (Chevalier e.a. 1964, Galichet 1968:127 Grevisse 1964:§ 212, rem. 4, Fischer & Hacquart 1959, Wagner & Pinchon 1968:149), the large collection of examples contained in Dessaintes 1962: 157, 182f, 188, 213, 215, and some examples I collected myself from a modern prose text, namely Boris Vian, *L'Arrache-coeur*, Paris 1962. Some of the data are self-made, but they all have been checked by a native speaker. – There are more examples of ADs in Pignon 1962,

ungrammatical:

> (6) Près de lui se tenait, <u>grande et souple</u>, une jeune femme
> '**adjunct**: Close to him **VP**: stood, **AD**: <u>tall-FEM/SG and supple-SG</u>, **subject**: a young woman'

b. Immediately following the subject:

> (7) Jeanne, <u>pleine d'énergie</u>, se mit au travail
> '**subject**: Jeanne, **AD**: <u>full-FEM/SG of energy</u>, **VP**: started to work'

This position is also possible when the subject follows the verb:

> (8) Et derrière s'ouvrait l'église, <u>immense et sombre</u>
> '**adjunct**: And behind **VP**: opened itself **subject**: the church, **AD**: <u>immense-SG and gloomy-SG</u>'

But the AD cannot stand in this position when the subject is a clitic pronoun:

> (9) * Il, <u>plein d'énergie</u>, se mit au travail
> '* **subject**: he[+CL], **AD**: <u>full-MASC/SG of energy</u>, **VP**: started to work'

c. After the verb phrase, at the end of the sentence

In (8), we already had an AD at the end of the sentence. In that case, it directly followed the subject noun phrase. It can also occur in final position, when the subject precedes the verb:

> (10) Elle se mit au travail, <u>pleine d'énergie</u>
> '**subject**: She **VP**: started to work, **AD**: <u>full-FEM/SG of energy</u>'

1.1.2 Agreement between the AD and noun or pronoun which is not the subject

Besides the subject, the element with which the AD agrees may be an object, an oblique or an adjunct. The latter cases are less frequent and

---

Glatigny 1966 and in Bredelite 1981.

less typical than those which are subject-related[5]. (Accordingly, examples (12)-(15) and (17)-(19) are not in my corpus of attested examples.) The typicality of the constructions decreases in the following order: agreement with

> the subject > the direct object > an oblique > an adjunct.

This decreasing frequency and typicality corresponds to an increasing difficulty in giving judgments on acceptability: as a general rule, it is impossible to decide clearly whether a marginal construction is grammatical or not.

In the cases discussed in this section, where the AD agrees with an element other than the subject, word order is more restricted: The AD must follow the agreement controller. In most cases it follows immediately, as in (11), or (14), but it may be separated from the agreement controller by an adverbial, as in (12). If the agreement controller is a clitic, there is no slot for an immediately adjacent position. In this case, the AD appears after the verb, as in (13). - Here are examples and further comments regarding constructions in which the agreement controller is not the subject:

a. The agreement controller is the object

(11) Il ramassa les branchages, <u>les uns verts, les autres desséchés</u>
'**subject**: He **V**: picked up **object**: the branches, **AD**: <u>some green-MASC/PL, others dry-MASC/PL</u>'

(12) Il revit Madame Dupont un an après, <u>plus belle encore qu'avant</u>
'**subject**: He **V**: again-saw **object**: Madame Dupont-FEM/SG **adjunct**: one year later, **AD**: <u>more beautiful-FEM/SG still than before</u>'

---

[5] It is interesting to see that the examples collected by Pignon 1962, Glatigny 1966 and in Bredelite 1981 almost exclusively have ADs which are related to the subject. Bredelite even explicitly claims that the construction is only possible with reference to the subject. But the paper contains an example of agreement with the object of *il y a* (which Bredelite may have analyzed as a "logical subject"): *Dans la hauteur du ciel, au-dessus, il y a, <u>suspendue</u>, une brume violette que le soleil déchire en ce moment* (Bredelite 1981:130). - Notice that this sentence is a counter-example to my claim that an object controlled AD must not precede its controller. This problem needs further investigation.

(13) Il la revit, <u>plus belle encore qu'avant</u>
'**subject:** He **object:** her[+CL] **V:** again-saw, **AD:** <u>more beautiful-FEM/SG still than before</u>'

Notice that in (12) there is an adjunct between the object and the AD. I will come back to this point in section 2.3.1.

b. The agreement controller is an oblique

(14) ? Il raconta tout à son amie, <u>très contente de ce qu'elle apprenait</u>
'**subject:** He **V:** told **object:** everything **oblique:** to his friend-FEM/SG, **AD:** <u>very happy-FEM/SG about what she heard</u>'

This sentence is not quite as clearly acceptable as the preceding examples, but it is far more acceptable than (15). If the oblique is a clitic, the sentence sounds very odd:

(15) * Il lui raconta tout, <u>très contente de ce qu'elle apprenait</u>
'**subject:** He **oblique:** her[+CL] **V:** told **object:** everything, <u>very happy-FEM/SG about what she heard</u>'

c. The agreement controller is an adjunct

(16) Un instant, la maison lui apparut tout entiére entre deux pitons de granit, <u>taillés par l'érosion en forme de sucette</u>
'**adjunct:** An instant, **subject:** the house **V:** completely appeared **oblique:** to him **adjunct:** between two peaks of granite-MASC/PL, **AD:** <u>carved-MASC/PL by erosion into the shape of nipples</u>'

(17) Contrairement à la plupart de ses amis, déçus par les événements, Jean-Charles a continué à faire de la politique
'**adjunct:** Unlike most of his friends-MASC/PL, **AD** <u>disappointed-MASC/PL by the events</u>, **subject:** Jean-Charles-MASC/SG **VP:** continued making politics'

If the agreement controller is a clitic, an AD sounds extremely odd; compare (18) which is grammatical, having a noun phrase as agreement controller, to (19), which is ungrammatical, the controller being *y* :

(18) Paul passa la journée dans sa chambre d'hotel, <u>spacieuse et ensoleillée</u>
'**subject**: Paul-MASC/SG **V**: passed **object**: the day **adjunct**: in his hotel room-FEM/SG, **AD**: <u>large-FEM/SG and sunny-FEM/SG</u>'

(19) *Paul y passa la journée, <u>spacieuse et ensoleillée</u>
'*****subject**: Paul **adjunct**: there [+CL, -GEND, -NUM] **V**: passed **object**: the day, **AD**: <u>large-FEM/SG and sunny-FEM/SG</u>'

Of all clitics, it is only the nominatives and the accusatives which can serve as controllers of the AD.

These observations suggest the following generalizations:
An AD may be linked

a. to subjects and to objects (either clitics or full noun phrases)

b. to any noun phrase it forms a constituent with.

This explains why only subject and object clitics can control an AD: clitics cannot form a constituent with a noun phrase.

Before closing the syntactic description, it should be mentioned that the agreement relation can be ambiguous, as in (18) above and in the following examples:

(20) André tenait à la main un chapeau haut de forme en toile d'argent, <u>orné d'un plumet</u>
'**subject**: André-MASC/SG **V**: held **adjunct**: in his hand **object**: a stove-pipe hat-MASC/SG of silver cloth, **AD**: <u>adorned-MASC/SG with a feather</u>'

(21) Mon amie Valentine disparait de ma vie, <u>discrète, effacée, pudique</u>
'**subject**: My friend-FEM/SG Valentine **V**: disappeared **oblique**: from my life-FEM/SG, **AD**: <u>discreet-FEM/SG, unobtrusive-FEM/SG, chaste-SG</u>'

In (20) the AD can be controlled by the subject as well as by the object. In (21) the subject or the oblique may control the AD. The reader's preference will be based upon reasons of plausibility. Since subject-controlled ADs are most frequent, the agreement with the subject probably is a default solution.

1.2 Semantics

In all the examples above, and this holds for the AD in general, the adjective phrase must be interpreted as specifying an adjective type property of the entity referred to by the agreement controller. Thus for

(18) Paul passa la journée dans sa chambre d'hotel, <u>spacieuse et ensoleillée</u>
'**subject**: Paul-MASC/SG **V**: passed **object**: the day-FEM/SG **adjunct**: in his hotel room-FEM/SG, **AD**: <u>large-FEM/SG and sunny-FEM/SG</u>'

we will understand that the room (*chambre*) is large and sunny. (*Paul* cannot be the controller because of the agreement facts; the day (*journée*) will not be understood as the controller for pragmatic reasons.)

Now if it is true that the AD specifies an adjective type property, we should expect that it admits of exactly those adjectives which can appear as predicatives after the copula. Conversely, we should expect that adjectives which cannot be predicatives will not occur as ADs. This is actually the case, cf. e.g.:

(22) * <u>Présumé</u>, ce docteur était un escroc
'* **AD**: Presumed-MASC/SG, **subject**: this doctor-MASC/SG **VP**: was a swindler' ; cf.

(22') * Ce docteur est présumé
 * 'This doctor is presumed'

(23) * <u>Equestre</u>, cette statue s'érige dans le parc
'* **AD**: <u>Equestrian-SG</u>, **subject**: this statue-FEM/SG **VP**: stands in the park'; cf.

(23') * Cette statue est équestre
 * 'This statue is equestrian'

If ADs express adjective type properties in very much the same way as predicative adjectives, then we can assume that they have the same semantic structure as predicative adjectives. Let us assume that predicative adjectives are one-place predicates, that is, that they have the general form $P(x)$, where P corresponds to the adjective and x to the subject. ADs then also have the general form $P(x)$, but here x is not overtly expressed, and it is "coreferential" with the referent of the agreement controller. (I do not want to discuss here the semantic structure of adjectives which have more than one argument. It may be assumed, however, that what is stated for the structure $P(x)$ also holds for structures of the form $P(x, ...)$).

We can now come to the question of the nature of this coreferentiality. Is the agreement anaphoric or grammatical? Anaphoric agreement is a morphological relationship, concerning number and gender, between an anaphoric expression and its antecedent. It must be accounted for on the text level. Grammatical agreement is a morphological relationship, concerning number, gender and possibly case, inside a constituent or between various constituents. It must be accounted for on the level of the sentence. Hence, if the agreement of the AD is grammatical, we will have to account for it in our syntactic analysis; if it is anaphoric, we will have to leave it to a theory of text coherence.

In order to answer this question, let us suppose for a moment what the argument of the AD is a zero pronoun, that is, that the general semantic form of an AD is $P(PRO)$. If the interpretation principles of this pronoun are analogous to those which hold for personal pronouns, then the relationship is anaphoric, otherwise it is grammatical.

The answer seems to be the following: In order to interpret a personal pronoun, I first have to search the preceding context, and I must be prepared to go beyond the sentence boundary. In order to interpret the argument of the AD, I do not necessarily start with the preceding context, and, above all, I must not go beyond the sentence boundary. Hence the coreferentiality (and consequently the agreement) seems to be grammatical rather than anaphoric.

But the facts of anaphoric "coreference" are not quite as clear: thus, in certain cases, the antecedent may follow the anaphoric expression. The only clear argument for deciding whether an agreement is anaphoric or grammatical is the presence or absence of case agreement, and French does not have case-marking, except with clitic pronouns. We could of course make an argument of analogy: if we translated our examples into Latin, the AD would receive the case of its controlling function: cf.

(13') Revidit **illam** ..., pulcherio**rem** quam prius
'He saw her-ACC/FEM again..., more beautiful-ACC/FEM than before'

It is thus plausible to assume that the process of interpreting the AD consists in applying the predicate expressed by the AD to the entity denoted by the agreement controller.

1.3 Pragmatics

It has frequently been observed that the AD may have an additional circumstantial meaning. Thus (1) has a quite reasonable paraphrase which expresses a causal relationship, namely:

(1) <u>Soulagé par la fraicheur</u>, il allait encore plus vite
'<u>Relieved by the coolness</u>, he went still faster'

(1') <u>Comme il était soulagé par la fraicheur</u>, il allait encore plus vite
'<u>Since he was relieved by the coolness</u>, he went still faster'

Other examples seem to denote a temporal relationship, cf.:

(24) <u>Arrivé presque en haut de la côte</u>, il se mit à courir
'<u>Arrived almost on top of the hill</u>, he started running'

(24') <u>Lorsqu'il fut arrivé presque en haut de la côte</u>, il se mit à courir
'<u>When he almost had arrived on top of the hill</u>, he started running'

If the additional value is adversative, it has to be overtly expressed, as in:

(25) <u>Même vaincus</u>, ils n'abandonneraient pas la partie
'<u>Even defeated</u>, they would not give up'
'<u>Bien que vide</u>, cette caisse est assez lourde
'<u>Although <it is> empty</u>, this box is rather heavy'

But in many other cases, there is no such additional meaning. This holds in particular for those ADs which *follow* their coreferential expression, as in:

(26) Apparait enfin au-dessus des sables une vieille cité blanche,
<u>plantée de rares palmiers jaunes</u>
'<There> appears finally above the sands an old white city,
<u>planted with rare yellow palm trees</u>'

And even in initial position, the AD may lack any circumstantial value, as in

(27) <u>Douce</u>, la nuit tombait
'<u>Softly</u>, the night fell'

From this it seems to follow that the additional circumstantial value doesn't belong to the AD constructions as such, but to the underlying propositions and their linear order. Analogously to what happens when we understand a sequence of sentences in a text in terms of causal or temporal relationships, the AD in initial position can be seen as inviting a possible causal or temporal interpretyion of the involved propositions.

2. LFG RULES FOR THE *adjectif détaché*

We can now discuss the problems which we need to resolve in order to account for the AD in the LFG framework. We will have to determine:
- the grammatical function of the AD
- the way in which the semantic relationship between the AD and the agreement controller can be expressed at the functional level
- the way in which the agreement facts are to be captured
- the way in which the relatively free word order can be accounted for.

We will not discuss the theoretical issues related to
- the prosodic detachedness of the AD, and
- the pragmatics of the AD.

I think in fact that both could in principle be treated in theories that might be directly linked to LFG syntax, but these theories still need to be formulated.

2.1 The functional status of the AD

We will try to determine the functional status of the AD by progressive elimination of solutions which, at first glance, might be considered as plausible.

We will first examine whether the AD is an argument function of the verb, that is an X-complement. X-complements associated to adjective phrases are in fact similar to ADs: sentences like the following seem to differ structurally only on the level of prosody:

(28) Je les croyais <u>contents de leur succès</u>
'I them[+CL] thought <u>happy-MASC/PL about their success</u>'

(29) Je les voyais rentrer, <u>contents de leur succès</u>
'I them[+CL] saw come-home, <u>happy-MASC/PL about their success</u>'

But there are three arguments against this hypothesis:

First, X-complements can be controlled only by argument functions, that is, the subject, the object and the oblique (cf. Bresnan 1982: 323). The AD, however, can also be controlled by adjuncts; see examples (16)-(18).

Second, X-complements are possible only if the verb has stored them in its lexical form. That is, they are lexically restricted, cf. the following examples:

(30) Je trouve ce prix <u>exagéré</u>
'I find this price <u>exaggerated</u>'

(31) * Je pense ce prix <u>exagéré</u>
'* I think this price <u>exaggerated</u>'

(32) Nous l'avons repêché <u>vivant</u>
'We fished him out <u>alive</u>'

(33) ? Nous l'avons regardé <u>vivant</u>
'? We looked at him <u>alive</u>'

Third, as we know, the X-complement constructions lack the pauses or commas which are typical for the ADs. If this were the only argument, it might be relegated to a possible pragmatic theory of intonation. But since this argument is obviously linked to the facts of control and of lexical restrictions we just discussed, it supports the syntactic argumentation.

Let us now examine the question of whether the AD, at least when it follows the agreement controller, is just a prosodic variety of the noun-modifying type of adjective phrase. In fact, the commas (or pauses) can be omitted; cf. pairs like the following:

(34) Une jeune femme, <u>grande et souple</u>, se tenait près de lui
 'A young woman, <u>tall-FEM/SG and supple-SG</u>, stood near him'

(35) Une jeune femme <u>grande et</u> souple se tenait près de lui
 'A young woman <u>tall-FEM/SG and supple</u>-SG stood near him'
 'A tall and supple young woman stood near him'

But there is one decisive argument against that hypothesis: As we have seen above, there is a subclass of adjectives which are exclusively adnominal, that is, which cannot occur as complements of the copula. Now if the ADs under discussion here were simple modifiers of the noun, these adjectives would expectedly occur after a noun, and it would be possible to separate them by a comma. But this is not the case; cf.:

(36) a. Ce présumé docteur était un escroc
 'This presumed doctor was a swindler'

 b. * Ce docteur, <u>présumé</u>, était un escroc
 '*This doctor, <u>presumed</u>, was a swindler'

(37) a. Cette statue équestre s'érige dans le parc
 'This equestrian statue stands in the park'

 b. * Cette statue, <u>équestre</u>, s'érige dans le parc
 '*This statue, <u>equestrian</u>, stands in the park'

Therefore, the AD, even when it follows its controller, does not have the same grammatical function as a modifier of the noun.

After having excluded the treatment of the AD as an X-complement and as a noun modifier, there remains the possibility of treating it as an adjunct. We can in fact conclude that the AD is an adjunct, but we have to add that it is of a very particular type, since it has this special relationship with an agreement controller. Adopting the analysis which has been made for English by Bresnan 1982: 325, we will **consider the AD as a controlled X-adjunct.**

In other words, an AD is an adjunct, which is realized, on the level of c-structure, by an adjective phrase and which is controlled by some other function. Technically speaking, in the LFG framework the AD is an adjective phrase which has two functional annotations. The first says that the adjective phrase is an X-adjunct, and the second says that the subject of the adjectival predicate equals some other grammatical function. This means that for a sentence like

(39) La pluie tombe, <u>vaporeuse</u>
 'The rain falls, <u>steamy</u>'

we want to have an f-structure of roughly the following type:

$$(39') \begin{bmatrix} \text{SUBJ} & \begin{bmatrix} \text{PRED} & \text{'PLUIE'} \\ \text{GEND} & \text{FEM} \\ \text{NUM} & \text{SG} \\ \text{SPEC} & \text{DEF} \end{bmatrix} \\ \text{PRED} & \text{TOMBE (SUBJ)} \\ \text{XADJ} & \begin{bmatrix} \text{PRED} & \text{'VAPOREUX (SUBJ)'} \\ \text{SUBJ} & \end{bmatrix} \end{bmatrix}$$

An f-structure of this type accounts for the semantic relationship between the AD and its agreement controller: The predicate 'VAPOREUX', being related by the arrow to the substructure which has 'PLUIE' as its main predicate, will be applied, in the process of semantic interpretation, to the entity to which 'PLUIE' is applied.

As to the morphological agreement between the AD and its controller, it is effected by operations on lexical information while building up the f-structure. The lexical entry for *vaporeuse* will in fact be something like:

(39") vaporeuse: A, (↑ PRED) = 'VAPOREUX <(SUBJ)>
 (↓ SUBJ NUMB) = SG
 (↓ SUBJ GEND) = FEM

Since the subject in (39') satisfies the agreement equations which are stated in (39"), *vaporeuse* is accepted as an AD linked to *pluie*.

When the agreement controller is a pronoun, there will be no essential difference in the f-structure. For a sentence like

(40) Elle tombe, <u>vaporeuse</u>
     'It falls, <u>steamy</u>'

we will get the following f-structure:

$$
(40') \begin{bmatrix} \text{SUBJ} & \begin{bmatrix} \text{PRED} & \text{'PRO'} \\ \text{GEND} & \text{FEM} \\ \text{NUM} & \text{SG} \\ \text{SPEC} & \text{DEF} \end{bmatrix} \\ \text{PRED} & [\text{TOMBE (SUBJ)}] \\ \text{XADJ} & \begin{bmatrix} \text{PRED 'VAPOREUX (SUBJ)'} \\ \text{SUBJ} \end{bmatrix} \end{bmatrix}
$$

Now, if in principle these are the correct f-structures, it is not yet clear how to ensure that the X-adjunct is controlled by the correct function.

For the control relationships, the solution is to specify them by equations. Since the control equations for adjuncts are by definition not lexically conditioned, they must be generated as annotations in the c-rules. Consequently we must now turn to the problems of c-structure.

2.3 C-structure rules for ADs

As a result of our analysis of the descriptive facts we can see that the A-adjunct is controlled in accordance with two different principles:
- a principle of **substantially specified control**, which works whenever the AD does not immediately follow the constituent which contains its controller, and
- a principle of **formally specified control**, which works whenever the AD immediately follows the constituent which contains its controller.

Accordingly, we will not try to account for the positions of ADs and for their control by just one rule, but rather will propose two sets of rules; one for those cases in which the AD does not immediately follow its controlling constituent, and another for the alternative case.

2.3.1 C-rules for non adjacent ADs

Bresnan 1982: 325 discusses functionally controlled adjuncts in English, as in (41), for example:

(41) Mary caught a glimpse of the fish lying on the
table, <u>tasty and fragrant with herbs</u>

In her analysis, the controlled X-adjunct has a non-overt subject, and the control relationship is expressed by an equation. We will follow the same basic approach.

Accounting for the facts of English, a language which has no adjective agreement, she proposes the following solution: For each controlled adjunct, several controlling functions are possible. Consequently, on the right hand side of the control equation there is a variable, which may be instantiaved by any grammatical function available in the sentence. But (still according to Bresnan 1982) there is one construction in English where the controlling function must be the subject, namely the case in which the controlled adjunct is in initial position. For this case, the control equation specifies that the subject of the adjunct equals the subject of the sentence. The relevant c-structure rule is as follows:

$$(42) \quad S \rightarrow \begin{bmatrix} AP \\ (\uparrow XADJ) = \downarrow \\ (\uparrow SUBJ) = (\downarrow SUBJ) \end{bmatrix} \quad \begin{matrix} NP \\ (\uparrow SUBJ) = \downarrow \end{matrix} \quad \begin{matrix} VP \\ \uparrow = \downarrow \end{matrix}$$

We will take this rule as a point of departure and change it in order to adapt it to the French facts. As has been shown above, French subject-controlled X-adjuncts have several positions, not just the one generated by rule (42). But I will not try to account for all these positions by expanding rule (42). I will, in fact, exclude from the rule those subject-controlled ADs which immediately follow their controlling constituent, treating them instead by a separate rule. What we have to do, then, is to ensure that the subject-controlled AD can occur not only before the subject noun phrase, but also

- before the subject and before another adjunct
- after the verb phrase

We must further account for the fact that, under certain conditions, the subject may follow the verb.

As Kayne 1972 has shown, one must distinguish between the inversion of the subject clitic, which occurs in interrogative sentences, and the inversion of a full noun phrase subject, which may occur in interrogative clauses, relative clauses and cleft sentences ("stylistic inversion").

Zaenen 1983 has proposed a treatment of French stylistic inversion in the LFG framework. In her analysis, the subject in its normal position is optional, and the inverted subject is part of the verb phrase. The consistency principle then filters out sentences with two subjects, and the completeness principle rules out sentences which have no subject. A feature "bounded" is attached to the verb node in order to constrain stylistic inversion to what she names a syntactic binding domain, i.e., intuitively speaking, the structure which the moved constituent runs through in wh-movement. The rules are:

(71) S   ->   (NP)   VP
                (↑ SUBJ) = ↓   ↑ = ↓

     VP   ->   V   X   NP   Y
                (↓ BOUNDED)   (↑ SUBJ) = ↓

But there are also other contexts in which subject inversion may occur. The presence of certain adjuncts at the beginning of the sentence makes it possible for the subject to follow the verb, as in examples (5), (6), and (8) above. Kayne 1972:109 mentions these facts. He points out that they are similar to stylistic inversion, since only full noun phrases are concerned; cf. his sentences:

(f') Demain reviendront les deux personnes
    to-morrow will-come-back the two persons
    'to-morrow the two persons will come back'
    Ici passera la nouvelle autoroute
    here will-pass the new freeway
    'the new freeway will pass here'

(h') *Demain reviendront-elles
*to-morrow will-come-back they[+CL]
'they will come back to-morrow'
*Ici passera-t-elle
*here will-pass she[+CL]
'she will pass here'.

He also mentions the possibility for certain verbs to stand in first position, causing inversion of the subject, as in example (26), above. But he did not try to include these types of subject inversion in his analysis. Even today, these facts are far from clear. Therefore it is not possible to give a full account of French subject inversion in this paper; the following rules are only a sketch.

The non-adjacent, subject-controlled AD is generated by the following rules:

$$(43) \quad S \rightarrow \begin{bmatrix} AP\ ! \\ (\uparrow XADJ) = \downarrow \\ (\uparrow SUBJ) = (\downarrow SUBJ) \end{bmatrix} \quad \underline{(PP)}\quad (NP) \quad \underline{VP}$$
$$\downarrow \in (ADJ) \quad (\uparrow SUBJ) = \downarrow \quad \uparrow = \downarrow$$

$$(44)\ VP \rightarrow \quad V' \qquad (NP)$$
$$\uparrow = \downarrow \qquad (\uparrow SUBJ) = \downarrow$$

I use the following conventions: The bold exclamation mark after a constituent means that the place which the constituent has in the rule is just one of the positions it may occupy; the horizontal lines indicate the other positions in which it may occur. A more elegant formulation would be possible if, as in General Phrase Structure Grammar, there was a way of separately stating relations of dominance and of precedence; cf. Gazdar e.a. 1985:44ff.

Rule (43) does not account for those cases in which the subject is a clitic pronoun, as in examples (1) and (3) above. The treatment of clitic subject pronouns still needs investigation. In any case, the clitic subject pronoun will be dominated by the first projection of the verb, and it will be annotated as being the subject of the sentence. That is, we will have something like:

(45) V' -> (CL$_1$) ... V
(↑SUBJ) = ↓

That is, the clitic subject pronoun can probably be treated by an expansion of the rule which Grimshaw 1982 proposes for the non-subject clitics of French. The category CL$_1$ comprises the forms *je, tu, il, elle, on, nous, vous, ils, elles* in their use as actual pronouns. I cannot discuss here the treatment of impersonal *il* and of the subject pronoun *ce*, neither of which can control an X-adjunct. At any rate, the functional information contained in the left hand bracket of rule (43) will also apply to most of the possible clitic subjects.

In the preceding discussion we have focussed on subject controlled ADs. We still have to provide for object control. As has been shown above, object controlled X-adjuncts, unlike the subject controlled ones, cannot precede their controller. Furthermore, we have to keep in mind that all ADs which immediately follow their controller will be accounted for by a separate rule. So what we have to add to rule (44) is a formulation for those cases in which an object controlled AD does not immediately follow its controller, as exemplified by

(12) Il revit Madame Dupont un an après, plus belle encore qu'avant
'**subject**: He **V**: again-saw **object**: Madame Dupont-FEM/SG
adjunct: one year later, **AD**: even more beautiful-FEM/SG than before'

This class of constructions includes the cases in which the controller is a clitic pronoun, as in

(13) Il la revit, plus belle encore qu'avant
'**subject**: He **object**: her[+CL] **V**: again-saw, **AD**: even more beautiful-FEM/SG than before'

So what we have to do is to add, on the right hand side of rule (44), the symbol for an optional adjective phrase, with functional annotations stating that this constituent is an X-adjunct and has a subject which equals the object of the sentence, namely:

(46) VP -> V'   (NP)   AP
         ↑ = ↓   (↑OBJ) = ↓   (↑XADJ) = ↓
                                    (↓SUBJ) = (↑OBJ)

We have to remember, however, that rule (43) provides, at the right hand side of the verb phrase, a slot for a subject controlled AD. Therefore, by adding rule (46), we generate a sequence of two ADs, one of them subject controlled, and the other object controlled, as for example in:

(47) ?? Il la revit, heureux, plus belle encore qu'avant
  'subject: He object: her[+CL] V: again-saw, AD: happy-MASC/SG AD: even more beautiful-FEM/SG than before'

Now we seem to have the choice of either deciding that (47) is grammatical, but not acceptable on stylistic grounds, or of changing rules (43), (44) and (46) in such a way that a subject controlled AD and an object controlled AD are mutually exclusive at the right hand side of the verb phrase. There are reasons to prefer the first solution; I will come back to that problem at the end of this paper.

For the convenience of the reader, I resume the rules for the non-adjacent AD:

$$(48)\ S \rightarrow \begin{bmatrix} AP\ ! \\ (\uparrow XADJ) = \downarrow \\ (\uparrow SUBJ) = (\downarrow SUBJ) \end{bmatrix} \quad \_(PP)\_ \atop \downarrow \in (ADJ) \quad NP \atop (\uparrow SUBJ) = \downarrow \quad VP\_ \atop \uparrow = \downarrow$$

$$VP \rightarrow V'\ \begin{Bmatrix} (NP) \\ (\uparrow OBJ) = \downarrow \\ (\uparrow SUBJ) = \downarrow \end{Bmatrix} \begin{bmatrix} PP \\ \downarrow \in (ADJ) \end{bmatrix} \begin{bmatrix} AP \\ (\uparrow XADJ) = \downarrow \\ (\downarrow SUBJ) = (\uparrow OBJ) \end{bmatrix} \begin{bmatrix} AP \\ (\uparrow XADJ) = \downarrow \\ (\downarrow SUBJ) = (\uparrow SUBJ) \end{bmatrix}$$
$$\uparrow = \downarrow$$

2.3.2 A rule for adjacent ADs

We have now to formulate a rule in order to generate the remaining ADs, namely those which immediately follow the constituent which contains their controller. This rule must operate in such a way that the :controller can be any grammatical function, and that it cannot be a clitic pronoun. It must express the fact that the subject of the X-adjunct equals the function realized by the immediately preceding noun phrase (cf. examples (7) and (11)) or prepositional phrase (cf. examples (14) and (18)).

Formulating the rule for adjacent ADs, it seems natural to postulate that the AD, together with the noun phrase by which it is preceded, forms a complex noun phrase. One might think, then, of directly exploiting the fact that the controller is the head of that noun phrase. Since the functional relationships must be expressed in the f-structure, we would have to introduce "head" as a new grammatical function.

But such a solution would not be very satisfactory. It would unnecessarily increase the number of primitives, and which is more, it would be in contradiction with the spirit of LFG: The relationship between the head and the rest of a constituent is a notion of constituent structure, not of functional structure. Therefore, introducing "head" as a grammatical function would mean to duplicate the c-structure on the level of f-structure. It is true that similar duplications are accepted, in LFG, for the various kinds of obliques and of complements. But increasing the range of parallelisms between constituent structure and functional structure certainly is not desirable: what would be the use of an f-structure which would be just a reflex of the c-structure?

Now there are various ways of expressing the functional and semantic relationship between the AD and its immediately preceding controller. All solutions must have in common that, on the level of c-structure, the adjacent AD is an adjective phrase dominated by a noun phrase. As to the nominal expression which is its left hand sister, it must be decided whether it is a noun (49) or a noun phrase (50):

(49) NP -> N (AP)

(50) NP -> NP (AP)

The answer is that the left hand sister is a noun phrase. This is justified by examples like:

(51) Trois cent tableaux rassemblés par José Pierre à la galerie Artcurial témoignent de l'aventure d'André Breton, <u>inlassablement poursuivie pendant un demi-siècle</u> (Le Monde)
'three hundred pictures brought together by José Pierre at the Artcurial gallery testify of André Breton's adventure, <u>unfatigably carried on throughout half a century</u>'

The AD is preceded, in this example, by *l'aventure d'André Breton*, which is clearly a noun phrase. Another argument[6] in favour of the noun phrase hypothesis is the possibility to link an AD to a (non-clitic) pronoun, as in (52), pronouns being noun phrases, not nouns:

(52) Près de lui, <u>grand et souple</u>, la jeune fille paraissait petite et timide
'close to him, <u>tall and souple</u>, the girl seemed small and timid'

If it is true that the nominal expression which preceeds an adjacent AD is a noun phrase, and not a noun, then the following hypothesis can be formulated: In adnominal adjective constructions, the categorial status of the nominal expression decides on the functional nature of the adjective phrase. The adjective phrase is a modifier (in a different terminology: a "restrictive adjective"), when its left hand sister is a noun. It is an adjunct (a "non-restrictive attribute"), when its left hand sister is a noun phrase.

Now for the functional annotations, one possibility is to state that the controller of the AD is the whole complex noun phrase (that is, not only the head)[7], as in

(53) NP -> NP   (AP)
         ↑ = ↓   ↓ ∈ (ADJ)
                  (↓SUBJ) = ↑

In f-structures based upon this rule the arrow points to the whole complex noun phrase; cf. (53'), which analyzes *...la chambre, large ...* '... the bed-room, large ...':

---

[6] I owe this argument to Annie Zaenen (personal communication).

[7] This solution has been suggested by Ronald Kaplan, who also was aware of the possible criticism (oral discussion).

$$(53') \begin{bmatrix} \text{PRED} & \text{'CHAMBRE'} \\ \text{GEND} & \text{FEM} \\ \text{NUM} & \text{SG} \\ \text{SPEC} & \text{DEF} \\ \\ \text{XADJ} & \begin{bmatrix} \text{PRED 'LARGE (SUBJ)'} \\ \text{SUBJ} \end{bmatrix} \end{bmatrix}$$

This solution has the advantage that no ad-hoc function has to be assigned to the head of the noun phrase.

It has the drawback, however, that it does not correspond to the intuitive understanding of the semantic relationship between the AD and its controller. In fact, one might object that, intuitively speaking, the AD is predicated of the preceding noun phrase, not of the whole complex noun phrase, and that, in a structure like (53'), a predicate modifies something it is part of, which is a circular relationship.

This objection is irrefutable if one postulates that control relationships must reflect predicate-argument structures. But if we do not claim this parallelism between functional structure and semantics, (53) just states that the subject of the AD has the same features as the noun phrase which it is part of. This assumption does not seem to raise any difficulties. The problem, then, is to decide to what extent functional structure should correspond to semantic structure. An alternative solution consists in stating that the subject of the AD is not the whole f-structure of the complex noun phrase, but only the main predicate of that structure[8], or, more precisely, that the subject predicate of the AD equals the predicate of the whole noun phrase. Since the f-structure of the complex noun phrase receives this predicate from the AD's left hand sister, that is, the noun phrase by which the AD is preceded, this solution corresponds more closely to an intuitive semantic analysis. The rule, then, is:

$$(54)\ \text{NP} \rightarrow \text{NP} \quad (\text{AP})$$
$$\uparrow = \downarrow \quad \downarrow \in (\text{ADJ})$$
$$(\downarrow\text{PRED}) = (\downarrow\text{SUBJ PRED})$$

---

[8] This was Klaus Netter's proposal in the oral discussion of this paper on the Friedenweiler conference.

The resulting f-structures, an example of which is (54'), are not in contradiction with semantic intuitions:

$$(54')\begin{bmatrix} \text{PRED} & \text{'CHAMBRE'} \\ \text{GEND} & \text{FEM} \\ \text{NUM} & \text{SG} \\ \text{SPEC} & \text{DEF} \\ \text{XADJ} & \begin{bmatrix} \text{PRED} & \text{'LARGE (SUBJ)'} \\ \text{SUBJ} & \end{bmatrix} \end{bmatrix}$$

But (54) does not account for agreement. This can be illustrated by (54'): The lexical entry for *large* requires that the subject of this form must be a singular. Now the subject of *large* is the predicate CHAMBRE. But since a predicate doesn't have number, the agreement requirement cannot be decided. Therefore we must complete (54) by an explicit agreement rule. This means that we have to treat the link between the AD and its controller not as a case of functional control, as we did for the non-adjacent ADs, but of anaphoric control.

This would require an expansion of the AP to a structure containing a null pronoun, namely

(55) AP ->   e   A
                 (↑ SUBJ PRED) = 'PRO'   ↑ = ↓

By this rule, the functional annotation of A would pass the number and gender constraints of the adjective to the AP, and the principles for finding the antecedent of 'PRO' would have to make use of this information.

But this solution contradicts what was said in section 1.2 in favour of a treatment of the AD as a case of functional control.

It should also be noted that (54) is not restricted to the case of adjacent adjective phrases: it apppplies indifferently to all adjective phrases. We would thus lose the advantage of functional control, which provides, as has been shown, an extremely simple treatment of agreement[9].

---

[9] Annie Zaenen (personal communication) drew my attention to the fact that the case

3. CLOSING REMARKS

The treatment of the AD which has been suggested above will not exclude all inacceptable sentences. The clearly acceptable sentences in the corpus do not have more than one AD, but the rules which have been formulated generate sentences with many ADs: The rule for non adjacent ADs, as formulated in (48), generates two ADs in the same sentence, one for the subject and another for the object, and makes it possible for the two ADs to follow each other at the end of the sentence. Furthermore, the rule for adjacent ADs generates, for each sentence, as many ADs as there are noun phrases in the sentence. (This happens independently of the treatment of the functional information, because both formulations which have been discussed here are based upon the rule NP -> NP AP.) And if the sets of rules for the non-adjacent ADs and for the adjacent ADs are both applied, they generate subjects and objects which control two ADs, one non-adjacent, the other adjacent. All these sentences are more or less unacceptable.

Obviously, it would be out of the scope of a syntax to account for the

---

for functional control might be strengthened by observing agreement in cases where natural and grammatical gender conflict. In fact words like *recrue* (f.) 'recruit', *sentinelle* (f.) 'sentry' may have agreement ad sensum in anaphoric relations which extend beyond the sentence, but require grammatical agreement in adnominal and predicative constructions; cf. a. and b. as opposed to c.:

    a. une nouvelle recrue
    'a new[FEM] recruit[FEM]'

    b. La sentinelle est intelligente
    'the sentry[FEM] is intelligent[FEM]'

    c. J'observais la sentinelle. Il semblait avoir froid.
    'I watched the sentry[FEM]. He[MASC] seemed to be cold'

Actually, there seems to be no agreement according to natural gender in AD constructions; cf.

    d. Impatiente, la sentinelle braqua son fusil
    'impatient[FEM], the sentry[FEM] levelled his gun'

    d'. *Impatient, la sentinelle braqua son fusil
    'impatient[MASC], the sentry[FEM] levelled his gun'

As has been pointed out in note 3, there are agreements ad sensum in AD constructions. But they are due to the absence of an explicit controller and have nothing to do with natural gender. Thus examples like a. - d'. actually strengthen the functional control hypothesis.

number of ADs in a sentence, and in the framework there are no instruments for doing so. Thus the fact that the rules generate too many ADs is not an objection: Their numeric limitations must be left to a stylistic component, which is not the object of this paper.

What I tried to show in this paper is that certain phenomena of free word order, which might easily be taken for mere stylistic facts, can be treated in a unification grammar like LFG.

As to the speficic properties of French, it has been shown that the degree in which adjectival adjuncts can be ordered freely is smaller than what appears from the data. There are three kinds of AD constructions: the non-adjacent subject controlled AD, the non-adjacent object controlled AD, and the adjacent head controlled AD. Of these three types, only the first has a certain freedom of ordering.

A more general point has been to show that all AD constructions can (and should) be treated as cases of functional control, and that the rules of functional control provide a very simple treatment of agreement, espacially if the adjective is distant from its controller.

Finally, an hypothesis has been formulated about the functional status of adnominal adjective phrases: Adnominal adjective phrases can be adjuncts or modifiers, depending on the category of the nominal expression. This hypothesis, of course, remains to be elaborated within the general structure of the French noun phrase.

BIBLIOGRAPHY:

Bredelite 1981 = Birute Bredelite, "Semanticeskaja svaz' mezdu podlezascim i obosoblennym opredeleniem", in: *Kalbotyra* 32 (1981), 123-133

Bresnan 1982 = Joan Bresnan, "Control and Complementation", in: Joan Bresnan (ed.), *The Mental Representation of Grammatical Relations*, Cambridge-London 1982, pp. 282-390

Chevalier e.a. 1964 = Jean-Claude Chevalier/Claire Blanche-Benveniste/ Michel Arrivé/Jean Peytard, *Grammaire Larousse du français contemporain*. Paris 1964

Dessaintes 1962 = Maurice Dessaintes, *L'Analyse grammaticale. Au seuil de la stylistique*. Namur-Bruxelles-Tournai 1962

Fischer & Hacquard 1959 = Maurice Fischer & Georges Hacquard, *A la découverte de la grammaire française*. Paris 1959

Galichet 1968 = Georges Galichet, *Grammaire structurale*, 2me éd., Montréal 1968

Gazdar e.a. 1985 = Gerald Gazdar, Ewan Klein, Geoffrey Pullum & Ivan Sag, *Generalized Phrase Structure Grammar*, Oxford 1985

Glatigny 1966 = M. Glatigny, "L'adjectif en apposition se rapporte-t-il au nom?" in: *Le Français Moderne* 34(1966) 264-279

Grevisse 1964 = Maurice Grevisse, *Le bon usage. Grammaire française, avec des remarques sur la langue française d'aujourd'hui*, 9me éd. revue, Gembloux 1969

Grimshaw = Jane Grimshaw, "On the Lexical Representation of Romance Reflexive Clitics", in: Joan Bresnan (ed.), *The Mental Representation of Grammatical Relations*, Cambridge-London 1982, pp. 87-148

Judge & Healey 1983 = Anne Judge & F.G. Healey, *A Reference Grammar of Modern French*. London 1983

Kayne 1972 = Richard S. Kayne, "Subject inversion in French interrogatives", in: Jean Casagrande & Bohdan Saciuk (eds.), *Generative Studies in Romance Languages*, Rowley (Mass.) 1972, pp. 70-126

Pignon 1962 = J. Pignon, "Discussion: l'Apposition", in: *Le Français Moderne* 30 (1962) 172-192 (This paper is a part of a discussion of the problems of apposition, by a group of French linguists (M. Arrivé, H. Bonnard, J. Chaurand, A. Chevalier, J.-C. Chevalier, J.-P. Mouchet, J. Pignon), published in *Le Français Moderne* 30 (1962) 172-192. This discussion was preceded by a note on apposition, in *Le Français Moderne* 29 (1961) 252-257)

Wartburg & Zumthor 1958 = Walter von Wartburg & Paul Zumthor, *Précis de syntaxe du français contemporain*, 2me éd., Berne 1958

Wagner & Pinchon 1968 = R. L. Wagner & J. Pinchon, *Grammaire du français classique et moderne*, 2me éd., Paris 1968

Zaenen 1983 = Annie Zaenen, "On syntactic binding", in: *Linguistic Inquiry* 14 (1983) pp. 469-504

DIETER WUNDERLICH
DÜSSELDORF

SOME PROBLEMS OF COORDINATION IN GERMAN

1. INTRODUCTION

The phenomenon I am going to discuss may be illustrated by sentence (1).*

(1) In den Wald ging der Jäger und fing einen Hasen.
('Into the forest went the hunter and caught a hare ')

At first sight, (1) seems to be a case of coordination. It is, however, a rather irregular case of coordination. The first 'conjunct' is a complete declarative sentence, whereas the second 'conjunct' is a verbal phrase. The unexpressed subject of the latter is identical with the expressed subject of the former. Obviously, an S and VP coordination cannot be an instance of the general coordination schema (see GKPS 1985:171), unless it can be shown that the VP is, in some way or other, the result of a deletion of the subject, or that its unexpressed subject is a proper instance of an empty category.

After the presentation of my paper in the conference, I became acquainted with an unpublished paper by Höhle (1983) dealing extensively with the phenomenon illustrated by (1). Höhle calls this phenomenon "subject gap in fronted finite verb coordination (SGF-coordination)". He shows that coordination of this kind is not only frequent in declarative

---

* My involvement with the problem I discuss in this article has been stimulated by remarks from Arnim von Stechow. My thanks go to Klaus-Dirk Smolka, Jürgen Pafel, and Christian Dütschmann, who contributed examples and insights into the structure of the problem in some seminar discussions. I want also to thank Tilman Höhle for his written comments on the problem, Therèse Torris, who called my attention to Höhle's paper, and Sue Olsen, Ray Fabri and an anonymous reader, who contributed some improvements of the written version.

sentences, but also in other sentence types of German (see below, section 4). He does, however, not offer any theoretical treatment of this phenomenon.

The first question I shall deal with, is whether (1) could be an instance of ellipsis, derived from (1a).

(1a) In den Wald ging der Jäger und [er] fing einen Hasen.
('...and [he] caught a hare')

For this reason, the general conditions of ellipsis in coordinate structures will be outlined in section 2. It will then be shown that the phenomenon of SGF-coordination does not conform to these conditions. This means that (1a), though itself being perfectly grammatical, should not be considered as the source of (1). We have to look for a non-ellipsis analysis of (1).

In section 3, I shall show that, within the standard assumptions of the Chomsky tradition, no solution is available. First, we will see that the unexpressed subject of the second conjunct can neither be PRO nor a trace. Second, any attempt to derive (1) by constituent coordination (e.g. VP or INFL coordination) will fail. This clearly shows that (1) cannot be an instance of regular coordination. Instead, we have to assume that the VP 'conjunct' is a sister of both the V and the subject NP of the first 'conjunct'. It still seems not to be possible to implement this insight within the proposals of government and binding theory. In particular, the assumption of the finite verb movement in German seems to prevent a solution.

In a GPSG analysis, however, the position of the finite verb can be treated as being a consequence of some of its head features. In section 4, I shall outline such a solution. This proposal can, without any further requirements, explain all properties of SGF-coordination in German.

Finally, in section 5, I shall present another problem of coordination in German. In contrast to Höhle's assumptions, it will be shown that it is not a cubcase of SGF-coordination. Here, a solution is not as easily at hand.

2. CONSIDERATIONS ABOUT ELLIPSIS

In the following, I take sentence (2) as the basis of my consideration.

(2) Die Tante hat den Korb in das Haus gelegt
und der Onkel hat den Sack in den Hof geworfen
('The aunt has put the basket into the house
and the uncle has thrown the bag into the yard')

(2) is a reasonably complex but not too complex instance of coordination of declarative sentences (assertion main clauses) in German: S_1 und S_2. Except for the finite auxiliary verb, each constituent of S_1 contrasts with a corresponding constituent of S_2. Both sentences exhibit the structure (3),

(3) [ ]$_{TOP}$ [ ]$_{+FIN}$ [ ]...[ ] [ ]$_{-FIN}$

where all non-verbal categories, including the topic, are arguments of the non-finite verb.

My assumption is that most of the interesting conditions on ellipsis in coordinate structures can readily be seen if we consider the possible deletions of the constituents in an example like (2), as well as deletions of the permuted constituents of (2). Moreover, if we need a contrast in the finite verb, we can replace the perfect auxiliary by a modal auxiliary (e.g. wollen vs. sollen 'will', 'must'). We'll arrive at interrogative structures if we have the topic empty. And if we want to have more structure in the constituents, we may introduce modifiers, etc.

Let us first consider four simple cases with gaps.

(4) a. In das Haus hat die Tante
[den Korb __ gelegt und den Sack __ geworfen].

b. Die Tante hat den Korb in das Haus gelegt
und der Onkel __ den Sack in den Hof __ .

c. Die Tante hat den Korb __
und der Onkel hat den Sack in den Hof geworfen.

d. Die Tante hat den Korb in das Haus gelegt
und __ den Sack __ .

In each sentence, the respective gap filling constituents have been underlined.

(4a) is an example of constituent coordination (X_1 und X_2, where X is a proper constituent of S), in this case of VP coordination. Any gap in X_1 must biuniquely correspond to a gap in X_2, and both gaps must be bound by one constituent of S (the topic of (4a)). This property of constituent coordination follows from the condition that coordinated phrases must be of the same category. In a movement analysis, this condition is specified as the condition of across-the-board rule application. In a GPSG analysis, it is specified by the condition that both phrases are heads of the coordinate structure with the same slash feature. In the following, I will restrict my considerations to those cases where an analysis as a constituent coordination is not possible.

(4b) is an example of gapping. If there is any position empty in S_2, then +FIN of S_2 must be empty, too. From this it follows that, on the surface, S_2 can consist of only a sequence of argument positions. But, since we have S-coordination, such a sequence must nevertheless syntactically constitute an S. Moreover, the gap-filling element cannot bind the gap here; and S_1 and S_2 cannot differ with respect to slash features. Figure (5a) vs. (5b) shows the difference between constituent coordination and gapping. The gap is illustrated by a white block, the gap filler by a black circle.

(5) a. Constituent coordination   b. Gapping

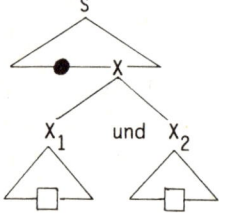
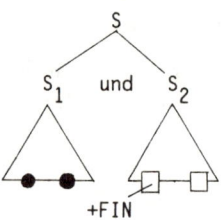

(4c) is an example of left deletion. In S_1, only the final sequence of constituents can be empty. Generally it is understood that this will be identical with the final sequence of constituents of S_2 (see (6a)), but it is also possible that the sequence of gap fillers is not final in S_2 (see (6b)).

(6) a. Max tritt für die große ___
   und Anna tritt für die kleine <u>Lösung</u> <u>ein</u>.
   ('Max prefers the big ___ and Anna prefers the small solution')

   b. Max tritt für die große ___
   und für die kleine <u>Lösung</u> tritt Anna <u>ein</u>.

Again, S_1 must syntactically be an S without any slash features, see figure (7a) below.

Finally, (4d) is an example of split coordination (in terms of Höhle 1983). In this case, <u>und</u> X_2 may be understood as an extraposed conjunct of a constituent coordination. It may also be considered an extreme case of gapping. As we shall see later, extraposed conjuncts seem to be possible in other circumstances too, but even there a gapping analysis is not excluded.

(7) a. Left deletion   b. Split coordination

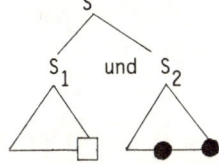 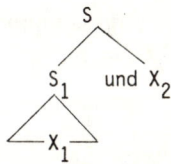

Gaps within constituent coordination (which always occur as twins) can be described by purely syntactic means. But this is not possible in the phenomena of gapping and left deletion. Here we must assume an underlying S_1 <u>and</u> S_2 coordination, where S_1 and S_2 must share the same syntactic features. We have two options at hand. Either we assume complete lexical insertion and then deletion of phonologically identical material by means of postlexical deletion rules. Or we assume incomplete lexical insertion and then reconstruction of the missing semantic material on the level of logical form (or semantics) by means of construal rules. The second option may be preferable. One argument in favor of it comes from the observation that left deletion can also affect word constituents (see (8)). It would be somewhat problematic if postlexical phonological rules were sensitive to word structure.

(8) Max liebt Herbst ___ und Anna liebt Frühlings<u>blumen</u>.
('Max prefers autumn ___ and Anna prefers spring flowers')

I will therefore assume the following:
  (i) Gaps due to gapping or left deletion are present as syntactic positions.
  (ii) These positions are not filled with lexical material, hence they can't contribute to the phonetic form.
  (iii) In the logical form of the dominating S, the semantic value of a gap of S_1 (S_2) is construed as identical with the semantic value of the corresponding gap filler of S_2 (S_1).
  (iv) Therefore, to each empty position in S_1 (S_2), there must correspond uniquely a non-empty position in S_2 (S_1).
  (v) In order to identify the empty and non-empty positions respectively, both S_1 and S_2 must have non-empty corresponding (contrastable) positions. (In a way, this conforms to the condition that both heads of a coordination must have identical syntactic features.)
  (vi) If S_1 and S_2 have a different order to the corresponding positions, the contrast must be marked by stress or special intonational means.

Clearly, the processing of gapping differs from that of left deletion. With respect to gapping, one has to copy the relevant features of the syntactic structure of S_1. (S_2 needs not be an exact copy of S_1 because the order of the elements can differ.) In a case of left deletion, however, it is S_1 that is phonetically incomplete. Therefore one has (i) to copy from S_1 the relevant features of its syntactic structure, and (ii) to copy from S_2 the additional features of the complete syntactic structure. Obviously, left deletion will be more easily processed, if exactly the right most sequence of constituents of S_2 is common to both S_1 and S_2 (see example (6a) from above).

Examples of gapping with a different order of constituents in S_1 and S_2 are presented in (9).

(9) Den Korb hat die Tante in das Haus gelegt

und $\begin{bmatrix} \text{in den Hof geworfen \_\_\_ der Onkel den Sack.} \\ \text{der Onkel \_\_\_ den Sack in den Hof \_\_\_.} \\ \text{den Sack \_\_\_ in den Hof der Onkel \_\_\_.} \end{bmatrix}$

But things are more complicated. (10) shows examples where both gapping and left deletion occur.

(10) In das Haus hat die Tante den Korb ___

und $\begin{bmatrix} \text{den Sack \_\_\_ in den Hof geworfen der Onkel.} \\ \text{der Onkel \_\_\_ den Sack in den Hof geworfen.} \\ \text{?in den Hof geworfen \_\_\_ der Onkel den Sack.} \end{bmatrix}$

Since it was not clear how gapping and left deletion are allowed to interact, I tried to find out by empirical generalization from the grammatical and ungrammatical coordinations, what restrictions have to be observed. These restrictions have to do with both the possibility of copying syntactic structure from S_1 or S_2 and the possibility of contruing a logical form for S. The restrictions I found out can be summarized as follows.[1]

(A) Every obligatory argument of a verb of S_1 or S_2 must be projectable onto S. (This condition follows from general principles of grammaticality, such as, e.g., the projection principle and the θ-criterion.)

(B) S_1 must have a non-empty initial sequence [ ]$_{TOP}$ [ ]$_{+FIN}$. (This gives the criterial features of a declarative sentence. It makes it possible to copy from S_1 some initial syntactic structure. In other words, left deletion is at most possible up to the finite verb.)

(C) If there is any position empty in S_2, then +FIN of S_2 must be empty, too. (This is exactly the condition of gapping. The finite verb, i.e. the bearer of the INFL category, can be considered the head of a sentence. There seems to be a structural condition to the effect that no gap filler from the left can control a gap in S_2 if +FIN is phonetically present, because +FIN defines the structurally closed domain of a sentence.)

---

[1] I do not intend to develop a theory of ellipsis here. The restrictions are found by empirical generalizations. The comments in brackets give some motivation, but clearly of different status. They are not meant as explanations.

(D) It must not be the case that both an argument position of S_1 and another argument position of S_2 are empty. (This turns out to the condition that the number of arguments must be read of from either S_1 or S_2. It seems that otherwise we won't be able to make the required copies in the processing of the coordinate structure.)

(E) An empty position of S_1 must not correspond to the topic position of S_2. (This means that you cannot topicalize something which has not been introduced in the relevant context. The relevant context of S_2 is here restricted to S_1.)

(F) If S_1 contains an empty position (by left deletion), then corresponding constituents of S_1 and S_2 must differ in their phonetic form or their referential value. (This means that left deletion requires strong contrast, maybe because the processing is more complex than in case of pure gapping.)[2]

The conditions (C) - (F) may be illustrated by some examples, which are clearly ungrammatical. It can easily be seen that they violate the respective condition.

ad (C):

(11) $\begin{bmatrix} \text{*Den Korb hat die Tante in das Haus gelegt} \\ \text{In das Haus gelegt hat die Tante den Korb} \end{bmatrix}$ und

$\begin{bmatrix} \text{der Onkel hat \_\_ in den Hof geworfen.} \\ \text{in den Hof hat \_\_ den Sack geworfen.} \\ \text{\_\_ hat der Onkel in den Hof \_\_} \\ \text{\_\_ hat der Onkel den Sack \_\_} \end{bmatrix}$

All combinations in (11) turn out to be grammatical if we drop <u>hat</u>, i.e. the finite verb in S_2. If, however, constituent coordination is possible, the finite verb in X_2 needs not be dropped. Consider (12).

(12) Den Korb [[hat die Tante __ in das Haus gelegt]
und [hat der Onkel __ in den Hof geworfen]]

---

[2] It may be the case that condition (F) must somehow be weakened, but this is not crucial to the following considerations.

ad (D):

(13) ⎡ *In das Haus gelegt hat die Tante __ ⎤
     ⎣ Den Korb hat die Tante __ ⎦

und __ den Sack in den Hof geworfen.

Here, in both S_1 and S_2 only two arguments of a 3-place verb are phonetically present. Though it might be possible, by purely semantic reasoning, to construe the missing argument from the other conjunct, the sentences are strictly ungrammatical. In case of the second combination of (13) there is, however, a possibly grammatical version, if und den Sack is realized by an intonationally marked parenthesis.

(14) Den Korb hat die Tante, und den Sack [%H], in den Hof geworfen.

In this case, und den Sack seems to be an extraposed or delayed constituent conjunct of den Korb. But even the gapping analysis is not fully excluded if we assume that the deletion of hat die Tante in S_2 results in the intonational boundary feature [%H].

Note that (15) is not a counterexample to condition (D).

(15) Den Korb hat die Tante in das Haus __
     und in den Hof __ den Sack geworfen.

Here, all 3 argument positions of S_1 are non-empty, though, of course, the verb is still missing.

ad (E):

(16) a. *Den Korb hat die Tante __
        und in den Hof hat der Onkel den Sack geworfen.

   b. *In das Haus gelegt hat die Tante __
        und den Sack hat der Onkel in den Hof geworfen.

   c. *In das Haus legen will __
        und den Sack soll der Onkel in den Hof werfen.

In all three examples the (underlined) topic of S_2 corresponds to an empty position of S_1.

ad (F):

(17) a. *Die Tante hat ___
und der Onkel hat den Sack in den Hof geworfen.

b. Die Tante will ___
und der Onkel soll den Sack in den Hof werfen.

(18) a. *Die Tante hat den Korb ___
und der Onkel ___ den Korb in den Hof geworfen.

b. Die Tante hat den Korb ___
und der Onkel ___ den Sack in den Hof geworfen.

(19) a. *Die Tante hat den Korb ___
und den Sack ___ die Tante in den Hof geworfen.

b. Die Tante hat den Korb ___
und den Sack ___ der Onkel in den Hof geworfen.

In (17a), the perfect auxiliary cannot be strongly contrastive but the modals in (17b) can. (18a) and (19a) are grammatical only if the determiners receive contrastive stress, meaning that you have to look for different referential values.

The most important point I want to stress in this section concerns the phenomenon of SGF-coordination illustrated by ex. (1) at the very beginning. It does not fit with conditions (A) - (F). More exactly, sentences such as (20) are perfectly grammatical but violate condition (C), which is otherwise strictly observed and also quite well motivated.

(20) ⎡ Den Korb hat die Tante in das Haus gelegt ⎤
⎢ In das Haus hat die Tante den Korb gelegt ⎥
⎣ In das Haus gelegt hat die Tante den Korb ⎦

und ___ hat dann den Sack in den Hof geworfen.

Here, S_2 has a finite verb but its subject is empty, so S_2 turns out in fact to be a VP. As far as I can see, examples of this kind are the only exceptions to conditions (A) - (F). We may add an additional clause to condition (C):

(C') If there is any position empty in S_2, then +FIN of S_2 must be empty too, unless S_2 is, on the surface, identical with VP.

But such a clause is completely unmotivated within a theory of ellipsis. Moreover, it won't suffice. It does not yet exclude the otherwise possible interaction with left deletion. But note that sentences such as (21) are ungrammatical.

(21) ⎡*Den Korb hat die Tante in das Haus __ ⎤
     ⎣ In das Haus hat die Tante den Korb __ ⎦

und __ hat dann den Sack in den Hof geworfen.

Therefore, we have good reasons to look for another solution to the phenomenon of SGF-coordination. It must be a base-generated phenomenon.

3. SGF-COORDINATION IN PROPOSALS OF THE CHOMSKY TRADITION

In the following, I consider the phenomenon of SGF-coordination as base generated. In this section, an analysis is looked for within the standard assumptions of the Chomsky tradition in dealing with German syntax.

Let us return to example (1) at the beginning.

(1) In den Wald ging der Jäger und fing einen Hasen.
    ('Into the forest went the hunter and caught a hare')

At least four things have to be explained:
  (i) The first conjunct has a topic which is an argument of the first verb (ging) but not the second one (fing), whereas the second conjunct has no topic (and, as we can add now, the lack of a topic is not a case of ellipsis).
  (ii) In both conjuncts, the finite verb is fronted.

(iii) The first conjunct has a subject, which is shared by both finite verbs.

(iv) The first conjunct is a complete sentence, whereas the second one is a VP.

According to the extended projection principle, every clause has to have a subject. The second conjunct might then, on the level of D-structure, be assigned the structure

(22) und [$_S$ [$_{NP}$ e] [$_{VP}$ einen Hasen fing]]

I assume that the basic word order in German is verb final.) The empty NP cannot be PRO, because PRO must be ungoverned, whereas in a tensed clause such as (22) it wold be governed by INFL (according to the principles of government and binding theory). Therefore the empty NP can only be a trace. (In German, we need not consider the possibility of 'pro' in this environment.) An NP trace must be an anaphora which is bound by an NP in an argument position. However the empty category in (22) is not bound in its minimal governing category. The final possibility is that the empty category in (22) is a wh-trace. However, the potential binder is in an argument position, and wh-traces must be bound by an element in a non-argument position.

Although we failed in the first attempt to provide an adequate representation of the empty subject-NP, there might be another solution. One may, e.g., explore whether (1) can be traced back to an underlying VP coordination. In any case, the interaction with finite verb movement in German has to be taken into account. The D-structure of a declarative sentence must prepare for a landing site of the finite verb. According to the most general accepted analysis of German (see, e.g. Thiersch 1978), the underlying structure of a declarative sentence is roughly the following:

(23)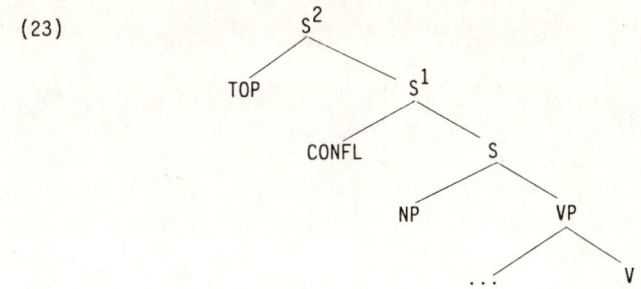

CONFL is either occupied by a lexical complementizer or it is designated as the landing site for the finite verb (the INFL category). With respect to this analysis, we may assume for sentence (1) an underlying coordination of S^2, or S^1, or S, or VP. None of these assumptions will work, however.
  (i) Assume underlying S^2 coordination. Then we could not explain why in the 2nd conjunct of (1), both TOP and the subject NP are empty.
  (ii) Assume underlying S^1 coordination. Again, we could not explain why the subject of the 2nd conjunct is empty. Moreover, topicalization would have to apply only to the 1st conjunct, which violates the principle of across-the-board application of rules (ATB principle).
  (iii) Assume underlying S coordination. Then both topicalization and FIN-fronting would violate the ATB principle; and we could not explain why the subject of the 2nd conjunct is empty and its finite verb is fronted.
  (iv) Assume underlying VP coordination. Again, the ATB principle would be violated, and FIN-fronting in the 2nd conjunct would remain mysterious.
The results won't be better if we take as basis, instead of (23), an analysis such as (24) (see Travis 1984).

(24)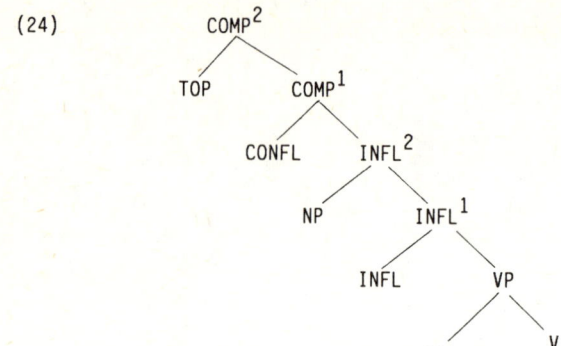

Let us assume an underlying $INFL^1$ coordination for (1). In this case, INFL would be a landing site for the finite verb in the 2nd conjunct, and NP would represent the position for the shared subject. But again, the ATB principle would be violated, since TOP and CONFL could only be filled from constituents of the 1st conjunct.

In the course of this wild-goose chase, the reader may have noted that we have run from a wrong starting-point. Sentence (1) is not an instance of regular coordination. Its structure may simply be this:

(25)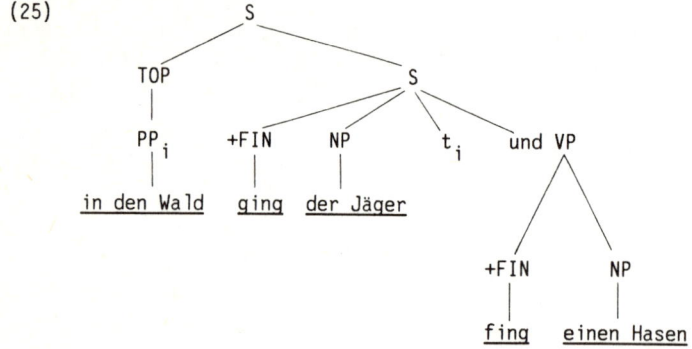

In this case, topicalization would not violate the ATB principle. The common subject c-commands both finite verbs. It is not clear, however, how the +FIN-fronting comes about.

With respect to the last point, a proposal might be made within the analysis (24). Let us assume (26) as the underlying structure of (1).

(26)

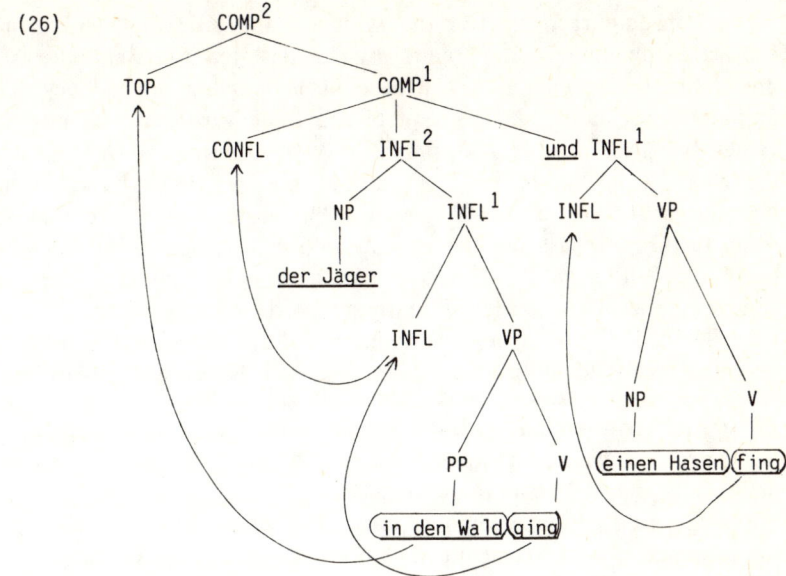

We may argue that +FIN-fronting can consist of two movements, one into INFL (which happens in both conjuncts) and another one into CONFL (which happens in the 1st conjunct only). And we may also argue that the ATB principle is not affected because there is no regular coordination; note that $INFL^2$ and $INFL^1$ are different categories. However, it is not quite clear why just $COMP^1$ consists of three constituents. This can only be stipulated. In any case, (26) must be ruled out because the shared subject does not c-command the verb of the 2nd conjunct. Therefore, the subject-verb agreement cannot be explained.

In summarizing this section, it seems that the Chomsky tradition does not look very happy in offering a solution to the problem posed here. A particular problematic point is the assumption of verb movement in German.

4. SGF-COORDINATION IN GPSG

Generalized phrase structure theory does not assume a movement rule. Extraction phenomena are treated by the slash-feature. But finite verb movement in German is not a case of unbounded dependency. The parameter regulating the position of the finite verb occupies just two values: being the head of a V^1, the finite verb has either the right-most or the left-most position in that V^1. The right-most position is basic because it is the position of a non-finite verb.[3] Therefore, we have to look for some feature of the syntactic configuration which triggers the left-most position. Within the Chomsky tradition, the position of the complementizer is considered to trigger verb fronting when it is not lexically filled. According to the grammar tradition of German, a sentence in which a complementizer is present is called 'Nebensatz' (subordinate clause). A sentence in which it is not present (and therefore verb fronting occurs) is called 'Hauptsatz' (main clause). The presence or absence of the complementizer turns out to have essential positional effects on the finite verb. At the same time, it relates the sentence semantically to a host sentence if lexically filled. Therefore, if we use a syntactic feature SC (for 'subordinate clause'), this will satisfy the expectation that the presence of a complementizer has both a specific syntactic effect and a specific interpretation. This does not exclude the possibility that there are clauses in German with [-SC] (i.e. main clause properties) which are semantically dependent.

Another property of German is the relatively free order of arguments. There is no fixed position of the subject-NP. GPSG allows flat V^n structures where the subject is sister of V^0. Such a flat structure can be induced by the application of a metarule. (In a head-driven PSG the metarule could be replaced by a lexical rule which rearranges the subcategorization frame.)

Along this line of reasoning, a GPSG analysis of German can easily represent a structure such as (25) with the required properties. We use the apparatus outlined in the work of Russell (1983) and Uszkoreit (1984).

---

[3] The non-finite verb does not interact with INFL (or agreement features). Therefore, it exhibits the most neutral word order of a a language. There are, however, more reasons why in German the right-most position of the verb is considered as basic.

(27) **ID rules**

    a. VP -> H^0 [i], ...   rule schema for verb subcategorization
    b. V^n -> XP, H^n/XP   topicalization
       +TOP -SC

metarule

    c. VP -> W ==> V^n -> NP , W
                     -SC   NOM

FC rule

    d. -SC -> +FIN

LP rules

    e. + TOP < X
    f. X < V
        +SC
    g. V < X
       -SC

H stands for the head category. Russell uses the feature [+INVERTED] instead of [-SC], Uszkoreit uses the feature [+MAIN CLAUSE].

In order to derive (25) we have to extend the metarule (27c) to the effect that VP adjunction is possible. One may hesitate to consider the possibility of a conjunct <u>und</u> VP as part of the extended subcategorization frame of the verb. The function of the metarule (27c) is, however, to introduce the subject into the extended frame. And the subject of a sentence with SGF-coordination obviously serves two functions: it must c-command two different finite verbs; in terms of GPSG, it must be the agreement target of both these verbs. The proposal is to replace (27c) by the metarule (28).

(28) VP -> W ==> V_n -> NP , W, $\begin{pmatrix} HP \\ CONJ\ \alpha_2 \end{pmatrix}$
                    -SC   NOM

The rules (27)(28) accept sentence (1) at the beginning with the following structure.[4]

(29)

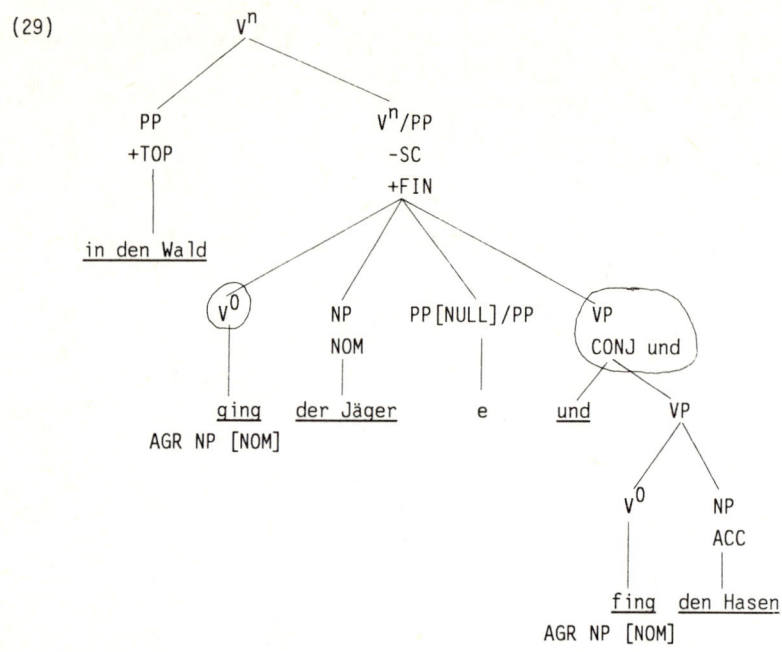

An important feature of this solution is that the V^n minus topic is biheaded. (In (29), the heads are encircled.) Therefore, both verbs are automatically marked as [-SC, +FIN], which means that they must both be finite and be fronted within the local structure they occur in. The Control Agreement Principle (GKPS: 89) guarantees that both verbs will find their agreement target in NP[NOM], the shared subject. Both heads of V^n/XP must have the same inherited features. Since the lexical head cannot be slashed (GKPS: 143), the same holds for the non-lexical head. Therefore, the slash-feature must be terminated in the local tree

---

[4] As a result of a rule such as (28) the V^n structure is somewhat flattened. But this does not mean that every structure in the so-called Mittelfeld of the German sentence is depressed. E.g., dependent VPs are still dependent. The arguments from coordination and topicalization in German are not convincing enough to assume a strong hierarchical structure of the Mittelfeld. On the contrary, they leave us with many conflicting structures. This is not the place to discuss this in detail. A flat structure such as (29) allows, however, to explain all the properties of the SGF-phenomenon we want to have explained.

dominated by V^n/XP, which means that only an argument (or a free adjunct) of the first verb can be left empty (topicalized, in this case).[5]

The output of rule (28) does not conform with the coordination schema (GKPS: 171). But if we rewrite it in the form of (30), it seems to be an instance of a generalized coordination schema.

(30) V^n -> V^0 , ..., VP
            $CONJ\alpha_1$ $CONJ\alpha_2$ where α_1 = NIL

Note that neither BAR nor CONJ are head features. This means that the two heads can differ with respect to their bar-level and in the value of the conjunction. The order of the constituents in the output of (30) is

---

[5] This explanation conflicts with the explanation of GKPS (176f.) regarding examples such as

(i) What did she go and buy?

GKPS assume a V and VP-coordination which resembles the SGF-coordination in German. They say that a SLASH-feature of the mother VP must be instantiated on the VP daughter only, because the V is lexical, and that this were required by the Head Feature Convention (HFC). I rather think that the HFC rules out a two-headed structure where a head feature is instantiated on just one daughter. A violation of the HFC in a case like this may possibly be tolerated, if no other daughter is present. In the German case, however, there are more daughters present, and the HFC in its strict form predicts then that we cannot extract from the VP head, if the other head is lexical.

Moreover, I guess that the English examples can be dealt with alternatively. Note that examples such as (ii) and (iii) are ungrammatical.

(ii) *what did she go or buy?

(iii) *what did she laugh and buy?

So extraction is heavily restricted. The first verb is restricted to very few verbs of motion, and the conjunction must be and. A sentence such as (i) seems to involve a complex verb go and buy which takes over the subcategorization of buy. Some complex verb rule of the following kind is needed.

(iv) VP -> H, W = = > VP -> go, H [CONJ and], W

Sentence (i) will then be accepted in the structure (v).

(v) VP / NP
    go
    buy [CONJ and]
    NP [+NULL]

regulated by the LP rule (31).

(31) $X < \text{CONJ}\alpha_2$

From (30) we get the prediction that SGF-coordination should also be possible with other values of α_2. The conjunction values in a two-place coordination of German are listed in (32).

(32) $\alpha = \{$<NIL, oder>, <NIL, aber>, <NIL, sondern>,
<weder, noch>, <sowohl, als auch>, <NIL, und>$\}$

In fact, we do find SGF-coordination in all cases where $\alpha_1 = $ NIL.

(33) a. In den Wald ging der Jäger oder setzte sich ins Wirtshaus.
('Into the forest went the hunter or placed himself into the inn')

b. In den Wald ging der Jäger, aber fing nichts.
('... but caught nothing')

c. Nicht in den Wald ging der Jäger, sondern setzte sich ins Wirtshaus.
('Not into the forest went the hunter but placed himself into the inn')

Another aspect of my analysis is that we cannot have iterative coordination. What we can have is a coordination within the 2nd conjunct.

(34) a. In den Wald ging der Jäger(und) fing einen Hasen oder jagte ein Wildschwein.
('... (and) caught a hare or hunted a wild boar')

b. In den Wald ging der Jäger (und) jagte einen Hasen, aber fing ihn nicht.
('... (and) hunted a hare but didn't catch it')

c. Einen Hasen verfolgte der Jäger (und/oder) fing ein Wildschwein oder erlegte einen Maulwurf.
('A hare pursued the hunter (and/or) caught a wild boar or killed a mole')

These sentences get the interpretation "(p conj (q conj r))" but not "(p conj q conj r)" or "((p conj q) conj r)", even if und or oder are missing. It is not clear to me why und or oder can be dropped, perhaps because of the interaction of two CONJ values in the structure [und [NIL VP oder VP]]. Another open problem concerns sentences such as (35).

(35) In den Wald ging der Jäger (und) fing weder einen Hasen, noch jagte er ein Wildschwein.
('... (and) neither caught a hare nor hunted he (sic!) a wild boar')

Note that the last conjunct contains a subject. Weder ... noch ('neither ... nor') exhibit more syntactic peculiarities than other conjunctions, which may be the source of this pecularity as well.

The only head feature introduced by (28) is the feature [-SC]. No mention has been made of a declarative sentence (assertion clause). Therefore we would expect that other types of [-SC] clauses will be subject to SGF-coordination as well. Höhle (1983) cites a lot of examples which convincingly show this. (Examples (36) are taken from Höhle.)

(36) a. Wann hat jemand einen Einfall und sagt uns die Lösung?
('When has somebody an inspiration and tells us the solution?')
[wh question]

b. Stehen da schon wieder welche rum und verteilen Flugblätter?
('Are standing there yet again some people and distribute leaflets?')
[yes-no question]

c. Gehen Sie lieber nach Hause und bringen Ihre Angelegenheiten in Ordnung!
('Go you better home and put your matters right')
[imperative]

d. Nimmt man den Deckel ab und rührt die Füllung um, (steigen übelriechende Dämpfe auf).
('(If) one takes the lid off and stirs the contents, (evil smelling fumes rise)')
[conditional clause].

Höhle (1983) summarizes the properties of SGF-coordination as follows.
  (i) <u>Weder</u> - <u>noch</u> and <u>sowohl</u> - <u>als auch</u> are not possible.
  (ii) In the second conjunct, no constituent can be deleted.
  (iii) The second conjunct cannot contain a trace.
  (iv) In the first 'conjunct', left deletion is not possible.
  (v) An adverbial in the first 'conjunct' can extend its scope to the second conjunct.
  (vi) The conjuncts will be interpreted as being merged, i.e. as standing in a natural connection.
  (vii) Sentences such as (37) are ungrammatical.

(37) a. *Ich hoffe, daß uns keiner sieht und zeigt uns an.
     (lit. 'I hope that us nobody sees and reports us')

   b. *Hoffentlich sieht uns keiner und uns anzeigt.
     (lit. 'Hopefully sees us nobody and us reports')

All these properties are explained by the analysis outlined here.
  ad (i) It lies in the nature of rule (28) that α_1 is restricted to NIL.

  ad (ii) Ellipsis or gapping presupposes the possibility of contrast between identical structures, it is therefore restricted to instances of the regular coordination schema.

  ad (iii) It has been shown that the 2nd conjunct cannot contain a subject trace. It cannot contain another trace, either, because a slash must be terminated in the local structure with both a lexical and a non-lexical head. Therefore, the empty position must be a sister of the 2nd conjunct.

  ad (iv) The same reason as in (ii).

  ad (v) This point has not yet been discussed. It has primarily to do with mapping onto logical form. Let us assume that an adverbial must c-command its scope. Then indeed the 2nd conjunct can belong to its scope.

  ad (vi) The 'merging' interpretation follows from the fact that the coordination predicates share the same subject.

ad (vii) Both finite verbs must be fronted, because they inherit the [-SC] feature from V^n.

Evidence has been given that in the SGF-coordination, a genuine VP is coordinated. If this is so, then SGF-coordination can be used as a test for VP in German. In circles of GB-orientated linguists the question has been raised whether the so-called 'ergative' verbs (obviously a misnomer: verbs without an agentive argument) subcategorize their surface subject as an internal argument. So we find the assumption that on the level of D-structure, the structure of a clause with <u>gefallen</u> ('like, please ') or with a passive verb should look like this:[6]

(38) a. weil [$_S$ e [$_{VP}$ dem^{DAT} Jungen die^{NOM} Rosen gefielen]]
('because the boy liked the roses' or 'because the roses pleased the boy')

b. weil [$_S$ dem Jungen [$_{VP}$ die Rosen gefielen]]

c. weil [$_S$ e [$_{VP}$ ihr^{DAT} das Fahrrad^{NOM} geklaut wurde]]
(lit. 'because from her the bike was stolen')

Now consider the following sentences.

(39) a. *Das Essen hat ihr geschmeckt und haben (ihm) die Rosen gefallen.
(lit. 'The food has tasted good to her and have (him) the roses pleased')

b. Auf dem Tisch standen Rosen und haben ihm gefallen.
(lit. 'On the table stood roses and have pleased him')

---

[6] Proponents of the 'ergativity' hypothesis claim that these verbs form a constituent together with their subject as well as transitive verbs do together with their object. It is, however, always an extracted constituent (e.g. in topic position), and there is no way to prove that it is a VP. In a movement analysis, we are indeed confronted with conflicting evidence. Generally, a verb can form a topic together with one or more of its arguments, but agentive subjects are always excluded. It seems that some semantically driven restructuring is at work. However, I cannot discuss this here in detail.

c. *Ein Fahrrad schenkte man ihm und wurde (ihr) dann das Fahrrad geklaut.
(lit. 'A bike one presented to him and was (from her) then the bike stolen')

d. Ihm wurde ein Fahrrad geschenkt und wurde ihr dann geklaut.
(lit. 'To him a bike was presented and was then stolen from her')

Both (38a) and (38b) are ruled out by the ungrammaticality of (39a). If there were no underlying subject according to (38a), then (39b) should be ungrammatical. But in fact, it turns out to be grammatical. It follows that the NP in the NOM case must be the subject. And even in the D-structure this NP must be outside of VP because the 2nd conjunct of (39b) cannot contain a trace. The same argument applies to the passive analysis of (38c). The ungrammaticality of (39c) shows that <u>ihr das Fahrrad geklaut wurde</u> cannot be a VP, whereas (39d) confirms that <u>ihr geklaut wurde</u> is a VP which cannot contain a trace.

5. AN UNSOLVED PROBLEM OF COORDINATION

There is a type of coordinate clauses in German which, on the first view, is quite similar to the SGF-coordination. It may be illustrated by (40).

(40) Wenn [wir in ein Kaufhaus <u>kommen</u>] [und <u>haben</u> kein Geld dabei], können wir nichts kaufen.
('If we into a department store come and have no money with us, we can buy nothing')

The two bracketed parts of (40) belong to the scope of the conditional complementizer <u>wenn</u>: first a subordinate clause V^n with the finite verb final, and second a VP conjunct with the finite verb fronted. (The finite verbs are underlined.) The shared subject is <u>wir</u>.

Höhle (personal communication) has suggested that (40) be an instance of the SGF-coordination. The second conjunct is indeed structurally identical with the VP conjunct in the SGF cases. The analysis I presented in the preceding section ,however, excludes (40) as a case of SGF-coordination. This analysis would require a bi-headed structure where the

two finite verbs are fronted. But in (40) the position parameter of +FIN is realized differently.
(40) might be a particular variant of (41),

(41) Wenn [*wir* in ein Kaufhaus <u>kommen</u>] [und *wir* <u>haben</u> kein Geld dabei] , ...

where the two conjuncts have a subject (italics in (41)), though again the position of +FIN (which is underlined) differs. One can show that in cases where a coordination like (41) is not possible, for semantical reasons, (see (42a)), a coordination like (40) is excluded as well (see (42b)), whereas SGF-coordination is fine (see (42c)).

(42) a. *Wenn uns *keiner* willkommen <u>heißt</u> und *er* <u>schließt</u> uns in die Arme, ...
('If nobody welcomes us and he embraces us, ...')

b. *Wenn uns *keiner* willkommen <u>heißt</u> und <u>schließt</u> uns in die Arme, ...

c. Uns <u>heißt</u> *keiner* willkommen und <u>schließt</u> uns in die Arme.

(<u>Keiner</u> ('nobody') cannot be the antecedent of <u>er</u> ('he').) This example makes the attempt to consider the VP conjunct in (40) as a case of SGF-coordination highly implausible.

Regarding (40) and (41), we have a further variant (43), which causes no problem, because here both finite verbs are final.

(43) Wenn wir in ein Kaufhaus <u>kommen</u> und kein Geld dabei <u>haben</u>, ...

Alongside with variants of the kind (43), coordination similar to (41) with different subjects is quite natural in German.

(44) Wenn wir in ein Kaufhaus <u>kommen</u> und niemand <u>hat</u> Geld dabei, ...
('... and nobody has money with them, ...')

This kind of coordination is also possible with the temporal complementizer <u>als</u> und <u>nachdem</u> ('when, after'), the concessive <u>obwohl</u> ('although'), and maybe more. It is only possible with the conjunctions und and aber ('and, but').[7]

The problem is that the two conjuncts are in the scope of the complementizer but differ in the position of the finite verb. They cannot be heads of a coordinate structure, because they realize different values of the SC-feature: The first conjunct is [+SC], whereas the second one is [-SC]. Moreover, the second conjunct involves topicalization, which is a property of assertion clauses [+AC]. ([+AC] implies [-SC].)

This particular property of clauses in the scope of complementizers such as wenn, als etc. seems to be a lexical property of these complementizers. But this is not always the case, as demonstrated by (45), where no complementizer is present.

(45) Kommen wir in ein Kaufhaus und niemand hat Geld dabei, ...

Here, the two clauses differ with respect to topicalization (or the AC-feature). Note that the fronted finite verb in the first conjunct serves here as a marker of a conditional clause. The conditional antecedent is, however, constituted by both of the conjuncts.

With regard to clauses of the kind (44), we may consider the complementizer as the head of the adverbial. (44) can then be represented by the ID-rule (46).

$$(46)\ \text{COMP}^1 \rightarrow H^0, \begin{array}{c} V^n \\ +SC \\ +FIN \end{array}, \left(\begin{array}{c} V^n \\ \text{CONJ } \alpha_2 \\ +AC \end{array} \right)$$

where α_2 = { und, aber }

The V^n clauses are not heads, therefore they need not have identical syntactic features. Since they are sisters of the complementizer, both of them fall in its scope.

In a clause such as (45), the complementizer is, however, replaced by the finite verb. Here we may assume a metarule quite similar to (28) in section 4.

---

[7] Höhle (personal communication) also cites examples with sondern and oder, which are rather odd in my view. It seems to me that Höhle is maximally tolerant in his grammaticality judgments. But nothing would change in principle if Höhle were right.

(47) VP -> W ==> V^n -> NP , W, $\begin{pmatrix} V^n \\ CONJ\ \alpha_2 \\ +AC \end{pmatrix}$
         -SC   NOM

where α_2 = { und, aber }

The difference to (28) is, that in (47), the V^n conjunct cannot be a head, because it is a complete assertion clause. Therefore, (47) seems not so well motivated. We should expect from (47) that, besides conditional clauses of the kind (45), other types of [-SC] clauses should display the described property as well. Höhle (personal communication) gives some evidence for this, though I am myself not so sure about his observations. (48) would be an interrogative with the described property, but it seems somewhat odd.

(48) Gehst du ins Büro und Max nimmt die Akten mit?
('Are you going into the office and Max takes the papers with him?')

Most problematic are clauses of the kind (40) found at the beginning of this section. The VP conjunct can neither be a result of gapping nor contain an empty subject. An analysis in the general spirit of this section would have to claim a structure such as (49).

(49)

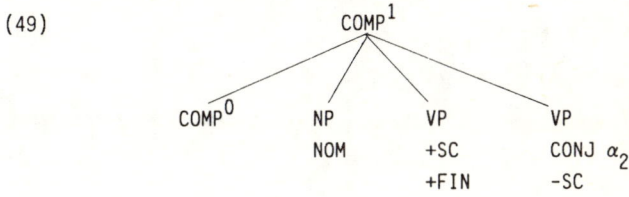

where α_2 = { und, aber }

Here, the complementizer is the only head. The shared subject c-commands the two VPs such that they will find their agreement target. So far the structure (49) may be alright. But if we compare (49) with the ID-rule (46), we will see that (49) claims something what we do not want to claim. In (46), the V^n conjunct is an optional constituent in a rule which we need independently. (A complementizer is subcategorized for a clause with a final finite verb, and some allow an additional conjunct.) In contrast, if we omit the VP conjunct from (49), we derive quite a strange structure. However, I have no solution to this problem.

Let me summarize. Evidence has been given in this paper that coordination outside of the generally assumed coordination schema is possible. The first part of the coordinate structure is a flat-structure with a lexical head to which a VP conjunct or an assertion clause conjunct can be added. In the so-called SGF-coordination, the conjunct is a second head, wheras in the various cases of coordination I considered in this section, the conjunct is a non-head. It is, however, still unclear to me what a general theory of coordination can do with these observations.

LITERATURE

Chomsky, Noam (1981) *Lectures on Government and Binding*. Dordrecht: Foris.
Gazdar, Gerald; Ewan Klein, Geoffrey Pullum, and Ivan Sag [GKPS](1985) *Generalized Phrase Structure Grammar*. Oxford: Basil Blackwell.
Höhle, Tilman (1983) *Subjektlücken in Koordinationen*. Unpublished Ms. Tübingen.
Russell, Graham (1983) *Compound Verbs and Constituent Order in German*. Unpublished Ms. Sussex.
Thiersch, Craig (1978) *Topics in German Syntax*. Ph.D.dissertation, MIT.
Travis, Lisa (1984) *Parameters and Effects of Word Order Variation*. Ph.D. dissertation, MIT.
Uszkoreit, Hans (1984) *Word Order and Constituent Structure in German*. Ph.D. dissertation, University of Texas at Austin.

GISBERT FANSELOW

LEHRSTUHL FÜR ALLGEMEINE SPRACHWISSENSCHAFT

UNIVERSITÄT PASSAU

GERMAN WORD ORDER AND UNIVERSAL GRAMMAR

0. INTRODUCTION AND OVERVIEW[*]

Within early generative grammar as developed in the sixties, grammatical rules and principles were exclusively formulated in terms of constituent structure, and there was no reference at all to grammatical functions like subject and objects, these terms being defined as the NP immediately dominated by S and VP, respectively (cf. e.g. Chomsky 1965). This fundamental claim of early generative grammar had some important implications for the linear ordering of constituents and words, because tangled trees were banned. Consequently, the theory made the prediction that the sequence "Object-Subject-Verb" could not show up, at least as a base structure, as no element which is not dominated by the VP can be positioned between two constituents of the VP. Linguists were very well aware of the existence of languages showing a considerable degree of freeness of constituent order, that are nowadays called non-configurational, like Japanese, Turkish, Warlpiri, Hungarian or German. For these languages, a special transformational device was invented, viz. the well-known scrambling rule permuting the elements of a fixed base

---

[*] With minor revision, this paper contains the major ideas of the paper I read at the Friedenweiler conference. A more elaborate treatment, dealing with more language and formulated in terms of the "barriers"- framework, is developed in Fanselow (1986f). I would like to thank the participants of the Friedenweiler conference and the audience of a talk I gave on a similar topic at the Max Planck Institute for Psycholinguistics at Nijmegen for helpful comments and valuable suggestions. In particular, I am indebted to Sascha Felix and Peter Staudacher. Thanks also go to Jane Garrett and Craig Mabrey for checking my English, and to Luise Haller for typing.

word order in some random fashion, or governed by thematic or other non-grammatical regularities. The most outstanding property of this treatment of free word order is its claim that there is no connection at all between grammar and linear order in non-configurational languages.

It is quite interesting to see that most modern approaches to word order phenomena share the latter property. McCawley (1982) and Falk (1983) proposed a redefinition of the notion "tree structure", taking apart the relations of "domination" and "linear precedence". Grammar is formulated in terms of the hierarchical dominance relations, and word order may be completely independent of these hierarchical configurations. Within Lexical Functional Grammar (cf. Bresnan 1982), most grammatical processes are either handled in the lexicon or in the so-called f-structure representing the assignment of undefined grammatical functions to the items in constituent structure. Some languages may spell out these grammatical functions in terms of configurational structures, while others do this using overt case marking, and for the latter there are no predictions at all about the linear arrangements of the various phrases of a sentence. Thus, again, the theory of grammar does not embody any claim about a connection between grammatical phenomena and word order.

Similar things could be said about other approaches to non-configurationality, like the ones developed by Hale (1983), Haider (1983), and Sternefeld (1984). There are, then, two assumptions shared by all these theories: that grammatical rules cannot be formulated in a fashion that explicitly or implicitly makes reference to facts about linear order and that linear order either is totally free in non-configurational languages, or constrained by extragrammatical principles only.

The theory of Government and Binding (Chomsky 1981, 1982, 1986a), however, does not share these claims. The basic notion of grammar is the relation of c-command, which plays a role in the definition of notions like binding or government, and thus functions as the fundament of the theory of Universal Grammar. Word order within maximal projections is not constrained by the X-bar-scheme itself, but other subtheories or principles of Universal Grammar may impose certain restrictions, as e.g. the parameter of the direction of government and case assigment, which requires all complements to appear on the right hand side of the verb in English, and on the left hand side in German. Elements from different maximal projections may not be mixed up, however, which again implies that the subject, being the specifier of the INFL-phrase IP, cannot appear between the verb and the object at least in base structure. Surface serializations like OSV must, therefore, have been derived by the rule of Move α, with a trace left in the pre-movement position. A German sentence like (1) therefore is assumed to have the structure given in (2):

(1) weil   den Mann niemand   mag
    because the$_{acc}$ man nobody$_{nom}$ likes
    "because nobody likes the man"

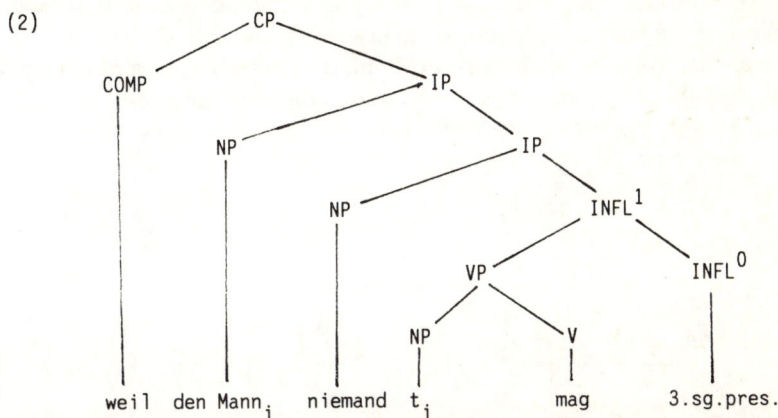

In this paper I want to argue for the viability of the approach of the theory of Government and Binding, showing that the non-grammatical approach to word order held by LFG or the other theories mentioned above is basically incorrect. As far as I can see, with a minimal change in the definition of variables, the apparently thematical restrictions in at least one free-word-order-language (namely German) follow from independently motivated principles of this theory, while they would have to be stipulated in some ad-hoc fashion in LFG or the other approaches.

The paper is organized as follows. In section 1 I will present the basic facts about German word order, and will develop a preliminary treatment in terms of a movement rule. Section 2 will investigate the properties of this rule more closely, showing that its domain of application is determined by the nature of the trace that is left in place. Section 3 introduces a minimal change in the definition of empty categories and will demonstrate that all the properties of the German re-ordering processes are direct consequences of principles of Universal Grammar. Section 4 is devoted to the treatment of some apparent counterexamples, whereas in section 5 I try to investigate the possible consequences of our findings for German, for the analysis of free-word-order-languages in general.

1. SOME BASIC FACTS ABOUT GERMAN WORD ORDER

The German language is, in fact, a good example for the (descriptive) category of non-configurationality, in that it not only shows freeness of constituent order, but also the rest of the syntactic properties that are normally seen in connection with non-configurationality (see Hale 1983 and Haider 1983, 1984, 1987):

a) *A rich system of case marking*
All the four morphologically distinct cases of German can be used for object marking.

b) *Discontinuous constituents*
They show up in constructions like the ones given in (3), which are dealt in some detail in Fanselow (1986a,f) and Haider (1987).

(3) Politiker   kenne ich nur   korrupte
politicians know I   only corrupts
"I know only corrupt politicians"

c) *No expletive subjects*
There are two types of expletive expressions: those that bear a quasi-theta-role in the sense of Chomsky (1981) (the wheather-*it*, e.g.) (4a) and those which lack thematic roles in an absolute sense (4b). While expletive subjects are necessary in those contexts where a quasi-theta-role has to be assigned, they may or must be absent in all other cases, e.g. in impersonal passive constructions, constructions with extraposed subjects etc. (cf. Pütz 1974).

(4a) weil es regnet
   because it rains

(4b) weil getanzt wird
   because danced is
   "because people are dancing"

(4c) *weil es getanzt wird
   because it danced is

d) *No movement on NP-type dependencies*
   The constructions *raising to subject* and *passive* do not involve movement processes in German, cf. Thiersch (1978); we will return to this point below.

e) *Freeness of word order*

f) *No apparent ECP-effects*
   Although German is not a pro-drop-language, it is possible to extract subjects from embedded clauses in German even if these are introduced by "daß", "that" or some other complementizer.

(5) wer$_i$ glaubst du daß t$_i$ die Wahlen gewinnen wird?
   who think you that the elections win will
   "who do you think will win the elections ?"

g) *Free drop of pronouns*
   Some of the non-configurational languages, e.g. Hungarian, allow for a free drop of pronouns, i.e. neither subject nor object pronouns have to show up in structures like (6):

(6) szeretlek
   love 1.sg.2.sg.
   "I love you"

This criterion for non-configurationality, however, is the most problematic one in Hale's list. First, there are a number of non-configurational languages like Latin which do not allow for constructions like (6), on the other hand, some clearly configurational ones like Chinese do. Two main processes seem to be responsible for the option of zero object pronouns. Languages like Hungarian (Horvath 1981) or Warlpiri (Jelinek 1984) have a system of inflection for objects and subjects, thus the free drop of object pronouns may be reducible to the so-called pro-drop-parameter of Chomsky (1981), cf. Fanselow (1986c). Huang (1985) has demonstrated, on the other hand, that there is no real "pronoun drop" in languages like Japanese or Brazilian Portuguese. Rather, the apparent lack of object pronouns is due to some general rule of deletion of topic phrases, which is applicable in German as well, cf. (7):

(7) hab ich schon   gesehen
    have I already seen
    "I have already seen it"

Thus, freeness of constituent order is in correlation with all the other crucial properties of non-configurational languages in German. But it is necessary to clarify the claim that German is a free-word-order-language.

As it is well known, there are two positional requirements that must be met by the finite verb in German. In subordinate clauses, the finite verb must occupy the final position, whereas it has to appear as the second constituent in main clauses, with all other non-finite verbal elements of the clause still being in sentence-final position:

(8a) (ich glaube), daß Hans das Buch lesen wird
     I believe   that Hans the book read will
     "I believe that Hans will read the book"

(8b) Hans wird das Buch lesen
     Hans will the book read
     "Hans will read the book"

There is some agreement among generative grammarians working on German that the final position of the verb is basic, i.e. to be generated by the X-bar-rule (cf. e.g. Koster 1975 or Thiersch 1978). In main clauses, the finite verb is moved into some COMP/INFL position, with a subsequent movement of some element from the sentence into the specifier-position of S' or CP[1], i.e. a German main clause will have the structure given in (9)[2]:

(9)
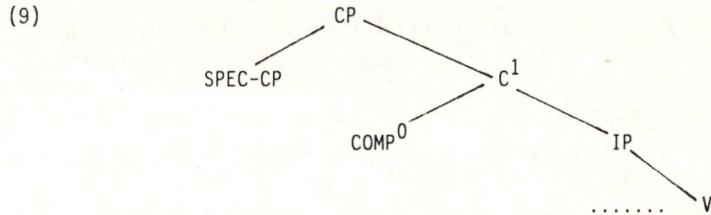

Movement to SPEC-CP is a subcase of *wh*-movement, insofar as it is a long distance phenomenon, but subject to the typical island constraints in general (cf. Thiersch 1978 and Fanselow 1986a). In this respect, then, German word order is not free: the finite verb must be in the second position in main clauses. But this is by no means unique to German, languages like e.g. Warlpiri, know a similar requirement of an AUX-element obligatorily in second position. The same appears to hold in a somewhat different fashion for Hungarian, cf. Kiss (1981).

What can be at question, then, is not the serialization of elements in the whole German main clause, but only the ordering of the elements that belong to IP/S, i.e. all constituents following the complementizer in subordinate clauses, and the finite verb in main clauses. Here, again, there appear to exist some restrictions insofar as the verbal elements may not precede NPs at all, with some options for post-verbal PPs and a full option for postverbal clauses, cf. (10):

---

[1] Following the approach developed in Chomsky (1986a), I have equated S with the maximal projection of INFL, and S' with the maximal projection of COMP. The VP is the complement of the INFL-phrase IP, the subject being its specifier. The specifier of CP/S' serves as the landing site of *wh*-movement processes, (cf. Chomsky 1986a and Fanselow & Felix 1987 for some details).

[2] But cf. Travis (1983) for an alternative treatment of subjects in the prefield position, cf. also Haider (1987) for an analysis differing in certain details. Furthermore, there is growing evidence that German main clause structure might be closely related to left dislocation structures (as discussed by Altmann 1981), cf. Chomsky (1977) and Koster (1978). The matter is, however, irrelevant for the topic of my paper.

(10a) *ich denke, daß Maria gekannt haben kann den Mann
       I think that Mary known   have may the man
      "I think Mary might have known the man"

(10b) ich denke, daß Peter die Frau eingeladen hat wegen ihrer
      I think that Peter the woman invited   has because of her
      Schönheit
      beauty
      "I think that Peter has invited the woman because of her beauty"

(10c) ich denke, daß Peter meint,   daß Maria schön   ist
      I think that Peter believes that Mary beautiful is
      "I think that Peter believes that Mary is beautiful"

Clearly, the data in (10) are due to a parametrization in the direction of government, hence case assigment. German verbs assign case to their left, implying that any NP standing to the right of the verb will be filtered out by the case filter, as they cannot be marked for case. PPs and clauses which do not have to bear case marking are, then, free with expand w.r.t. ordering. Similar restrictions on the position of the verb are common in other non-configurational languages as well, the verb must be clause-final in Japanese, e.g.

Within the limits presented so far, word order appears to be free in German clauses, however. To be more precise, we have to say that there are grammatical examples for all conceivable orderings of the subject, the direct object, the indirect object and adverbials in German. Thus, e.g. all the permutations of the constituents of (11) yield a grammatical structure, cf. (12):

(11) daß ein Mann   dem Mädchen den Ball   gestern gab
     that a   man$_{nom}$ the girl$_{dat}$ the ball$_{acc}$ yesterday gave
     that a man gave the ball to the girl yesterday

(12a) daß dem Mädchen ein Mann gestern den Ball gab

(12b) daß dem Mädchen den Ball ein Mann gestern gab

(12c) daß gestern dem Mädchen den Ball ein Mann gab

(12d) daß gestern den Ball dem Mädchen ein Mann gab

It might thus appear hopeless to formulate German grammar in terms of constituent structure because of the seemingly incorrect predictions made for the serialization of the constituents. In fact, linear order does not seem to have any consequences for the grammaticality of some standard structures, e.g. the binding of anaphora and pronouns is not affected by ordering facts, cf. (13), in particular, weak crossover seems to be absent in German (cf.14):

(13a) weil   jeder   sich   liebt
 because everybody himself loves
 "because everybody loves himself"

(13b) weil sich jeder liebt

(14) wen$_i$ hat seine$_i$ Frau betrogen ?

In particular if one considers (13b), it seems to be impossible to construct a constituent structure in which the subject *jeder* asymmetrically c-commands the object anaphor *sich*, as would be required by principles A and C of Binding theory (cf. Chomsky 1981). Only (15) might serve as a correct structural representation if we accept Koster's principle of chain transfer (cf. Koster 1982), according to which the relevant c-command-relations of a trace are inherited by its antecedent. Thus, in (15), the trace in object position is c-commanded by the subject as required by Binding theory, and the anaphor *sich* in presentential position shares this property by virtue of inheritance from the trace it binds.

(15)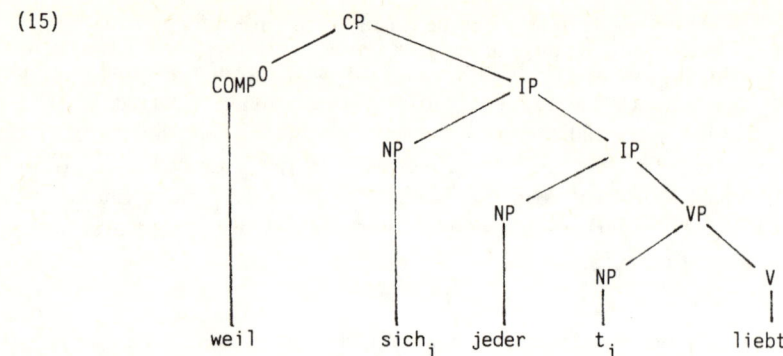

Note in this respect that Koster's principle of chain transfer is independently motivated in German syntax because anaphora can be subject-bound in the SPEC-COMP-prefield as well, although there cannot be any direct relation of c-command between elements in SPEC-COMP and the subject in structures like (16). The only way to explain the possibility of anaphors in structures like these appears to be the transfer of properties from the trace to its antecedent as proposed by Koster.

(16)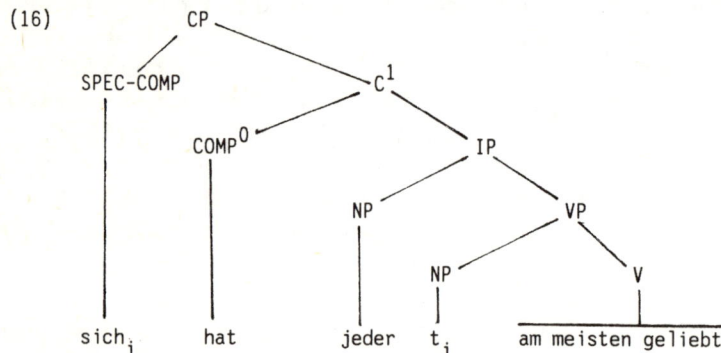

Although this approach seems to work quite nicely, one might wonder why it should be preferred to a non-configurational theory formulating, e.g. a Binding theory in terms of case or grammatical functions.

There are, now, some restrictions on the serializations of constituents in German clauses which are relevant in this respect, although they seem to be of a thematic nature at a first glance. As was noted by Lenerz (1977) in his important study on German word order, adverbials and objects may not precede the subject in the IP-domain of German clauses if they carry main stress and if the subject does not. This fact is illustated by the examples given in (17) and (18), where italicization should be taken to stand for main stress:

(17a) weil   im   Hilton *der Präsident* wohnt
because in-the Hilton the president resides
"because the president resides in the Hilton"

(17b) *weil *im Hilton* der Präsident wohnt

(18a) weil   dem Minister   *der Präsident*   eine Tasche gab
because the minister$_{dat}$ the president$_{nom}$ a bag$_{acc}$ gave
"because the president gave a bag to the minister"

(18b) *weil *dem Minister* der Präsident eine Tasche gab

Note that this distribution of the data cannot be due to some mysterious constraint against elements bearing main stress in the first position of IP, because main stress elements are not banned there if they are subjects:

(19a) weil *der Präsident* im Hilton wohnt

(19b) weil *der Präsident* dem Minister eine Tasche gab

Furthermore, the subject needs not to bear main stress if it is in sentence-initial position:

(20a) weil der Päsident *im Hilton* wohnt

(20b) weil der Präsident *dem Minister* eine Tasche gab

If we equate - following Abraham (1984) - main stress with focus, the descriptive generalization about German word order appears to be the following: non-focus or thematic elements may either occupy the position you would expect for them if a configurational SOV-base ordering is assumed, or they may precede the subject. Focus elements, however, may appear only in the position reserved for them under a basic SOV-hypothesis. Sentence initial position, then, is reserved for thematic elements with the exception of subjects, for which the sentence initial slot is the basic one. It would be correct, then, to describe the data presented so far in the following way: the X-bar-scheme generates SOV-orderings only, and there is a special instance of Move α, which we may tentatively identify as "IP-internal re-ordering" (IIR), which optionally moves non-focus elements to some pre-IP position.

German, then, resembles Hungarian which is also of the "free-word-order-type". As was demonstrated by Kiss (1981), a Hungarian clause is organized into fields similar to the ones we can find in German. At the beginning of the sentence, there is a slot for topicalized phrases, which may be filled by one or more items. The same is true for the German S/IP-node, insofar as two or more constituents of the sentence may be placed in front of the subject.

(21) weil   dem Minister   die Tasche   niemand   geben   konnte
 because the minister$_{dat}$ the bag$_{acc}$ nobody give could
"because nobody could give the bag to the minister"

However, the position for topicalized phrases is followed in Hungarian by a slot for one focussed phrase, which appears to be absent in German. Focussed phrases have to remain in their base position here. German, then, again appears to be in conformity with the standard type of non-configurational languages.

2. SOME PROPERTIES OF RE-ORDERING IN GERMAN

If what we have said so far is correct, German clauses with some elements preceding the subject position bear a structure like (22):

(22)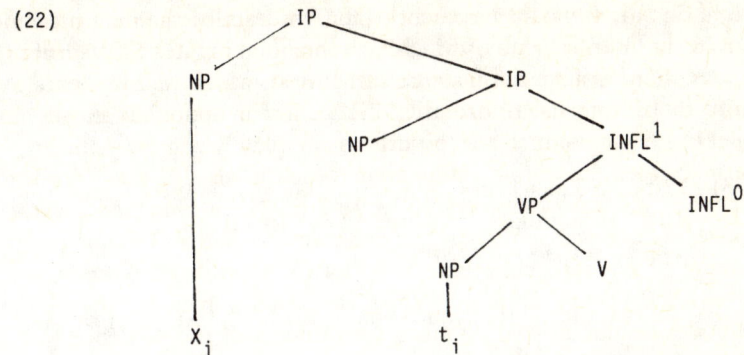

It is a crucial fact about (22) that there is a trace left in the base position of the preposed element. Within the framework of the GB-theory, most of the properties of the movement rule are determined by the nature of this trace, which, in turn, is fixed by independently motivated principles. According to Chomsky (1982), an empty category is a variable if and only if it is locally bound[3] by some element in an A-bar-position[4]. It is an anaphor if it is not a variable, and it is also pronominal if it is free or if its binder bears a thematic role of its own. Obviously, the trace in (22) is neither free nor does its binder bear a separate thematic role, hence t_i cannot be a pronominal anaphor. Note that this is a welcome result because pronominal anaphors cannot be governed by a verb because of Binding theory, as it is the case for the trace in (22). Its binder being adjoined to IP, the trace left behind seems to fulfill the requirements for being a variable, because adjoined positions are no likely candidates for A-positions.

There are, however, some empirical data which cast some doubt on the correctness of this result. If t_i were a variable, the scope of the re-ordering rule should be constrained by subjacency only, but not by Binding theory. Furthermore, parasitic gaps should be possible for the IIR rule, because these are licensed for variables only.

---

[3] x is locally bound by y if and only if y binds x and there is no z that binds x but does not bind y.

[4] Normally A-positions are those slots in a tree to which thematic roles can be assigned, i.e. the subject position, the object position etc. All other positions (e.g. the specifier slot of CP/S') are held to be A-bar-position.

Felix (1985) has given an account of the few parasitic gap constructions that occur in German, one of which is exemplified in (23)[5]. If the rule IIP would create a variable as a gap, constructions similar to (23) should also occur in these contexts. But clearly, this prediction is not borne out. (24), parallel to (23) in the relevant respects, is completely ungrammatical.

(23) LI ist eine Zeitschrift [$_{CP}$ die$_i$ [$_{IP}$ man anstatt PRO t$_i$ zu
    LI is a   journal   which$_i$ one instead   to
    kopieren t$_i$ abonnieren sollte]]
    copy   subscribe should
    "LI is a journal that you should subsribe to instead of copying"

(24) *ich habe LI$_i$ anstatt t$_i$ zu kopieren t$_i$ abonnieren müssen
    I have LI$_i$ instead   to copy   subscribe must
    "I had to subscribe to LI instead of copying it"

Although most speakers of German agree w.r.t. to the ungrammaticality of (24), Felix (1985) states that (24) does not sound that bad at all to some speakers of the Bavarian dialect. If his theoretical conclusions from this fact were true, we would have to assume that the trace left in (22) is a non-variable for most speakers of German and a variable for part of the Bavarian speech community, clearly an undesirable result. The crucial difference between those Bavarian speakers and the majority of fluent Germans rather seems to lie in the fact that people who accept (24) also find (25) grammatical, a construction which cannot involve movement at all, because *jede Zeitschrift* is a non-thematic element, and thus cannot have been affected by IIR.

(25) *ich habe jede Zeitschrift anstatt zu kopieren
    I have every journal   instead to copy
    abonnieren müssen
    subscribe must
    "I had to subscribe to every journal instead of copying it"

As was pointed out to me by Karin Donhauser, there are no real infinitival constructions in Bavarian (cf. also Merkle 1975), rather

---

[5] Cf. also Bennis & Hoekstra (1985) and Koster (1984). Bordelois (1986) gives an interesting account of parasitic gaps in Spanish which appear to share certain properties of similar German structures.

constructions with *zu* are nominalized forms normally. Thematic roles do not have to be expressed as full NPs or empty category within nominal constructions. There is no compelling evidence, then, to insert variable-traces into the infinitival constructions of Bavarian exemplified in (24) or (25). They are no counterexamples to the claim that preposing of elements in the middle field does not involve parasitic gaps at all. The absence of the parasitic gap constructions, however, counts against the assumption that the trace in (22) is a variable.

The same is true for the character of boundedness we can identify for the IIR rule. If a variable were left in place, the rule IIR should be constrained by subjacency only, i.e. we should expect that the domains of *wh*-movement (which moves elements to the prefield/COMP-position of German main clauses) of the rule IIR should be identical. This prediction is not borne out. As in most other languages, *wh*-movement can leave a finite complementizerless clause in German (26a), any non-finite clause (26b), and finite clauses with complementizers at least in the dialects spoken in the south of Germany (26c).

(26a) den Hans$_i$ denke ich [$_{CP}$ t$_i$ hat [$_{IP}$ t$_i$ jeder gemocht]]
the$_{acc}$ Hans think I has everyone liked
"I think everyone liked Hans"

(26b) die Bücher$_i$ haben sie mich [$_{IP}$ PRO t$_i$ zu lesen] gebeten
the books have they me to read asked
"They have asked me to read the books"

(26c) den Hans$_i$ denke ich schon [$_{CP}$ daß jeder t$_i$ gemocht hat]
the$_{acc}$ Hans think I ptc that everyone liked has
"I think that everyone liked Hans"

Finite and non-finfite clauses, however, are absolute barriers for the rule IIR, as is exemplified by the ungrammaticality of the examples given in (27):

(27a) *daß diesen Politiker$_i$ der Senator einem Mann [$_{IP}$ PRO t$_i$
that this politician$_{acc}$ the senator$_{nom}$ a man$_{dat}$
zu helfen] vorwarf
to help accused
"that the senator accused a man of helping this politician"

(27b) *daß diesen Mann$_i$ niemand dachte [$_{CP}$ t$_i$ einlädt Karl t$_i$]
      that this man$_{acc}$ no one$_{nom}$ thought   invites Karl
      "that no one thought Karl would invite this man"

(27c) *daß diese Frau$_i$ du schon dachtest [$_{CP}$ daß Karl t$_i$ einlädt]
      that this woman$_{acc}$ you$_{nom}$ ptc thought that Karl$_{nom}$ invites
      "that you thought that Karl would invite this woman"

There is one apparent exception to the generalization implicit in (27): Certain infinitival constructions seem to permit that the rule IIR causes an element to leave an embedded clause, cf. e.g. the data given in (28):

(28a) daß den Mann$_i$ gestern niemand (t$_i$ einzuladen) versuchte
      that the man$_{acc}$ yesterday noboby$_{nom}$ invite tried
      "that noboby tried to invite the man yesterday"

(28b) daß den Brief Karl niemandem aufzugeben versprochen hatte
      that the letter$_{acc}$ Karl$_{nom}$ nobody$_{dat}$ to post promised has
      "that Karl had not promised to anybody to post the letter"

Gestern and *niemandem* are elements that belong to the main clause, which implies that any element preceding them must form part of it as well. *Den Mann* and *den Brief*, however, are objects of the embedded verbs, which seems to indicate that IIR also can affect elements of embedded infinitival clauses in German. Arguing that way, however, would mean overlooking the well-known fact that verbs like *versuchen* or *versprechen* trigger some reanalysis rule in the sense of Rizzi (1982), which removes the intervening S-boundary. The application of reanalysis is inevitable for the account of certain pecularities of these constructions, e.g. with respect to the scope of negation. A negation operator like *nicht* "not" immediately preceding the verbal complex of the embedded infinitival in constructions governed by *versprechen* or similar verbs will have an option for wide scope negation in constructions like (28), which is impossible in data which contain verbs like *vorwerfen* or similar predicates (cf. Haider (1987) for some discussion). Moreover, the embedded objects in sentences parallel to (28) can even move to subject position in some dialects of German (cf. 29), which is even more compelling evidence for the absence of a clause boundary in (28). We can thus maintain the generalization that IIR cannot leave clauses in German, in contrast to *wh-*

movement.

(29) der Wagen wurde zu reparieren versprochen
the$_{nom}$ car was to repair promised
"it was promised to repair the car"

It is therefore highly implausible that the gap created by the application of IIR is a variable. If it were, we should find parasitic gap constructions in exactly those contexts in which they are possible for the variable gaps created by *wh*-movement in German, and if it were, there should be no additional locality restrictions on the range of rule application above the general subjacency condition. On the other hand, entirely correct predictions follow from the assumption that IIR is a process creating an anaphoric empty element in the base position of the moved phrase. Anaphors exclude parasitic gap constructions for principled reasons, because otherwise both the requirements imposed by the definition of chains and the criterion of thematic roles would be violated (cf. Chomsky 1982). If the trace in (22) is anaphoric, there can be no parasitic gap constructuctions with the IIR rule i.e. the anaphoric option makes correct predictions in this domain.

Furthermore, anaphors are subject to the condition A of Binding theory, implying that an anaphor must be bound within its minimal governing category[6], i.e. the S- or NP-node containing the anaphor in the standard case. If the trace left in (22) is an anaphor, IIR is constrained in a fashion implying that S-nodes cannot be crossed in the standard case simply for the reason that the anaphoric trace must be bound by its moved antecedent within its minimal governing category. This restriction on movement within a single clause is, however, what we have found to be true for German in the context of examples (28). Note again that German is by no means exceptional in this respect. There are no attested examples of languages in which elements from different clauses could be mixed up in general[7].

---

[6] The minimal governing category for some element x is the smallest projection containing x; a subject accessible to x and a governor for x, according to the definition of the Chomsky (1981) framework. There are some modifications in Chomsky (1986a), however, to which we will return below.

[7] This claim has to be qualified, however. Turkish scrambling processes are not strictly clause-bound, a fact, that appears to be connected to the peculiar behavior of Turkish

Of course, the fact that processes preposing elements within the middle field of German sentences are clause bound is not a new discovery. A constraint on clausemates appears to be part of any description of "scrambling processes". But note that the predictions made by the two alternatives "clausemateness" and "anaphoric trace" differ in subtle respects. The approach I propose here claims that IIR may create any dependency between the antecedent moved to the front of the middle field and the trace in the original position which is licensed with respect to principle A of Binding theory, the trace being an anaphor. This dependency, however, does not have to be identical with any notion of "clausemateness", although it will be so in the standard cases. There are some contexts in which an anaphor can be bound "one clause higher up", or in which the anaphor is no immediate constituent of the sentence. My theory predicts that IIR may affect NPs in exactly those cases, whereas a clausemate condition would predict no re-ordering to occur in these cases. There are three sets of data where the different claims of these two approaches can be evaluated. Let us consider them in turn.

Anaphora embedded in PPs and NPs can be bound by the clausal subject quite generally in German, with the restriction that the NP may not have a subject of its own. The approach claiming that the application of IIR is only governed by the anaphoric nature of its trace thus predicts that scrambling should also affect complements of PP and NP. In general, however, any movement operation applying to complements of prepositions or nouns will lead to bad results cf. (30):

(30a) *[dem Brief von Monika]$_i$ habe ich nicht mehr
the letter of Monika have I not more
(mit e$_i$)gerechnet
with reckoned
"I have not reckoned with Monika's letter any more"

(30b) *[nach Riedering]$_i$ ist (ein Zug e$_i$) entgleist
to R. is a train derailed
"a train to R. has been derailed"

Note that this is a property of all movement processes in German, i.e.

---

anaphors. Other languages, like Hungarian or Makua have further COMP-like positions, which yield a slightly different pattern of reordering. Cf. Fanselow (1986f) for more details.

both NP-movement and *wh*-movement are inapplicable in these cases; German therefore both lacks prepositional passives and preposition stranding. It does not count as evidence against the anaphoric status of the trace in (22) then, that IIR is not applicable in contexts like (31) either.

(31a) *daß dem Brief von Monika ich nicht mehr mit gerechnet habe

(31b) *daß nach Riedering ein Zug entgleist ist

There are, however, some exceptions to the general restriction we are talking about. There is preposition stranding with the pro-PPs *da* "there" and *wo* "where", which may be used instead of the normal pronouns *es* "it" and *was* "what" within PPs. This appears to be obligatory in certain dialects of German. Thus we find structures like (32) and (33), but preposition stranding is restricted to the constructions in (33) (cf. Koster (1984) for some details).

(32a) ich habe für es viel Geld ausgegeben
 I have for it much money paid
 "I have paid much money for it"

(32b) für was hat er viel Geld ausgegeben?
 for what has he much money paid
 "what has he paid much money for?"

(33a) ich habe dafür viel Geld ausgegeben
 I have there-for much money paid
 (=32a)

(33b) wofür hat er viel Geld ausgegeben?
 where-for has he much money paid
 (=32b)

(34a) *es_i habe ich für t_i viel Geld ausgegeben
 it have I for much money paid
 (=32a)

(34b) *was$_i$ hat er für t$_i$ viel Geld ausgegeben
what has he for much money paid
(=32b)

(35a) da$_i$ habe ich viel Geld (t$_i$ für) ausgegeben
there have I much money for paid
(=32a)

(35b) wo$_i$ hat er viel Geld t$_i$ für ausgegeben?
where has he much money for paid
(=32b)

If re-ordering is restricted to clausemates in general, *wo* and *da* should not be able to precede the subject in German clauses, whereas the approach I develop here makes exactly the opposite predictions. The grammaticality of (36) is corroborating evidence for my proposal.

(36) ich habe da$_i$ schon gar nicht mehr t$_i$ mit gerechnet
I have there yet no more with reckoned
"I haven't reckoned with that any more"

Similarly, those contexts which allow *wh*-movement to leave NPs also tolerate application of IIR.

(37a) von Becker will niemand ein Autogramm bekommen
of Becker wants nobody an autograph to get
"nobody wants to get an autograph of Becker"

(37b) daß von Becker niemand ein Autogramm haben möchte
that of Becker nobody an autograph have wants
"that nobody wants to have an autograph of Becker"

The theory claiming that IIR is constrained by the anaphoric nature of the trace it leaves thus makes far better predictions than any clausemate approach on scrambling could do. Note that this in itself counts as evidence in favor of a movement analysis of free word order in German. We can capture the generalization that "move topic" is applicable in all those contexts where anaphors could be bound only if there is an anaphor present in move topic structures. Any theory operating with unordered base structure would have to stipulate *ad hoc*-constraints on the scope of re-ordering which are completely unnecessary within the GB-framework. All that must be said about the scope of re-ordering is a simple consequence of the anaphoric nature of the trace left behind. If you look at the constraints on free word order you cannot escape the conclusion that linear order is determined by syntactic factors even in free-word-order-languages.

The data from contexts of exceptional case marking are still more persuasive. Although this construction is quite rare in German, there are a few verbs like *lassen* "let", *sehen* "see" or *hören* "hear" which mark the subject of an embedded infintivial clause for case. As was demonstrated by Reis (1976), the arrangement of data for the binding of anaphors is quite complex here.

First, the subject of the embedded clause is always accessible to binding from the matrix clause, as should be expected.

(38a) weil   die Männer$_i$ sich$_i$ die Hymne   singen ließen
      because the men$_{nom}$ themselves$_{acc}$ the hymn$_{acc}$ sing let
      "because the men let each other sing the hymn"

(38b) weil   die Männer$_i$ sich$_i$ die Hymne singen hörten
      because the men$_{nom}$ themselves$_{acc}$ the hymn$_{acc}$ sing heard
      "because the men heard each other sing the hymn"

Object anaphors embedded in the complement clause may also find their binder in the matrix clause. The relevant condition is that the embedded clause may not contain a deep structure subject, cf. the contrast given in (39):

(39a) *weil   das Kind$_i$ den Mann die Geschichte sich$_i$
       because the child$_{nom}$ the man$_{acc}$ the story$_{acc}$ himself$_{dat}$
       vorlesen läßt
       read   lets
       "because the child lets the man read the story to him"

(39b) weil   das Kind$_i$ die Bücher sich$_i$ entgleiten ließ
      because the child$_{nom}$ the books$_{acc}$ himself$_{dat}$ slip from let
      "because the child lets the books slip from him"

Note that *entgleiten* is an ergative verb in the sense of Burzio (1981), i.e.

a verb whose subject is a deep structure object. There are several proposals to cope with data like (39b), (cf. Grewendorf 1983, Sternefeld 1984), but we need not go into details here.

Lastly, anaphors embedded within adverbial parts of the complement infinitival clause can always be bound from some position in the matrix clause[8]:

(40a) weil   niemand$_j$ den Mann für sich$_i$ arbeiten läßt
       because nobody the man for himself work   lets
       "because nobody lets the man work for him"

(40b) weil   Maria$_i$ eine Bombe neben sich$_i$ platzen hörte
       because Mary   a   bomb   near herself explode heard
       "because Mary heard a bomb exploding near her"

Our approach allows us to derive clear predictions for the scrambling options we should be able to find in German ECM-contexts. Re-ordering should be grammatical for elements of the embedded clause in just those cases where an anaphor can be bound from the matrix clause. To be more concrete, subjects of embedded infinitivals are predicted to be able to precede the matrix clause subject, and so are the objects of ergative or passivized verbs. On the other hand, preposing of an object in all the other constructions should yield ungrammatical results, whereas adverbials originating in the embedded infinitival are claimed to undergo IIR freely. It will come as no great surprise that all these predictions are borne out in detail.

(41a) daß den Mann$_i$ niemand [$_S$ t$_i$ schlafen] sah
       that the man$_{acc}$ nobody$_{nom}$ sleep   saw
       "that nobody saw the man sleeping"

---

[8] Within the Barriers-framework, there is an explanation at hand for the long-distance-binding of adverbial anaphors in German ECM-context. According to Chomsky (1986a), anaphors have to undergo LF-movement to the INFL-node they are co indexed with, leaving a gap subject to the ECP. If an anaphor is embedded in the VP, there will be at least two barriers between the gap and the anaphor at LF with long-distance-binding: the VP of the anaphor has left and the IP-node immediately dominating it, because IP inherits bar rierhood from VP. On the other hand, if we consider adverbial anaphors, both VP and IP will not count as barriers. VP cannot do so for the trivial reason that the anaphor or its trace does not form part of it. IP, however, is a barrier only in a derivative sense, and as VP is no barrier in the case we consider, IP cannot inherit barrierhood from any position.

(41b) *daß dem Mädchen$_i$ niemand [$_S$ einen Mann t$_i$ helfen] ließ
　　　 that the girl$_{dat}$ nobody$_{nom}$ a man$_{acc}$ help let
　　　 "that nobody let a man help the girl"

(41c) *daß dem Kind$_i$ niemand [$_S$ einen Mann t$_i$ gratulieren] sah
　　　 that the child$_{dat}$ nobody$_{nom}$ a man$_{acc}$ congratulate saw
　　　 "that nobody saw a man congratulate the child"

(41d) daß dem Kind$_i$ niemand ($_S$ die Bücher t$_i$ entgleiten) ließ
　　　 that the child$_{dat}$ nobody$_{nom}$ the books$_{acc}$ slip-from let
　　　 "that nobody let the books slip from the child"

(41e) daß dem Diener$_i$ niemand ($_S$ einen Apfel t$_i$ bringen) ließ
　　　 that the servant$_{dat}$ nobody$_{nom}$ an apple$_{acc}$ bring let
　　　 "that nobody let an apple be brought to the servant"

(41f) daß für Hans$_i$ niemand ($_S$ seine Frau t$_i$ arbeiten) lassen würde
　　　 that for Hans nobody his wife work   let would
　　　 "that nobody would let his wife work for Hans"

(41g) daß neben Maria niemand eine Bombe platzen sah
　　　 that near Mary nobody a bomb explode saw
　　　 "that nobody saw a bomb exploding near Mary"

The data given in (41) clearly demonstrate that IIR may create exactly those dependencies between trace and antecedent that are licensed for anaphoric binding in general. Note that (41f) and (41g) are most crucial in that respect. There may be some sort of clausal reanalysis responsible for the "long binding" of objects in (39) (cf. Grewendorf 1983), such that data like (41d) and (41e) might be in the scope of a clausemate approach as well. But Haider (1984) has argued convincingly that there is no clausal reanalysis to be found with *lassen*-complements that have a deep structure subject and with *sehen*-complements in general. If "scrambling" were a process restricted to clausemates in some fashion, (41f) and (41g) should be as ungrammatical as (42), which they definitely are not. They constitute most crucial evidence, then, for the fact that re-odering in German is not restricted by clausemateness, but by Binding theory for anaphoric traces[9].

(42a) *weil neben Maria niemand Karl eine Bombe zu sehen glaubte
because near Mary nobody Karl a bomb to see believed
"because nobody believed K. that he saw a bomb near Mary"

(42b) *weil niemand$_i$ Karl neben sich$_i$ eine Bombe zu sehen glaubte
because nobody Karl near himself a bomb to see believed
"because nobody believed K. to have seen a bomb near him"

It should also be stressed that the data that we have discussed in order to demonstrate that re-ordering is subject to the condition A of Binding theory cleary shows that free constituent order must be a syntactic movement process.

---

[9] Martin Everaet has pointed out to me in personal communication that one should expect scrambling to have a greater range of application in those languages which have long distance anaphora. Indeed, this appears to be the case for Turkish, cf. Fanselow (1986f). Grewendorf (personal communication) notes the following contrasts:

(i) er$_i$ sah den Braten sich$_i$ gelingen
he saw the roast himself succeed
"he saw himself succeeding in preparing the roast"

(ii) er$_i$ sah den Braten ihm$_i$ gelingen
him

(iii) er$_i$ sah sich$_i$ den Braten gelingen

(iv) *er$_i$ sah ihm$_i$ den Braten gelingen

gelingen is an ergative verb. In (iii) and (iv), *den Braten*, i.e. the direct object of this verb, has not been preposed to the subject position of the embedded infinitival. This clause is subjectless, then, which seems to account for the fact that a pronoun coreferent with the matrix clause subject is impossible here. However, if *den Braten* has been preposed, both a coreferent anaphor and a coreferent pronoun are possible. If the direct object could be advanced to subject position only, (i) should be ungrammatical, since now the embedded clause would have a subject. As Grewendorf points out, the grammaticality of (i) suggests that there must be a further position an object could be advanced to. Thus, data like (i)-(iv) provide further corroborating evidence for my proposal.

3. MOVE TOPIC IN UNIVERSAL GRAMMAR

Although the properties that we have attributed to the rule IIR, i.e. the anaphoric nature of the gap created by it, make correct predictions about the applicability of the process in question, we still have to answer two questions: why does IIR leave an anaphoric trace, and why is IIR constrained to topic elements, in other words why is it impossible to apply the rule to focus elements? It will turn out that the answer to both questions is the same.

According to the definitions developed in Chomsky (1981, 1982), an empty element is a variable if it is locally A-bar-bound, and a non-pronominal anaphor if it is A-bound from an A-position without an independent thematic role. While the latter of the two conditions for anaphoricity is clearly fulfilled by the topic slot at the beginning of IP, one might wonder why this position should count as an A-position, which is necessary for the empty category to be an anaphor.

There are, then, two options open to us. First, we might subsume any adjoined position under the label "A-position", which would imply that elements bound from that slot are anaphors. On the other hand, we might slightly revise the conditions developed by Chomsky and claim that an empty element is a variable if and only if it is locally operator-bound, and anaphoric otherwise. SPEC-COMP is the standard case for operator-slots. It is not quite clear how to decide between the two options. What we can be sure of, however, is that the assumption that traces bound from positions adjoined to IP are anaphora and not variables, is completely unproblematic in the general context of what we know about universal grammar[10].

If slots adjoined to IP do not count as operator positions, the trace bound by any element occupying them will be an anaphor in the sense of principle A of Binding theory, and this will yield the locality constraints on re-ordering that we have discussed in the above paragraph. We may also claim that languages may differ with respect to the possible existence of a position Chomsky-adjoined to IP. If there is none, the language in

---

[10] Cf. Chomsky (1986b) for some comments on the exceptional nature of positions adjoined to IP and Cinque (1985) for some arguments demonstrating that variables must be locally operator-bound. Fanselow (1986f) tries to integrate the theory proposed here into the general framework of Chomsky (1986b).

question would not allow for clause-internal "scrambling"[11], if there is one, it would resemble German in the relevant respects. Freeness of word order, then, appears to be a question of the existence of certain positions in clausal structure.

Its relevant properties being determined by independent properties of Universal Grammar, IIR can be viewed as an instance of the general rule "Move α". There is one problem still left open however: why is this subcase of Move α restricted to topic phrases? The answer to this can be found by a closer inspection of the properties of the adjunction slot of IP.

Being adjoined to IP, there is no lexical element governing the landing site of intra-clausal re-ordering. This makes the strong implication that - all other things being equal - no empty category may appear in that slot, because these are subject to the ECP. ECP requires that empty categories must be properly governed, where government by a lexical element is the standard case of the latter notion[12]. One might wonder what the import of this observation could be, because empty categories can be created by movement processes in this context only, and there is no position but the specifier of COMP that might serve as the landing position of an element having left the pre-IP-slot.

It is quite important to realize, however, that the ECP is a principle applying at LF- and not at S-structure. This means that any empty category created by LF-movement is also subject to the ECP, and, in particular, that no process of LF-movement may leave the pre-IP topic slot. In other words, the Theory of Government and Binding makes the strong prediction that any element that must occupy an operator position at LF cannot stand in the pre-IP-slot at S-structure. If that were the case, the NP in question would have to be moved to some operator position at LF, leaving an ungoverned empty category, which implies a violation of the ECP.

The existence of weak-crossover effects is one of the standard test cases for NPs undergoing LF-movement. As was pointed out by Chomsky (1972, 1981), NPs show weak crossover effects if they bear main stress, i.e.

---

[11] Cf. Fanselow (1986f) for some more elaborations.

[12] Proper government via antecedent-binding would then be excluded in a strict sense. Of course, this is not in the spirit of Chomsky (1986b). As remarked above, Fanselow (1986b) shows how to integrate the theory developed here into the Barriers-framework.

if they are in focus, cf. (43):

(43a) his$_i$ mother loves John$_i$

(43b) *his$_i$ mother loves *John*$_i$

The claim that elements in focus undergo LF-movement is in line with the fact noted recently by Chomsky and others that languages do not appear to differ with respect to the question which elements undergo movement processes, but only at which structural level these movement processes apply. Thus, there is no syntactic *wh*-movement in Chinese or Japanese, but Huang (1982) has demonstrated that *wh*-movement must apply at LF in these languages. Anaphors are moved syntactically to the INFL-position in the Romance languages, and there is growing evidence that the same must be true at LF for English anaphors (Chomsky 1986a). Since there are languages which have a syntactic process of focus-movement (Hungarian, and Hawaiian Creole), we should expect that languages without overt focus movement should apply this rule at LF, and this is in fact required by data like (43).

Having already established that the pre-IP position is not properly governed, we can derive that re-ordering is restricted to non-focus elements in German. If a phrase in focus were moved into the pre-IP-slot, it would stand in the ungoverned position indicated in (44a), and no longer in its base position (44b).

(44a)

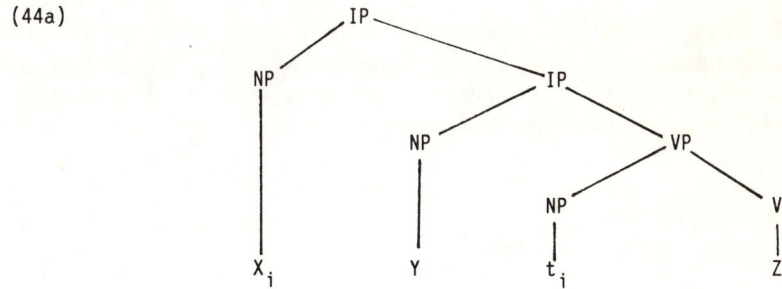

(44b)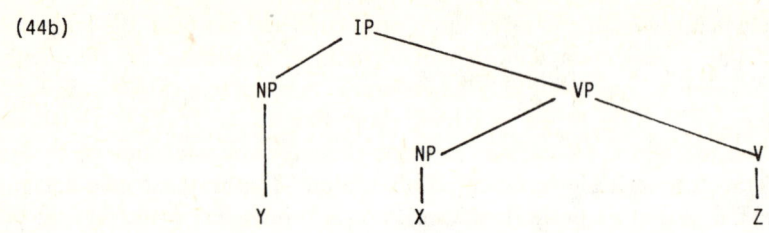

Being a focus element, it must be moved farther at LF in order to reach an operator position, which we have to identify with some slot connected to SPEC-COMP. We therefore will derive structures like (45a) and (45b), respectively.

(45a)

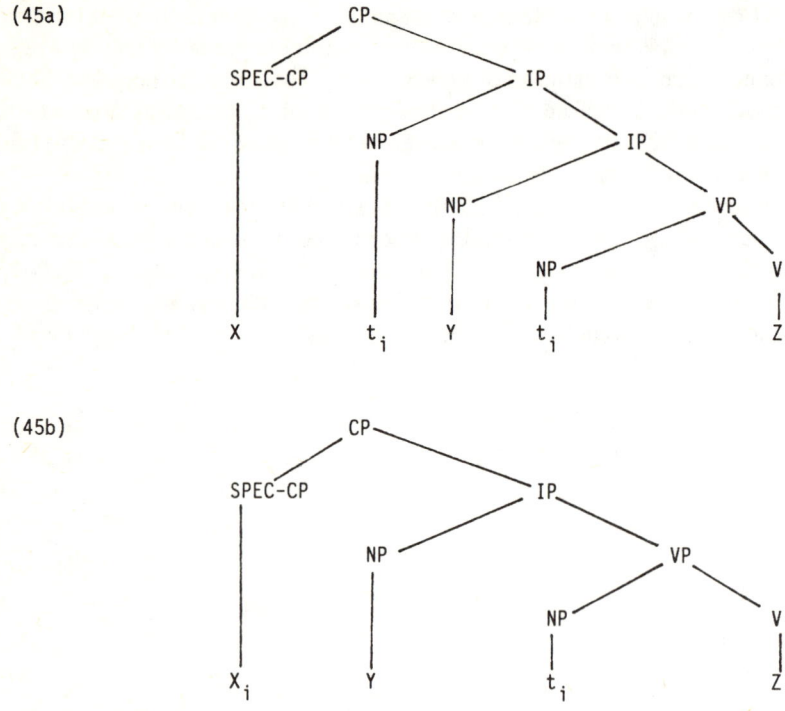

(45b)

Consider first (45b). The trace left behind by the application of Move α at LF is properly governed by the verb. If we stick to the formulation of the ECP developed by Kayne (1983), the structure will be grammatical only if it is possible to unify the g-projection set of t_i with the antecedent X. The g-projection set of some element is constituted by the element itself and the g-projection of its governor. X is in the g-projection of some element Y if X is the maximal projection of Y. If Y is a structural governor, all the projections in which the maximal projection of Y stands in the "canonical government configuration" (i.e. in the configuration of typical governors in the language), are also included in the g-projection-set. V is a structural governor of the trace in (45), therefore the VP is in the g-projection of V, but also any maximal projection in which the VP is on the right hand side, i.e. both IP and CP. The g-projection-set of the trace is the whole sentence, which its antecedent is part of for trivial reasons. Therefore, (45b) does not contradict the ECP.

But consider now (45a). The variable in question is the first occurence of t_i, because the second occurence is anaphoric in nature and thus cannot count in the computation of g-projections. The variable is governed by the INFL-node, therefore IP is in its g-projection. The crucial difference lies in the fact that INFL is not a structural governor in German, which implies that the g-projection of INFL will not include the CP-node although IP is on the left hand side of CP. Thus the g-projection-set of the trace in the pre-IP position does not include its antecedent, which implies that (45a) constitutes an ECP-violation. It has been proved, then, that focus elements cannot be preposed in the middle field because this would lead to a contradiction with the ECP. We do not have to stipulate at all, that the rule generating free word order only involves topic elements. It is consequence of the Theory of Government and Binding.

Of course, there are more elements that have to undergo movement at LF, e.g. this is true of quantified noun phrases is the sense of Hornstein (1984). Thus we make the prediction that there should be no re-ordering for NPs containing a quantifier in German, and this prediction is borne out. OSV-orderings are quite odd and close to ungrammaticality if the object contains a quantifier.

(46a) ?*weil   jede Frau   der Mann   liebt
      because every woman$_{acc}$ the man$_{nom}$ loves
      "because the man loves every woman"

(46b) ?*weil   jede Frau   ein Mann   liebt
       because every woman$_{acc}$ a man$_{nom}$ loves
       "because a man loves every woman"

(46c) ?*weil   viele Frauen jeder Mann liebt
       because many women$_{acc}$ every man$_{nom}$ loves
       "because every man loves many women"

(46d) ?*weil   viele Frauen ein Mann   liebt
       because many women$_{acc}$ a man$_{nom}$ loves
       "because a man loves many women"

We may conclude, then, that the limitations on free worder in German are fully predicted by the Theory of Government and Binding. Free word order is not a phenomenon that is problematic for the GB-theory, rather it is problematic for any theory that does not share the crucial properties of GB.

4. SOME APPARENT DESCRIPTIVE PROBLEMS

Let us now turn to some data which appear to be problematic for the account we gave for German word order so far. There are two main classes of data which do not fall in the lines of our predictions at a first glance. First, there is a class of verbs governing the dative which allow for an object preceding the nominative NP even if the object is quantified or bears main stress. Second, quantified objects may be preposed if the subject is a quantified NP as well. The two facts are exemplified in (47) and (48) respectively.

(47a) weil   einem Mädchen der Schlüssel ins Wasser fiel
       because a   girl$_{dat}$ the key$_{nom}$ into-the water fell
       "because the key fell into the water"[13]

---

[13] The NP *dem Mädchen* is a so-called ethical dative quite common in German, but unfortunately untranslatable to English in this case. Here, the dative expresses the experiencer role of the falling of the key, i.e. the person who it slipped from.

(47b) weil   einem Mann   das Fahrrad gestohlen wurde
      because a   man$_{dat}$ the bike$_{nom}$ stolen   was
      "because a bike was stolen from a man"

(48a) weil   keinem Arzt   jeder Patient   vertraut
      because no   doctor$_{dat}$ every patient$_{nom}$ trusts
      "because every patient doesn't have confidence in any doctor" [14]

(48b) weil   jeden Studenten   kein Professor   mag
      because every student$_{acc}$ no   professor$_{nom}$ likes
      "because no professor likes every student"

The option to precede the subject even if quantified is by no means a property we could ascribe to dative NPs in general. If the verb in question is a transitive active one, data like (47a) are ungrammatical, and there are many verbs with a dative object which do not tolerate constructions like the ones given above, cf. (49):

(49a) *weil   einem Mädchen   der Mann   half
      because a   girl$_{dat}$ the man$_{nom}$ helped
      "because the man helped a girl"

(49b) ?*weil   einem Mann   das Kind   folgte
      because a   man$_{dat}$ the child$_{nom}$ followed
      "because the child followed a man"

The class of verbs which may be inserted in structures like (47a) is well-defined: it comprises all verbs forming their perfect with the auxiliary *sein*, and all verbs in passive voice. Similar to the situation in Italian, verbs forming their perfect with *sein* are ergative in German, (cf. Grewendorf 1987 for some details). The condition for the grammaticality of (47a) thus comes up to the requirement that a dative NP may precede a nominative NP if the latter is not a deep structure subject, this being the case in ergative and passive constructions.

---

[14] Due to the option for re-ordering if both subject and object are quantified, quantifier scope always corresponds to linear order in German, in contrast to English. Cf. Fanselow (1986f) for some more discussion.

Although it is a standard assumption, explicitly argued for by Reis (1984), that any nominative NP is a S-structure-subject in German, this turns out to be false on closer examination, (cf. Sternefeld 1985 and Fanselow 1986c). Nominatives which correspond to deep structure objects do not show any of the typical properties of S-structure-subjects in German apart from case marking. They are S-structure-objects as well, but marked for nominative, a phenomenon not uncommon among the languages of the world (it is also attested for Icelandic, cf. Andrews 1982 for Georgian, Anderson 1984 and many other languages). E.g. there are no ECP-effects for D-structure-objects even if they are nominatives at S-structure, as can be seen in the examples given in (50).[15]

(50a) was$_i$ denkst du, daß t$_i$ ihm passiert sein könnte?
what think$_{2sgpres}$ you$_{nom}$ that him$_{dat}$ happened be could
"what do you think might have happened to him?"

(50b) *wer$_i$ denkst du, daß t$_i$ einen Wagen gekauft haben könnte?
who$_{nom}$ think$_{2sgpres}$ you$_{nom}$ that a car$_{acc}$ bought have could
"who do you think might have bought a car?"

(50c) was$_i$ denkst du, daß Dagmar t$_i$ gekauft haben könnte?
what$_{acc}$ think$_{2sgpres}$ you$_{nom}$ that D$_{nom}$ bought have could
"what do you think Dagmar might have bought?"

But if nominative NPs are objects in constructions with ergative verbs and verbs in the passive voice, data like (47) do not contradict the approach developed here at all. The dative NPs in (47) have not left the VP at all and can precede the direct object within the VP in any case.

Let us now turn to the second set of examples. We have proposed an account for the impossibility of placing quantified NPs in front of the subject in terms of the ECP. If this explanation is correct, it must share all the peculiarities that follow from the ECP. As was noted by Kayne (1983), there is a number of constructions which constitute ECP-violations but

---

[15] German *wh*-extraction data are a quite complex matter. Extraction of subjects is constrained in the way indicated in the text in standard German and the northern German dialects only. In southern German, especially in the dialects spoken in Bavaria and Austria, subjects may freely leave *that*-clauses. ECP-effects show up too, however, in these dialects, but in a much more subtle fashion only, cf. Fanselow (1986a,b).

which are considerably improved if a second gap is created in the sentence. This is exemplified by the pair of data in (51):

(51a) *a person who$_i$ people that talk to t$_i$ usually end up fascinated with him$_i$

(51b) ?a person who$_i$ people that talk to t$_i$ usually end up fascinated with t$_i$

Let us first have a glance at (51a). The trace in question is properly governed by the preposition *to* and the PP is on a right branch, i.e. in the standard government configuration in the VP, and so is the latter in the IP and CP of the relative clause modifying *people*. But the subject of the relative clause modifying *person* is on a left branch in the IP, hence the IP of the greater relative clause will not be part of the g-projection of *to*. It follows that the g-projection-set of the trace will not include more material than the subject of the larger relative clause. In particular, it will not comprise the relative pronoun *who*, in contradiction to what is required by the ECP. Thus (51a) is ruled out. The situation should be the same one for the first occurence of the trace in (51b), but the crucial difference rests in the fact that there is a second gap bound by *who* in this example, which is in object position of the relative clause, which implies that its g-projection-set will contain all the material found in the whole construction. In a sense, the two g-projection-sets unite, and all that is required by the ECP is that the unification of the g-projection-sets of all the traces bound by some element also contain the antecedent.

The same, however, appears to be true of cases where the variables are bound by different operators provided that the latter have scope over the same domain. There is an improvement of grammaticality similar to the one found in (51) in constructions with multiple interrogation.

(52a) *we are trying to find out which man said that which woman was in love with him

(52b) ?we are trying to find out which man said that which woman was in love with which boy

It should have become obvious by now what is responsible for the improvement of grammaticality in constructions with preposed quantified

NPs. If the subject is quantified, too, it will create a g-projection-set that will reach the CP-node, and because the g-projection-set of the element in the pre-IP-position will be included in the former g-projection, the ECP will not block these constructions. (48) is no counterexample to our approach, rather the data have to be that way.

5. IMPLICATIONS FOR UNIVERSAL GRAMMAR

In the above paragraphs, we have considered some of the properties of the serialization of elements in one of the so-called free-word-order-languages. There is no way to escape the conclusion that "free word order" is nothing but an euphemism for a system governed by a strict base ordering and the application of the rule Move α, which is constrained by the fact that positions adjoined to IP are not operator slots. All the constraints on the re-ordering of elements will then turn out to be consequences of the application of the ECP and Binding Theory's principle A.

Even if theories like LFG which ground their grammars in terms of grammatical functions instead of constituent structures, or GB-versions with a flat clausal structure, could handle all grammatical phenomena in a fashion that comes close to the explanatory power of the standard GB-system (which they don't), we would have to give up these approaches - somewhat ironically - because they are not able to handle satisfactorily the phenomenon they were invented for: the existence of languages with free word order. Crucially, any connection between grammar and serialization must be stipulated in an *ad hoc fashion* in these frameworks. This connection has proven to be a strict one, namely the one you would expect to exist if the GB-theory is correct.

The main objection one could make here would be that German is not a typical free-word-order-language. In order to counter this argument, I have stressed above again and again that the properties of German are not uncommon at all. What distinguishes the GB-approach from LFG is that it makes predictions about the possible arrangement of elements, whereas LFG does not. The serialization component is completely independent of grammar in that framework. Thus you can test GB but you cannot test LFG.

There are two answers that can be given to the objection, an empirical and a conceptual one. Empirically, we have seen what the predictions are that GB makes about possible free-word-order-languages, and we can check these predictions in other languages that can be labeled nonconfigurational as well[16]. Hungarian is one of the cases that are well studied, so let us see if anything incompatible with our GB-approach happens there.

At a first glance, Hungarian appears to be a language with totally free ordering of elements, but the important study by Kiss (1981) has demonstrated that this is not quite so. There is a topic slot similar to the one identified for German which may accept any of the topicalized unquantified phrases of the sentence, followed by a focus position which can be shown to be filled by the *wh*-version of the rule Move α. Both positions are followed by the finite verb, which in turn precedes the "rest" of the sentence, i.e. the IP-node. The crucial difference between Hungarian and German, now, lies in the fact that there are no apparent restrictions on the ordering of the subject and the object in the sequence of elements following the verb, i.e. within IP. Kiss (1985) uses this data to conclude that IP is flat in Hungarian, i.e. that there are no structural differences between subject and object in this language. She tries to corroborate this claim by presenting data which show that there are no subject-object asymmetries with respect to *wh*-extraction or similar processes in Hungarian.

Kiss and many researchers working with Hungarian or languages like Japanese or Warlpiri seem to overlook the important fact that Hungarian, Japanese or Warlpiri are pro-drop-languages. As the pro-drop-parameter is responsible for the absence of ECP-effects on subject extraction in Italian or the Celtic languages, one might wonder why it should not do the same job in Hungarian and Japanese. Thus, the primary syntactic differences between Hungarian and, e.g. English are due to the pro-drop-parameter and not to the alleged structural differences. Horvath (1981) has pointed out that any pro-drop-language is predicted to show a free inversion of subjects and verbs *within* the IP/S-nodes. She correctly draws the conclusion that SO- and OS-ordering should occur in Hungarian IP

---

[16] As noted above, I have tested the predictions made by my system in Fanselow (1986f) with languages as diverse in nature as Greenlandic, Turkish, Hungarian, Makua, Icelandic.

because it is a *pro-drop-language*. Pro-drop-languages, then, are no good testing ground for the question of what is responsible for free word order. One has to look at languages in which no other factor interferes with the operation of the free ordering parameter, i.e. at least at some non-pro-drop-language like German. We must conclude that nothing unexpected happens in Hungarian syntax.

Perhaps, Latin or Warlpiri are greater stumbling blocks. One should not forget that there is a story about Warlpiri in particular which began with the claim that it shows a totally free ordering of *words*, and passing intermediary stations like the rule "auxililiary must be second" or "no interclausal scrambling" now seems to end with some thematic constraints on word order which, perhaps, may not be that far away from what we can find in German. Again, one should stress that Warlpiri is a pro-drop-language, and in a very specific sense: the verbs do not only agree with the subject, but with the object, such that we should expect the pro-drop-effects for both subjects and objects. According to Jelinek (1983), full noun phrases may be nothing but free adjuncts to the sentence. Fanselow (1986f) tries to show that Warlpiri very well falls into what we should expect within the theory of Government and Binding.

There is a conceptual point also. The most important constraint grammars of natural languages must fulfil is learnability, and this means that any parameter with respect to which languages are said to differ must be learnable on the basis of positive data only, simply because of the fact that children do not have access to negative data. Chomsky (1986a) and Williams (1984) have pointed out in this respect that we cannot decide the question of the existence of a VP-node without considering learnability, i.e. learnability is crucial also for free word order as a result of Move α on the one hand and a totally unorderd base on the other, as proposed by the LFG. The above paragraphs have shown that there are enough data which tell the child that there is freeness of word order in German. Ultimately, however, the child develops a grammar which rules out certain serializations. As these serializations are ungrammatical, i.e. negative data, the child cannot have learned anything about them. Knowledge that you have not learned must be innate. It is thus a *logical* conclusion to be drawn from what we know about the process of language acquisition that a strict base ordering responsible for the limitations of serializations must be innate. A child acquiring German just cannot learn anything about them.

Two reservations come to mind. On the one hand, UG, i.e. the innate initial state the child uses to interpret the data it hears and to ultimately construct the grammar of its language is a highly complicated system, which constitutes intricate connections between data. The pro-drop-parameter is a case in point. If there is a free inversion of subject and verb in a language, UG forces that null subject pronouns and the free extraction of subjects are realized all the same. Thus it could be the case that other data of German will tell the child that German has a fixed base order. But this is only a theoretical option. As I have shown in Fanselow (1986a,b), referring to a set of data containing diverse construction types, positive data in German always appear to tell the child "you are learning a language without structural differences between subjects and objects", but in every case there are negative data (i.e. data to which the child does not have access) which cannot be accounted for without the assumption that German base structure comes quite close to the NP-VP-configuration we are familiar with from English. There is no data at all which could tell the child that German has a VP.

On the other hand, a defender of the free-base-order-hypothesis might withdraw to the somewhat weak position that a fixed base word order is the unmarked value of the parameter, i.e. the one that is assumed by the child to be true unless there is some really hard evidence against it. As there is no German sentence at all which would turn out to contradict the strict base-order-hypothesis upon closer inspection, the child will never give up this formulation of grammar. But there might be languages which show data incompatible with a strict basic order. Well, as the GB-Theory is a predictive system, there are possible data which would show it to be incorrect. Time has come to stop promising data of that kind and to present them. We are still waiting.

BIBLIOGRAPHY

Abraham, W. ed. 1982, *Satzglieder im Deutschen*. Tübingen. Narr.
Abraham, W. 1984, Word order in the middle field of the German sentence. *Groninger Arbeiten zur Germanistischen Linguistik* 25:1-22.
Abraham, W. 1985a, Transitivitätskorrelate und ihre formale Einbindung in die Grammatik. *Groninger Arbeiten zur germanistischen Linguistik* 26:1-60.
Abraham, W. ed. 1985b, *Erklärende Syntax des Deutschen*. Tübingen. Narr.

Altmann, H. 1981, *Formen der Herausstellung im Deutschen*.Tübingen, Niemeyer.
Andrews, A. 1982, The representation of case in modern Icelandic. In: Bresnan, J. ed. 1982:427-503.
Anderson, S.R. 1984, On representations in morphology: case marking, agreement and inversion in Georgian. *Natural Language and Linguistic Theory* 2:157-228.
Baker, C. & McCarty J. eds. 1981, *The logical problem of language aquisition*. Cambridge, Mass. MIT Press.
Baltin, M. 1981, Strict bounding. In: Baker, C. & McCarthy, J. eds. 1981:257-295.
Bennis, H. & Hoekstra, T. 1985, Gaps and parasitic gaps. *The Linguistic Review* 4:29-87.
Bordelois, I. 1986, Parasitic gaps: extensions of restructuring. In: Bordelois et al. eds., 1986:1-24.
Bordelois, I. & Contreras, H. & Zagona, K. eds. 1986, *Generative studies in Spanish syntax*. Dordrecht, Foris.
Bresnan, J. ed. 1982, *The mental representation of grammatical relations*. Cambridge, Mass. MIT Press.
Burzio, L. 1981. *Intransitive verbs and Italian auxiliaries*. Ph.D. Dissertation, MIT.
Chomsky, N. 1965, *Aspects of the theory of syntax*. Cambridge, Mass. MIT Press.
Chomsky, N. 1972, *Studies on semantics in generative grammar*. The Hague. Mouton.
Chomsky, N. 1977. On *wh*-movement. In: Culicover et al., eds. 1977:71-132.
Chomsky, N. 1981, *Lectures on governement and binding*. Dordrecht. Foris.
Chomsky, N. 1982, *Some concepts and consequences of the theory of government and binding*. Cambridge, Mass. MIT Press.
Chomsky, N. 1986a, *Knowledge of language*. London.
Chomsky, N. 1986b, *On barriers*. Cambridge, Mass. MIT Press.
Cinque, G. 1985, Bare quantifiers, quantified NPs and the notion of operators at S-structure. Paper presented at the *Tromso Workshop on Romance Syntax*.
Culicover, P. & Wasow, T. & Akmajian, A. eds., 1977, *Formal syntax*. New York. Academic Press.
Falk, Y. 1983, Constituency, word order and phrase structure rules. *Linguistic Analysis* 11:311-360.
Fanselow, G. 1986a, *Konfigurationalität*. Tübingen. Narr (in press).
Fanselow, G. 1986b, *The proper treatment of configurationality and the German language*. Ms. submitted to NLLT.
Fanselow, G. 1986c, *Kasus*. Untersuchungen zur Universalgrammatik am Beispiel des Deutschen. Ms. Passau.
Fanselow, G. 1986d, On the sentential nature of prenominal adjectives in German. *Folia Linguistica* (in press).
Fanselow, G. 1986e, *Subjekte vs. Nominative, oder: Wieviel Ebenen hat ein deutscher Satz?* Ms. Passau.
Fanselow, G. 1986f, *Scrambling and barriers*. Paper read at the GGS-conference at Regensburg, October 1986.
Fanselow, G. & Felix, S. 1987, *Sprachtheorie*. München, UTB (in Druck).
Felix, S. 1985, Parasitic gaps in German. In: Abraham, W. ed. 1985b:173-200.
Grewendorf, G. 1983, Reflexivierung in deutschen AcI-Konstruktionen - Kein transformationsgrammatisches Dilemma mehr. *Groninger Arbeiten zur germanistischen Linguistik* 23:120-196.
Grewendorf, G. 1987, *Ergativität im Deutschen*. Ms. Frankfurt.
Haider, H. 1983, The case of German. *Groninger Arbeiten zur Germanistischen Linguistik* 22:47-100.
Haider, H. 1984, *Was zu haben ist und was zu sein hat*. Ms. Wien.

Haider, H. 1987, *Deutsche Syntax - generativ*. Tübingen. Narr.
Hale, K. 1983, Warlpiri and the grammar of non-configurational languages. *Natural Language and Linguistic Theory* 1:5-48.
Hornstein, N. 1984, *Logic as grammar*. Cambridge, Mass. MIT Press.
Horvath, J. 1981, *Aspects of Hungarian syntax and the theory of grammar*. Ph.D. Dissertation. UCLA.
Huang, J.T. 1982, Move *wh* in a language without *wh*-movement. *The Linguistic Review* 1:369-415.
Huang, J.T. 1985, On the distribution and reference of empty pronouns. *Linguistic Inquiry* 16:531-573.
Jelinek, E. 1984, Empty Categories, case and configurationality. *Natural Language and Linguistic Theory* 2:39-76.
Kayne, R. 1983, Connectedness. *Linguistic Inquiry* 14:223-250.
Kiss, K. 1981, Structural relations in Hungarian. A "free" word order language. *Linguistic Inquiry* 12:185-213.
Kiss, K. 1985, *Is the VP universal?* Ms. submitted to LIn.
Koster, J. 1975, Dutch as an SOV-language. *Linguistic Analysis* 1:11-136.
Koster, J. 1978, *Locality Principles in Syntax*. Dordrecht. Foris.
Koster, J. 1982, Enthalten syntaktische Repräsentationen Variablen? *Linguistische Berichte* 80:70-100.
Koster, J. 1984, *Global Harmony*. Ms. Tilburg.
Lenerz, J. 1977, *Zur Abfolge nominaler Satzglieder im Deutschen*. Tübingen. Narr.
McCawley, J.D. 1982, Parentheticals and discontinuous constituent structure. *Linguistic Inquiry* 13:91-105.
Merkle, H. 1975, *Bairische Grammatik*. München. Heimeram.
Pütz, H. 1974, *Über die Syntax der Pronominalform es*. Tübingen. Narr.
Reis, M. 1976, Reflexivierung in deutschen AcI-Konstruktionen. Ein transformationsgrammatisches Dilemma. *Papiere zur Linguistik* 9:5-82.
Reis, M. 1982, Zum Subjektbegriff im Deutschen. In: Abraham, W. ed. 1982:171-211.
Rizzi, L. 1982, *Issues in Italian syntax*. Dordrecht. Foris.
Sternefeld, W. 1984, On case and binding theory. *Working papers of the Sonderforschungsbereich* 99, University of Konstanz.
Sternefeld, W. 1985, Deutsch ohne grammatische Funktionen. Ein Beitrag zur Rektions- und Bindungstheorie. *Linguistische Berichte* 99:394-438.
Thiersch, C. 1978, *Topics in German syntax*. Ph.D. Dissertation. MIT.
Williams, E. 1984, Grammatical Relations. *Linguistic Inquiry* 15: 639-673.

KLAUS NETTER

INSTITUT FÜR MASCHINELLE SPRACHVERARBEITUNG

UNIVERSITÄT STUTTGART

NONLOCAL-DEPENDENCIES AND

INFINITIVAL CONSTRUCTIONS IN GERMAN

SUMMARY[0]

Drawing on the example of infinitival constructions in German this paper will contrast two different approaches to the treatment of non-local dependencies within the framework of Lexical Functional Grammar. The essential difference between the two accounts is that the first and older approach, Constituent Control (CC), operates on phrase structure, whereas the second approach, Functional Uncertainty (FU), operates on functional structure. A further difference between the two approaches is that FU allows one to do without empty strings (as traces), which are indispensable in CC for purely technical reasons. This paper concentrates on the linguistic aspects rather than the mathematical properties of FU, arguing in favour of FU on the basis of linguistic data.

To compare the two approaches a small fragment of German infinitival constructions will be described. The phenomena considered are primarily extraposition and 'wh-movement'.

A grammar for basic clauses is presented in section 1., which illustrates the underlying grammatical relations. It will be argued that, given these basic assumptions, in LFG extraposition to the right in LFG must be

---

[0] For helpful discussions and critical support I would like to thank G. Bouma, G. Fanselow, W. Frey, H. Haider, M. Reis, J. Wedekind and A. Zaenen. The research underlying this paper was carried out by support of the Bundesminister für Forschung und Technologie (Grant No. FKZ 1013207 0) and the ESPRIT - ACORD project (P393).

treated as a kind of non-local dependency in German. To introduce and compare the mechanisms of CC and FU, the grammar is extended in section 2. for both mechanisms, to cover the extraposition phenomena. The simple case of extraposed infinitival clauses governed by verbs serves to show that for a CC-based analysis, an equivalent grammar based on FU can be constructed.

By expanding the grammar further to include infinitival clauses subcategorized for by nouns (section 3.), evidence is presented which suggests that grammatical relations rather than the phrase structure configuration determine the grammatical process of extraposition. For these phenomena, the FU approach permits to capture certain generalizations more directly than the phrase structure oriented CC.

In section 4., a more classical type of non-local dependencies, wh-movement, illustrated by German relative clauses, will be discussed. Certain restrictions on wh-movement with respect to its interaction with extraposition are described. It will be shown that, given the correctness and adequacy of the generalizations outlined in the previous sections, FU allows the formulation of restrictions which cannot be expressed in the traditional approach of constituent control.

0. INTRODUCTION

One of the foremost aims of syntactic frameworks is to capture the underlying grammatical relations between the parts of a sentence, in particular the predicate argument structure, as well as the possible linear order in which these parts may occur in different surface realizations.

In many grammatical frameworks both the relations between the parts of a sentence and their linear order are determined by tree or phrase structure configurations. Specific phrase structure positions defined by dominance and precedence are assumed to encode grammatical relations. (A possible definition for the 'direct object' relation in English, for example, could be "the NP right-adjacent to V dominated by VP".) In some cases, however, a surface substring cannot be derived under a phrase structure node for which local dominance and precedence relations suffice to determine its grammatical function.

As a consequence, these displaced constituents cannot be interpreted at the position where they occur in the surface string; to receive their interpretation they must somehow be linked to their corresponding argument positions in the tree. In most frameworks, this linkage has been considered to be best represented by movement or some other notation that indicates the relation between the respective nodes in the tree.

In earlier transformational frameworks, for example, it was assumed that this linkage was constituted by (cyclic) transformations that moved a constituent from its deep structure position, which determined its grammatical relation, to its surface structure position.

In more recent versions of generative grammars, this linkage does not necessarily involve actual movement transformations. Rather, it can be expressed by means of well-formed binding relations, which to a large extent are defined over admissible phrase structure paths connecting the dislocated constituent with the phrase structure node which determines its grammatical relation. Since this node has no correspondence in the surface string, yet must be present in some form in order to determine the grammatical relation of the displaced constituent, it is derived and expanded to an empty string or trace. Thus, the interpretation of a dislocated constituent may be read off the S-structure of a sentence. This account, however, involves empty nodes as well as the concept of admissible phrase structure paths.

Within the framework of *Lexical Functional Grammar* (*LFG*)[1] the original account of non-local dependencies given in KAPLAN/BRESNAN (1982: 231-263) can be regarded as some version of this latter 'representational' conception of 'movement'. In the so-called mechanism of *constituent control* (*CC*) the correspondence between a dislocated constituent and the node determining its grammatical function, which can be arbitrarily structurally distant, is established by specific *bounded domination metavariables*.

In its most usual application the *controller* metavariable (⇓), is assigned to the node representing the dislocated constituent. The corresponding *controllee* metavariable (⇑) is assigned to an empty node dominated by a node which determines the dislocated constituent's function. Configurationally, the corresponding controller and controllee metavariables are connected by a specific c-command relation between

---

[1] cf. KAPLAN/BRESNAN (1982), BRESNAN (1982), SELLS (1985)

the nodes annotated by the metavariables. The *control domain*, i.e. the partial tree that contains the controllee, is defined as being dominated by a daughter node of the mother node of the controller annotated node. The condition holds that the path connecting the root node of the control domain and the node annotated by the controllee must not contain any nodes marked as *bounding nodes*.

However, this mechanism exhibits some properties that have often been felt to be out of place in a theory such as LFG, since it introduces a certain amount of inhomogeneity into the theory: unlike other theories, LFG explicitly does make use of grammatical functions (such as SUBJect, OBJect etc.) as primitives of the theory along with the phrase structure configuration. Although the two levels of representation, *constituent* or *c-structure* and *functional* or *f-structure*, are more or less closely connected by the conditions for the syntactic encoding of grammatical functions, there is a clear division of labour between the two levels. Whereas c-structure in LFG has always been primarily designed to determine the surface phrase structure configuration, the grammatical relations are represented by the f-structure, built up from functional equations annotated on the c-structure nodes.

Thus, with the exception of dislocated constituents, whose functions can be determined only by means of the corresponding controllees, all other constituents are assigned their functions directly through equations annotated on the roots of the constituents.

Besides the influence of transformational frameworks, one of the primary reasons for putting up with this inhomogeneity seems to have been a technical problem: for some phrase structure positions the function of a constituent cannot be determined within a local structural domain, but may depend on lexical items or predicates unpredictably deeply embedded in the structure:

(1) $[_i$ What $]$ did Mary tell Peter $[_i$ $]$?

(2) $[_i$ What $]$ did Mary promise to try to tell Peter $[_i$ $]$?.

Whereas it would be possible in principle to assign to the wh-phrase *what* in (1) the function OBJ relative to the local predicate *tell*, there is no such function for *what* relative to the local predicate *promise* in (2): the function of the wh-phrase in this case is determined by the local predicate of the infinitival complement (XCOMP) of the complement *to tell* of the complement of *promise*. Since the chain of intervening predicate-argument relations (argument of a predicate of an argument of a predicate of an argument ... of the local predicate) is taken to be unpredictably long in principle, this kind of dependency has to be considered as being 'unbounded'.

Thus, if one wanted to determine the possible functions of the dislocated constituent in situ, this could not be done by a finite number of disjunctive statements such as 'This constituent is the OBJ of the local predicate', 'This constituent is the OBJ of the XCOMP of the local predicate' etc., or their formal equivalents $\{/(\uparrow \text{OBJ}) = \downarrow / (\uparrow \text{XCOMP OBJ}) = \downarrow / ... /\}$.

This uncertain number of embeddings of a function in the f-structure is accounted for by CC, since the recursions during the derivation of the controller generate a non-finite number of c-structure paths and thus a non-finite number of sequences of function assigning equations (annotated on the nodes of the paths) which determines the specific embedding in an f-structure.

Recently, this technical problem has been overcome in a proposal by Kaplan and Zaenen[2] to represent unbounded dependencies by annotating dislocated constituents with rule schemata of the form $(\uparrow R) = \downarrow$, where R is a regular expression over the functional vocabulary, say 'XCOMP* OBJ' or XCOMP* OBJ/OBJ2/POBJ. This allows a non-finite number of disjunctive function assigning equations to be specified in a finite way.

Beyond the solution of a technical problem however, this approach called *Functional Uncertainty* opens up a somewhat, possibly even radically, different view of the description of word order variations in LFG: phrase structure becomes even more surface oriented, since every sub-structure is recognizably realized in the surface string. FU also renders the interpretation of annotated rule schemata more homogeneous: every constituent in the phrase structure configuration can now be assigned its (potentially uncertain) function directly. This is done either by a single function designator or a (potentially non-finite) set of designators specified by means of a regular expression. In the latter case,

---

[2] cf. KAPLAN/MAXWELL/ZAENEN (1987). The proposal has also been taken up by KARTTUNEN (1986), who incorporates the mechanism in a Categorial Unification Grammar.

the selection of the correct function assigning expression, out of the set of possible expressions, is determined by well-formedness conditions (coherence and completeness) in a similar way as it is done in the first case.

This approach, of course, also raises a number of questions and problems from the linguistic point of view: One must ask whether two grammars using CC and FU, respectively, are strongly equivalent on the level of f-structure, i.e. whether they describe the same set of sentences and assign the same f-structure to a given sentence. CC involves the notion of bounding categories on the level of phrase structure, i.e. some phrase structure nodes are marked as boundaries or islands for 'extraction'. The generalizations expressed by this concept have to find a re-formulated equivalence on the level of f-structure. In fact, to motivate the change in the theory, it should be plausible that f-structure relations rather than phrase structure relations determine the possible link between a dislocated constituent and its governing predicate.

This paper will present linguistic evidence bearing on some of these questions. Since very little is known about the description of German within the framework of LFG and since the working of two mechanisms should be compared relative to a given grammar, a grammatical description for a fragment of German, covering some infinitival constructions, is given below. For some of the constructions (extraposition of complements of verbs), it will be shown that functional uncertainty will yield the same results as constituent control.

Extraposition phenomena involving the complements of nouns will serve to illustrate that functional information plays a crucial role. An analysis of the interaction of extraposition and wh-movement in the final section will demonstrate that, given the present definition of constituent control, functional uncertainty allows restrictions to be expressed which are impossible to express with the mechanism of constituent control.

1. BASIC CLAUSE STRUCTURE

In this section some assumptions about the basic clause structure in German will be outlined. The main purpose of the proposed analysis is to motivate the claim that, within a framework such as LFG, right extraposition of infinitival clauses in German should be considered a kind of non-local dependency.

Irrespective of the question of whether there is a VP-constituent in German or not[3], it is a quite uncontroversial assumption that the basic position of verbal elements is to the right of their complements. This assumption can be extended to cover not only the nominal and prepositional complements but also the verbal complements of a verb. Thus, as a starting point, it can be assumed that the basic position of the infinitival complement of a verb should be to the left of the verb. Structures of this type are given in (3) and (4):

(3) dass [er [[[von ihr gesehen] worden] sein] kann].
   that he by her seen passive be can
   that he could have been seen by her

(4) dass [er [[sie zu sehen] zu versuchen] wagte].
   that he her to see to try dared

For these so-called *coherent* infinitival constructions (be they obligatorily (3) or optionally (4) coherent), it is crucial to ask how the various verbal elements should be represented on the level of f-structure and whether (or not) they should have a similar representation. At least for the first construction, involving verbs which mark modal, passive and perfect, one could argue that it should be represented by a flat f-structure, i.e. an f-structure which contains only one semantic form, the 'main' verb's PRED-entry, while the other verbs are represented by features. The alternative analysis, which will be argued for in the following, assigns a semantic form to every verb, resulting in a hierarchical f-structure.

For sentence (5) these alternative analyses are exemplified by the f-structures (F1) and (F2).

(5) weil er geschlafen haben kann.

---

[3] An FU-based LFG approach which represents infintival constructions by means of a verb complex rather than by VP recursion is outlined in NETTER (1986) and NETTER (1987). Cf. EVERS (1975) for an early transformational account. Verb Raising phenomena in Dutch are analyzed in BRESNAN et al. (1982) and JOHNSON (1986a), who also bases his anlysis on FU.

(F1)

$$\begin{bmatrix} \text{TENSE} & = \text{present} \\ \text{PERFECT} & = + \\ \text{MODAL} & = \text{können} \\ \text{PRED} & = \text{schlafen} < (\text{SUBJ}) > \\ \text{SUBJ} & = [\text{PRED} = \text{pro}] \end{bmatrix}$$

(F2)

$$\begin{bmatrix} \text{XCOMP} & = \begin{bmatrix} \text{XCOMP} & = \begin{bmatrix} \text{INF} & = \text{ge} \\ \text{PRED} & = \text{schlafen} < (\text{SUBJ}) > \\ \text{SUBJ} & = [1] \end{bmatrix} \\ \text{PRED} & = \text{haben} < (\text{XCOMP}) > (\text{SUBJ}) \\ \text{SUBJ} & = [1] \\ \text{INF} & = \text{en} \end{bmatrix} \\ \text{PRED} & = \text{können} < (\text{XCOMP}) > (\text{SUBJ}) \\ \text{SUBJ} & = 1[\text{PRED} = \text{pro}] \end{bmatrix}$$

The answer to this question has important consequences for the analysis of extraposed or *non-coherent* infinitival constructions such as in (7), since in the second approach extraposition must be considered as a construction involving non-local dependencies.

(6) dass er [ihr zu helfen] überredet worden zu sein scheint.

(7) dass er [$_i$] überredet worden zu sein scheint, [$_i$ ihr zu helfen].

The arguments against the former analysis, which leads to structures like (F1) are among others the following:

- There is little reason and less evidence to assume a categorial distinction between auxiliary and main verbs: all potential auxiliary categories have a full inflectional paradigm. Unlike English modal verbs, which have the distribution of finite verbs only, German modals (with the exception of the future modal *werden*) also occur in non-finite verb forms. Similarly, there is no clear auxiliary category in German comparable to English *do*, whose only purpose is to take up the finite features in the case of AUX-inversion, in the absence of other auxiliaries. German auxiliaries, just like main verbs, take non-verbal complements and may appear as the only verbal element in a clause.

- Given that all verbs are categorized as V, it is difficult to determine the correct word order in the first approach: an annotated phrase structure from which f-structure (F1) could be derived would be (C1).

(C1)

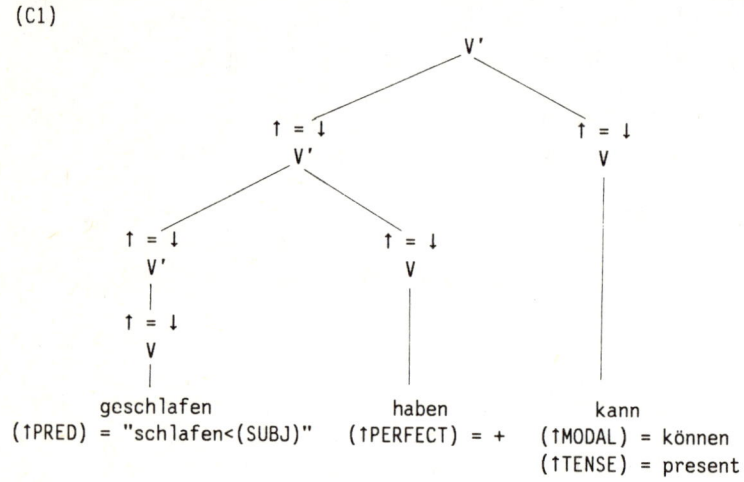

Yet the same f-structure would obviously also result from a structure like (C2), no matter what specific constraints are expressed in the lexical entries.

(C2)

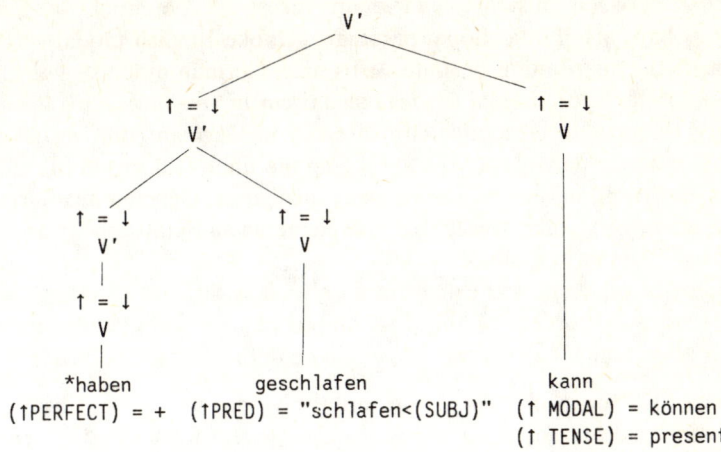

Of course one could express certain restrictions by marking the PS-rules in a specific way rather than formulating constraints in the lexical entries. It is clear, however, that this would cause a considerable loss of generality as well as disallow a uniform account for the phenomena in question.

- Non-finite verbs occur in three different morphological forms: the *pure infinitive* (*schlafen*), the *perfective / passive participle* (*geschlafen*) and the *zu-infinitive* (*zu schlafen*). This morphological form is determined, or 'governed' in the sense of LFG, by the verb which is right-adjacent to the infinitive.

Whereas in the first analysis there is no obvious and adequate way to maintain this local government relation (a verb could equally well govern an infinitive which is once removed to its left or even to its right), it is a relatively trivial task in the second approach: every non-finite verb can be marked in the lexicon by a morphological feature 'INF' which selects an atomic value from the set {*en, ge, zu*}, e.g.:

(L1) schlafen: V,
                 ...
                 (↑ INF) = en

(L2) geschlafen: V,
                 ...
                 (↑ INF) = ge

Verbs which may take an infinitival complement are then marked accordingly, e.g.:

(L3) kann: V,   (↑ PRED) = "können < (XCOMP) > (SUBJ)
                    (↑ TENSE) = present
                    (↑ XCOMP SUBJ) = (↑ SUBJ)
                    (↑ XCOMP INF) = en
                    ...

(L4) haben: V,   (↑ PRED) = "haben < (XCOMP) > (SUBJ)
                    (↑ INF) = en
                    (↑ XCOMP SUBJ) = (↑ SUBJ)
                    (↑ XCOMP INF) = ge
                    ...

- In the first approach there is no intuitively adequate way to capture certain differences in meaning which are clearly determined by the order of verbs:

(8) weil er geschlafen haben kann.
          he slept   have can
    he could have slept

(9) weil er schlafen gekonnt hat.
          he slept   can   have
    he has been able to sleep

If the modal (*können*) and the verb which marks perfect (*haben*) were only represented by means of two different feature value pairs in the same f-structure (F1), there would be no way to tell which one had 'scope' over the other in the (unambiguous) surface strings[4]. Leaving it to the semantics to determine the differences in meaning would mean that the syntax first blurs a semantic distinction, which was reflected in the syntax to start off with, and then puts the burden onto the semantics of figuring

---

[4] The difference in meaning referred to here is not the difference between the epistemic and deontic reading of the modal verbs in these examples. Although this difference seems to manifest itself to some extent in the syntactic structure, - the preferred reading for *können* is the epistemic reading in (8) and the deontic reading in (9) - , it appears to be much more a matter of semantics. For some further syntactic differences see also fn.6 below.

out from, an ambiguous f-structure, which is the meaning of an originally unambiguous string.
 - If the government relation is not expressed as a strictly local relation, a large number of potential feature conflicts is to be expected. Most obviously there would be the question of the infinitival status of the governed infinitive, but this is not the only generalization to be lost.

The verb *haben* for example, in different readings, may govern a participle or a *zu*-infinitive, imposing the restriction on the governed verb that it must not have a passivized predicate argument structure:

(10) weil er das Buch gelesen hat

(11) weil er das Buch zu lesen hat

(12) *weil das Buch zu lesen / gelesen hat.

(13) weil das Buch zu lesen / gelesen ist

Werden as a passive marker, on the other hand, requires a passivized participle verb form:

(14) weil das Buch gelesen wird.

However, if *werden* intervenes between *haben* and the main verb, the passivization of the main verb is obviously no longer relevant, i.e. *haben* becomes insensitive to the predicate argument structure of the main verb in such cases:

(15) weil das Buch gelesen zu werden hat.

For these and other reasons, it clearly appears to be preferable to treat all verbs which stand in a governing relation to an infinitive, as described above, as full-fledged main verbs.

All verbs that can be combined with a non-finite verb phrase are assumed to be subcategorized for the open predicative function XCOMP, and determine the infinitival form and other properties of this XCOMP complement. (This is an over-simplification which ignores the possibility of anaphoric control.) The only distinction made for the time being is the traditional distinction between *raising* and *equi verbs*.[5]

Specifically for all auxiliary-like verbs it will be assumed that they can be analyzed as raising verbs.[6]

These sketchy assumptions about the adequate f-structure representation of infinitival constructions bias to a certain degree the issue of how the phrase structure rules ought to be designed.

Basically the infinitival complements can be separated into those which must appear in a left-adjacent position to their respective governing verb, and those which may occur in this position but need not necessarily do so. This property is determined by the governing verbs, which, accordingly, can be classified either as requiring a *coherent* construction or as permitting a *non-coherent* construction.[7]

---

[5] It should be noted that the transformational analysis on which these terms are based has little in common with the way the phenomena in question are treated in LFG. In BRESNAN (1982) the difference between the lexical entries for raising and equi verbs is expressed by the way the syntactic functions are interpreted in the semantic form of the verb: in the semantic form for raising verbs the function which controls the SUBJ of an XCOMP is not assigned an argument position or thematic role in the verb's semantic form. Notationally this is indicated by assigning this function a position outside the pointed brackets of the semantic form.

(↑ PRED) = "... < (XCOMP) > (SUBJ)"   vs.

(↑ PRED) = "... < (SUBJ) (XCOMP) >"

Apart from this difference, both cases are treated identically, i.e. by means of *functional control*, expressed by the *control equations* (↑ G) = (↑ XCOMP SUBJ), where G is a governable function SUBJ, OBJ or OBJ2. The question of whether the assumptions made in BRESNAN (1982) carry over to German is beyond the scope of this paper.

[6] A notable exception here might be certain modal verbs: The distinction between the epistemic and non-epistemic reading of some modals seems to coincide with the distinction between raising and equi verbs, as certain data involving coordination and the proform *es* suggest:

(a) Peter versucht ein Buch zu lesen und Maria versucht es auch.

(b) *Peter scheint ein Buch zu lesen und Maria scheint es auch.

(c) Peter kann Klavier spielen und Maria kann es auch.

(d) *Peter kann in der Bibliothek sein und Maria kann es auch.

Cf. also ASKEDAL (1982: 299ff)

[7] Cf. especially BECH (1955). The terms *coherent/non-coherent* are the descriptive terms traditionally used for this kind of construction. They should not be confused with the

Verbs which govern the participle or the pure infinitive always require their complements to appear in a left-adjacent position. Among the verbs which govern the zu-infinitive one can distinguish between raising verbs (16)-(21) (*scheinen, pflegen, sein, haben; versprechen* and *drohen* in some specific readings) and equi verbs (22)-(25) (*versuchen, wagen, überreden, versprechen*). By and large one can make the generalization that the complements of raising verbs must appear in a coherent construction, whereas equi verbs governing the zu-infinitive will also allow a non-coherent construction.

(16) weil er das Buch zu lesen hat.

(17) *weil er hat, das Buch zu lesen.

(18) weil er zu schlafen scheint.

(19) *weil er scheint, zu schlafen.

(20) weil das Baby sich gut zu entwickeln versprach.

(21) *weil das Baby versprach, sich gut zu entwickeln.

(22) weil er zu schlafen versucht hat.

(23) weil er versucht hat, zu schlafen.

(24) weil er gesehen worden zu sein behauptet.

LFG internal *coherence condition*.

The only non-coherent construction that will be considered in the following will be right-extraposition, as the most frequent case. Other non-coherent constructions involve *pied-piping* (a) and the so-called *medial* position of infinitival complements (b):

(a) Das Buch, [$_i$ das zu lesen] [ich [ihm [$_i$] empfehlen] wuerde].

(b) weil [$_i$ ich [es zu lesen] [ihm nicht [$_i$] empfehlen] wuerde].

Additional distinctions have been made by GREWENDORF (1984) and HAIDER (1986), who point out that not every infinitival complement that appears in a coherent position necessarily exhibits all the properties that are predicted for the genuine coherent constructions. This exceptional status is claimed in particular for equi verbs with subject control. I will ignore these distinction in the following.

(25) weil er behauptet, gesehen worden zu sein.[8]

The crucial point here is not that some verbs will allow a non-coherent construction, but rather that all verbs which govern some non-finite structure will allow a coherent construction, in the sense that the complement appears in a left-adjacent position. As a consequence, coherent constructions could be regarded as the basic structure for all infinitival constructions, all others (extraposition, topicalization etc.) being derived by some means or other.

Given the specific assumptions in the LFG-framework that the difference between raising verbs and equi verbs is to be represented in the semantic form rather than on the categorial level, I will assume that all coherent constructions are derived by the same rule system:[9]

---

[8] There are some notable exceptions to this generalization in both directions:

G. Fanselow suggested (peronal communication) that *anfangen* and *beginnen* should be treated as raising verbs in one of their readings, although they permit a non-coherent construction. The main argument for his assumption seems to be that these verbs are compatible with the subjects of 'weather verbs' which are difficult to imagine as thematic arguments:

(a) als [es [[zu regnen] begonnen / angefangen] hatte]

(b) als [es [[$_i$] begonnen / angefangen] hatte], [$_i$ zu regnen]

However, if these verbs were genuine raising verbs, they should accept subjectless complements, which appears to be doubtful, at least for the case of passivized complements:

(c) weil gearbeitet zu werden schien

(d) *weil gearbeitet zu werden anfing

M. Reis has raised some doubts on the basis of verbs such as *wissen* which could be argued to assign a thematic role to their subjects, but will not permit a non-coherent construction:

(e) weil er gut zu leben weiss.

(f) *weil er weiss, gut zu leben.

Wissen in this reading will not allow a subject-less construction (g), which suggests an equi reading, yet it will not permit the kind of coordination (h) discussed in fn.6:

(g) *weil gearbeitet zu werden wusste.

(h) *weil Maria zu arbeiten wusste und Hans es auch wusste.

[9] In the rules given below the phrase structure categories are written in vertical

(R1)   S'   ->   C   ↑ = ↓
                           (↑ TENSE)
                 S   ↑ = ↓.

(R2)   S   ->   [NP   (↑ SUBJ) = ↓]
                 [NP   (↑ OBJ2) = ↓]
                 [NP   (↑ OBJ) = ↓]
                 [VP   (↑ XCOMP) = ↓]
                 [V   ↑ = ↓].

(R3)   VP   ->   [NP   (↑ OBJ2) = ↓]
                 [NP   (↑ OBJ) = ↓]
                 [VP   (↑ XCOMP) = ↓]
                 V   ↑ = ↓ .

The existential constraint on the feature TENSE, annotated on the complementizer position C, guarantees that the V immediately dominated by S will be a finite verb. Since the finite verb only occupies the clause-final position under certain conditions, it is marked as optional (V-second clauses can be introduced through a particular expansion of C.). The non-finite verbs, introduced by VP-recursion, are obligatory constituents of VP.

An application of these rules is illustrated by the c- and f-structure derivations (C3), (F3) and (C4), (F4).

---

columns, the functional annotations appear to the right of the symbols. Square brackets [ ] mark optional constituents, disjunctions of rule schemata are indicated by {/ ... / ... / }. In the f-structures, functional control relations between partial f-structures are marked by coindexing the f-structures with single numerals.

(C3)

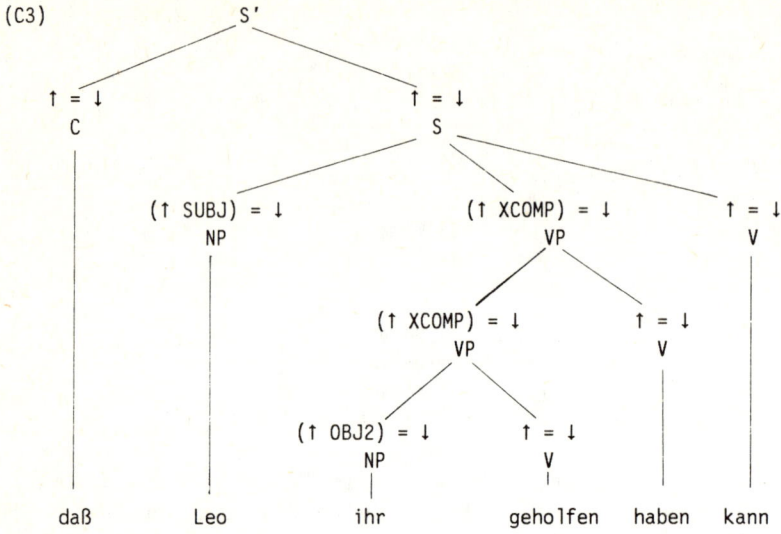

daß Leo ihr geholfen haben kann

(F3)

$$\begin{bmatrix} \text{TENSE} & = \text{present} \\ \text{XCOMP} & = \begin{bmatrix} \text{XCOMP} & = \begin{bmatrix} \text{INF} & = \text{ge} \\ \text{PRED} & = \text{helfen} < (\text{SUBJ}), (\text{OBJ2}) > \\ \text{SUBJ} & = [1] \\ \text{OBJ2} & = [\text{PRED} = \text{pro}] \end{bmatrix} \\ \text{PRED} & = \text{haben} < (\text{XCOMP}) > (\text{SUBJ}) \\ \text{SUBJ} & = [1] \\ \text{INF} & = \text{en} \end{bmatrix} \\ \text{PRED} & = \text{können} < (\text{XCOMP}) > (\text{SUBJ}) \\ \text{SUBJ} & = 1 | \text{PRED} = \text{leo} | \end{bmatrix}$$

(C4)

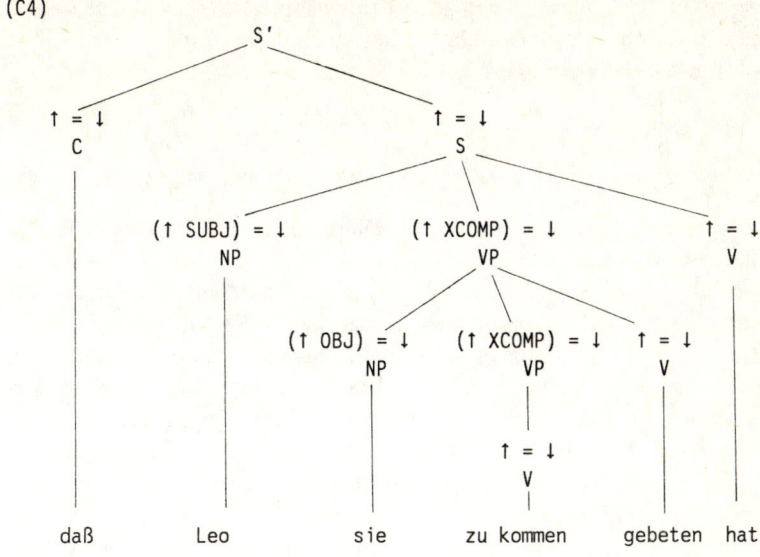

daß	Leo	sie	zu kommen	gebeten	hat

(F4)

$$\begin{bmatrix} \text{XCOMP} & = & \begin{bmatrix} \text{XCOMP} & = & \begin{bmatrix} \text{INF} & = & \text{zu} \\ \text{PRED} & = & \text{kommen} < (\text{SUBJ}) > \\ \text{SUBJ} & = & [3] \end{bmatrix} \\ \text{PRED} & = & \text{bitten} < (\text{SUBJ}), (\text{OBJ}), (\text{XCOMP}) > \\ \text{SUBJ} & = & [1] \\ \text{OBJ} & = & 3\begin{bmatrix} \text{PRED} & = & \text{pro} \end{bmatrix} \\ \text{INF} & = & \text{ge} \end{bmatrix} \\ \text{PRED} & = & \text{haben} < (\text{XCOMP}) > (\text{SUBJ}) \\ \text{SUBJ} & = & 1\begin{bmatrix} \text{PRED} & = & \text{Leo} \end{bmatrix} \end{bmatrix}$$

Given that the assumptions made in this chapter are correct, it follows that extraposition, as discussed in the next section, has to be regarded as a case of non-local dependency.

2. EXTRAPOSITION OF INFINITIVAL COMPLEMENTS

After a short description of data involving the extraposition of infinitival complements of verbs in 2.1., the CC and FU approach for the analysis of extraposed infinitival clauses will be contrasted. Section 2.2.1. will demonstrate that a CC approach allows two different sets of phrase structure rules for the description of these phenomena, one yielding a left recursive, the other a right recursive phrase structure. Both rule sets are strongly equivalent on the level of f-structure (*strongly f-equivalent* in the following), i.e. they allow the derivation of the same set of sentences, and each of the rule systems will assign the same f-structure to a given sentence. It is argued that only the right-recursive rule set is empirically adequate. In 2.2.2. an equivalent grammar based on FU is constructed, which in a sense is more restrictive, since it is compatible only with one set of phrase structure rules.

2.1. The Data

As mentioned above, the non-finite complement of an equi verb which governs a *zu*-infinitive may appear either in an embedded coherent position or the complement can be derived in a non-coherent position. One such non-coherent construction results when the complement is *extraposed* in the sense, that it takes the position to the right of the structure that contains its governor (27)/(29):

(26) weil [er [[das Buch zu lesen] versucht] hat]

(27) weil [er [[$_i$] versucht] hat] [$_i$ das Buch zu lesen]

(28) weil [er [[[das Buch gelesen] zu haben] behaupten] will]

(29) weil [er [[$_i$] behaupten] will] [$_i$ [das Buch gelesen] zu haben]

It is not quite clear how deep the governor of an extraposed constituent may be embedded. For infinitives which must obligatorily occur in a coherent verb-complex, the number of embeddings can be relatively high (31). In the case of equi verbs, however, the acceptability seems to decrease with the depth of embedding (32)/(33)

(30) weil [er [[[[der Frau zu helfen] gebeten] worden] sein] könnte]

(31) weil [er [[[[$_i$] gebeten] worden] sein] könnte] [$_i$ der Frau zu helfen]

(32) weil [er [[[$_i$] zu behaupten] wagte] [$_i$ das Buch gelesen zu haben]

(33) ?weil [er [[[[$_i$] zu behaupten] zu beginnen] wagte] [$_i$ das Buch gelesen zu haben]

It is arguable, however, whether this difference should be described as a restriction on the grammatical system or whether it should be considered as a pragmatic and stylistic restriction. Obviously, right-recursive structures are easier to process than left-recursive structures. Thus, if extraposition is available as an optional variant, one would expect it to apply whenever possible, in order to improve the processability of a sentence.

It is important to note that extraposition does not mean that the complement appears to the right of its governor: the complement has to appear to the right of any verb f-commanding its governor. This restriction holds for both obligatorily (34)-(36) and optionally coherent (37)-(39) constructions:

(34) weil [er [[das Buch zu lesen] versuchen] kann]

(35) weil [er [[$_i$] versuchen] kann] [$_i$ das Buch zu lesen]

(36) *weil [er [[$_i$] versuchen [$_i$ das Buch zu lesen]] kann]

(37) weil [er [[ein guter Mensch zu sein] zu behaupten] versuchte]

(38) weil [er [[$_i$] zu behaupten] versuchte] [$_i$ ein guter Mensch zu sein]

(39) *weil [er [[$_i$] zu behaupten [$_i$ ein guter Mensch zu sein]] versuchte]

Extraposition is an operation that may be applied recursively, in that the complement of an extraposed complement may be extraposed as well (42):

(40) weil [er [[[zu schlafen] versucht] zu haben] behauptet]

(41) weil [er [$_i$] behauptet] [$_i$ [[zu schlafen] versucht] zu haben]

(42) weil [er [$_i$] behauptet] [$_i$ [[$_j$] versucht] zu haben] [$_j$ zu schlafen]]

To summarize: the depth of embedding of the governor of an extraposed constituent is uncertain (30)-(33). Extraposition is restricted to the complements of equi verbs governing the zu-infinitive (16)-(25). The extraposed complement must be adjoined to the right of any verb f-commanding its governing verb (34)-(39). Extraposition is an optional operation and may be applied recursively (40)-(42).

2.2. The Grammatical Description

According to the generalizations made over the data in section 1. and 2.1., a rule system which covers extraposition will have to cope with the following problems:

Obviously the extraposed complement cannot be derived as a co-constituent to its governor, i.e. the subcategorization of a verb for an XCOMP-complement on the f-structure level cannot (always) be fulfilled by a VP-constituent c-commanded by this verb.

Since the governing verb can be arbitrarily deeply embedded, the f-structure level to which the extraposed complement must be assigned is uncertain and not predictable within the rule system.

The rule introducing extraposed constituents must be restricted to the XCOMP-complements of an adaquate subset of verbs, which is hypothesized to be the class of equi verbs which govern a zu-infinitive, and it must not apply within the self-embedding VP-recursion itself.

2.2.1. CONSTITUENT CONTROL

For the CC approach there are basically two ways to represent the c-structure of extraposed constituents. The first is more in line with X-bar-principles and involves *Chomsky-adjunction* of VP to S. Recursive extraposition of VP in this approach is represented by a left-recursive structure. The second approach is based on right recursion of a VP'-symbol which dominates the extraposed constituents together with all recursively extraposed constituents.

The treatment of extraposition by means of Chomsky-adjunction of VP to S comes closer to traditional approaches to this phenomenon. It involves the extension of the rules (R1) - (R3) by the following two rules, which automatically prevent extraposition from occuring within a self-embedding VP-recursion:

(R4)   S   -> $\boxed{S}$ $\uparrow = \downarrow$

                VP $\Downarrow^S_{vp} = \downarrow$

                     $(\downarrow \text{COHERENCE}) = -$.

(R5)   VP ->   e $\Uparrow_{vp} = \uparrow$.

The adjoined VP serves to derive the extraposed constituent; it is annotated by a rule schema which introduces a controller. The control domain for this controller is its left sister node S, which is marked as a bounding node.

This has the effect of *bounding* the *control domain* such that it comprises all constituents dominated by the *domain root* S except constituents which are dominated by another S.

The corresponding controllee is introduced by (R5), which expands an (XCOMP annotated) VP - node to the empty string. By definition, two correponding bounded domination metavariables are instantiated by the same variables. Thus, in the f-description solution, the partial f-structure built up from the extraposed constituent is treated as if it were derived in the embedded position.

To prevent extraposition of an arbitrary VP, a binary valued feature "COHERENCE = +/- " is assumed. All verbs which require an obligatory coherent position for their complements will be marked by an equation (↑ XCOMP COHERENCE) = + in the lexicon.[10]

The VP node which represents the extraposed infinitive is annotated by a respective equation (↓ COHERENCE) = - , causing a feature clash if the 'wrong' complement is extraposed. When a VP governed by a verb which permits both coherent and non-coherent constructions is extraposed, there is no clash, since these verbs do not mark their complements in the lexicon for any value of COHERENCE.

The structure (C5) illustrates the recursive extraposition of two VP-complements. The metavariables in the functional schemata are instantiated in parallel by variables only for the relevant parts of the structure.

---

[10] This can be done by means of a lexical redundancy rule, or, if one considers coherence to be an ideosyncratic and unpredictable property (see fn.8), this equation must be assigned directly to the (presumably) closed set of respective verbs. I have chosen the use of a feature here, since it involves the least changes of in LFG theory of control and complementation. Other solutions, such as the use of different functions, could be contrived, but would require a more detailed discussion than is within the scope of this paper.

(C5)

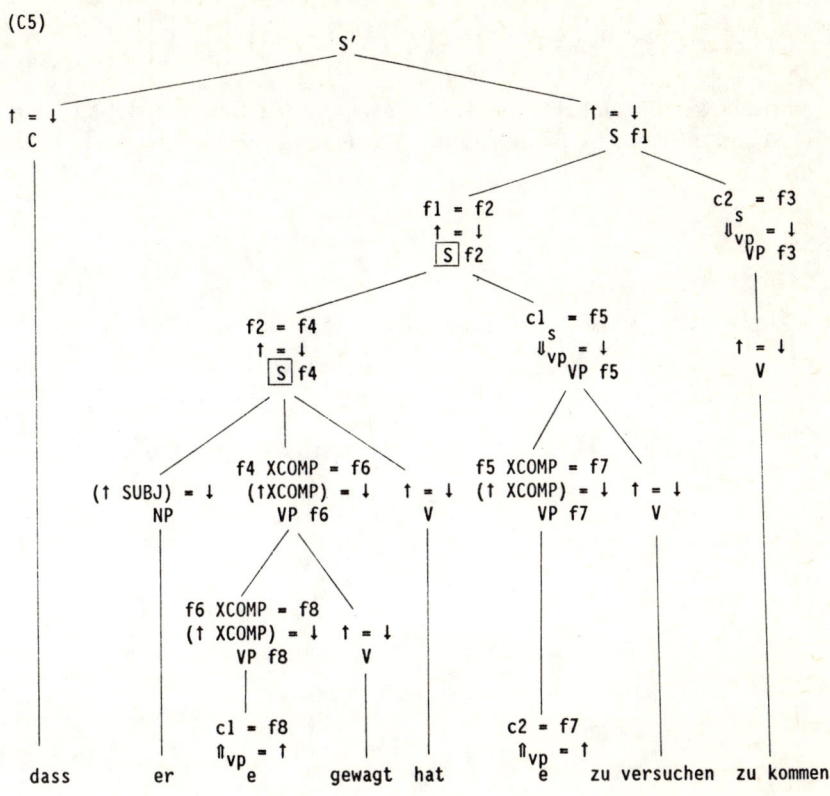

The relevant subset of the f-description contains the following equations:

f1 = f2	f2 = f4
f4 XCOMP = f6	f6 XCOMP = f8
c1 = f8	c1 = f5
f5 XCOMP = f7	c2 = f7
c2 = f3	

from which the partial f-structure (F5) can be built, illustrating the embedding of the extraposed constituents' f-structure:

(F5) f1 [XCOMP [XCOMP f5 [XCOMP f3 [ ]]]]
     f2   f8   f7
     f4   f6   c1   c2

(F6) shows the global f-structure, incorporating the partial f-structure (F5) and enriched by the functional information carried by lexical entries etc.

(F6)

```
      ⎡ TENSE    =  present                                                              ⎤
      ⎢ XCOMP    =  ⎡ XCOMP  =  ⎡ XCOMP   =  ⎡ INF       =  zu              ⎤ ⎤ ⎤ ⎥
      ⎢             ⎢           ⎢            ⎢ COHERENCE =  -               ⎥ ⎥ ⎥ ⎥
      ⎢             ⎢           ⎢         f7 ⎢ PRED      =  kommen < (SUBJ) > ⎥ ⎥ ⎥ ⎥
      ⎢             ⎢           ⎢         f3 ⎢                              ⎥ ⎥ ⎥ ⎥
      ⎢             ⎢           ⎢         c2 ⎣ SUBJ      =  [1]             ⎦ ⎥ ⎥ ⎥
      ⎢             ⎢           ⎢  SUBJ   =  [1]                              ⎥ ⎥ ⎥
      ⎢             ⎢           ⎢  INF    =  zu                               ⎥ ⎥ ⎥
      ⎢             ⎢        f5 ⎢  COHERENCE = -                              ⎥ ⎥ ⎥
      ⎢             ⎢        f8 ⎢                                             ⎥ ⎥ ⎥
      ⎢             ⎢        c1 ⎣  PRED   =  versuchen < (SUBJ), (XCOMP) >    ⎦ ⎥ ⎥
      ⎢             ⎢  SUBJ      =  [1]                                         ⎥ ⎥
      ⎢             ⎢  PRED      =  wagen < (SUBJ) (XCOMP) >                    ⎥ ⎥
      ⎢             ⎢  COHERENCE =  +                                           ⎥ ⎥
      ⎢          f6 ⎣  INF       =  GE                                          ⎦ ⎥
      ⎢ PRED     =  haben < (XCOMP) > (SUBJ)                                      ⎥
      ⎢ SUBJ     =  1 ⎡ PRED  =  pro ⎤                                            ⎥
   f1 ⎢                ⎢ NUM   =  sg  ⎥                                            ⎥
   f2 ⎢                ⎣ CASE  =  nom ⎦                                            ⎥
   f4 ⎣                                                                            ⎦
```

The rule system (R1)-(R5), although sufficiently restricted and theoretically valid for the cases considered until now, has certain disadvantages on a broader empirical level: there are some constructions in German which suggest that a non-finite clause forms a constituent together with all the material extraposed from underneath it. In V-second clauses the same substring that occurs in an extraposed position at the end of the sentence (43) may also occur in the *topic* position in front of the finite verb (44):

(43) Hans hat sich geweigert, [dem Richter zu gestehen, die Tat begangen zu haben].

(44) [Dem Richter zu gestehen, die Tat begangen zu haben,] hat Hans sich geweigert.

Given the traditional LFG assumption that non-finite clauses of this type must not be S, it is quite unclear what the category of the topicalized constituent should be. If it were analyzed as VP, one would have to allow adjunction to VP to account for the extraposed constituent. Yet the result of a rule which would allow Chomsky-adjunction to VP would be that extraposition within the self-embedding VP recursion under S would also be allowed.

A similar problem arises in connection with the infinitival complements of nouns (45)/(46):

(45) Hans hat den Befehl, wenigstens zu versuchen, die Hunde zu füttern, nicht akzeptiert.

(46) Hans hat den Befehl nicht akzeptiert, wenigstens zu versuchen, die Hunde zu füttern.

Again, one could argue that the infinitives are (recursively) Chomsky-adjoined to some projection of N. However, in this case some *freezing principle*[11] would have to be invoked, which would prevent the top-most adjoined infinitive from being extraposed on the sentence level (47):

(47) *Hans hat den Befehl, wenigstens zu versuchen, nicht akzeptiert, die Hunde zu füttern.

In other words, there seems to be some evidence for a rule in German which allows the derivation of a non-finite clause together with extraposed

---

[11] Devices of this kind are argued for by e.g. WEXLER/CULLICOVER (1980) but appear to be out of place in a non-transformational theory such as LFG.

constituents as a single constituent.

For this reason, I will assume a c-structure analysis which derives the extraposed VPs by means of a right recursive rule, rather than by left recursive adjunction.[12]

One of the most crucial differences between the approach described above and the analysis proposed in the following is the postulation of a specific category symbol VP' which is the righmost daughter of S and which may be expanded right recursively.[13]

Besides the addition of a rule (R7) for VP' the rule (R2) is modified to allow the derivation of a VP' constituent under S (R6). The complete grammar consists of the rules (R1), (R3), (R5), (R6) and (R7).

(R6)   S   ->   [NP   ($\uparrow$ SUBJ) = $\downarrow$]
                   ...
                   [VP   ($\uparrow$ XCOMP) = $\downarrow$]
                   [V $\uparrow$ = $\downarrow$]

                   [VP' $\Downarrow_{vp}^{vp}$ = $\downarrow$

                             ($\downarrow$ COHERENCE) = -]

---

[12] The criticism of certain insufficiencies in the mechanism of constituent control in section 3. and 4. is not affected by this difference.

[13] Note that a VP immediately dominated by VP' cannot be expanded to the empty string right away. A partial tree such as (Ci) is excluded by the condition that every control domain must have a *lexical signature*, i.e. a distinct word in the terminal string which guarantees decidability. (cf. KAPLAN/BRESNAN (1982: 246f)).

(Ci)

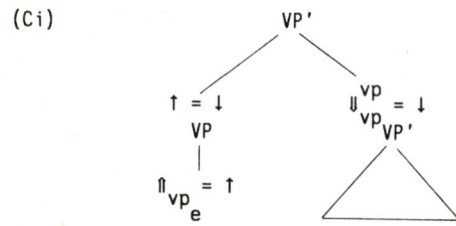

(R7)   VP' -> VP $\uparrow\ =\ \downarrow$

   [VP' $\Downarrow_{vp}^{vp} = \downarrow$

   ($\downarrow$ COHERENCE) = -]

The feature which serves to distinguish non-coherent from coherent complements is used here in the same way as described above. To prevent extraposition within the self-embedding VP-recursion, the (controller annotated) node dominating the extraposed infinitive is labelled with the symbol VP'. Since the controller metavariable carries a vp-symbol as subscript, indicating that this controller must be identified with a VP-dominated controllee, this symbol has no further consequences.

Besides the empirical motivation discussed above, the VP' symbol is also technically motivated by the conditions for constituent control: since the extraposed infinitive is derived as the right-most daughter of S, the control domain for the controller must be the VP-sister node to its left. The definition of the control domain, however, only requires that the root node of the control domain be a daughter node to the mother node of the node annotated by the controller. Therefore, the category symbol of the extraposed category has to be distinct from the category VP specified as control domain, otherwise it could be its own control domain. I.e. the situation could arise in which a controller annotated VP-node exhaustively dominates an empty string which is annotated by a controllee satisfying the constraint of its mother's controller.

That the two rule systems are strongly f-equivalent is demonstrated by structure (C6). (For the purpose of illustration, the instantiations of the meta-variables in this structure are chosen to be compatible with the variables in f-structure (F6) above.)

(C6)

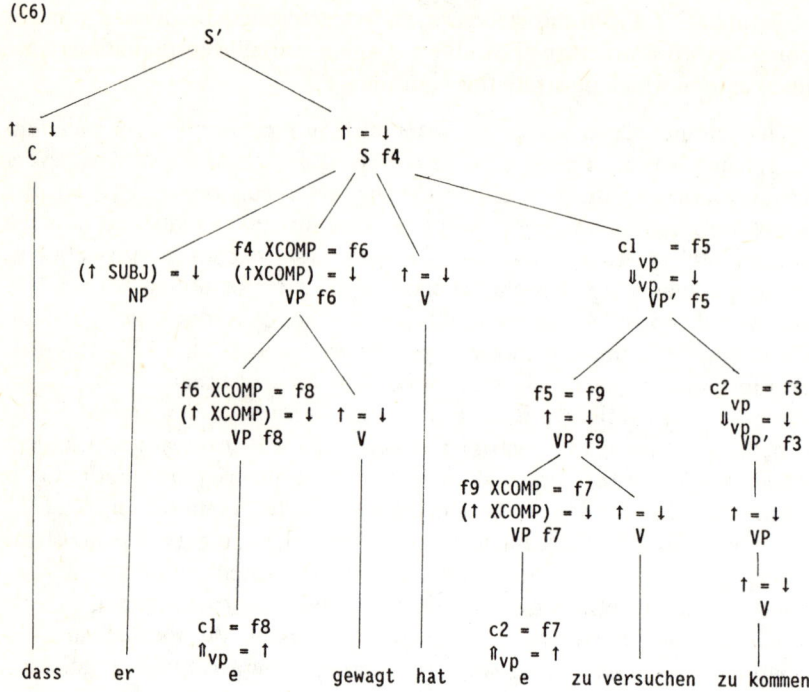

In the next section it will be shown that an LFG can be constructed using the mechanism of FU which is strongly f-equivalent to both approaches discussed above.

2.2.2. FUNCTIONAL UNCERTAINTY

The working of the mechanism of FU is once more illustrated by the sample sentence in (C6). The context free base of the rules used below is similar to the rules deriving the right-recursive structures above.[14]

Suppose that the VP-nodes dominating the empty strings in (C6) are

---

[14] Although the matter will not be discussed much further, it appears impossible that a similar LFG based on FU can be constructed which builds up c-structures analogously to the analysis based on Chomsky adjunction.

removed and that the annotations on the VP'-nodes introducing the controller metavariables in (C6) are replaced by the equations given in structure (C7). From this structure, an f-structure can be derived which is equivalent to f-structure (F6) above. (Again, variable instantiations have been chosen which illustrate this equivalence.)

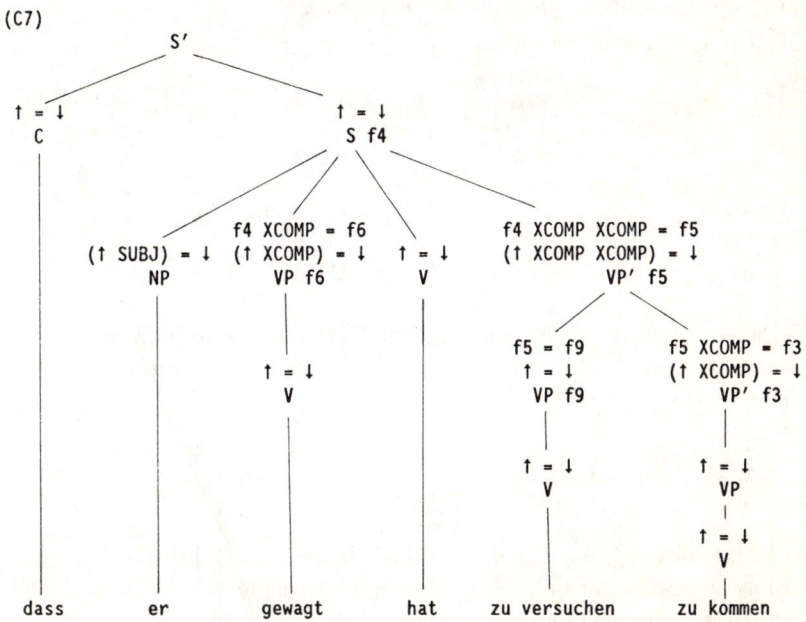

Whereas the bounded domination metavariables do not make any reference to the mother node of the node on which they are annotated, the equations annotated on the VP' nodes in (C7) contain a *mother variable* (↑), which locates the starting point of an f-structure path which embeds the extraposed constituents' f-structures.

Now, of course the rule schemata annotated on the extraposed VP's in (C7) are 'hand-made', i.e. these annotations will not always produce the correct result. The XCOMP function represented by a VP' could be the complement of a predicate higher up or deeper down in the global f-structure. Still, for the data given, one can predict that a VP' will always fulfill the function of an XCOMP with respect to a predicate that can be reached along a path of XCOMPs starting from the f-structure node onto which the mother node of this VP' is mapped. In other words, we can predict that the VP' must have the function of an XCOMP, of an XCOMP's XCOMP, of an XCOMP's XCOMP's XCOMP etc. One preliminary way of representing this regularity is to annotate the VP' nodes with a finite disjunction of rule schemata:

```
(R8)    S       ->      [NP       (↑ SUBJ) = ↓ ]
                        ...
                        [VP       (↑ XCOMP) = ↓]
                        [V        ↑ = ↓ ]
                        [ VP'     {/ (↑ XCOMP) = ↓
                                   / (↑ XCOMP XCOMP) = ↓
                                   / (↑ XCOMP XCOMP XCOMP) = ↓
                                   / ... / }
                                  (↓ COHERENCE) = - ]
```

Suppose, then, that a partial f-structure (F7) has been built up from the structure to the left of this VP' node (irrelevant details ommitted).

(F7)

$$
f4\begin{bmatrix} \text{XCOMP} & = & f6\begin{bmatrix} \text{XCOMP} & = & \begin{bmatrix} \text{SUBJ} & = & [1] \end{bmatrix} \\ \text{SUBJ} & = & [1] \\ \text{PRED} & = & \text{wagen} < (\text{SUBJ}) > \end{bmatrix} \\ \text{PRED} & = & \text{haben} < (\text{XCOMP}) > \\ \text{SUBJ} & = & 1\begin{bmatrix} \text{PRED} & = & \text{pro} \end{bmatrix} \end{bmatrix}
$$

The partial f-structures built from the VP'-node f5 can be represented by a disjunction of partial f-structures following the form of (F8):

(F8)

$$f4\left[\begin{array}{l}\overbrace{\text{XCOMP} \ldots}^{\text{n-times, } n \geq 0} \left[\text{XCOMP} = \begin{array}{l} f5 \end{array}\left[\begin{array}{l}\text{PRED} = \text{versuchen} < (\text{SUBJ}), (\text{XCOMP}) > \\ \text{COHERENCE} = -\end{array}\right]\right]\right]$$

The correct instance of n will then be determined by an interaction of the *completeness, coherence* and *consistency conditions* and unification. As indicated in (F6) the correct instance for n must be 1.

What happens in the cases where n < 1 and n > 1?

In the case where n < 1 unification obviously fails, since f-structure (F7) already contains a value for the attribute 'f4 XCOMP PRED'. An f-structure such as (F9) is blocked for being inconsistent:

(F9)

$$f4\left[\text{XCOMP} = \begin{array}{l} f5 \\ f6 \end{array}\left[\begin{array}{lll}\text{PRED} & = & \text{versuchen} < (\text{SUBJ}), (\text{XCOMP}) > \\ \text{PRED} & = & \text{wagen} < (\text{SUBJ}), (\text{XCOMP}) > \end{array}\right]\right]$$

For n > 1, unification succeeds, but the completeness and, more important, the coherence condition is violated. For example n = 2 yields the f-structure (F10).

(F10)

$$f4\left[\begin{array}{lll}\text{XCOMP} & = & \left[\text{XCOMP} = \left[\begin{array}{l}\text{XCOMP} = \begin{array}{l} f5 \end{array}\left[\begin{array}{l}\text{PRED} = \text{versuchen} <(\text{SUBJ}), (\text{XCOMP})> \\ \text{COHERENCE} = -\end{array}\right] \\ \text{SUBJ} = [1] \end{array}\right]\right. \\ & & \left. \begin{array}{l} \text{SUBJ} = [1] \\ f6 \end{array}\left[\text{PRED} = \text{wagen} < (\text{SUBJ}) > \right]\right] \\ \text{PRED} & = & \text{haben} < (\text{XCOMP}) > \\ \text{SUBJ} & = & 1\left[\text{PRED} = \text{pro}\right] \end{array}\right]$$

Since the unindexed local f-structure in (F10) contains two governable functions (SUBJ and XCOMP) but no predicate to govern these functions, it fails the coherence condition. The f-structure indexed f5 violates the completeness condition, since it contains a predicate which is subcategorized for SUBJ (and XCOMP) but does not contain a SUBJ - f-structure.

In other words, a well-formed f-structure can be produced only by unifying (F7) with a partial f-structure of the form (F8) where n = 1 and this is exactly the desired result, represented by f-structure (F6).

Of course, the disjunctive set annotated on VP' is a finite set of equations. If we assume that extraposition is a non-local and potentially unbounded dependency phenomenon, this finite set will be insufficient. A corresponding non-finite set of equations, however, can be specified in a finite way by a regular expression ' XCOMP* XCOMP '.

```
(R9)    S       ->      [NP     (↑ SUBJ) = ↓ ]
                        ...
                        [VP     (↑ XCOMP) = ↓]

                        [V      ↑ = ↓ ]
                        [ VP'   (↑ XCOMP* XCOMP) = ↓
                                (↓ COHERENCE) = - ]


(R10)   VP'     ->      VP      ↑ = ↓
                        [ VP'   (↑ XCOMP* XCOMP) = ↓
                                (↓ COHERENCE) = - ]
```

With this extension one can show that the CC grammar given by the rules (R1), (R3), (R5), (R6), (R7) is equivalent to the FU grammar with rules (R1), (R3), (R9), (R10).

This equivalence is best illustrated by the construction of the correct FU-annotation for the metavariable c1 in (C6)/(F6). All the rules which can be applied to derive the controllee from the root node of the control domain ((R3) and (R5)) and the rule introducing the controller (R6), build up all possible paths from the domain root's mother to the controllee.

All c-structure paths leading from the domain root's mother to the controllee are generated by (R5) (expanding VP to the empty string) and the unitary parts (R6') and (R3') of the rules (R6) and (R3), respectively.

```
(R6')   S       ->      VP      (↑ XCOMP) = ↓
```

(R3')   VP   ->   VP   (↑ XCOMP) = ↓

This grammar ((R3'), (R6'), (R5)) implicitly describes a regular language over the functional vocabulary. This language can be specified explicitly by a regular grammar (R3''), (R5'), (R6''), which is constructable from (R3'), (R5) and (R6') respectively, by attaching the annotated function to the left of the righthand category:

(R6'')   S   -   XCOMP   VP

(R3'')   VP   ->   XCOMP   VP

(R5')   VP   ->   e

This regular grammar describes the regular language denoted by the regular expression "XCOMP* XCOMP". In the FU grammar, this regular expression is annotated by a function assigning equation on the category originally annotated by the controller. The VP-deletion rule (R5) is eliminated. Since the VP, which is deleted by (R5) is optional in rule (R3) it is not necessary to take additional steps to ensure weak equivalence of the two grammars.

In the next sections some cases will be described where an equivalence of this kind no longer exists.

In 3. some data are considered where c-structure nodes with the same categorial label can have different grammatical functions. (E.g. PP nodes can have the grammatical function POBJ (prepositional object) or ADJ (adjunct or adverbial)). In this case, regular expressions over the functional vocabulary can be constructed which denote only a subset of the regular languages described by the corresponding c-structure paths.

Section 4. will demonstrate that cases may arise in which the c-structure path connecting controller and controllee no longer contains any of the relevant information necessary for excluding ungrammatical constructions.

3. EXTRAPOSITION OF NP-COMPLEMENTS

The following discussion serves to illustrate that extraposition involving infinitival complements of nouns is restricted by functional distinctions rather than by phrase structure configurations. Although the phenomena can be accounted for by CC a grammatical description within this approach must make recourse to two levels of grammatical representation, one of which can be argued to be irrelevant. FU, on the other hand, lends itself quite naturally to the description of the phenomena in question, making use of the relevant level of representation only.

In German, there is quite a number of nouns that take an optional infinitival complement, which has a *zu*-infinitive as the morphological default value for sentential infinitival complements:

(48) der Versuch, eine Lösung zu finden,

(49) die Annahme, die Lösung gefunden zu haben,

(50) die Anordnung, die Hunde zu füttern,

Since many of these nouns can be derived from equi verbs it will be assumed for the sake of simplicity[15] that they maintain a subcategorization frame similar to that of equi verbs:

```
(L5)   Versuch:  N,      (↑ PRED) = "versuch < SUBJ , XCOMP >"
                         (↑ SUBJ PRED) = pro
                         (↑ SUBJ) = (↑ XCOMP SUBJ)
                         (↑ XCOMP INF) = zu.
                         ...
```

There is no restriction on the function, that these complex NPs may fulfill in a sentence. They may be assigned a *governable function* SUBJ (51), OBJ (52), OBJ2 (53) or POBJ (54) or a *non-governable function*

---

[15] I am well aware that this assumption touches on a much debated question, cf. e.g. RAPPAPORT (1983), who argues that nominals take only closed functions. However, it is of little relevance here whether one chooses an alternative analysis which subcategorizes nouns for an (anaphorically controlled) *closed function* COMP, or whether one assumes these nouns to have an *anaphorically controlled* PRO subject themselves. Issues of this kind can be left to further discussion and do not affect the problems in question.

ADJ(unct) (55)/(56):

(51) dass der Versuch, dafür eine Lösung zu finden, jeden reizen würde

(52) dass er den Versuch, dieses Problem zu lösen, abgelehnt hat

(53) dass er sich der Anordnung, die Hunde zu füttern, widersetzte

(54) dass er auf die Anordnung, die Hunde zu füttern, wartete

(55) dass er trotz der Anordnung, die Hunde zu füttern, ging

(56) dass er nach dem Versuch, die Hunde zu füttern, ging

However, if these infinitival complements are extraposed, there is a clear difference between infinitival complements embedded under a governable function (SUBJ, OBJ, etc) and the complements of ADJuncts. Extraposition is grammatical in the former cases (57)-(60), but not in the latter (61)/(62):[16]

(57) dass allein der Versuch mich reizen würde, dafür eine Lösung zu finden,

(58) dass er den Versuch abgelehnt hat, dieses Problem zu lösen

(59) dass er sich der Anordnung widersetzte, die Hunde zu füttern

(60) dass er auf die Anordnung wartete, die Hunde zu füttern

(61) *dass er trotz der Anordnung ging, die Hunde zu füttern

---

[16] A. ZAENEN arrives at a similar generalization for Icelandic (cf. KAPLAN / ZAENEN (1987)). Apparently, in this respect there are no SUBJect OBJect asymmetries in German, comparable to those in the English data. Extraposition of infinitival complements out of SUBJ-NPs in English seems to be unacceptable.

(a) The mere attempt, to solve this problem, made him furious.

(b) *The mere attempt annoyed him, to solve this problem.

(62) *dass er nach dem Versuch ging, die Hunde zu füttern

It is important to note that there is no reason to assume PPs with an adverbial function take a different phrase structural position than those with a subcategorized (prepositional object) function. Both may occur between the verb and its subcategorized OBJects (63)/(64), i.e. there is little evidence for the assumption that adverbials are adjoined to a VP node or some other projection of V, whereas prepositional objects are sisters to the governing V. Thus a phrase structure based account for the ungrammaticality of (64) must be rejected.

(63) dass er [Maria [auf [den Versuch [$_i$]]] vorbereitete],
 [$_i$ sie zu küssen]

(64) *dass er [Maria [trotz [seines Versprechens [$_i$]]] küsste], [$_i$ sie nicht anzufassen].[17]

The infinitival complements of nouns are apparently best described by the VP' rules (R7)/(R10) above, since they (optionally) allow recursive extraposition:

(65) dass er [die Anordnung, [[das Problem zu lösen] zu versuchen]], nicht befolgte.

(66) dass er [die Anordnung,[[[$_i$] zu versuchen], [$_i$ das Problem zu lösen,]]] nicht befolgte.

However, if an infinitival complement embedded under an NP is to be extraposed on the sentence level, it must always be the one immediately subcategorized for by the noun, together with all its complements:

(67) dass er [die Anordnung [$_i$]] nicht befolgte,
 [$_i$ [wenigstens [$_j$] zu versuchen] [$_j$ das Problem zu lösen]]

---

[17] This would imply that HUANG's (1982) definition of extraction domains as domains which are 'properly governed' falls short of accounting for the German data. Needless to say, a distinction between arguments and non-arguments exclusively on the basis of phrase structure configuration runs into trouble with these data in any case.

(68) *dass er [die Anordnung [[$_i$] zu versuchen],] nicht befolgte, [$_i$ das Problem zu lösen]

Beyond these restrictions it should be taken into account that, although NP and PP (in non-ADJunct functions) in German are not boundaries for extraposition of clauses, they are normally bounding nodes for NP-extraction:

(69) *[$_i$ Seines Freundes] hat er [das Auto [$_i$]] gesehen.

(70) *[$_i$ Maria] hat er [auf [$_i$]] gewartet.

What would an LFG analysis for these phenomena look like in the two approaches under discussion?

Within the CC approach, the last restriction mentioned must be expressed by marking all NPs and PPs as bounding nodes. The distinction between those NPs and PPs which allow extraposition and those (adjunctive PPs) which do not, leads to rather complex expressions, which intuitively do not look very attractive, but will do the job:

Every NP and PP which qualifies for extraposition must be annotated by a so-called *linking schema* which neutralizes the boundary for extraction of VP'-constituents. This is done by equating the controller metavariable 'coming down' from above with a controllee derived somewhere under the NP- or PP-node. Since not all NPs will contain a respective controllee, the linking rule must be made an optional rule schema. (The extension is exemplified only for the VP-rule here):

(R11)   VP   ->   [NP]   ($\uparrow$ OBJ2) = $\downarrow$

                               [$\Uparrow_{vp}$ = $\Downarrow_{vp'}^{np}$]]

               [NP]   ($\uparrow$ OBJ) = $\downarrow$

                               [$\Uparrow_{vp}$ = $\Downarrow_{vp'}^{np}$]]

               PP* $\uparrow$ ele ($\uparrow$ ADJ)

               [PP]   ($\uparrow$ POBJ) = $\downarrow$

                               [$\Uparrow_{vp}$ = $\Downarrow_{vp'}^{pp}$]]

               V $\uparrow$ = $\downarrow$

To express the restriction that it is always the topmost VP'-constituent under an NP which is optionally subject to extraposition, this VP' must also be a bounding node for all kinds of extraction:

(R12)   NP   ->   ...
                  N $\uparrow$ = $\downarrow$
                  ...
                  [VP']   ($\uparrow$ XCOMP) = $\downarrow$]

Again, this is not a very 'natural' thing to do, since, as we will see below, VP' is not always a boundary for extraction. In other words, it has to be stipulated in a rather unnatural way that VP' is a bounding node only in this specific position, just as it has to be stipulated that there is a difference between PPs in the function of POBJects and those in the function of ADJuncts.

A well-formed derivation for a sentence like (58) is given in (C8):

(C8)

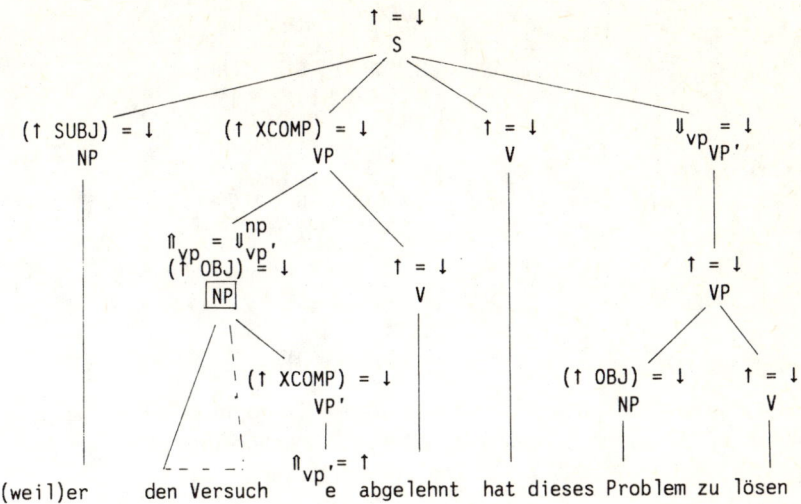

Even if the generalization that only a sequence of governable functions forms an admissible path for extraction must also be stipulated within the FU approach, the restrictions mentioned above may be formulated more directly.

Within this approach we do not have to express the (functional) difference between governable functions and ADJuncts by stipulating that categorially identical phrase structure constituents behave in different ways with respect to extraction. Instead, it suffices to extend the regular expression annotated on the extraposed infinitives so that it contains the governable functions SUBJ, OBJ, OBJ2 and POBJ. This leads to the prediction that an extraposed VP' constituent can fulfill the function of an XCOMP with respect to a verbal predicate or a SUBJ/OBJ/OBJ2/POBJ noun phrase which can be reached along a path of XCOMPs. In short:
(↑ XCOMP* [SUBJ/OBJ/OBJ2/POBJ] XCOMP) = ↓

To simplify the rules a variable G can be defined ranging over the (sub)set of governable functions {SUBJ, OBJ, OBJ2, POBJ}. The regular expression which is used to designate the function of the extraposed infinitival clause will then have the form "XCOMP* [G] XCOMP".

(R13) S   ->   [NP   (↑ SUBJ) = ↓]
                 ...
                 [VP   (↑ XCOMP) = ↓]
                 [V   ↑ = ↓]
                 [VP'   (↑ XCOMP* [G] XCOMP) = ↓
                         (↓ COHERENCE) = -]

(R14) VP' ->   VP   ↑ = ↓
                 [VP'   (↑ XCOMP* [G] XCOMP) = ↓
                         (↓ COHERENCE) = -]

(R15) VP   ->   [NP   (↑ OBJ2) = ↓]
                 [NP   (↑ OBJ) = ↓]
                 PP*   (↓ ele (↑ ADJ)
                 [PP   (↑ POBJ) = ↓
                 V   ↑ = ↓

(R16) NP   ->   DET   ↑ = ↓
                 N   ↑ = ↓
                 [VP'   (↑ XCOMP) = ↓]

(R17) PP   ->   P   ↑ = ↓
                 NP   ↑ = ↓

The extension of the rule system is illustrated in (C9), again by example (58).

NONLOCAL-DEPENDENCIES 397

(C9)

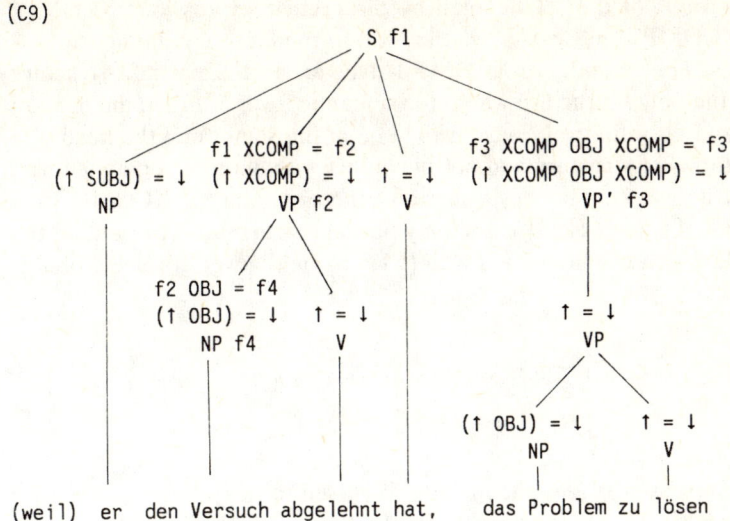

(weil) er den Versuch abgelehnt hat, das Problem zu lösen

Suppose again that all the information introduced by the substring *er den Versuch abgelehnt hat* is collected to form the partial f-structure (F11):

(F11)

$$
f1 \begin{bmatrix} \text{XCOMP} & = & f2 \begin{bmatrix} \text{OBJ} & = & f4 \begin{bmatrix} \text{XCOMP} & \begin{bmatrix} \text{SUBJ} & = & [2] \end{bmatrix} \\ \text{PRED} & = \text{versuch} < (\text{SUBJ}) \, (\text{XCOMP}) > \\ \text{SUBJ} & = 2[.\text{PRED} = \text{pro}] \end{bmatrix} \\ \text{PRED} & = \text{ablehnen} < (\text{SUBJ}), (\text{OBJ}) > \\ \text{SUBJ} & = [1] \end{bmatrix} \\ \text{PRED} & = \text{haben} < (\text{XCOMP}) > (\text{SUBJ}) \\ \text{SUBJ} & = 1[\text{PRED} = \text{pro}] \end{bmatrix}
$$

If the partial f-structure corresponding to the structure dominated by the VP'-node is built up separately, only one designator formed from an expression out of the set denoted by the regular expression "XCOMP* [G] XCOMP" will satisfy all the well-formedness conditions over f-structures. The un-indexed XCOMP f-structure in the partial f-structure (F11) is the only f-structure where the semantic form of *lösen*, the head of the extraposed infinitival clause, would be at the same time the head of a subcategorized f-structure and not in conflict with another semantic form. This f-structure can be designated by the equation f1 XCOMP OBJ XCOMP = f3. Thus (F12) is the only partial f-structure, representing the VP' node, which can be unified with (F11) to yield a well-formed global f-structure.

(F12)

$$f1\left[\text{XCOMP} = \left[\text{OBJ} = \left[\text{XCOMP} =_{f3} \left[\begin{array}{l} \text{PRED} = \text{loesen} < (\text{SUBJ})\ (\text{OBJ}) > \\ \text{OBJ} = [\ \text{PRED} = \text{problem}\ ] \end{array} \right] \right] \right] \right]$$

The comparison of the phenomena discussed in this section shows that some syntactic processes clearly rely on functional distinctions such as *governable function* vs. *adjunct*, rather than categorial distinctions such as NP vs. PP. Even though it is possible to handle the phenomena in question by means of constituent control, it is neccessary to take into account both the functional and the phrase structure level. Functional uncertainty, on the other hand, allows one to express the relevant generalizations directly, on a single level of representation (f-structure), without redundantly making reference to c-structure.

4. 'WH-MOVEMENT'

The same mechanisms that were applied to treat dislocations to the right, can also be used for the more classical cases of non-local dependencies, *topicalization* or *WH-movement*, involving the clause initial C(omplementizer) - position.

The crucial issue will be whether and how the interaction of WH-movement with extraposition can be described in the two approaches under discussion. In particular it will be demonstrated that the present definition of constituent control does not suffice to express the restriction commonly known as *complex-NP-constraint*.

Although the discussion here is restricted to the analysis of some simple relative clauses, it could easily be extended to cover *w-interrogatives* and the position in front of the finite verb in V-second *declaratives*.

4.1. The Data

In German, the left-peripheral position in finite sentences may be occupied by a relative pronoun which exhibits the properties of non-local dependencies.

Any complement of a verbal predicate which appears in a chain of (obligatorily) coherent infinitives (71) may appear in this position as a relative pronoun (72) - (74):

(71) dass [er [[der Frau das Buch geben] zu wollen] scheint]

(72) der Mann, [$_i$ der] [[$_i$] [[der Frau das Buch geben] zu wollen] scheint]

(73) Das Buch, [$_i$ das] [er [[der Frau [$_i$] geben] zu wollen] scheint]

(74) Die Frau, [der] [er [[[$_i$] das Buch geben] zu wollen] scheint]

WH-movement is also possible for constituents fulfilling a function within an infinitival clause governed by an equi verb (75), irrespective of whether this clause is extraposed (77) or not (76):

(75) dass [er [ihr [[dem Mann zu helfen] versprochen] hat]

(76) der Mann, [$_i$ dem] [er [ihr [[$_i$] zu helfen] versprochen] hat]

(77) der Mann, [$_j$ dem] [er [ihr [[$_i$] versprochen] hat [$_i$ [$_j$] zu helfen]]

What indisputably qualifies WH-movement as a non-local dependency phenomenon in German is that the number of recursively extraposed infinitival clauses intervening between the relative pronoun and the verb determining its function appears to be unlimited in principle:

(78) das Problem, [$_i$ das] er behauptet hat, ihr versprochen zu haben, zu versuchen, [$_i$] zu lösen.

However, besides the constructions which allow WH-movement out of an infinitival clause there is a considerable number of 'islands' which are closed for extraction of complements.

The most relevant cases analyzed below are the complex noun-phrases discussed in section 3. As it seems extraction is blocked if the infinitive is subcategorized for by a noun which is the head of some closed function (SUBJ, OBJ, OBJ2 etc.). Again it seems to be irrelevant whether the infinitival clause occurs in an embedded position (80)/(83) or whether it is extraposed (81)/(84):

(79) dass er sich [der Aufgabe, [dieses Problem zu lösen]], widmete]

(80) *das Problem, [$_i$ das] [er sich [der Aufgabe, [[$_i$] zu lösen], widmete]

(81) *das Problem, [$_j$ das] [er sich [der Aufgabe, [$_i$]] widmete, [$_i$ [$_j$] zu lösen],]

(82) dass er vor [die Aufgabe, [dieses Problem zu lösen]], gestellt wurde

(83) *das Problem, [$_i$ das] [er [vor die Aufgabe, [[$_i$] zu lösen] gestellt wurde]

(84) *das Problem, [$_i$ das] [er [vor die Aufgabe, [$_i$]] gestellt wurde, [$_i$ [$_j$] zu lösen],]

Other well-known islands for extraction are infinitival clauses in ADJunct (or better XADJunct) (85)-(88) and SUBJect functions (89)-(92).

(85) dass er aufgegeben hat, [ohne das Problem gelöst zu haben]

(86) *das Problem, [$_i$ das] er aufgegeben hat, [ohne[$_i$]gelöst zu haben]

(87) dass er gegangen ist, um seine Freundin abzuholen.

(88) *die Frau, [$_i$ die] er gegangen ist, [um [$_i$] abzuholen.]

(89) dass ihm schwerfiel, den Artikel zu Ende zu schreiben.

(90) *der Artikel, [$_i$ den] ihm schwerfiel, [[ ] zu Ende zu schreiben].

(91) weil ihm sicherlich missfiel, diesen Artikel lesen zu müssen.

(92) *der Artikel, [$_i$ den] ihm missfiel, [$_i$]lesen zu müssen.]^{18}

Again, most of these data suggest that grammatical functions rather than phrase structure configurations play a crucial role for the question of whether WH-extraction out of a constituent is grammatical or not. For the data given above one can make the generalization that the WH-constituent in the C - position may fulfill a governable function at any f-structure level which is accessible along a path which exclusively consists of XCOMPs. If a closed function such as SUBJ, OBJ, OBJ2, POBJ, or one of the adjunct functions, XADJ or ADJ occurs on this path, topicalization is blocked.

4.2. C-Structure vs. F-Structure Paths

In the previous section, the generalization was made that a WH-proform may appear in the left-peripheral complementizer position if it fulfills a function in an f-structure which can be reached along a path of

---

[18] Contrary to expectations, the extractions out of infinitives in a SUBJect-function are claimed to improve somewhat if the extraposed clause leaves behind a dummy proform *es* (M. Reis, indirect personal communication):

(a) ?der Artikel, [$_i$ den] es ihm missfiel, [[$_i$]lesen zu muessen.]

(b) ?[$_i$ Wen] wuerde es dich freuen, [dort [$_i$]wiederzusehen.]

These data are even more remarkable in light of other (case-marked) dummy proforms in an OBJ or POBJ function, which apparently block extraction:

(c) weil er es gewagt hat, den Artikel zu schreiben

(d) *der Artikel, [$_i$ den] er es gewagt hat, [[$_i$] zu schreiben],

(e) weil er ihn darum gebeten hat, den Artikel zu schreiben

(f) *der Artikel, [$_i$ den] er ihn darum gebeten hat, [[$_i$] zu schreiben],

XCOMPs. For all infinitival clauses which are the XCOMP-complements of some noun dominated by a node which is assigned a closed (non-propositional) function (SUBJ, OBJ, POBJ etc), it was hypothesized that extraction would be blocked.

Of course the way this generalization is expressed somewhat favours the functional uncertainty approach: the island constraints mentioned can easily be expressed by annotating the complementizer position with a regular expression XCOMP* G', where G' is a variable ranging over the set {SUBJ, OBJ, OBJ2}:[19]

```
(R18)    S'      ->      NP      (↑ TOPIC) = ↓
                                 (↓ WH) = +
                                 (↑ XCOMP* G') = ↓
                         S       ↑ = ↓.
```

In the complete rule system we now have two regular expressions which can interact, since their mother variables (↑) are instantiated by the same value (C10).

```
(R14)    S       ->      [NP     (↑ SUBJ) = ↓ ]
                         ...
                         [V      ↑ = ↓ ]
                         [ VP'   (↑ XCOMP* [ G ] XCOMP ) = ↓
                                 (↓ COHERENCE) = - ]
```

---

[19] It is of little relevance here exactly how the structure of the clause initial Comp-position is spelled out.

(C10)

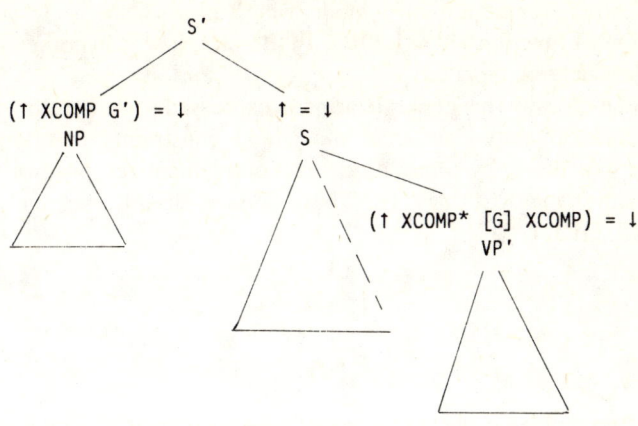

The interaction of these regular expressions can be illustrated by the following two examples:

(93) Das Problem, [$_j$ das] [er [[$_i$] versucht] hat, [$_i$ [$_j$] zu lösen]].

(94) *Das Problem, [$_j$ das] [er [[den Versuch [$_i$]] abgelehnt] hat [$_i$ [$_j$] zu lösen]].

Irrespective of the mathematical problem of two interacting regular expressions (cf. JOHNSON (1986)) it is obvious that there can only be a well-formed f-structure for (93), not for (94). It is only for the first sentence that equations among the two sets of equations generated by the regular expressions can be found which satisfy the coherence, completeness and consistency conditions (C11).

(C11)

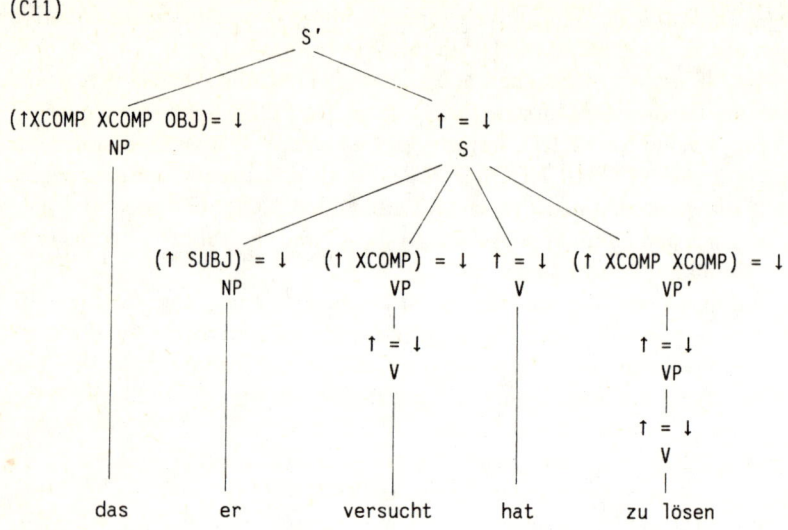

(C12)

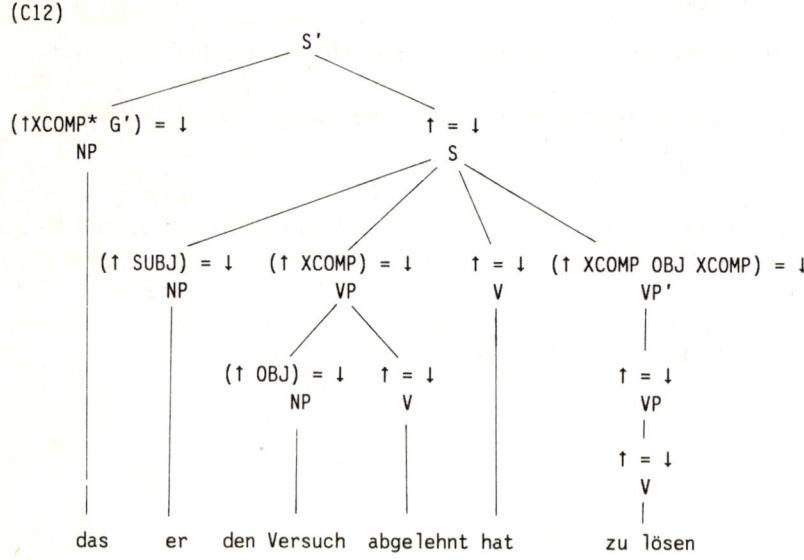

In the second case (C12), although there is an adaequate equation to denote the extraposed infinitive's function, there is no adaequate equation which can be assigned to the NP in the WH-position.

If the NP *das* were assigned a designator (↑ XCOMP OBJ) this would yield an inconsistent f-structure, since the OBJ-f-structure already contains a value for PRED, introduced by *Versuch*. If it were assigned the designator (↑ XCOMP XCOMP OBJ), both consistency and coherence would be violated, since the second embedded XCOMP-function would not be governed by an appropriate predicate and the subcategorization of *lösen* would not be satisfied.

In other words, the dislocated NP cannot become the OBJ of the extraposed infinitive, since the regular expression assigned to it does not allow it to cross the boundary that the OBJ-NP *den Versuch* presents. The only equation annotated on the topicalized NP which would allow the derivation of a well-formed f-structure is the equation (↑ XCOMP OBJ XCOMP OBJ) = ↓, which cannot be constructed from any element out of the set denoted by the regular expression XCOMP* G.

Thus, although the constraint we are dealing with is known as the 'complex NP constraint', suggesting that it is a constraint defined over phrase structure configurations, it can be expressed on the level of f-structure, by means of FU, in a quite straightforward way.

Of course, one would expect that a phrase structure oriented mechanism such as CC would allow this constraint to be equally well encoded. However, this is by no means the case.

The following rules correspond to the expansion made by rule (R18) above and allows the NP in the WH-position to be linked with a position where it can be interpreted:

(R19) S' -> NP $\Downarrow^{S}_{np} = \downarrow$

   (↑ TOPIC) = ↓

   S   ↑ = ↓

(R20) NP -> e $\Uparrow_{np} = \uparrow$

Given the bounding node character of PP and NP, the domain in which a corresponding controllee may be found is restricted to all NP nodes dominated by S which are not dominated by a NP or PP node themselves. This gives the correct predictions for sentences such as (95)/(96), since the controllees in these cases are embedded under NP or PP nodes, respectively:

(95) *das Problem, [$_i$ das] [er [den Versuch [[$_i$ e] zu lösen]] abgelehnt hat.]

(96) *die Lösung, [$_i$ die] [er [auf [$_i$ e]] gewartet hat.]

However, looking at structures (C13) and (C14), we are faced with a dilemma:

(C13)

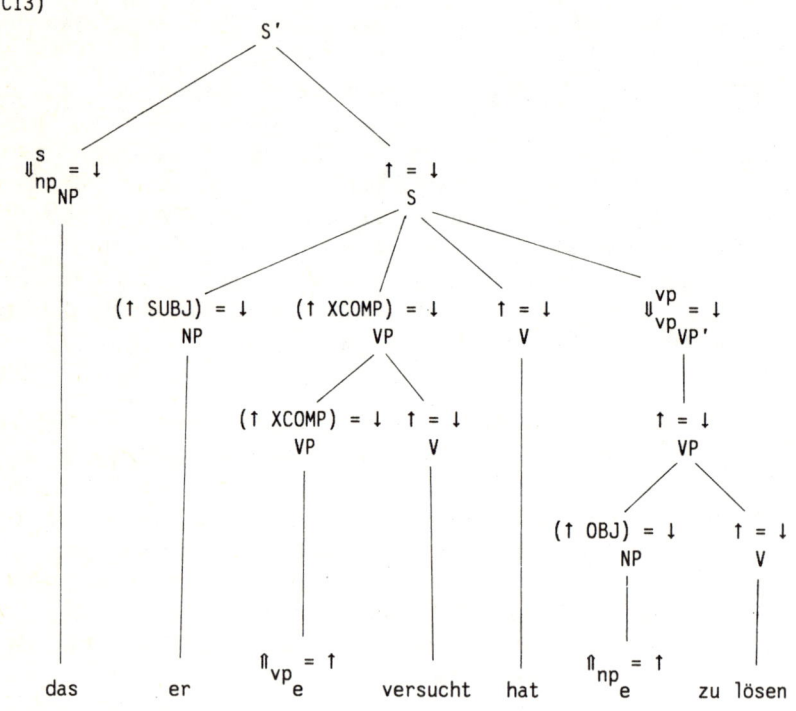

(C14)

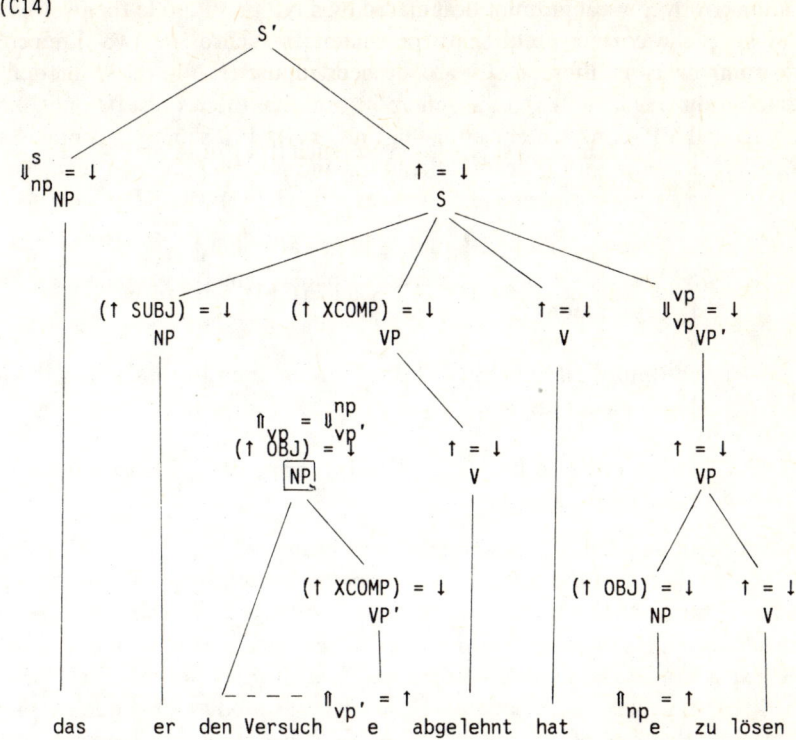

In both cases, the c-structure path leading from the root node S of the NP-controller's bounding domain to the controllee dominated by the OBJ-NP in the extraposed infinitive does not cross any bounding nodes, NP or PP, but consists of a sequence S - VP' - VP. As a consequence, the information that the WH-proform violates something like a Complex-NP-Constraint in the second case cannot be read off the c-structure any more.

Of course one could make the VP'-node a bounding node too, but this would imply that grammatical constructions such as (C13) would be also excluded. That is for a theory which generally claims
    a) that 'adjunction' (in this case extraposition) is defined over phrase structure configurations and
    b) that any adjoined constituent is an island for extraction
the problem would not be how to avoid ungrammatical extraction but

rather how to permit grammatical extractions.

A simple way out would be to postulate that there are two different positions or two different types for the extraposed VP'-nodes. Yet this assumption runs counter to the generalization that there must be only one extraposed VP'-complement after the finite verb. If a sentence contains a verb and a noun, both subcategorizing for an infinitival complement, only one of these complements may be extraposed (97)/(98), but not both (99).

(97) weil [die Hoffnung, [sie wiederzusehen]], ihn [$_i$] veranlasste],
[$_i$ zu kommen]

(98) weil [nur die Hoffnung [$_i$]] [ihn [zu kommen] veranlasste],
[$_i$ sie wiederzusehen]

(99) *weil [nur die Hoffnung [$_i$]] [ihn [$_j$] veranlasste], [$_j$ zu kommen],
[$_i$ sie wiederzusehen]

An additional (technical) complication for any redefinition of CC arises due to the fact that the NP nodes must be annotated by a linking schema which neutralizes these nodes as bounding nodes for VP' extraction. As a consequence, the information that the VP' nodes are bounding nodes for NP-extraction would be lost in any case. Thus, once the infinitival clause is extraposed, we have little means of marking it as a bounding node for any extraction that one of the mothers of its controllee is a bounding node for.

In short: Unless the definition of constituent control is radically altered, functional uncertainty appears to be a superior approach since it tackles the problem on a level of representation on which all the relevant information can be made available.

5. CONCLUSION

The range of phenomena considered in this paper is quite limited. Moreover it contains many tacit assumptions on control, the distribution of grammatical functions etc. which certainly need further elaboration.

At this stage, however, this paper was simply an attempt to demonstrate that within the framework of LFG a treatment of non-local dependencies on the basis of grammatical functions could represent a promising and superior alternative to an approach relying exclusively on phrase structure configurations. It was shown that functional distinctions such as governable vs. non-governable functions are relevant for some syntactic processes. Likewise, it was argued that a surface phrase structure configuration does not suffice to determine admissable phrase structure paths for WH-extraction. The level of functional structure, on the other hand, which represents grammatical relations at a much deeper level, could contain all the information necessary to express the relevant restrictions.

Explanatory adequacy was not the primary concern of the proposals made in this paper. None of the analyses based on functional uncertainty was shown to follow from 'independently motivated principles'. However, at least for the range of phenomena considered a higher observational and possibly even descriptive adequacy could be claimed for functional uncertainty relative to constituent control. Although little reference was made to other frameworks, it is a question of further reflection whether the problems outlined in this paper are LFG specific problems or whether they present a difficulty for any grammatical framework based exclusively on phrase structure configurations.

BIBLIOGRAPHY

ASKEDAL, J. O. (1982): "Über den Zusammenhang zwischen Satztopologie und Statusrektion im Deutschen." in: *Studia Neophilologica*, vol 54, 287 - 308

BECH, G. (1955, 1983): *Studien über das deutsche Verbum Infinitum*. 2nd ed., Tübingen

BRESNAN, J. ed. (1982): *The Mental Representation of Grammatical Relations*. Cambridge, Mass.

BRESNAN, J. / R. KAPLAN / S. PETERS / A. ZAENEN (1982): "*Cross Serial Dependencies in Dutch*." LI 13

BRESNAN, J. (1982): "On Control and Complementation." LI 13, 343 - 434; also in: BRESNAN ed. (1982: 282 - 390)

EVERS, A. (1975): The Transformational Cycle in Dutch and German. Reproduced by IULC, Bloomington, Indiana

GREWENDORF, G (1984): "Kohaerenz und Restrukturierung. Zu verbalen Komplexen im Deutschen." To appear in: B. ASBACH-SCHNITKER / J. ROGGENHOFER eds., *Festschrift für H. Brekle*.

HAIDER, H. (1986): "Nicht-Sententiale Infinitive." *Groninger Arbeiten zur Germanistischen Linguistik* 27

HUANG, J. C.-T. (1982): *Logical relations in Chinese and the Theory of Grammar*. PhD-Thesis, MIT.

JOHNSON, M. (1986): The LFG Treatment of Discontintuity and The Double Infinitive Construction in Dutch. CSLI report CSLI-86-65
JOHNSON, M. (1986): *Computing With Regular Path Formula*. Ms., Stanford
KAPLAN, R. / J. BRESNAN (1982): "Grammatical Representation." in: BRESNAN ed. (1982: 173 - 281)
KAPLAN, R. / J. MAXWELL / A. ZAENEN (1987): "Functional Uncertainty." in: CSLI Monthly, 01-87
KAPLAN, R. / A. ZAENEN (1987): "Wh-Constructions and Constituent Structure."To appear in: M. BALTIN / A. KROCH eds., *Alternative Conceptions of Phrase Structure*.
KARTTUNEN, L. (1987): "Radical Lexicalism". To appear in: M. BALTIN / A. KROCH eds., *Alternative Conceptions of Phrase Structure*.
NETTER, K. (1986): "Getting Things Out Of Order". COLING 11.
NETTER, K. (1987): "Wortstellung und Verbalkomplex im Deutschen." To appear in: SCHERBER et. al., eds. (1987): *Computerlinguistik und Philologische Datenverarbeitung*. Hildesheim
RAPPAPORT, M (1983) "On the Nature of Derived Nominals", in: L. LEVIN / M. RAPPAPORT / A. ZAENEN eds. (1983): *Papers in Lexical Functional Grammar*. IULC, Bloomington, Indiana.
SELLS, P. (1985): *Lectures on Contemporary Syntactic Theories*. Stanford

CHRISTA HAUENSCHILD

TU BERLIN

GPSG AND GERMAN WORD ORDER

0. ABSTRACT

In this paper*, my main concern is raising questions rather than giving answers. My starting point is Hans Uszkoreit's revised version of the LP (linear precedence) component (cf. Uszkoreit 1984 and 1986) within the GPSG formalism (cf. Gazdar et al. 1985). I shall discuss some problems of Uszkoreit's approach that result from the fact that the whole complex phenomenon of German word order is described at a unique level of linguistic representation. I shall then propose a somewhat speculative solution to some of these problems, which is based on a multi-level approach to analysis and generation within the context of machine translation (which is the setting of the project KIT/NASEV and its successor KIT/FAST[1]).

---

* A first version of this paper was read at the Friedenweiler workshop on "Word Order and Parsing in Unification Grammars" organized by the complementary research project or EUROTRA-D, April, 7th to 11th, 1986. I thank the participants of that workshop for many useful remarks; I am even more obliged to Klaus Brockhaus, Stephan Busemann, James Kilbury and Peter Pause for their patience in several discussions and their critical as well as encouraging comments.

[1] KIT/NASEV (NASEV = Neue Anlyse- und Syntheseverfahren zur maschinellen Übersetzung = New Methods of Analysis and Synthesis for Machine Translation; KIT = Künstliche Intelligenz und Textverstehen = Artificial Intelligence and Text Understanding) as well as the successor project KIT/FAST (FAST = Functor-Argument Structure for Translation) constitute the Berlin component of the complementary research project of EUROTRA-D, which is sponsored by the Federal Minister of Research and Technology. KIT/NASEV has been and KIT/FAST is located at the Technical University of Berlin within the Department of Applied Computer Science and, more precisely, within the project group KIT (director: Prof.Dr. H.-J. Schneider), which means that we try to make artificial intelligence methods available for machine translation.

U. Reyle and C. Rohrer (eds.),
Natural Language Parsing and Linguistic Theories, 411–431.
© *1988 by D. Reidel Publishing Company.*

1. THE ID/LP FORMAT OF GPSG

One of the essential merits of the GPSG formalism is, in my view, the distinction between immediate dominance and linear precedence. This means that information about mother-daughter relationships on one hand, and about linear ordering among sisters in local trees (=trees of depth 1) on the other hand, is coded in two different components of the grammar, namely in the ID (immediate dominance) rules and in the LP (linear precedence) statements respectively. As the LP statements do not refer to single ID rules but to the whole set of rules in a grammar, the ID/LP device allows to express generalizations about the linear order of sisters in trees that cannot be encoded by usual context-free grammars. This fact is illustrated by the following comparison between a traditional phrase structure grammar and an ID/LP grammar, which I repeat from (Uszkoreit 1986):

(1) <u>Traditional PSG</u>   and <u>corresponding ID/LP grammar</u>

A -> BCD	<u>ID rules</u>	<u>LP statements</u>
A -> BDC	A -> B,C,D	B < C
B -> BD	B -> B,D	B < D
C -> ABC	C -> A,B,C	
C -> BAC		
C -> BCA		

Moreover, the ID/LP device leads to the empirically interesting hypothesis that natural languages have the property of Exhaustive Constant Partial Ordering (ECPO, cf. Gazdar et al. 1985), which means that sister categories in independently motivated linguistic structures are ordered (or unordered) in the way predicted by the LP component[2], irrespective of the structural context.

---

[2] It is important that the structures assigned to sentences be linguistically motivated because otherwise the claim of the ECPO hypothesis would be trivial: (Shieber 1984) has shown that it is possible to construct a weekly equivalent GPSG syntax (with the ECPO property) to any context-free syntax with the aid of (not linguistically motivated) additional nodes in the trees labelled with arbitrary auxiliary categories.

2. THE REVISED VERSION OF LP STATEMENTS

The ECPO hypothesis becomes critical in the case of languages with (relatively) free word order, where rather flat syntactic structures can be independently motivated (German is such a language). In binary structures there are just two possibilities: either the two sisters are strictly ordered or they are not (the problem with the ECPO property - or the interesting hypothesis - lies then in the fact that the ordering vs. non-ordering has to be the same in any structural context, i.e. independent ot the mother); in the case of three or more sisters in a local tree, however, there are more possibilities of partially free ordering. Thus, if we assign rather flat structures to the sentences of a language, this constitutes an interesting test case for the ECPO hypothesis.

In his thesis (Uszkoreit 1984) as well as in (Uszkoreit 1986), Hans Uszkoreit argues for a revised version of the LP component within GPSG. His analysis of German word order is essentially based on the findings of Lenerz (cf. Lenerz 1977), where different competing principles of linearization in German sentences are described. These ordering principles seem to interact in a way that cannot be accounted for by LP statements of the form proposed in (Gazdar et al. 1985) because the principles do not apply conjunctively (as it is assumed in the "classical" version) but (partially) disjunctively.

For the linear ordering of the complements of verbs in the middle field of German sentences[3] Hans Uszkoreit assumes the following ordering principles (cf. Uszkoreit 1986):

(2) OP 1: The agent precedes the theme.
OP 2: The agent precedes the goal.
OP 3: The goal precedes the theme.
OP 4: Focused constituents follow other consituents.
OP 5: Personal pronouns precede nonprominal constituents.

These are, in principle, the same assumptions as in (Uszkoreit 1984) with the exception of the fact that "unmarked order" is now coded in

---

[3] The middle field of German sentences is defined as follows: in sentences with verb-first or verb-second position it is the span between the finite verb and the (optional) verbal complex of non-finite verbs; in verb-last sentences it is the span between the introductory conjunction (if such is present) and the verbal complex, the last element of which is normally the finite verb.

terms of thematic roles, whereas it was expressed with the aid of surface case in (Uszkoreit 1984), where it was argued (in the section on possible extensions of the fragment described by the grammar) that both types of information seem to be relevant (see also the arguments on arguments in Wunderlich 1985).

In the GPSG formalism these statements would be coded in the following way (the entities on both sides of the PRECEDES relation are minimal categories consisting of just one feature-value pair):

(3) 1. {<TR,AGENT>}   < {<TR,THEME>}
    2. {<TR,AGENT>}   < {<TR,GOAL>}
    3. {<TR,GOAL>}   < {<TR,THEME>}
    4. {<FOCUS,->}   < {<FOCUS,+>}
    5. {<PPRN,+>}   < {<PPRN,->}

The main thesis that Uszkoreit extracts from (Lenerz 1977), namely that sentences are grammatical if and only if at least one of the (possibly conflicting) principles is complied with, is nicely reflected by the revised version of the LP component proposed in (Uszkoreit 1984) and (Uszkoreit 1986) by the complex LP statements that function as follows: a local tree is admitted by a complex LP statement (consisting of different LP clauses) if and only if the following holds for every pair of sisters: at least one of the LP clauses applying to that pair is fulfilled by it (simple LP statements consisting of just one clause are defined as a special case of complex LP statements and function as the "classical" LP statements in (Gazdar et al. 1985)). The fact that different linearization principles have different degrees of obligation is proposed to be reflected by different weights assigned to the single clauses of a complex LP statement. These weights may differ depending on stylistic properties of a given type of texts.

3. PROBLEMS WITH USZKOREIT'S PROPOSAL

Hans Uszkoreit's revised version of the LP component of GPSG is really an ingenious solution to the problem of partially free word order in German (and probably in many other languages), but unfortunately things are even more complicated. Natural language being an essentially conventional phenomenon, the range of rational principles governing it must be expected to be limited; some arbitrary grammatical restrictions may always come in (at least if we look at a natural language from a purely synchronical point of view).

Obviously, the domains of strict ordering and partially free ordering overlap in German sentences; thus they cannot be described in separate types of LP statements as easily as it is suggested by Uszkoreit's proposal, where he assumes partially free word order for all kinds of arguments in the middle field on one hand (which is accounted for by his complex LP statements) and a strictly defined position for the verb as well as e.g. for the determiners in NPs on the other hand (which is described by singleton LP statements of the "classical" form: $\{\{<MC,+>\} < X\}$ vs. $\{X < \{<MC,->\}\}$, which means that the finite verb precedes all its arguments in main clauses and follows them in subordinate clauses). Pronouns, however, seem to be subject to strict ordering in some cases where full noun phrases are not, whereas in other cases the rules for both types of complements are the same: the former holds for the order among direct and indirect objects - the latter holds for the relative position of prepositional objects (Marga Reis in Reis 1986 suggests that this might be dependent on the fact that the unmarked order of direct and indirect objects is essentially less strict than the order between e.g. prepositional and direct objects).

As the complex LP statement in (Uszkoreit 1986) stands, it does not account correctly for the relative position of pronominal direct and indirect objects (as it is acknowledged in his footnote 4). Thus the following sentence would not be admissible unless the pronominal indirect object is focused:

(4) Sie   gab   es   ihm.
    (she gave   it   to-him)
                 TR:THEME   TR:GOAL
                 PPRN:+   PPRN:+

There are, however, many possible contexts where 'ihn' is not focused (if FOCUS is not just intended as a syntactic trick, which it is not if I understand Hans Uszkoreit correctly).

The problem results from the fact that the unmarked order of pronominal direct and indirect objects is the reverse of the unmarked order in cases where both objects are full nouns (as Hans Uszkoreit puts it, starting from the analysis of unmarked order between direct and indirect objects as given in (Lenerz 1977), which has been disputed since (see below); I should prefer to assume a strict ordering in cases with two pronouns).

How might the complex LP statement for the complements of verbs in the middle field of German sentences be adjusted to cope with examples like (4)? A first step would consist in including a special LP clause for the case of two pronominal objects into the complex LP statement:

$$(5)\begin{bmatrix} 1. & \{<TR,AGENT>\} & < \{<TR,THEME>\} \\ 2. & \{<TR,AGENT>\} & < \{<TR,GOAL>\} \\ 3a. & \{<TR,GOAL>\} & < \{<TR,THEME>\} \\ 3b. & \{<TR,THEME>,<PPRN,+>\} & < \{<TR,GOAL>,<PPRN,+>\} \\ 4. & \{<FOCUS,->\} & < \{<FOCUS,+>\} \\ 5. & \{<PPRN,+>\} & < \{<PPRN,->\} \end{bmatrix}$$

This revised version of the complex LP statement would still admit some sentences that ought to be ruled out, e.g.:

(6)* Sie gab   ihm   es.
    (she gave to-him   it)
               TR:GOAL   TR:THEME
               PPRN:+   PPRN:+

This sentence is accepted by (5) because it suffices for a pair of sisters to fulfil one of the relevant ordering clauses, which is 3a. in this case. The problem with (6) is that the order of pronominal direct and indirect objects is strict (the only possible context for (6) would be a very odd case of correction, where 'es' is substituted for some other item in a preceding utterance).

Another problematic example is the following:

(7)* Sie gab   dem Mann   es.
    (she gave to-the man   it)
               TR:GOAL   TR:THEME
               PPRN:-   PPRN:+

(7) is admitted by clause 3a., too, while it ought to be ruled out as ungrammatical because the ordering of a personal pronoun and a full

noun phrase can be overridden by focusing of the pronoun only; but in the case of 'es' focusing is impossible (in the sense of carrying the intonation focus, which seems to be the interpretation of the FOCUS feature in (Uszkoreit 1986), though I am not quite sure about that) with the exception of very special contexts of correction or the like.

We shall have to return to the problem of an appropriate interpretation of the FOCUS feature, but first let us look at a further step in the revision of the complex LP statement that is to account for the inadmissibility of (6) and (7):

(8)
1. {<TR,AGENT>}   < {<TR,THEME>}
2. {<TR,AGENT>}   < {<TR,GOAL>}
3a. {<TR,GOAL><PPRN,->}   < {<TR,THEME><PPRN,->}
3b. {<TR,THEME>,<PPRN,+>}   < {<TR,GOAL>,<PPRN,+>}
4. {<FOCUS,->}   < {<FOCUS,+>}
5. {<PPRN,+>}   < {<PPRN,->}

The most important question with respect to this version of the complex LP statement is whether the ordering of goals and themes is really dependent on focusing in cases where at least one of them is realized as a personal pronoun - it seems unquestionable in cases with two pronound that the ordering must not be relativized by the FOCUS feature specification. If these ordering regularities are totally or partially independent of focusing (i.e. categorical orderings), then the corresponding LP clauses cannot be simply included into the complex LP statements for the complements of verbs in the middle field.

The answer to the given question is, of course, strongly affected by the notion of focus we want to use. (Lenerz 1977) offers several convincing arguments against a notion of focus that comprises contrastive and emotive focus as well: he argues that nearly no sentence could then be ruled out as ungrammatical on the basis of extremely odd relative positions of the verb's arguments because nearly every ordering can be compensated by extreme stress in very special situations.

If we follow this proposal, then the ordering of goals and themes in all the cases where at least one of them is realized by a personal pronoun must obviously not be relativized by the FOCUS clause in the complex LP statement. This would mean that LP clause 5. (with the feature PPRN) would have to be strict in some cases and relativized by other clauses in other cases (the latter would be necessary for the relative positions of prepositional and non-prepositional objects). This would probably lead to problems in the revised version of the LP component as it is proposed by Hans Uszkoreit. A potential solution might consist in additional conditions for the application of LP statements.

Thus there seem to be left two possibilities:

- either we must allow even more complex relations between single LP clauses than is proposed in Uszkoreit's revised version of the LP component

- or we must adopt an extremely wide notion of focus, which comprises "ordinary" focus as well as contrastive and emotive focus: this solution would necessitate the acceptance of very odd sentences without a chance of accounting for their oddness by weight differentiation because there would be just one FOCUS feature and just one corresponding LP clause.

The whole foregoing argumentation is based on many if's, thus it cannot be intended to claim that an analysis of the ordering regularities of German is not at all possible in the conception of Hans Uszkoreit. I just wanted to argue that there are some serious problems left, which are essentially connected with the fact that strict and relative ordering principles seem to have overlapping domains in German sentences.

There are other difficulties, some of them were mentioned already:

- the "unmarked ordering" of arguments of the verb in the middle field is not at all uncontroversial, neither with respect to the facts nor with respect to the conception (the judgements on "facts" are, of course, not really independent of the underlying conception);

- as for the facts: the unmarked order of the direct and indirect objects is described in (Hoberg 1981) as DO before IO, which corresponds to the unmarked (vs. strict) order of pronominal objects in (Lenerz 1977), but is the reverse of his description of the ordering of nonpronominal DO and IO (according to Hoberg 1981 this order is influenced strongly by the factor of animateness, which is not at all considered in Uszkoreit's proposal);

- Marga Reis in (Reis 1986) even supposes that the unmarked order of direct and indirect objects might be dependent on individual verbs, which would suggest a "lexical" solution[4] of the problem; such a solution might also cope with the cases of experiencer verbs or verbs without an agent, where the unmarked order of IO and DO seems to differ from the "normal" cases;

- <u>as for the conception</u>: (Reis 1986) questions the conception of "unmarked order" that underlies Lenerz's analysis (and thus, indirectly, Uszkoreit's proposal), which considers as unmarked the order of two constituents A and B if that order is not restricted by additional conditions, whereas an ordering is said to be marked if it is possible under special conditions only;

- an alternative conception is that of (Höhle 1982), which defines as unmarked that ordering of constituents of a sentence (not just the ordering of pairs of constituents) which can occur in the maximal number of possible contexts;[5] the most important feature of this conception lies in the fact that it considers real sentences (with lexically realized constituents) in contexts and not just sentence types and constituent types (the latter is characteristic for Lenerz's approach);

- the most important problem, however, is that of the role of the FOCUS feature: (Reis 1986) argues that the topic-focus dichotomy is not really the decisive factor of linearization; much more important is the factor of intonation (this would suggest an interpretation of the FOCUS feature as marking the intonation focus); but if we analyze written texts, the information on intonational features of sentences is not directly available.

---

[4] By "lexical" solution I mean an approach where the information about the unmarked order of the complements of a verb is coded in the lexicon together with the corresponding subcategorization information.

[5] In fact, the definition in (Höhle 1982) is not as straight forward as that: his definition connects unmarked order via the concepts of focus and focus projection with the maximal number of possible contexts.

I shall return to the last problem in the next section, where I argue for an alternative framework for the solution of some of the ordering problems where the analysis of written texts is one of the central tasks. Thus a different conception of focus is needed which allows to infer the focus of a sentence on the basis of word order and context.

4. OUTLINE OF AN ALTERNATIVE SOLUTION

As I already mentioned, the argumentation given so far is not intended to maintain the claim that an analysis of word order regularities in the spirit of Hans Uszkoreit is impossible. I just wanted to show that a more exhaustive analysis of the ordering principles governing the linearization of verb complements in the middle field of German sentences will probably not look as nice as is suggested by Uszkoreit's proposal.

I am not pretending to offer a really nice solution either, but I should like to point out to an alternative way of coping with some of the problems raised so far. The solution I want to propose is mainly motivated by the context in which we are using the GPSG formalism in our project, namely that of machine translation. We have developed a conception of the translation process that is based on a multi-level representation of the input and output texts. This multi-level representation corresponds to a multi-level conception of transfer as indicated in (9).

A more detailed motivation of this conception is to be found in (Hauenschild 1986). It is analogous to some relevant approaches in translation theory. Many authors assume different aspects of translation equivalence (e.g. Pause 1983 considers formal value, semantic meaning and communicative function; quite a number of similar approaches are described in Koller 1979). Some definitions of translation equivalence are even directly based on a notion of levels of equivalence (e.g. Komissarov 1973 or Darbelnet 1977), which corresponds directly to our conception of transfer levels.

(9) Levels of Representation and of Transfer

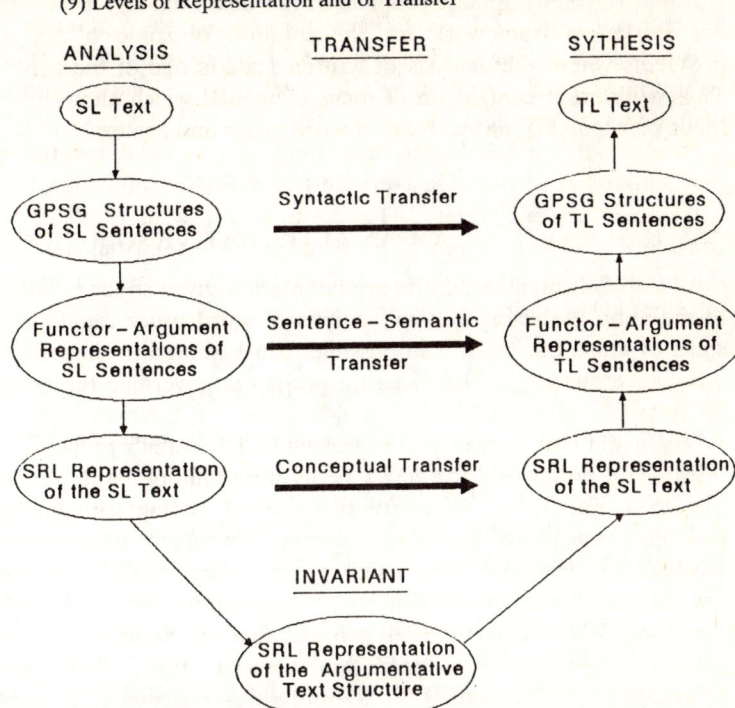

SL = Source Language
TL = Target Language
SRL = Semantic Representation Language
    (a network language that allows to represent the content of a text as
    well as extra-linguistic knowledge)
x -> y = x is precondition of y
x ➔ y = x influences y

(9) is, in fact, not quite the version of (Hauenschild 1986): the original IL (intensional logic) representations of SL and TL sentences have been replaced by a functor-argument representation in the spirit of (Sgall et al. 1973) because the latter offer a better way of connecting the different levels.

The division of labour among the different levels of representation vs. of transfer is not finally fixed, nor is the appropriate number of levels. Schema (9) is just a first approximation that is oriented towards the traditional division into syntax, semantics and pragmatics although it is not a direct reflex of this division. There may be reasons to alter the number and definitions of levels, but after all, it seems sensible to split up the enormous complexity of the whole process of translation into different components of transfer.

In my view, an analogous argumentation is valid for the complex problems of word order in German (as well as in other languages with partially free word order). The basic idea I want to discuss here is considering different types of linearization principles that fulfil different functions in the processes of analysis and synthesis and that refer to different levels of linguistic representation.

4.1 Syntactic Level

In the first step of approximation I shoul like to assume a syntactic level that is relatively liberal with respect to ordering regularities. This means that only the really "hard" syntactic facts are represented by the LP statements at this level, e.g. the order of determiners and nouns, the position of finite verbs in main vs. subordinate clauses etc. These are exactly the facts about ordering that are reflected by simple LP statements in Hans Uszkoreit's revised version of the LP component as proposed in (Uszkoreit 1984) and (Uszkoreit 1986). The ordering of pronominal direct and indirect objects in the middle field must probably also be accounted for by singleton LP statements, which correspond to strict linearization rules.

It is important to point out the fact that, in the field of machine translation, the main interest is not in excluding inacceptable (or marginally acceptable) sentences from the realm of syntactic well-formedness, but rather in analyzing whatever sentence is presented as input and in assigning it the most probable reading. I am not quite sure how far the conception of a "liberal" syntax might carry over to other fields of application. In the underlying theory, it has, of course, to be compensated for by other components that account for the different degrees of acceptability.

However, there seem to be some important advantages in such a conception:

- we can probably get by with the "classical" version of LP statements as they were proposed in (Gazdar et al. 1985), which is desirable from an implementional point of view, too;

- we are not forced to just include or exclude some marginally acceptable sentences from the language generated by the syntax, but we can account for the fact that such sentences may have sensible interpretations in special contextual circumstances (see below on the use of backtracking mechanisms);

- such essentially contextual phenomena as topic and focus can be treated at a level of representation where contextual information is explicitly available.

4.2 Sentence-Semantic Level

The tentative solution to some of the problems of word order in German sentences that I want to present here uses argument roles at the sentence-semantic level for the assignment of preferred readings to sentences like

(10) Die Mutter zeigt das Kind dem Arzt.
(the mother shows the child to-the doctor)

In this case, the most probable interpretation would assign nominative to the first noun phrase and accusative to the second. Both noun phrases are ambiguous, and the alternative reading, where the mother is the object or theme and the child is the agent of the showing action, is less probable, but nevertheless possible, e.g. in contexts with a double contrast:

(11) Die Mutter zeigt das Kind dem Arzt.
Den Vater zeigt es dem Lehrer
(the father shows it to-the teacher)

where the first noun phrase in the second sentence is not ambiguous with respect to surface case, but can only be accusative. The parallel construction of the two sentences suggests the assignment of accusative case to the first noun phrase of the first sentence, too. The unusual fronting of the direct objects is plausible here because of the contrast between 'die Mutter' and 'den Vater'.

The fact that such cases are rather rare and that the reading with the first noun phrase denoting the agent is highly preferred for (10), is to be reflected in my suggestion of a solution in the following way: the sentence-semantic level of representation contains linearization principles referring to argument roles that say e.g. "The agent tends to precede the theme"; this leads to the corresponding preferred interpretation of sentences like (10). This interpretation is pursued until there is any evidence coming up that suggests an alternative interpretation as in the case of parallel constructions like (11). The two alternatives need not be pursued in parallel because, in our approach, backtracking is possible. Backtracking is to be triggered by special clues in the following text or by the constatation that an integration of the sentence meaning into the representation of the whole text is impossible for reasons of consistency[6].

By the way, such sentence-semantic preference rules of the type "The agent tends to precede the theme" seem to be relevant not only for the middle field of German sentences but for the whole sentences. This is suggested by our examples (10) and (11) as well as by similar cases. The interplay between preferred orderings in the middle field and "topicalization" (i.e. position in front of the inflected verb), however, is still subject to further research.

4.3 Textual Level

As I have mentioned already, the phenomenon of focusing ought to be treated at a level of representation where the linguistic and extra-linguistic context comes in explicitly, i.e. at the level of the semanto-pragmatic representation of the whole text. The linear order of constituents will then

---

[6] Such a suggestion sounds, of course, rather futuristic at the given moment because the whole mechanism of backtracking and effective testing for consistency, and even more so the complex interplay of different relevant factors, is not yet very well understood. However, it seems to be the only way of approaching the phenomena of text understanding that does not cut short too many facts of the language, considered from a procedural point of view. I ought to draw the attention of the reader to the fact that I use 'backtracking' and 'procedural' in a somewhat metaphorical sense; especially the theoretical concept of backtracking is not necessarily implemented with the aid of the technical backtracking mechanisms of programming languages like PROLOG.

be used as a starting-point for a first hypothesis about the thematic ordering of the elements of a sentence, given the fact that we cannot rely on information about intonation in the case of an automatic analysis of written texts. The resulting hypothesis must then be checked for consistency with what has already been said in the preceding text.

The corresponding rules of interpretation have not been formulated yet: the whole process of assigning a thematic structure to sentences and texts will be in some respects analogous to that of assigning preferred readings to sentences considering the argument roles at the sentence-semantic level of representation: a first hypothesis will be created on the basis of facts about the normal ordering of constituents ("Focused constituents tend to follow non-focused constituents", and other regularities of contrasting etc. that would account for the fronting of the direct objects in (10) and (11)); this hypothesis will be pursued as far as possible, i.e. as far as no conflict with contextual information arises. In the case of a conflict, backtracking will again be triggered in order to search for a viable alternative.

4.4 The Concept of Thematic Structuring of Sentences and Texts

We base our analysis of the thematic structuring of sentences and texts on a conception of functional sentence perspective that is similar to the approach of (Sgall et al. 1973) in that it combines structural and contextual features of the thematic structuring and in that it has scalar as well as dichotomic characteristics. Some modifications seem to be necessary that will be along the lines of (Hauenschild 1982) and (Hauenschild 1985): the most relevant feature for the application to (machine) translation seems to be the scalar ordering of the main constituents of a sentence. The interaction of structural and contextual features of the thematic ordering of sentences and whole texts has to be made more precise than it is done in (Sgall et al. 1973): there is not a simple one-one-correlation between the two types of factors, but a much more complicated interplay. A first version of a theory that distinguishes between sentential themes and textual themes has been developed in (Hauenschild 1985).

The background of the following schematic definitions is the text understanding model of Con^3Tra (Constance Concept of Context-

Oriented Translation, see Engelberg et al. 1984), a theoretically oriented machine translation project. Our starting point has been the assumption that the thematic structuring of sentences and of whole texts have to be preserved in the translation process (Hauenschild 1982 gives an extensive argumentation for the sentential aspect of the phenomenon); moreover, both types of thematic structuring play a decisive role in the interpretaion of anaphoric expressions (see Hauenschild & Pause 1983 as well as Hauenschild 1985 for an explicit argumentation).

(12) Sentential Themes and Textual Themes

Sentential Themes	Textual Themes
Dynamic view (during the process of text understanding): In which order are the referents introduced or recalled?	Static view (after a (partial) result of the understanding process has been reached): Which referents have been mentioned in the text?

Reconstruction in the Text Understanding Model	
Ordering of the constituents in the semanto-thematic sentence structure = order in which the constituents are considered in the construction of the text model	Thematic text structure = the textual themes with their hierarchical and conceptual relations

Scalarity or Dichotomy?
Primarily, the thematic structure of a sentence is represented as a scalar ordering of its constituents at the different levels of the functor-argument hierarchy; but dichotomic structures for special cases (e.g. negated sentences) are not excluded.

There are different degrees of textual thematicity, as textual themes may be more or less prominent; but this does not yield a simple ordering of textual themes: the prominence of a textual theme is determined in a complex way by its position in the thematic hierarchy of the text and by, the density of its conceptual relations with other textual themes.

Criteria (not necessarily absolute)
As far as possible "objectivity", i.e. structural criteria only:
- word order
- anaphoricity (as a property of expressions, without reference to the actual antecedent in the text)
- definiteness
- certain configurations or particles

...

Combination of "objectivity" and "subjectivity", i.e. structural criteria in combination with criteria depending on special interpretations:
- direct recurrence (e.g. nominal or pronominal anaphors with identity of reference with their antecedent)
- indirect recurrence (e.g. "contiguity" anaphors, i.e. anaphors without identity of reference)
- certain configurations or particles (yielding e.g. "expected textual themes")

...

Contribution to the Interpretation of Anaphoric Relations

Relevance of the sentential themes of the sentence or clause just being analyzed	Relevance of the textual themes of the (part of) text already analyzed in prior steps of interpretation

Prototypical Anaphoric Relation

The antecedent is a (relatively) prominent textual theme - the anaphor is (relatively) thematic in its sentence or clause.

Interaction Between Sentential and Textual Themes

If textual themes of the preceding text are (directly or indirectly) referred to in a sentence, they are (relatively) thematic in that sentence or they take a neutral position (cases of contrasting, correcting etc. are considered as an additional level of the thematic sentence structure that may override the primary scalar ordering). Sentential themes are typical candidates for textual themes of the following text, but it is also possible for sentential rhemes or for the relations between themes and rhemes of sentences to be thematized in the following text (certain linguistic cues may yield specific expectations as to what will be thematized).

These schematic definitions of sentential and textual themes give us no more than a rough framework for the formulation of linearization principles accounting for the thematic relations in sentences and texts. At least, they make it obvious that word order is just one of the factors relevant for the thematic structuring (we suppose it to be decisive in some types of written texts!). The interplay between word order and other criteria like definiteness or anaphoricity (which is connected with textual themeness in many cases) has to be investigated in much more detail before we can start to formalize the underlying linearization principles. However, it is important that we start from an independently motivated conception of thematic structuring, and not from something tailored to the solution of specific word order problems, which would probably not fit into a more comprehensive model of text understanding and production - and, of course, translation.

5. CONCLUSION

As a conclusion, let me first resume the problems that I found in Hans Uszkoreit's proposal for a revised version of the LP component in GPSG:

- the problem with the relative positions of pronominal and nonpronominal arguments of the verb in the middle field of German sentences, which is connected with the overall concept of unmarked vs. strict word order, might be solved by more complex conditions for the LP statements (vs. clauses);

- the second problem seems to me even more serious because, in my view, it is impossible to find an adequate conception of topic and focus (or - as I put it - of the thematic structuring of sentences and texts) at a purely syntactic level; the difficulty is even harder to cope with if we cannot rely on information on the intonation focus of sentences, which is the case in the analysis of written texts.

The alternative solution of (some of) the word order problems that has been argued for in this paper is essentially dependent on a multi-level concept of representational as well as procedural aspects of natural-language modeling. The different levels of representation vs. analysis (and - of course - of transfer and synthesis) are conceived to describe different types of linearization principles: syntactic, semantic and pragmatic ones. One of the main points in our conception is the availability of all sorts of information, including information about the preceding text and about the factual knowledge that is necessary for understanding (and translating) natural-language texts.

Interestingly, our approximate formulations of linearization principles at the sentence-semantic level and the textual level referring to argument roles and focused constituents just have the form of their very first version in (Uszkoreit 1986): they are relativized by the verb 'tend': "The argument tends to precede the theme" or "Focused constituents tend to follow non-focused constituents". In the proposal of Hans Uszkoreit, the relativization is accounted for in the complex LP statements by other LP clauses, whereas our multi-level approach allows for a more sophisticated relativization by all sorts of facts that are available in the course of analysis, which means that information about the linguistic and non-linguistic context can be considered if necessary.

By the way, the conception of a first interpretation hypothesis that can be revised in case of counter-evidence showing up seems to be plausible from a psycholinguistic point of view, too: humans seem to use analogous strategies of a first more or less good guess (which can be seen e.g. from the normal reaction of readers that are confronted with the sentences of our example (11) one by one). This strategy includes backtracking in case of inconsistency or other counter-evidence.

However, I do not want to speculate further on this issue, which seems to me too futuristic at this given moment. I hope to be able to continue this discussion in future papers.

REFERENCES

Darbelnet, J. (1977): *Niveaux de la traduction*. Babel 23: 6-17

Engelberg, K.-J., C. Hauenschild, S. Knöpfler & P.E. Pause (1984): Con^{3}Tra: ein prozedurales Modell des Textverstehens für die Übersetzung. *Papers of the Sonderforschungsbereich 99*, Konstanz

Gazdar, G., E. Klein, G.K. Pullum & I.A. Sag (1985): *Generalized Phrase Structure Grammar*. Oxford, Blackwell

Hauenschild, C. (1982): Zur Rolle der Thema-Rhema-Gliederung in der automatischen Übersetzung. E. Stegentritt (ed.): *Maschinelle Sprachverarbeitung 1981*. Vorträge auf der 12. Jahrestagung der GAL, Mainz 1981. Sektion "Maschinelle Sprachverarbeitung". Dudweiler, AQ-Verlag: 103-117

Hauenschild, C. (1985): Zur Interpretation russischer Nominalgruppen: Anaphorische Bezüge und thematische Strukturen im Satz und im Text. München, Sagner (*Slavistische Beiträge* 186)

Hauenschild, C. (1986): KIT/NASEV oder die Problematik des Transfers bei der maschinellen Übersetzung. I.S. Batori & H.J. Weber (eds.): *Neue Ansätze in Maschineller Sprachübersetzung: Wissensrepräsentation und Textbezug*. Tübingen, Niemeyer: 167-195

Hauenschild, C. & P.E. Pause (1983): Fakktoren-Analyse zur Modellierung des Textverstehens. *Linguistische Berichte* 88: 101-120

Hoberg, U. (1981): Die Wortstellung in der geschriebenen deutschen Gegenwartssprache. München, Hueber (*Heutiges Deutsch* 1/10)

Höhle, T.N. (1982): Explikationen für "normale Betonung" und "normale Wortstellung". W. Abraham (ed.): *Satzglieder im Deutschen. Vorschläge zu ihrer syntaktischen, semantischen und pragmatischen Fundierung*. Tübingen, Narr: 75-153

Koller, W. (1979): *Einführung in die Übersetzungswissenschaft*. Heidelberg, Quelle & Meyer (UTB 819)

Komissarov, V.N. (1973): Slovo o perevode. Moskau, Izdatel'stvo "Mezdunarodnye otnosenija"

Lenerz, J. (1977): *Zur Abfolge nominaler Satzglieder im Deutschen*. Tübingen, Narr

Pause, P.E. (1983): Context and Translation. R. Bäuerle, C. Schwarze & A. v.Stechow (eds.): *Meaning, Use, and Interpretation of Language*. Berlin-New York, de Gruyter: 384-399
Reis, M. (1986): Die Stellung der Verbargumente im Deutschen. Stilübungen zum Grammatik-Pragmatik-Verhältnis. To appear in: I. Rosengren (ed.): *Sprache und Pragmatik*. 5. Lunder Symposium. Stockholm (Lunder Germanistische Forschungen)
Sgall, P., E. Hajicova & E. Benesova (1983): *Topic, Focus and Generative Semantics*. Kronberg/Taunus, Scriptor
Shieber, S.M. (1984): Direct Parsind of ID/LP Grammars. *Linguistics and Philosophy* 7: 135-154
Uszkoreit, H. (1984): *Word Order and Constituent Structure in German*. PhD thesis. University of Texas, Austin, Texas
Uszkoreit, H. (1986): Constraints on Order. To appear in: *Linguistics* 24/5
Wunderlich, D. (1985): Über die Argumente des Verbs. *Linguistische Berichte* 97: 183-227

WILLIAM R. KELLER

NESTED COOPER STORAGE:
THE PROPER TREATMENT OF QUANTIFICATION
IN ORDINARY NOUN PHRASES

ABSTRACT

A technique devised by the linguist Robin Cooper provides a means of desribing quantifier scope without the need for otherwise unmotivated syntactic ambiguity.It can be shown that certain complex noun Phrases may exhibit quantifier scope ambiguity, but that Cooper's strategy tends to overgenerate in such cases. A consideration of the reasons for this suggests a modification of Cooper's theory which overcomes the problem. The result is a principles approach to quantifier scope generation which is more restrictive than 'naive' techniques in that it predicts fewer readings. The strategy offers computational benefits which may make it more suitable for implementation in natural language processing systems.[0]

1. INTRODUCTION

Certain kinds of ambiguity in natural languages arise from the interaction of quantified noun phrases. According to the grammar of PTQ [Montague 1974b], a sentence such as *John seeks a unicorn* has two interpretations depending soley on the scope assigned to the quantified noun phrase *a unicorn*. In fact the sentence is regarded as syntactically ambiguous, having the two distinct analysis trees shown below. The analysis in (1a) is intended to represent the so-called narrow-scope, or *de*

---

[0] I would like to thank Gerald Gazdar, Stuart Shieber and Hans Uszkoreit for comments and discussions relating to this paper.

dicto reading on which John has no particular unicorn in mind, whilst (1b) corresponds to the wide-scope, or *de re* interpretation.

(1) a.   b.

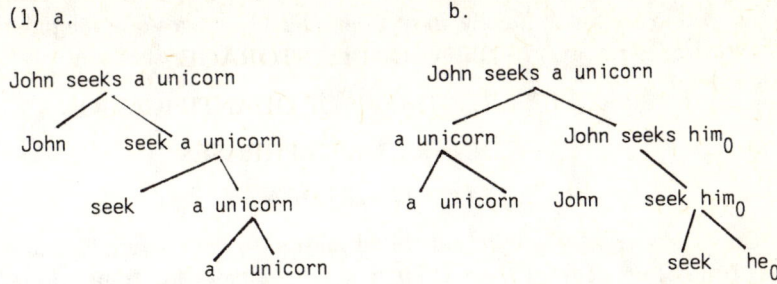

The advantage of disambiguating natural language in this way is that it allows semantic interpretation to be treated as a function: a one-one mapping from structural descriptions to objects in a suitable domain of discourse [Montague 1974a]. The signal disadvantage is that structural ambiguity may not always be well-motivated on syntactic grounds.

The linguist Robin Cooper was able to show that the need for such syntactic disambiguation could be avoided without loosing the essence of Montague's approach [Cooper 1975]. Cooper chose to define semantic interpretation not as a function but as a relation between structures and meanings. Following PTQ, in [Cooper 1975] this relation is defined in two stages: structural descriptions are first translated into one or more expressions of intensional logic (IL) and these latter are then given a fairly standard model-theoretic interpretation. Cooper has since provided a more comprehensive version of his theory which rejects translation in favour of direct interpretation of phrase structure [Cooper 1983]. It is arguable that direct interpretation emphasizes that what is being defined is a meaning relation. However, for ease of exposition the presentation of Cooper's strategy given in this papaer will be more in the spirit of his earlier work. We shall thus be concerned with a technique for translating structural descriptions into IL. It is important to note that the criticisms of Cooper's strategy and the modifications subsequently proposed carry over just as well to the later theory.

In the rest of this paper Cooper's strategy is looked at in more detail. Particular attention is paid to the technique used to relate parse trees to logical expressions, and this is outlined in the next section. Following a consideration of quantifier scope ambiguity arising in noun phrases, in section 3 it will be demonstrated that Cooper's strategy can give rise to incorrect results. The reasons for this are discussed and a solution proposed in section 4. Finally, in section 5 the advantages of implementing the revised strategy in natural language processing systems are briefly considered.

2. COOPER STORAGE.

Coopers's strategy will be illustrated informally with a simple example, the translation of *John seeks a unicorn*. As a basis for translation, the syntax tree in (2) should suffice.

(2)
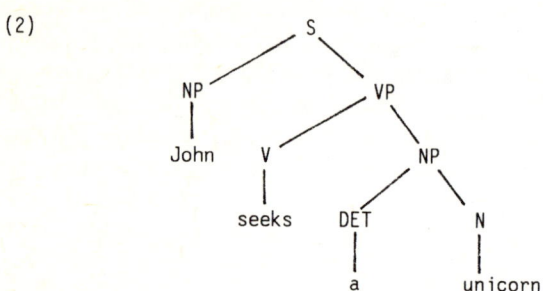

The adopted strategy will be to work from the leaves to the root, assigning interpretations to successively higher nodes. In accordance with the principle of semantic compositionality, the representation associated with some given node in the tree will always be a function of the interpretations of its daughters. An interpretation of a phrase structure node is itself a n-place sequence, the first element of which is a suitable denotation for the node in question: in this paper an expression of IL. Subsequent elements, if any, represent stored *binding operators*. Each binding operator is derived from the denotation of a previously encountered NP node and carries a unique index. Indexes themselves refer to free variables occuring in the denotation assigned to the node.

For example, the representation for the DET node will be the one-place sequence <a'>. The first, and only element of this sequence is the denotation of the determiner *a* and there are no binding operators in store. Similarly, the interpretation associated with the N node in (2) will be the one-place sequence <unicorn'>.

To obtain an interpretation for the NP *a unicorn* the interpretations of the DET and N nodes must now be combined. This is achieved by combining the denotations for the nodes after the fashion of PTQ, and forming a new sequence with hte resulting expression as first element. Any binding operators in store at either the DET or N nodes are also to be included in the interpretation. In this case there are none, and the result is therefore a new one-place sequence <a'(unicorn')>.

Once the V node has been assigned the interpretation <seek'>, the VP node may be dealt with. At this point according to Cooper, the option of storing the NP translation also arises. Ignoring this alternative for the moment, the result of combining the V and NP interpretations will be <seek'(^a'(unicorn'))>. Next, the NP *John* is assigned the interpretation <λP.P{j}> which may be combined with that of the VP to yield <seek'(a'(unicorn'))(j)> as the interpretation associated with the S node. Since there are no binding operators in store, the denotation seek'(^a'(unicorn'))(j) may be regarded as a valid translation for the whole tree. Note that it corresponds to the narrow-scope, or *de dicto* reading of the sentence.

To generate the *de re* reading translation proceeds just as before until the option of storing the translation of *a unicorn* arises. At this point the NP-Storage rule is invoked:

> NP-Storage:
> If α is an NP node with meaning (i.e. denotation) α', then the sequence <λP.P{x_i},[α']$_i$>, for some unique index i, is a valid interpretation for that node. (The variable x_i will be called an *address variable*).

Application of this rule associates with the NP node an additional interpretation <λP.P{x_0},[a'(unicorn')]$_0$>, where x_0 is the chosen address variable. Combining this new sequence with that of the V node <seek'>, gives rise to a further interpretation for the whole VP <seek'(^λP.P{x_0}),[a'(unicorn')]$_0$>. It should be noted that the stored binding operator derived from the NP translation is carried up the tree to the VP node. Similarly, combining the NP interpretation with that of *John*, <λP.P{j}>, yields a new interpretation for the sentence as a whole

$<\text{seek'}(^\wedge\lambda P.P\{x_0\})(j),[a'(\text{unicorn'})]_0>$.

This time there is a binding operator in store corresponding to the meaning of the NP node. Furthermore the partial translation seek'$(^\wedge\lambda P.P\{x_0\})(j)$ contains a free occurrence of the address variable x_0. In order to complete the translation it is necessary to retrieve the binding operator by a process which will here be named Storage Retrieval. An appropriate retrieval rule for S nodes is given below.

S-Retrieval:
If α is an S node and the sequence $<\phi, \sigma^1,[NP']_i, \sigma^2>$ is an interpretation for α, then the sequence $<NP'(^\wedge\lambda x_i.\phi), \sigma^1 \sigma^2>$ is also an interpretation for α. (Where σ^1 and σ^2 are sequences of stored binding operators and ϕ is an expression of IL)

Applying S-Retrieval yields the one-place sequence $<\text{a'}(\text{unicorn'})(^\wedge\lambda x_0.\text{seek'}(^\wedge\lambda P.P\{x_0\})(j))>$. The denotation thus constitutes a further translation for the whole tree. Assuming the usual PTQ translation for the determiner *a* it may be reduced to the logically equivalent (3), which corresponds to the wide-scope, or *de re* reading as required.

(3) $\text{Ex}[\text{unicorn'}(x) \& \text{seek'}(^\wedge\lambda P.P\{x\})(j)]$

In this way both interpretations of the sentence *John seeks a unicorn* may be obtained without the need for otherwise unmotivated syntactic ambiguity.

The technique may also be applied to cases where ambiguity arises from the interaction of two or more quantified NP's. For example, one possible representation for *every man finds a unicorn* is shown below.

(4) $<\text{find'}(^\wedge LP.P\{x_0\})(x_1),[\text{every'}(\text{man'})]_0,[\text{a'}(\text{unicorn'})]_1>$

In this instance there are two stored binding operators, and two address variables (x_0 and x_1) occur unbound in the partial translation. To empty the store it is therefore necessary to apply the S-Retrieval rule twice. But now note that there are two ways of going about this. Either the binding operator corresponding to *every man* may first be retrieved, followed by that of *a unicorn*, or alternatively the opposite ordering may be chosen. Whichever way, the result will be a one-place sequence, and in both cases the expression of IL will be a valid translation for the sentence. The two translations will however differ in the relative scope assignments to the NP denotations every'(man') and a'(unicorn'), and accordingly represent different model-theoretic interpretations.

3. COMPLEX NOUN PHRASES AND SCOPE AMBIGUITY.

Noun phrases often exhibit a fair degree of structure involving modifiers such as adjectival phrases and relative clauses, and complements including prepositional phrases, non-finite verb phrases and *that* clauses [Chomsky 1970], [Gazdar et al 1985]. It is interesting to note that where the structure is rich enough, quantifier scope ambiguities may show up apparently similar to those arising in clauses. The NP's italicised in (5a) to (5d) exhibit such ambiguity.

(5)   a. *An agent of every company* arrived
        b. They disqualified *a player belonging to every team*.
        c. *Every attempt to find a unicorn* has failed miserably.
        d. Fortunately, *every recommendation that a hospital be demolished* was ignored.

The NP underlined in (5a) involves a PP acting as a complement of the noun *agent*. There are clearly two distinct readings: one on which there is a single agent, as well as the perhaps more natural interpretation involving many agents, one for each company. The ambiguity presumably arises from the scope given to the quantified NP *every company*. Likewise in (5b) there may be a single player or many. In this case a quantified NP *every team* occurs as a constituent of a modifying VP.

The examples in (5c) and (5d) illustrate cases involving VP and S complements respectively. In (5c) both *de dicto* (no particular unicorn) and *de re* (one, alternatively many unicorns) readings seem to be available. In this respect there is a striking similarity between (5c) and the sentence *John seeks a unicorn*. The italicised NP of (5d) evinces the same kind of semantic ambiguity.

The foregoing examples indicate a rather general phenomenon operating across a variety of structures. In each case it appears that an embedded quantified NP may plausibly be given overall wide-scope with respect to the entire NP. Admittedly, for many NP's similar to those above, narrow-scope readings often seem to be preferred. On the whole it appears that examples involving PP modifiers or complements give rise to wide-scope readings most readily. It is a little harder to find convincing examples where VP modification or complementation occurs, and quite difficult in the case of S complements and relative clauses. Why this should be so is not immediately obvious and merits further attention, but for the present it will be accepted that with more or less ease, wide-scope readings may be obtained in sufficiently many cases to justify some kind of general treatment.

Consider now the examples in (6) below.

(6)   a. John seeks *an agent of a company.*
       b. John seeks *a company agent.*

Given that the NP's italicised in (6a) and (6b) might initially appear synonymous, it is rather surprising to find that sentence (6a) may be read in three different ways. Not only can the object term be given *de dicto* and *de re* interpretations as in (6b), but additionally *a company* may be read wide of *seek,* whilst *an agent (of it)* retains narrow-scope. This might be paraphrased: 'There is a particular company such that John seeks some or other agent of that company'. Here there is evidence that the scope assigned to an embedded NP is relatively independant of that given to the larger NP. This fact must be properly accounted for by any proposed translation strategy.

Suppose that Cooper's strategy is adopted to induce an appropriate set of translations for (6a). It can first be assumed that the sentence has the structure shown below.

(7)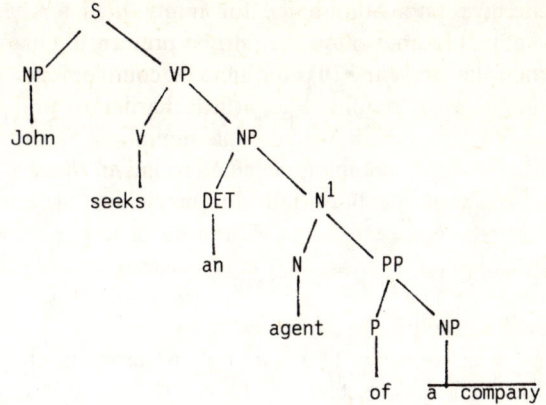

By analogy with the translation of *John seeks a unicorn* given in section 2, it is immediately clear that a *de dicto* reading for *an agent of a company* may be obtained without invoking the NP-Storage rule. Similarly, if it is chosen to store the whole object NP, then S-Retrieval will lead to the *de re* interpretation. In order to obtain the third reading mentioned above it is necessary to store the embedded NP *a company* as in (8)[1].

(8) $<a'(\text{agent}'(^\wedge\lambda P.P\{x_0\})),[a'(\text{company}')]_0>$

Translation now continues as for the narrow-scope reading, with the result that the S node has the following sequence assigned to it.

(9) $<\text{seek}'(^\wedge a'(\text{agent}'(^\wedge\lambda P.P\{x_0\})))(j),[a'(\text{company})]_0>$

This completed, the stored NP translation may be retrieved giving *a company* wide-scope, whilst *an agent(of it)* remains narrow with respect to *seek*.

So far then, it appears that Cooper Storage works, but closer inspection reveals that there is a further reading for (6a) licenced by the storage mechanism. This involves storing both the translation of *a company* as well as the larger NP of which it forms a part.

---

[1] The analysis of relational nouns assumed here is that of [Gazdar *et al* 1985]. A relational noun such as *agent* will (logically speaking) be of type $<<s,\text{Type}(NP)>,<e,t>>$, that is, a function from the intensions of term phrases to sets of individuals. It should further be noted that the preposition *of* is to be treated as the identity function on term phrases.

Starting with the representation previously obtained for *an agent of a company* shown in (8) above, NP-Storage is now invoked for a second time to yield the following further three-place sequence shown in (10).

(10) $<\lambda Q.Q\{x_1\},[a'(agent'(^\wedge\lambda P.P\{x_0\}))]_1>,[a'(company')]_0>$

Combining this with the meaning of the V node and the result with that of *John* produces a new interpretation to be associated with the sentence as a whole.

(11) $<seek'(^\wedge\lambda Q.Q\{x_1\})(j),\{<a'(agent'(^\wedge\lambda P.P\{x_0\}))]_1,$
    $[a'(company')]_0>$

The resulting sequence has two binding operators in store, but it is notable that the expression $seek'(^\wedge\lambda Q.Q\{x_1\})(j)$ contains only one free address variable (x_1). The second address variable x_0, occurs free in the binding operator $[a'(agent'(^\wedge\lambda P.P\{x_0\}))]_1$.

An immediate consequence of this is that the S-Retrieval rule is no longer guaranteed to produce sensible results. To see that this is so, it may be noted that if $[a'(company')]_0$ is retrieved first, then the resulting translation will be as shown in (12a). Substituting the PTQ translation for the determiner *a* and simplifying, this reduces to the logically equivalent (12b).

(12) a. $a'(agent'(^\wedge\lambda P.P\{x_0\}))(^\wedge\lambda x_1.a'(company')(^\wedge\lambda x_0.seek'$
      $(^\wedge\lambda Q.Q\{x_1\})(j)))$
      b. $Ex[agent'(^\wedge\lambda P.P\{x_0\})(x)\&Ey[company'(y)\&seek'$
      $(^\wedge\lambda Q.Q\{x\})(j)]]$

Roughly speaking, the problem with this 'translation' is that it still contains a free occurrence of the address variable x_0. This is since the retrieval of the translation of *a company* made it impossible to bind the variable with the lambda abstraction operator as would normally happen.

It is easily seen that performing retrieval in the opposite order does not lead to the same problem, since both address variables become bound. The translation and its simplified equivalent are shown in (13a) and (13b) respectively[2].

---

[2] The observant reader will have noticed that the interpretation obtained in this way is synonymous with the *de re* reading already mentioned. This is since the NP *an agent of a company* is itself unambiguous. Ambiguous NP's (e.g. *an agent of every company*)

(13) a. a'(company')($^\wedge\lambda x_0$.a'(agent'($^\wedge\lambda P.P\{x_0\}$)))($^\wedge\lambda x_1$.seek' ($^\wedge\lambda Q.Q\{x_1\}$)(j))))
b. Ex[company'(x)&Ey[agent'($^\wedge\lambda P.P\{x\}$)(y)&seek' ($^\wedge\lambda Q.Q\{y\}$)(j)]]

4. NESTED COOPER STORAGE.

From the foregoing discussion it should be clear that Cooper Storage depends for its success on the way in which address variables are utilised during translation. Intuitively, each address variable acts as a kind of semantic place-holder, relating an indexed binding operator to the role it will eventually play in the final translation. To illustrate, the representation for *every man finds a unicorn* is reproduced in (14) below. Inspection of the address variables reveals that the 'something doing the finding' corresponds in some sense to the stored item every'(man'), whilst the 'thing being found' corresponds to a'(unicorn').

(14) $<$ find'($^\wedge\lambda P.P\{x_0\}$)($x_1$),[every'(man')]$_0$,[a'(unicorn')]$_1 >$

The representation of *John seeks an agent of a company*, which is reproduced in (15), may be read in a similar fashion. Here the 'thing being sought' corresponds to a'(agent'($^\wedge\lambda P.P\{x_0\}$)), but notice that the role of a'(company'), indicated by the address variable x_0, is 'that thing the agent is an agent of'. Importantly, it does **not** play a (direct) role in the expression seek'($^\wedge\lambda Q.Q\{x_1\}$)(j) as evidenced by the absence of the address variable x_0.

(15) $<$ seek'($^\wedge\lambda Q.Q\{x_1\}$)(j),[a'(agent'($^\wedge\lambda P.P\{x_0\}$))]$_1$,]a' (company')]$_0 >$

The problem thus seems to be that the S-Retrieval rule is insensitive to the precise roles of the stored NP translations which it must operate on. In (15) there is nothing to prevent [a'(company')]$_0$ being retrieved first, despite the fact that it has no direct contribution to make to the partially complete sentential translation.

The obvious solution would be to amend the S-Retrieval rule so that it

---

would give rise to distinct readings.

checks for the free occurrence of an address variable, prior to retrieving a given NP translation. An appropriate formulation is the following:

> S-Retrieval (with free variable check):
> If a is an S node and the sequence $<\phi, \sigma^1, [NP']_i, \sigma^2>$ is an interpretation for α, and x_i occurs unbound in ϕ, then the sequence $<NP'(^\wedge\lambda x_i.\phi), \sigma^1 \ \sigma^2>$ is also an interpretation for α.

Aside from the fact that the new rule relies on a purely syntactic property of the logic used (i.e. whether or not an arbitrary expression of IL contains a given free variable), there is at least one place where it may still fail to produce sensible results. Such a case would be the sentence given in (16a) below, where the pronoun *him* is to be read co-referentially with *a boy*. The reason is that the usual translation given to a pronoun is an expression of the form $\lambda Q.Q\{x_i\}$, for some free variable x_i. To produce a logical translation for the sentence having the required interpretation this variable must be captured as a result of performing Storage Retrieval for the *binding operator corresponding to a boy*. A possible representation for (16a) which would achieve this is given in (16b), with *him* translated as $\lambda Q.Q\{x_0\}$[3].

(16)   a. Every sister of a boy hates him.
       b. $<$hate'$(^\wedge\lambda Q.Q\{x_0\})(x_1)$,[every'(sister'$(^\wedge\lambda P.P\{x_0\}))]_1$, [a'(boy')]$_0>$
       c. Ex[boy'(x)&Vy[sister'$(^\wedge\lambda P.P\{x\})(y) = >$ hate'$(^\wedge\lambda Q.Q\{x\})(y)]]$
       d. Vx[sister'$(^\wedge\lambda P.P\{x_0\})(x) = >$ Ey[boy'(y)&hate' $(^\wedge\lambda Q.Q\{y\})(x)]]$

If *every sister (of him)* is retrieved first then everything works out fine, with the result as shown in (16c). This reading might be paraphrased: 'there is some particular boy and every sister of his hates him'. On the other hand, since x_0 now occurs free in hate'$(^\wedge\lambda Q.Q\{x_0\})(x_1)$ on account of the translation of *him*, then the amended S-Retrieval rule can still apply first to *a boy* leading to the anomalous (17d). A possible paraphrase for the latter would be: 'Every sister of him hates a boy'.

---

[3] Clearly this is not intended to be a particularly sophisticated treatment of pronouns, for one thing, the translation of *him* given in the text makes no attempt to deal with matters of gender agreement. However, it does serve to illustrate the point.

Fortunately there is an alternative approach to translation which neither relies on syntactic properties of the logic, nor falls foul of pronouns. The proposed solution is to introduce enough structure into the store to make explicit the order in which binding operators may be retrieved. Similar suggestions have been made by Elizabet Engdahl [Engdahl 1980, 1986] in her work on the semantics of questions. To begin with a new NP-Storage rule is required:

NP-Storage (Nested Store):
If α is an NP node, and the sequence $<\alpha',\sigma>$ is an interpretation for α, then the sequence $<\lambda P.P\{x_i\}, [<\alpha',\sigma>]_i>$ for some unique index i is also an interpretation for α.

Rather than simply putting the denotation of an NP node into store, along with anything else that happens to be there, the revised rule creates a completely new store and places in it the whole representation for the NP: $<\alpha',\sigma>$. The intention is to record the fact that any binding operator in the sequence SIGM has a direct role to play in in the expression α, though not necessarily in any larger expression prior to retrieving α itself. Clearly a new S-Retrieval rule is also required:

S-Retrieval(Nested Store):
If α is an S node and the sequence $<\phi,\sigma^1,[<\beta,\sigma>]_i,\sigma^2>$ is an interpretation for α, then so is the sequence $<\beta(\char`\^\lambda x_i.\phi),\sigma^1\sigma\sigma^2>$.

The modified S-Retrieval rule need make no reference to free variables. Note that whenever some item β is retrieved from store, then its associated sequence of binding operators σ is 'added' to the the items remaining in store at the S node. This Storage Promotion, to give it a name, ensures that anything stored during the translation of β becomes accessible to the S-Retrieval rule once β itself has been retrieved. Significantly, S-Retrieval cannot apply to the sequence of stored binding operators associated with β prior to Storage Promotion.

To see how this works in practice the troublesome example of section 3 -- *John seeks an agent of a company* -- will be re-analysed. It will be remembered that Cooper's strategy failed when both NP translations were stored. This leads to the possibility of retrieving the translation of *a company* first, resulting in a spurious interpretation of the sentence. Before describing how the new storage strategy overcomes this problem, it should first be checked that the three valid readings can still be obtained.

Firstly it is clear that without invoking NP-Storage the narrow-scope reading of the sentence may be obtained as before. Modulo some very minor changes of detail, the wide-scope interpretation is also produced as previously with a single application of NP-Storage to the whole object term. Likewise, the third reading (on which *a company* is read *de re*) will result just in case NP-Storage is only applied to the embedded NP.

Choosing to store both NP denotations, the sequence below is first constructed for *an agent of a company*.

(17) $<\text{a'}(\text{agent'}(^\wedge\lambda P.P\{x_0\})), [<\text{a'}(\text{company'})>]_0>$

Here there is a single binding operator in store corresponding to the interpretation of *a company*. Storing (17) in turn results in (18).

(18) $<\lambda Q.Q\{x_1\}, [<\text{a'}(\text{agent'}(^\wedge\lambda P.P\{x_0\})), [<\text{a'}(\text{company'})]_0>]_1>$

The new sequence again has a single item in store derived from the previous interpretation (17). Translation now continues as before yielding the result:

(19) $<\text{seek'}(^\wedge\lambda Q.Q\{x_1\})(j), [<\text{a'}(\text{agent'}(^\wedge\lambda P.P\{x_0\})), [<\text{a'}(\text{company'})>]_0>]_1>$

At this stage, the S-Retrieval rule can be applied, but note that there is no longer any choice as to how to proceed. In fact only the expression $\text{a'}(\text{agent'}(^\wedge\lambda P.P\{x_0\}))$ is initially accessible to the rule. Following the first application the result is as shown in (20a), with Storage Promotion ensuring that a'(company) becomes available for retrieval. A further application and the store is empty as in (20b) signaling that translation is complete.

(20) a. $<\text{a'}(\text{agent'}(^\wedge\lambda P.P\{x_0\}))(^\wedge\lambda x_1.\text{seek'}(^\wedge\lambda Q.Q\{x_1\})(j)), [<\text{a'}(\text{company'})>]_0>$
b. $<\text{a'}(\text{company'})(^\wedge\lambda x_0.\text{a'}(\text{agent'}(^\wedge\lambda P.P\{x_0\}))(^\wedge Lx_1.\text{seek'}(^\wedge\lambda Q. Q\{x_1\})(j)))>$

The translation thus obtained is equivalent to (13) of section 3. The fact that S-Retrieval cannot proceed in the opposite order guarantees that the unwanted reading (12) cannot arise.

The example involving a pronoun can be treated in a like manner. The sentence is repeated below along with a suitable representation.

(21) a. Every sister of a boy hates him.
b. $<\text{hate'}(^\wedge\lambda Q.Q\{x_0\})(x_1),[<\text{every'}(\text{sister'}(^\wedge\lambda P.P\{x_0\})),[<\text{a'}(\text{boy'})>]_0>]_1>$

Once again there is no choice as to which stored NP denotation may be retrieved first. It is only possible to start with $\text{every'}(\text{sister'}(^\wedge\lambda P.P\{x_0\}))$ and then retrieve a'(boy') following Storage Promotion. In consequence both occurrences of x_0 will become bound as required.

5. COMPUTATIONAL ISSUES AND SUMMARY

Computational linguists have already taken advantage of Cooper's storage technique for dealing with quantifier scope ambiguity in the design of natural language processing systems [Gavron *et al* 1982] [Keller 1984]. The strategy is particularly appealing because it relies on the principle of surface compositionality, enabling semantic representations to be built up in parallel with syntactic analysis. In the Hewlett-Packard system of Gavron *et al*, Cooper Storage is utilised in the generation of first order Logical Representations during parsing. These Logical Representations are then mapped into expression of the query language for HIRE, a relational database. This allows the further possibility of a principled approach to ambiguity resolution on the basis of 'state of the world' knowledge as, say, reflected in the database.

Nested Cooper Storage presents no particular difficulties with regard to implementation. Indeed, a substantially correct treatment of quantifier scope ambiguity which is more restrictive than competing aproaches in that it predicts fewer readings is clearly to be favoured computationally. This point has been stressed by Hobbs and Shieber in a recent paper [Hobbs and Shieber 1986] which presents a new algorithm for generating quantifier scopings. Hobbs and Shieber specifically consider noun phrases introducing multiple quantifiers of the kind exemplified in section 3 of this paper. It is shown that in contrast to 'naive' algorithms which generate all possible permutations of quantifiers, the new algorithm represents a considderable saving in computational effort. For example, a naive approach to sentence (22) below, which introduces the five quantifiers *some*, *every*, *most*, *a* and *each* predicts that it has no fewer than 120 (i.e. 5 factorial) readings.

(22)   Some representatives of every department in most
       companies saw a few samples of each product.

It should be clear from the discussion of Cooper Storage in section 2 of this paper that any faithful implementation of Cooper's strategy will also be naive in this sense. Module *de dicto/de re* ambiguities it will make precisely the same predictions. In fact, of these 120 readings, only those 42 generated by the algorithm of Hobbs and Shieber turn out to be valid.

In summary, it has been demonstrated that Cooper Storage fails to provide a satisfactory treatment of quantifier scope ambiguity in certain cases. More specifically, over-generation can arise in the context of complex NP's. A proposed modification of Cooper's translation strategy, involving a nested store and Storage Promotion overcomes this problem.

Aside from some limited assumptions regarding constituent structure Nested Cooper Storage is not dependant upon a particular view of syntax nor even particular syntactic analyses. The result is a principled approach to quantifier scope ambiguity compatible with much contemporary research on syntax. As such it should be clear that Nested Cooper Storage makes no claims with regard to preferred readings. Yet a systematic account of how native speakers choose a particular interpretation must surely proceed from an empirically justified account of the available choices.

Finally it is noted that a substantially correct treatment of quantifier scope ambiguity which is more restrictive than previous approaches (in the sense that it predicts fewer readings) is clearly to be favoured computationally. For this reason it is expected that Nested Cooper Storage will also be of interest to computational linguists.

REFERENCES

Chomsky, N. (1970). Remarks on nominalization. In Roderick A. Jacobs and Peter S. Rosenbaum, eds. *Readings in English Transformatorial Grammar*. Waltham, Massachusetts: Ginn and Company, pp.184-221.

Cooper, R. (1975). *Montague's semantic theory and transformatorial syntax*. Ph.D dissertation, University of Massachusetts at Amherst.

Cooper, R. (1983). *Quantification and Syntactic Theory*. D. Reidel Dordrecht Holland.

Engdahl, E. (1986). *The Syntax and Semantics of Question in Swedish*, unpublished Ph.D dissertation. University of Massachusetts Amherst.

Engdahl, E. (1986). *Constituent Questions: The Syntax and Semantics of Questions with Special Reference to Swedish*. D. Reidel Dordrecht Holland.

Gawron, J. M., J. King, J. Lamping, E. Loebner, A. Paulson, G. Pullum, I. Sag & T. Wasow (1982). Processing English with a Generalised Phrase Structure Grammar. *Proceedings of the 20th Annual Meeting of the Association for Computational Linguistics*, University of Toronto, June.

Gazdar, G., E. Klein, G. Pullum and I. Sag (1985). *Generalized Phrase Structure Grammar*. Oxford: Basil Blackwell.

Hobbs, J. and S. Shieber (1986). *An Algorithm for Generating Quantifier Scopings*. SRI Research Paper.

Keller, W. R. (1984). Generating Logic from ProGram Parse Trees. *Cognitive Studies Research Paper*, Serial no. CSRP 39. University of Sussex.

Montague, R. (1974a). Universal Grammar. In Thomason, Richmond, ed. Formal Philosophy: *Selected Papers of Richard Montague*. New Haven: Yale University Press, 1974, pp.222-246.

Montague, R. (1974b). The Proper Treatment of Quantification in Ordinary English. In Thomason, Richmond, ed. Formal Philosophy: *Selected Papers of Richard Montague*. New Haven: Yale University Press, 1974, pp.247-270.

UWE REYLE

INSTITUT FÜR MASCHINELLE SPRACHVERARBEITUNG

UNIVERSITÄT STUTTGART

COMPOSITIONAL SEMANTICS FOR LFG

1. INTRODUCTION

The two levels of syntactic representation induced by lexical functional grammars (LFG) consist of c-structures and sets of attribute-value pairs called f-structures. F-structures are built up from the syntactic surface structure of a sentence by unification of the attribute-value graphs that are associated with each word and each constituent of the c-structure of that sentence. Thus (2) shows an f-structure for the sentence (1).

(1) Dov loves logic

(2) $\begin{bmatrix} \text{SUBJ} & [\text{PRED Dov}] \\ \text{PRED} & \text{love} < \text{SUBJ,OBJ} > \\ \text{OBJ} & [\text{PRED logic}] \end{bmatrix}$

If one uses the (typed) lambda-calculus for constructing the interpretation of a sentence, the result depends on the order in which arguments are provided for functions. This information about order can be provided in many ways. In approaches which make use of surface structure interpretation of phrase structure trees, the order of the arguments is determined in part by the linear order of constituents, and in part by the hierarchical structure of constituents. F-structures have dominance but not precedence defined on them. But the information that is represented in terms of linear precedence in phrase structure trees is encoded by the attribute names of the f-structures.

Therefore, a common practice in computing the interpretation of f-structures is to make the composition determinate. If, for the moment, we suppose that *love'* is of type $<e,<e,t>>$, then this is easily achieved by using attribute names ARG1 and ARG2 to encode within the attribute value graph (3) the correct order of the two steps of functional application yielding the result love'(l)(d).

(3) $\begin{bmatrix} \text{ARG1} & d \\ \text{PRED} & \text{love'} \\ \text{ARG2} & l \end{bmatrix}$

Thus, from the point of view of constructing the interpretation of (1), (3) is regarded as binary rather than ternary - still under the presupposition that the functions figuring in the interpretation are curried.

The present paper suggests an extension of the λ-calculus to admit reference to the attribute names associated with the values which are to be interpreted. The reflection of attribute names in the λ-expressions does not make the composition determinate. This means that there might be different sequences of lambda-conversions. However, they yield a unique result in cases where there are no semantic distinctions. Thus, for the interpretation of (2) the extended calculus gives the result love'(l)(d) from the two possible calculations. In cases where the compositional semantic structure is underdetermined by the f-structure, different calculations might lead to different interpretations. I will show to what extent scope ambiguities can be accounted for by this indeterminacy.

The present approach differs from the proposals given by Halvorsen (1983) and Fenstad et al (1985). Halvorsen gives rules which translate f-structures into attribute value graphs with implicit information about the order of applications of lambda-conversions (as in (3)). Scope ambiguities are dealt with by means of a Cooper storage mechanism. The extension of the lambda-calculus presented here permits a direct interpretation of f-structures. Sentential scope ambiguities arise in a very natural way from the fact that the f-structure underdetermines the order of composition, as is shown in sections 4 and 6. The contrast between the approach presented here and the one proposed by Fenstad et al. lies in the way of relating syntax and semantics. Fenstad et al. use constraint propagation in order to establish a structural relation between c-structures, f-structures, and semantic structures. In section 5 the interpretation mechanism is modified in order to satisfy the rule-to-rule hypothesis. This means that we associate a semantic construction rule with every rule of an LF-grammar. F-structures are no longer the input to the semantic construction component. They only restrict the set of possible analyses for syntactic reasons. In this spirit the fragment is extended to cover control phenomena in section 6.

The appendix gives the formal definition of the syntax and semantics of the extended lambda calculus. An informal introduction is given in section 2. Aspects of encoding λ-calculus within a unification framework are addressed in section 7. It is shown that a copying operation is needed to express the whole (typed) λ-calculus.

2. INTERPRETATION OF ATTRIBUTE-VALUE GRAPHS

The interpretation of a semantic representation is constructed by means of an operation FR which, given as input a set S, has as output a set of elements, each of which belongs to the bounded closure of S under the operation of functional application.[1]

In the present proposal, the meaning of (3) is calculated by FR(<ARG1,d>,love',<ARG2,l>), i.e. by taking the ARGi-attributes themselves to be part of the translations from which the translation of the whole is built up. Given an appropriate semantics, the argument positions of a relation will be independent of the order in which the arguments come.

The result of the application of FR to the set {<ARG1,d>,love',<ARG2,l>} is represented syntactically as love'{<ARG1,d>,<ARG2,l>} (which is equivalent to love'{<ARG2,l>,<ARG1,d>}).

Semantically this independence is achieved by taking the <u>denotation of a two-place relation</u> not to be a subset of the cartesian product UxU of the domain of individuals U but to be a subset of the set

$\{g \mid g:\{1,2\} \to U\}$

of partial functions from a set of indices IND into U. IND comprises attribute names ARGi as well as names of grammatical functions SUBJ, OBJ, VCOMP etc.

---

[1] For an exact definition of FR see Klein and Sag (1985).

The denotation of an individual constant or individual variable x is a function from the set of indices into the domain U.[2]

$[x] = g:IND \to U$

The denotation of a pair $<ARG_i,x>$ (written as $[<ARG1,x>]$) will be the value of the function $[x]$ at the index i, i.e. an element of the domain U.

The result of reducing a two-place relation to a one-place relation by functional application of an argument, e.g. $<ARG2,x>$, is defined as a subset of

$[love'\{<ARG2,x>\}] =$
  $\{g \mid dom(g)=\{1\}$ and there is a function $h \in [love']$
    that extends g such that $h(2)=[<ARG2,x>]\}$.

Therefore $[love'\{<ARG2,x>,<ARG1,y>\}]$ is true iff there is a function $h \in [love']$ such that $h(1)=[<ARG1,x>]$ and $h(2)=[<ARG2,y>]$.

This allows a direct interpretation of (3) but not yet of (2). In order to apply the modification to (2) we must take into account the fact that the pair $<PRED,love<SUBJ,OBJ>>$ encodes the information that the subject-NP is mapped onto the first argument and the object-NP onto the second argument of the two-place relation love'. The translation of $<PRED,love<SUBJ,OBJ>>$, therefore, involves a function t that maps the grammatical functions SUBJ and OBJ to the attributes ARG1 and ARG2, respectively. Syntactically, this information is represented by the following λ-term:

$\lambda\{<SUBJ,x>,<OBJ,y>\}love'\{<ARG1,x>,<ARG2,y>\}$

The corresponding entry for the passive voice will be

$T(<PRED,love<by-OBJ,SUBJ>>) =$
  $\lambda\{<SUBJ,x>,<by-OBJ,y>\}love'\{<ARG1,y>,<ARG2,x>\}$

Thus, we can extend the proposal and allow λ-terms to contain unordered λ-prefixes. Reduction is guided with the help of indices as follows.

---

[2] One could consider restricting the denotation of individual constants to certain indices, i.e. allowing partial functions on IND, especially if one thinks of the domain IND as containing additional features, as well as a (lattice-) structure defined on them to express selectional restrictions.

$\lambda\{<\text{SUBJ},y>,<\text{OBJ},x>\}\text{love'}\{<\text{ARG1},x>,<\text{ARG2},y>\}\ (<\text{OBJ},u>)$
$= \lambda\{<\text{SUBJ},y>\}\text{love'}\{<\text{ARG1},u>,<\text{ARG2},y>\}$

$\lambda\{<\text{SUBJ},y>,<\text{OBJ},x>\}\text{love'}\{<\text{ARG1},x>,<\text{ARG2},y>\}(<\text{SUBJ},v>)$
$= \lambda\{<\text{OBJ},x>\}\text{love'}\{<\text{ARG1},x>,<\text{ARG2},v>\}$

To simplify the notation I will write love'(x,y) for love'$\{<\text{ARG1},x>,<\text{ARG2},y>\}$ in the following.

The denotation of a pair $<\text{GF},x>$, where GF is a grammatical function, is taken to be the function g with domain {GF} and value [x]. The denotation of $\lambda\{<\text{SUBJ},y>,<\text{OBJ},x>\}\text{love'}\{<\text{ARG1},x>,<\text{ARG2},y>\}$ is therefore defined as a subset of

{g | dom(g) = {SUBJ,OBJ} and
there is a function h ∈ [love'] such that
h(1)=g(SUBJ) and h(2)=g(OBJ) }.

<u>Reduction</u> works as follows.

$[\lambda\{<\text{SUBJ},y>,<\text{OBJ},x>\}\text{love'}\{<\text{ARG1},x>,<\text{ARG2},y>\}\ (<\text{OBJ},u>)]$

= {g | dom(g) = {SUBJ} and there is a function
h ∈ $[\lambda\{<\text{SUBJ},y>,<\text{OBJ},x>\}\text{love'}\{<\text{ARG1},x>,<\text{ARG2},y>\}]$
such that h extends g and h(OBJ)=[<OBJ,u>] }

The general definition of the syntax and semantics of this calculus is given in the appendix.

3. A MINIMAL FRAGMENT

First of all the notion of type driven translation must be extended to take the indices into account. As in Montague Grammar, I will associate types with lexical categories by means of a type assigning function TYP.

TYP(PN)   = e
TYP(N)   = $<e,t>$
TYP(IV)   = $<e,t>$
TYP(TV)   = $<e,e,t>$
TYP(DET) = $<<e,t>,<<e,t>,t>>$

The translation T is defined recursively over the set of attribute-value pairs.

<u>Definition:</u>

T(<PRED,form>) = form'
   for lexical forms that do not subcategorize for any grammatical function

T(<PRED,form<$GF_1,...,GF_n$>>) =
   $\lambda\{<GF_1,x_1>,...,<GF_n,x_n>\}$form'$(x_1,...,x_n)$
   for lexical forms that subcategorize for grammatical functions $GF_1, ..., GF_n$

T(<GF,value>) = <GF,value>
   for attribute-value pairs the attribute of which is a grammatical function GF[3]

T(<$ATT_1,value_1$>,<$ATT_2,value_2$>,...,<$ATT_n,value_n$>) =
   FR(T(<$ATT_1,value_1$>),T(<$ATT_2,value_2$>),...,T(<$ATT_n,value_n$>))
   for f-structures <$ATT_1,value_1$>,...,<$ATT_n,value_n$>)

Now we are ready to calculate the translation of example (1) in detail. The first step is to translate all the attribute-value pairs in f-structure (4) which have atomic values.

(4) $\begin{bmatrix} \text{SUBJ} & [\text{PRED Dov}] \\ \text{PRED} & \text{love<SUBJ,OBJ>} \\ \text{OBJ} & [\text{PRED logic}] \end{bmatrix}$

⇓

(5) $\begin{bmatrix} \text{SUBJ} & [d] \\ \lambda\{<\text{SUBJ},x>,<\text{OBJ},y>\}\text{love'}(x,y) \\ \text{OBJ} & [l] \end{bmatrix}$

---

[3] This translation will be generalized in the next section.

The second step is to apply FR to all (sub-)f-structures in which all attribute-value pairs have been translated. The result of these applications of FR are the new values for the attribute-value pairs, the old values are the sub-f-structure. Since the f-structures to which FR is applicable in (5) are singletons, the transition to (6) is trivial.

(6) $\begin{bmatrix} \text{SUBJ} & d \\ \lambda\{<\text{SUBJ},x>,<\text{OBJ},y>\}\text{love'}(x,y) \\ \text{OBJ} & l \end{bmatrix}$

By recursion, the first and second step are applied to (6) again, which leads to the (unique) result love'(d,l).

Note that we adopted the following convention: when FR(input) is a singleton the calculation is carried out for the element of that singleton. Otherwise we get n>1 non-equivalent readings and must split the translation set into n translations.

4. QUANTIFICATIONAL NPS

In order to extend the fragment to quantificational NP's one must consider two points. The first is the independence of the translation of the determiner from the grammatical functions, and the second is the implementation of a type raising principle.

In the traditional translation $\lambda P \lambda Q \forall x(P(x) \rightarrow Q(x))$ of the determiner "every" the argument position of the quantified variable within the relation Q is specified by simply stipulating that "it is the last one". Within our LFG framework, the position is non-configurationally determined by the grammatical function that is associated with the NP. The argument of the predicate Q in the translation of the determiner must be a pair <GF,x> rather than the variable x alone. In addition, since the value of the grammatical function is determined independently, we must abstract from GF in the translations of the <SPEC,value> pairs.

T(<SPEC,every>) = $\lambda P \lambda GF \lambda Q \forall x(P(x) \rightarrow Q\{<GF,x>\})$

The translation of the OBJ-NP *every man*, for example, is

T{ <OBJ, {<SPEC,every>, <PRED,man>} > } =
   T{ <OBJ, FR{ T(<SPEC,every>), T(<PRED,man>) }>} =
   T{ <OBJ, FR(λP λGF λQ $\forall$x(P(x)$\rightarrow$Q{<GF,x>}), man')>} =
   T{ <OBJ, λGF λQ $\forall$x(man'(x) $\rightarrow$ Q{<GF,x>}) >} =
   λGF λQ $\forall$x(man'(x) $\rightarrow$ Q{<GF,x>}) (OBJ) =
   λQ $\forall$x(man'(x) $\rightarrow$ Q{<OBJ,x>})

Here we made use of a slight generalization of the translation rule for pairs of the form <GF,value>, namely T<GF,value> = value(GF). This modification will lead to the same result for the case of proper names above if we assume that in the f-structure of an NP that is a proper name, the SPEC has a value, and translate the pair <SPEC,pn> as λxλGF<GF,x>.[4]

As for the second point, note that we take proper names to be of type e. Therefore, in order to extend the fragment to quantificational NPs we must apply some type raising principle, e.g. the following rule of Geach's.

(G) If an expression occurs in type <a,b> then it may also occur in any type <<c,a>,<c,b>> (c arbitrary).

Within our framework we have to modify G, which I have stated in the form corresponding to a nondirectional categorial grammar, so as to depend on indices in addition. If the value of an attribute-value pair occurs in type <a,b>, where the index associated with a is k, then it may also occur in any type <<c,a>,<c,b>> (c arbitrary) where the index j, associated with c, is different from k.

(IG) $<a_k,b>$ ==> $<<c_j,a_k>, <c_j,b>>$, where j ≠ k

In terms of indexed λ-calculus we can give a general translation for IG by the following schema:

$\lambda R^{<c,a>} \lambda \{<j_1,z_1>...<j_n,z_n>\}^c (P^{<a,b>} (R^{<c,a>}(\{<j_1,z_1>...<j_n,z_n>\}^c)))$

If no indices were used to trigger the right combinations, the choice of the correct term would again depend on the order of the arguments. In

---

[4] If IND is finite we still have first order, because quantification goes over tuples of fixed length.

cases where the verb is combined with the subject NP first, the following index-less term would yield the correct result.[5]

$$\lambda R^{<e,<e,t>>} \lambda z^e (\lambda P^{<<e,t>,t>} (\forall x(boy(x) \to P(x)) (R^{<e,<e,t>>} (z^e)))$$

For the combination with the object first, however, the following translation must be used.

$$\lambda R^{<e,<e,t>>} \lambda z^e (\lambda P^{<<e,t>,t>} (\forall x(boy(x) \to P(x))$$
$$(\lambda w^e R^{<e,<e,t>>} (w^e)(z^e)))$$

$$\lambda^{<c,a>} \lambda z^c (P^{<a,b>} (R^{<c,a>} (z^c)))$$

The application of these two rules must be restricted according to which NP is combined with the verb first. The application of IG, on the other hand, is completely determined by the attribute of the argument. Let us see how IG is applied in the derivation of example (7).

(7) A woman loves every man

After having calculated the translations of the subject and object NPs, we get the set of expressions (8), the associated types of which are $<<e,t>,t>$, $<e,<e,t>>$, and $<<e,t>,t>$, respectively.

(8) { $\lambda Q \forall x(man'(x) \to Q\{<OBJ,x>\})$,
$\lambda\{<SUBJ,z>,<OBJ,w>\}love'(z,w)$,
$\lambda Q \exists y(woman'(x) \to Q\{<SUBJ,x>\})$ }

First, we need to apply the translation of the object NP $\lambda Q \forall x(man'(x) \to Q\{<OBJ,x>\})$ to the predicate's translation $\lambda\{<SUBJ,z>,<OBJ,w>\}$ love'(z,w). In order to do that we must lift the type of the NP to $<<e,<e,t>>,<e,t>>$, where the index associated with the introduced e is OBJ. This gives us the following expression

$$\lambda R \lambda<SUBJ,v> \lambda Q \forall x(man'(x) \to Q\{<OBJ,x>\}) (R\{<SUBJ,v>\}))$$

which is applied to $(\lambda\{<SUBJ,z>,<OBJ,w>\}love'(z,w))$ and finally reduced to

---

[5] For singletons {<j,z>} I will simply write <j,z>.

λ<SUBJ,v> λQ$\forall$x(man'(x)→Q{<OBJ,x>}) (λ{<OBJ,w>}love'(v,w))
= λ<SUBJ,v> λQ$\forall$x(man'(x)→λ{<OBJ,w>}love'(v,w){<OBJ,x>}
= λ<SUBJ,v> $\forall$x(man'(x)→love'(v,x))

This, in turn, will be the argument of the translation of the subject NP

λQ $\exists$y(woman'(y) & Q{<SUBJ,y>})
              (λ<SUBJ,v> $\forall$x(man'(x)→love'(v,x)))
= λQ $\exists$y(woman'(y) & λ<SUBJ,v>
        $\forall$x(man'(x)→love'(v,x)){<SUBJ,y>})
= $\exists$y(woman'(y) & $\forall$x(man'(x)→love'(y,x))

If we applied the translation of the subject NP to the predicate's translation first (via type lifting) and then the result to the translation of the object NP, we would get the second reading of (7).

$\forall$x(man'(x)→$\exists$y(woman'(y) & love'(y,x)))

Thus, the translation procedure gives us all the quantifier scope readings of a sentence that arise by permutation of the quantifiers of one clause.[6] In order to distinguish this mechanism for getting scope ambiguities from others (e.g. Cooper Storage) that are not limited to clauses, I will call it <u>quantifier scrambling</u>.

An argument for quantifier scrambling is that, although the indefinite NP *a girl* must have wide scope over the universally quantified NP *every boy* in the sentence

If every boy loves a girl then she must be quite beautiful.

it does not have wide scope over the *if...then* construction, i.e. does not imply existence.

---

[6] Note that it is not possible to generate the two different readings for (7) by using rule G together with Montague's rule (a --> <<a,b>,b>) within the framework of categorial grammar. In this case all the power of Lambek-calculus is needed (see van Benthem (1983)).

5. COMPOSITIONALITY IN LFG

What we have gained so far is a direct interpretaton of f-structures, but not yet a compositional semantics for our minimal natural language fragment. In order to achieve this, we must associate with every rule in the syntax which combines syntactic items to produce a new item a corresponding semantic rule which gives the meaning of the produced item from the meanings of the input terms. Within the framework of LFG this means that we must associate meanings with the annotated phrase structure rules.

$$S \rightarrow \quad NP_{\uparrow SUBJ=\downarrow} \quad VP_{\uparrow=\downarrow}$$
$$VP \rightarrow \quad V_{\uparrow=\downarrow} \quad NP_{\uparrow OBJ=\downarrow}$$

Let NP', VP' and V' be the translations of NP, VP and V, respectively. We know that the translations have the following form:

NP': $\lambda GF\ NP''$, where NP'' is of type $<e,t>$
V': $\lambda\{<SUBJ,x>\}verb'(x)$, for intransitive verbs
$\lambda\{<SUBJ,x>,<OBJ,y>\}verb'(x,y)$, for transitive verbs

Loosely speaking, the meaning of the equation $\uparrow OBJ=\downarrow$ in the VP-rule is that the role the NP plays in the VP (or sentence) is that of the object. The trivial equation $\uparrow=\downarrow$ indicates that the meaning of the verb is incorporated into the meaning of the VP without any additional information added. Since λ-conversion should not be applied until sentence level[7], the translations we associate with the above rules are the following.

$$S \rightarrow NP_{\uparrow SUBJ=\downarrow}\ VP_{\uparrow=\downarrow} \qquad FR(\ \{\ NP'(SUBJ)\ \} \cup \{\ VP'\ \}\ )$$

$$VP \rightarrow V_{\uparrow=\downarrow} \quad NP_{\uparrow OBJ=\downarrow} \qquad \{\ NP'(OBJ)\ \} \cup \{\ V'\ \}$$

---

[7] In non-configurational languages without VP we directly have

$$S \rightarrow NP_{\uparrow SUBJ=\downarrow}\ VP_{\uparrow=\downarrow}\ NP_{\uparrow OBJ=\downarrow} \qquad FR(\ \{NP'(SUBJ)\}\ \{NP'(OBJ)\}\ \{V'\}\ ).$$

6. CONTROL PHENOMENA AND LONG DISTANCE DEPENDENCIES

The treatment of control and complementation in LFG is based on so-called control equations associated with the lexical entries of the control verbs (cf. Bresnan (1982)). These equations express the relation of referential dependence between an unexpressed subject (i.e. the *controlled* element of the embedded clause) and an expressed or unexpressed constituent (the *controller*) in the matrix clause. We will consider the LFG-treatment of 'equi'- (e.g. *promise, persuade*) and 'raising'-verbs (e.g. *expect*) within our compositional semantics. The lexical entries LFG provides for these verbs are the following:

V, promise<SUBJ,OBJ,VCOMP> , ↑VCOMP SUBJ = ↑SUBJ
V, persuade<SUBJ,OBJ,VCOMP> , ↑VCOMP SUBJ = ↑OBJ
V, expect<SUBJ,VCOMP>OBJ , ↑VCOMP SUBJ = ↑OBJ

Raising verbs occur with an NP that bears only a *grammatical* relation to the matrix verb, but does not play a *semantic role* in the relation expressed by the raising verb. This fact is represented by not including the OBJ in the argument list of the verb, but rather by listing it <u>outside</u> the brackets. Equi verbs, on the other hand, have a grammatical argument that plays a semantic role both in the matrix clause and in the clause nucleus associated with the complement. This leads to the well known differences between the two types of verbs regarding the existential entailments of an indefinite object NP.

Given the syntactic rules (9), these control equations give rise to so-called reentrancy structures, as shown in the f-structure (11), for sentence (10).

(9) VP --> $V_{\uparrow=\downarrow}$ $NP_{\uparrow OBJ=\downarrow}$ (...) $VP'_{\uparrow VCOMP=\downarrow}$

  VP' --> (to) $VP_{\uparrow=\downarrow}$

(10) Every man persuades an American to sin.

(11) $\begin{bmatrix} \text{SUBJ} & \text{[every man]} \\ \text{PRED} & \text{persuade}<(\text{SUBJ}),(\text{OBJ}),(\text{VCOMP})> \\ \text{OBJ} & \text{[an American]} \\ \text{VCOMP} & \begin{bmatrix} \text{SUBJ} & [\ ] \\ \text{PRED} & \sin<(\text{SUBJ})> \end{bmatrix} \end{bmatrix}$

We will associate the following translations with the entries in the lexicon.

V, persuade<SUBJ,OBJ,VCOMP> , ↑VCOMP SUBJ = ↑OBJ -->
  λ{<SUBJ,x>,<OBJ,z>,<VCOMP,y>}persuade'(x,z,w),
        where w ∈ FR{y,<SUBJ,z>}

V, promise<SUBJ,OBJ,VCOMP> , ↑VCOMP SUBJ = ↑SUBJ -->
  λ{<SUBJ,x>,<OBJ,z>,<VCOMP,y>}promise'(x,z,w),
        where w ∈ FR{y,<SUBJ,x>}

V, expect<SUBJ,VCOMP>OBJ , ↑VCOMP SUBJ = ↑OBJ -->
  λ{<SUBJ,x>,<OBJ,z>,<VCOMP,y>}expect'(x,w),
        where w ∈ FR{y,<SUBJ,z>}

This means that, in general, we do not have one but a set of translations associated with each verb. I will abbreviate this by writing λ{<SUBJ,x>,<OBJ,z>,<VCOMP,y>}expect'(x,*FR{y, <SUBJ,z>}*),where *FR{y, <SUBJ,z>}* represents some element of *FR{y,<SUBJ,z>}*, and y is of type <e,t>.[8] For the translations associated with the syntax, we have:[9]

VP --> $V_{\uparrow=\downarrow}$ $NP_{\uparrow OBJ=\downarrow}$ (...) $VP'_{\uparrow VCOMP=\downarrow}$

     { V' } ∪ { <OBJ,NP'> } ∪ ... ∪ { <VCOMP,(VP')'> }

---

[8] Within the scope of this paper, I cannot address the question of whether control verbs should be translated by taking as the translation of the infinitival complement a property or a proposition (see e.g. Chierchia (1984)).

[9] If we were to translate (11) directly, we would have to deal with the problem of nodes that are the value for more than one edge labeled by grammatical functions. In (11) this node is the f-structure for 'an American', which is the value for both the SUBJ and OBJ attributes. An algorithm that takes this approach is given in Reyle (1985) and Asher, Wada (1986).

VP' -->   (to) VP'$_{\uparrow=\downarrow}$ { VP' }

Let us calculate the semantics for (10) step by step. For building up the semantic $VP' = \{V\} \cup \{<OBJ,NP'>\} \cup ... \cup \{<VCOMP,(VP')'>\}$ associated with the VP-rule above we have the following translations:

$<OBJ,NP'>$ = $\lambda Q \exists o(American'(o) \& Q\{<OBJ,o>\})$

V' = $\lambda\{<SUBJ,x>,<OBJ,z>,<VCOMP,y>\}$
           $persuade'(x,z,\underline{FR\{y,<SUBJ,z>\}})<VCOMP,(VP')'>$
    = $\lambda\{<SUBJ,s>\}sin'(s)$

$\underline{FR\{y,<SUBJ,z>\}}$ cannot be reduced until y is replaced by a λ-term. Therefore, we must apply the S-rule and extend the set of translations for VP' by the translation of the subject of the main clause.

$S' = FR\{<SUBJ,NP'>,<OBJ,NP'>,V',<VCOMP,(VP')'>\}$

The following sequences, (a) to (f), of λ-conversions are consistent with the types of our translations. Note that we must apply the type shifting principle IG. For the present example, the indexed types $\{<SUBJ,x>,<VCOMP,y>\}$ and $\{<VCOMP,y>\}$ for the relation R are relevant. For the derivation that converts the object NP with the translation of the verb first, we need the following term as translation of $<OBJ,NP>$.

$IG<OBJ,NP'>$ =
    $\lambda R \lambda\{<SUBJ,x>,<VCOMP,y>\}\lambda Q$
        $\exists w(American'(w)\&Q\{<OBJ,w>\}) R\{<SUBJ,x>,<VCOMP,y>\})$

For the derivation that converts the subject NP with the translation of the verb first we need the following term as translation of $<OBJ,NP>$.

$IG<OBJ,NP'>$ =
    $\lambda R \; \lambda\{<VCOMP,y>\} \; \lambda Q$
        $\exists w(American'(w)\&Q\{<OBJ,w>\})(R\{<VCOMP,y>\})$

Which result is chosen depends on the type of Q. In the following calculation (a) the second translation is used.

(a) IG<OBJ,NP'> (IG<SUBJ,NP'> (V')) (<VCOMP,(VP')'>)

First, we need the raised translation of the subject NP that corrresponds to the first translation given for the object above.

IG<SUBJ,NP'> =
  λR λ{<OBJ,v>,<VCOMP,w>} λQ ∀s(man'(s) → Q{<SUBJ,s>})
                      (R{<OBJ,v>,<VCOMP,w>})

IG<SUBJ,NP'>(V') =
  λR λ{<OBJ,v>,<VCOMP,w>} λQ ∀s(man'(s) → Q{<SUBJ,s>})
   (R{<OBJ,v>,<VCOMP,w>})
   (λ{<SUBJ,x>,<OBJ,z>,<VCOMP,y>}persuade'(x,z,FR{y,<SUBJ,z>}) =

  λ{<OBJ,v>,<VCOMP,w>} λQ ∀s(man'(s) → Q{<SUBJ,s>})
      λ{<SUBJ,x>,<OBJ,z>,<VCOMP,y>}persuade'(x,z,FR{y,<SUBJ,z>})
             ({<OBJ,v>,<VCOMP,w>}) =

  λ{<OBJ,v>,<VCOMP,w>} λQ ∀s(man'(s) → Q{<SUBJ,s>})
             (λ{<SUBJ,x>}persuade'(x,v,FR{w,<SUBJ,v>})) =

  λ{<OBJ,v>,<VCOMP,w>} ∀s(man'(s) →
      λ{<SUBJ,x>}persuade'(x,v,FR{w,<SUBJ,v>}){<SUBJ,s>}) =

  λ{<OBJ,v>,<VCOMP,w>} ∀s(man'(s) → persuade'(s,v,FR{w,<SUBJ,v>}))

IG<OBJ,NP'> (IG<SUBJ,NP'> (V')) =

  λR λ{<VCOMP,y>} λQ ∃x(American'(x) & Q{<OBJ,x>}) (R{<VCOMP,y>})
  λ{<OBJ,v>,<VCOMP,w>} ∀s(man'(s) → persuade'(s,v,FR{w,<SUBJ,v>})) =

  λ{<VCOMP,y>} λQ ∃x(American'(x) & Q{<OBJ,x>})
      (λ{<OBJ,v>,<VCOMP,w>} ∀s(man'(s) →
              persuade'(s,v,FR{w,<SUBJ,v>})){<VCOMP,y>}) =

  λ{<VCOMP,y>} λQ ∃x(American'(x) & Q{<OBJ,x>})
      (λ{<OBJ,v>} ∀s(man'(s) → persuade'(s,v,FR{y,<SUBJ,v>}))) =

λ{<VCOMP,y>} ∃x(American'(x) & λ{<OBJ,v>}∀s(man'(s) →
    persuade'(s,v,FR{y,<SUBJ,v>})){<OBJ,x>})   =

λ{<VCOMP,y>} ∃x(American'(x) & ∀s(man'(s) →
    persuade'(s,x,FR{y,<SUBJ,x>})))

IG<OBJ,NP'> (IG<SUBJ,NP'> (V')) (<VCOMP,(VP')'>) =

∃x(American'(x) & ∀s(man'(s) →
    persuade'(s,x,FR{λ{<SUBJ,u>}sin'(u),<SUBJ,x>}) =

∃x(American'(x) & ∀s(man'(s) → persuade'(s,x,{sin'(x)}))

(b) (IG<SUBJ,NP'> (IG<OBJ,NP'> (V'))) (<VCOMP,(VP')'>) =
    ∀w(man'(w) → ∃x(American'(x) & persuade'(w,z,{sin'(x)}))

(c) IG<OBJ,NP'> ((IG<SUBJ,NP'> (V')) (<VCOMP,(VP')'>)) =
    (a)

(d) IG<SUBJ,NP'> ((IG<OBJ,NP'> (V')) (<VCOMP,(VP')'>)) =
    (b)

(e) IG<OBJ,NP'> (IG<SUBJ,NP'> (V'(<VCOMP,(VP')'>)) = (a)

(f) IG<SUBJ,NP'> (IG<OBJ,NP'> (V'(<VCOMP,(VP')'>)) = (b)

The readings resulting from the different positions of the VCOMP are equivalent, simply because the translation of VCOMP does not allow for 'quantifying into' it. Raising verbs may allow additional ambiguities if we let the type of the argument that is controller be raised to <<e,t>,t>. This means the translation of e.g. *expect* would allow both types <e,<e,t>,t> and <<<e,t>,t>,<e,t>,t>. The translations given further predict that the object of an infinitival complement cannot take wide scope over the control verb. Of course this is far too restrictive. Note, however, that these ambiguities arise only via what I called quantifier scrambling in section 4 and that we need additional mechanisms to be able to treat the whole range of scope phenomena.[10]

7. IMPLEMENTATION

In this section we will describe how λ-expressions and λ-conversion can be encoded within a slightly extended unification framework. That means that rather than parse the λ-expressions and use a subroutine to deal with the λ-conversion rules throughout the entire calculation, we will encode the conversion rules directly by means of the unification operation. We will first show for which fragment of the traditional λ-calculus the unification operation is sufficient and then add a copying operation in order to cover the whole language.

The first problem we must deal with is the renaming of bound variables. For untyped λ-calculus in which all functions are curried, De Bruijn (1970) (see Barendregt (1981)) defines a kind of λ-term, so-called nameless terms, that are syntactic objects where no names are given to bound variables. These objects are introduced in such a way that an a-congruence class (two terms are a-congruent if they result from each other by a series of changes of bound variables) of ordinary λ-terms corresponds exactly to one nameless term. The syntax of the untyped λ-calculus is given by the following definition.

Definition: The set of λ-terms Λ is inductively defined as follows:
    (i) any variable x, y, ... is a λ-term
    (ii) if M, N ∈ Λ then MN ∈ Λ; M is called *functor* and N *argument* of the λ-term MN
    (iii) if M ∈ Λ then (λxM) ∈ Λ (for any variable x); M is called *body* of (λxM)

Consider the term M = λxx(λyxyy). This term may be represented by the following tree, in which the nodes labeled with λ dominate unlabeled

---

[10] One such phenomenon is the asymmetry in the behaviour of universally versus existentially quantified NPs, which cannot be explained by their pure quantificational force, but must be accounted for by other means of semantic differentiation among determiners. The limitations of pure quantification theory become particulary clear when one looks at such non-quantificational distinctions as referential/attributive readings of definite NPs, distributive/non-distributive readings of plural NPs or the differences in indefinite, definite and demonstrative reference.

nodes (according to part (iii) of the definition) which in turn dominate functor argument pairs (according to part (iii)).

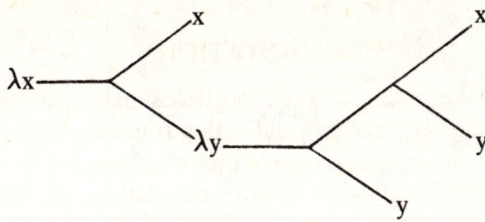

The nameless term for M, namely λ1(λ211), has the following tree.

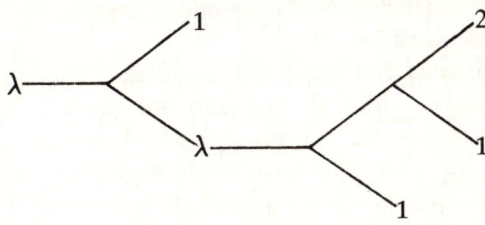

A number occurrence n in the nameless term represents the fact that the variable in the corresponding place in M is bound by the λ which is n λ-labeled nodes away (along a path in the tree) from that place.

I will modify de Bruijn's approach for a <u>fragment</u> of the λ-calculus. The fragment is syntactically defined by exactly those formulas, whose bound variables only occur once within the scope of their binders. Thus, the above formula M is not contained in the fragment, but the formula N=λx(λyxy) is. This restriction allows the number occurrences to be eliminated by taking the directed acyclic graph N" instead of the tree N' for N, where N" results from N' simply by adding an edge which ends at the node of the number occurrence n and starts at the node labeled with its corresponding λ.

N'

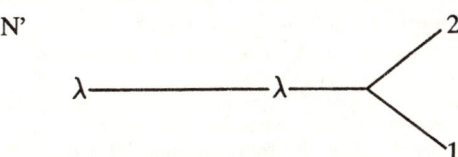

N"

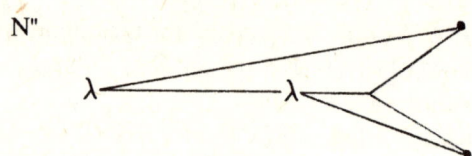

N" might also be written as a set of attribute-value pairs N*, where \<i\> and \<j\> are coindexing devices and *bod*, *fun* and *arg* stand for the body, functor and argument of a λ-term, respectively.

$$N^* \begin{bmatrix} \lambda & <i> \\ bod & \begin{bmatrix} \lambda & <j> \\ bod & \begin{bmatrix} fun & <i> \\ arg & <j> \end{bmatrix} \end{bmatrix} \end{bmatrix}$$

Before we can explain why we needed to restrict the fragment to the special sort of terms with only one occurrence of bound variables, we must explain how we deal with λ-conversion within the unification framework. λ-conversion is achieved by the unification of the meaning of an argument with the value of the (outermost) λ-attribute. Let us do this for the conversion of N* with λxx, which has the attribute-value form M*.

$$M^* \begin{bmatrix} \lambda & <k> \\ bod & <k> \end{bmatrix}$$

The result of this conversion is

$$\begin{bmatrix} bod & \begin{bmatrix} \lambda & <j> \\ bod & \begin{bmatrix} fun & \begin{bmatrix} \lambda & <k> \\ bod & <k> \end{bmatrix} \\ arg & <j> \end{bmatrix} \end{bmatrix} \end{bmatrix}$$

The motivation for the mentioned restriction is that we want to deal with secondary conversions too. When secondary conversions come into play is best illustrated with the simple example *every man sleeps*. After the conversion of *every man* with *sleeps* we get ∀y(man(y) → λ{\<SUBJ,x\>}sleep'(x){\<SUBJ,y\>}) which further reduces to ∀y(man'(y) → sleep'(y)). Although the last two expressions are logically equivalent, we are in general interested in the simpler one. Therefore, we must somehow prepare the translation of *every man* to take care of such

COMPOSITIONAL SEMANTICS FOR LFG

additional conversions. In order to do this, we consider a <u>typed</u> λ-calculus and make use of the information available about the types of variables as well as the position they take within the term itself.

Suppose Q is a variable which has a type of the form <a,b>. Then we can distinguish two cases, where Q either occupies the position of a functor or the position of an argument in the λ-term. In the latter case we get the following schema, which obviously also applies for atomic types.

$$\lambda Q \ldots F Q \ldots \quad \longrightarrow \quad \begin{bmatrix} \lambda & <Q> \\ bod & \begin{bmatrix} \ldots & \begin{bmatrix} fun & F \\ arg & <Q> \end{bmatrix} \end{bmatrix} \end{bmatrix}$$

When Q occupies an argument position, we make the functional structure of Q explicit in the value of the λ-attribute.

$$\lambda Q \ldots Q A \ldots \quad \longrightarrow \quad \begin{bmatrix} \lambda & \begin{bmatrix} \lambda & <A> \\ bod & <Q> \end{bmatrix} \\ bod & \begin{bmatrix} \ldots & \begin{bmatrix} fun & <Q> \\ arg & <A> \end{bmatrix} \end{bmatrix} \end{bmatrix}$$

The rationale behind this is the following: if the λ-term λQ...QA... is applied to an argument P of type <a,b>, the argument P takes in the secondary conversion is A. Therefore, the result of the conversion is the node labeled by <Q>. In the example where *every man* is applied to *sleeps* we start with the following translations, in which the attributes *quan* and *form* have as values the quantifier prefix and the matrix of a formula, respectively:

every man
$$\begin{bmatrix} \lambda & \begin{bmatrix} \lambda & <y> \\ bod & <j> \end{bmatrix} \\ bod & \begin{bmatrix} form & \begin{bmatrix} quan & \forall <y> \\ form & \begin{bmatrix} conn & \rightarrow \\ arg1 & \begin{bmatrix} pred & man' \\ arg & <y> \end{bmatrix} \\ arg2 & <j> \end{bmatrix} \end{bmatrix} \end{bmatrix} \end{bmatrix}$$

sleep
$$\begin{bmatrix} \lambda & <k> \\ bod & \begin{bmatrix} form & \begin{bmatrix} pred & sleep' \\ arg & <k> \end{bmatrix} \end{bmatrix} \end{bmatrix}$$

After the conversion, the resulting formula is the value of the outermost attribute *bod* in the structure associated with *every man*.

$$\begin{bmatrix} \text{form} & \begin{bmatrix} \text{quan} & \forall <y> \\ \text{form} & \begin{bmatrix} \text{conn} & \to \\ \text{arg1} & \begin{bmatrix} \text{pred} & \text{man'} \\ \text{arg} & <y> \end{bmatrix} \\ \text{arg2} & \begin{bmatrix} \text{pred} & \text{sleep'} \\ \text{arg} & <y> \end{bmatrix} \end{bmatrix} \end{bmatrix} \end{bmatrix}$$

To be precise, we give the rule of λ-conversion.[11] The easiest way to do this is to associate with the formation rule X → F A, which corresponds to part (ii) of the definition of λ-terms above, a set of constraints in the same format as the functional equations in LFG. We assume that the result of the λ-conversion (↑sem) as well as the terms which play the roles of the functor and argument categories (↓sem), are values of an attribute *sem*.

$$\begin{array}{ccc} X & \to & F \quad , \quad A \\ & \uparrow\text{fun} = \downarrow\text{sem} & \uparrow\text{arg} = \downarrow\text{sem} \\ & \uparrow\text{fun } \lambda = \uparrow\text{arg} & \\ & \uparrow\text{sem} = \uparrow\text{fun bod} & \end{array}$$

For syntactic reasons we assume that the translations of the lexical entries always make their types explicit by means of λ-abstractions. The translation for e.g. *man*, therefore, will be λx man'(x) and not simply *man*'.

---

[11] This rule does not specify linear precedence. Which position of a given string is identified with the functor F or argument A is determined by the types of the translations associated with F and A. For the sake of readability we do not make this restriction explicit in what follows. What it amounts to is replacing the value <v> of attribute λ, with type <a,b>, by

$$\begin{bmatrix} \text{type} & <a,b> \\ \text{var} & <v> \end{bmatrix}$$

COMPOSITIONAL SEMANTICS FOR LFG

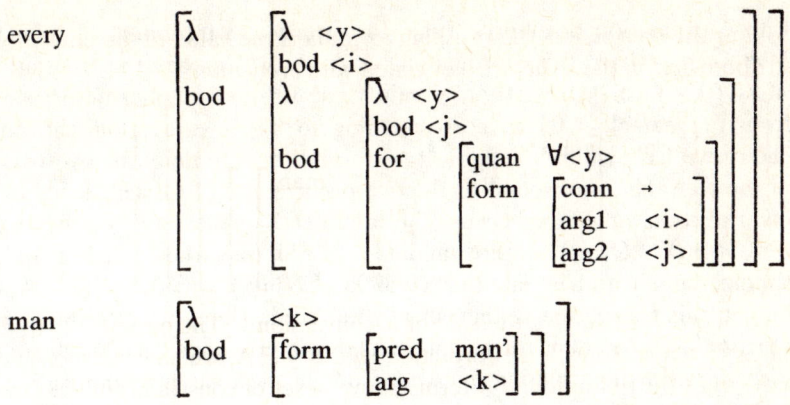

Conversions that arise from the functor-argument structure of λ-terms are handled as shown in the following example for type raising.

λRλPPλxRλylove(x,y)

$$\begin{bmatrix} \lambda & \begin{bmatrix} \lambda & <r> \\ bod & <R> \end{bmatrix} \\ bod & \begin{bmatrix} \lambda & \begin{bmatrix} \lambda & <p> \\ bod & <P> \\ fun & <P> \\ arg & \begin{bmatrix} \lambda & <x> \\ bod & \begin{bmatrix} fun & <R> \\ arg & \begin{bmatrix} \lambda & <y> \\ bod & \begin{bmatrix} form & \begin{bmatrix} pred & love' \\ arg1 & <x> \\ arg2 & <y> \end{bmatrix} \end{bmatrix} \end{bmatrix} \end{bmatrix} \end{bmatrix} \end{bmatrix} \end{bmatrix}$$

This should suffice to show how the fragment of the traditional λ-calculus can be handled within the unification framework itself. I do not have an answer to the question of what expressive power the fragment has. Furthermore I do not know whether the fragment is adequate for describing the semantics of natural language fragments. Although both questions are subjects for further research, I would like to make a few remarks on the latter one here.

The fact that the fragment is too restricted is illustrated by examples with coordination or ellipsis. Take, for example, a treatment of *John or Max sleeps*, where the coordinated NP *John or Max* has the translation $\lambda Q(Q(j) \vee Q(m))$. If we try to eliminate de Bruijn's number occurrences from the nameless term corresponding to this λ-expression, the only choice we have within the unification formalism is to unify the two nodes of the tree that correspond to the two occurrences of Q. This leads to a contradiction, however, because the arguments of these two occurrences in $\lambda Q(Q(j) \vee Q(m))$ are not unifiable. In this case, the remedy is quite simple, namely, to translate the NP as $\lambda Q \exists x((m(x) \vee j(x)) \& Q(x))$. And, in fact, this translation is linguistically more adequate, because the x can function as antecedent for singular anaphoric pronouns, such as in *He is dreaming*. But this solution does not work in the case of quantificational NPs, such as *A girl or every boy is dreaming*. A translation such as $\lambda Q(\text{quant}(z)(\exists x(\text{girl}(x) \& x=z) \vee \forall y(\text{boy}(y) \rightarrow x=z)) \& Q(z))$ would give the wrong truth conditions for any choice of quantification quant(z) over z. The only solution I see is to copy the VP into the disjuncts. But $\lambda Q(\lambda P \exists x(\text{girl}(x) \& P(x))(Q) \& \lambda P \forall y(\text{boy}(y) \rightarrow P(y))(Q))$ ($\lambda x \text{sleep}'(x)$) leads to the same problems with unification as above.

This example shows that it is not enough to extend the fragment of the λ-calculus so that several occurrences of some variable under the scope of its binder are allowed in cases where every occurrence is in an argument position and does not take any arguments itself.

Therefore we need to implement a copying mechanism that creates different nodes for multiple occurrences of the same variable. The simplest way of doing this, while keeping the property of dealing with nameless terms without number occurrences, is the following. Suppose a term t is given, in which a variable x occurs n times under the scope of its binder. Then we make n copies of an argument y, which, after conversion, occupy the n positions of x. The copying is triggered by writing $\lambda < x_1,...,x_n >$ instead of λx in t and substituting each occurrence of x in t by one of the x_i. Thus we replace $\lambda Q(Q(j) \vee Q(m))$ by $\lambda < Q_1, Q_2 > (Q_1(j) \vee Q_2(m))$.

When y is to be unified with the value $< x_1,...,x_n >$ of attribute λ then an n-tuple $< y_1,...y_n >$ is created by copying that will be unified with $< x_1,...,x_n >$ instead of y.

Note that the transitions from the form $\lambda Q(Q(j) \vee Q(m))$ to $\lambda < Q_1, Q_2 > (Q_1(j) \vee Q_2(m))$ are given a priori by simple changes in the translations of the lexical entries and templates. The transitions from y to $<y_1,...y_n>$, however, must be executed dynamically by a unification operation with a built-in copying-mechanism.

8. CONCLUSION

We have shown how the proposed extension of the λ-calculus can be used to formulate a semantics for LFG's that satisfies the rule-to-rule hypothesis. We achieved this by allowing, in the λ-expressions themselves, reference to the attribute names appearing in the equations associated with the phrase structure rules.

The main characteristic of the present approach is that the problem of scope ambiguities is solved without adopting Montague's view that syntax is only an auxiliary science for semantics. F-structures are autonomous within our system. Although the requirements that f-structures be coherent and complete no langer have to be tested on the f-structures themselves - these restrictions simply fall out of the reduction process for our *indexed* λ-expressions - f-structures are still the place for expressing syntactic constraints for, e.g., agreement, binding, gapping etc. F-structures (and c-structures), however, do not determine the order in which the arguments of the verb must be bound during the construction of the semantic representation, and thus do not determine the scope of quantifiers.

9. APPENDIX: DEFINITION OF THE INDEXED λ-CALCULUS

8.1 Syntax:

<u>Definition:</u> Let I be any set and e, t be the basic types. Then ITYP, the set of indexed types, is inductively defined as follows.

(i) $<i,e>$, $<i,t> \in$ ITYP for all $i \in I$

(ii) if $<i_1,s_1>, ..., <i_n,s_n>, <i,s> \in$ ITYP and $i_j \neq i_k$ for all $j \neq k$,

then $<h, \{<i_1,s_1>, ..., <i_1,s_n>\}; <i,s>> \in$ ITYP

<u>Definition:</u> The set of terms of indexed type $<i,s>$ (notation $T^{<i,s>}$) is inductively defined as follows.

(i) $v^{<i,s>} \in T^{<i,s>}$ for all variables v of type $<i,s>$

(ii) if $M \in T^{<h,\{<i1,s1>,...,<in,sn>\};<i,s>>}$
     and $N^j \in T^{<jm,rm>}$ for $m = 1,...,m' < n+1$
     such that $<j_m,r_m> \in \{<i_1,s_1>,...,<i_n,s_n>\}$,

then if m' < n:

$M\{N^{j_1},...,N^{j_{m'}}\} \in$

$T^{<h,\{<i_1,s_1>,...,<i_1,s_1>\}\setminus\{<j_n,r_n>,...<j_{m'},r_{m'}>\};<i,s>>}$

and if m' = n:

$M\{N^{j_1},...,N^{j_{m'}}\} \in T^{<i,s>}$.

(iii) if $M \in T^{<i,s>}$ and $v_k \in T^{<i_k,s_k>}$ for $0<k<n+1$ then

$$\lambda\{v_1,...,v_n\}M \in T^{<h,\{<i_1,s_1>,...,<i_n,s_n>\};<i,s>>}$$

Note: The set of terms of traditional typed k-calculus is a subset of the set of terms with indexed types: take only singletons in (ii) and (iii).

8.2 Reduction and Substitution

<u>Definition:</u> Reduction is defined as usual (see e.g. Barendregt (1981)) except for:

if $\lambda\{v_1,...,v_n\}M \in T^{\{h,<i_1,s_1>,...,<i_n,s_n>\};<i,s>>}$ and

$N^jm \in T^jm$ for $m = 1,...,m' < n+1$,

then if $m'<n$:

$$\lambda\{v_1,...,v_n\}M \{N^j1,...,N^jm'\} = \lambda\{v_1,...,v_n\}\backslash\{v^j1,...,v^jm'\} M [v:=N]$$

and if $m'=n$:

$$\lambda\{v_1,...,v_n\}M \{N^j,...,N^j\} = M[v:=N]$$

where $M[v:=N]$ is the abbreviation for $M[v^j1 := N^j1, ..., v^jm' := N^jm']$, which means substitution of all variables v^jm' in M by N^jm'.

8.3 Interpretation

<u>Definition:</u> Let X be any set. By induction on $s \in$ ITYP sets X^s are defined.

(i) $X^{<i,t>} = \{0,1\}$ for all $i \in I$

(ii) $X^{<i,e>} = X^i$ for all $i \in I$

(iii) $X^{<h,\{<i_1,s_1>,...,<i_n,s_n>\};<i,s>>} =$

$X^h\{X^{<i_1,s_1>},...,X^{<i_n,s_n>}\},$

where $\{X^{<i_1,s_1>},...,X^{<i_n,s_n>}\}$ is the set of all functions f from $\{i_1,...,i_n\}$ to the union of the X^{s_j} such that $f(i_j) \in X^{s_j}$

for all j = 1,...,n.

REFERENCES

Asher, N., Wada, H. (1986) 'Buildrs: an Implementation of DR Theory and LFG', *Proceedings of the 11th International Conference on Computational Linguistics*, August 1986, Bonn

Barendregt, H.P. (1981) *The Lambda Calculus*, Studies in Logic, Vol. 103, North Holland, Amsterdam

van Benthem, J. 'The Semantics of Variety', report 83-29, Dept. of Mathematics, Simon Fraser University, Burnaby

Bresnan, Joan W. (1982), 'Control and Complementation', *Linguistic Inquiry*, 13, 343-434

De Bruijn, N.G. (1972) 'Lambda calculus notation with nameless dummies', *Indag Math*, 34, pp. 381-392.

Fenstad, J.E., Halvorsen P.-K., Langholm T., van Benthem, J. (1985) 'Equations, Schemata and Situations: a Framework for Linguistic Semantics', CSLI-report 85-29, Stanford

Halvorsen, P.-K. (1983) 'Sematics for Lexical Functional Grammar', *Linguistic Inquiry*, Vol 14, Fall 1983, pp. 567-615

Klein,E., Sag,I. (1985), 'Type Driven Translation', *Linguistics and Philosophy*

Reyle, U. (1985) 'Grammatical Functions, Discourse Referents and Quantification', *Proceedings of IJCAI*, LA 1985

INDEX

Adjectif détaché	25f, 262, 272, 288
Adjective phrase	262f, 269, 274f, 280, 282f
Adjunct	9, 17, 25, 193, 264ff, 274ff, 280f, 283, 307, 389, 393, 398, 400f
Adjunction	305, 342, 377, 381f, 384, 407
Adnominal constructions	24
Agreement	4, 6f, 14, 54, 67, 100, 110, 114, 122, 262ff, 274ff, 285ff, 303ff, 315, 322, 354, 442
Algorithm for unification	5
Aliases	100, 102, 126
Alvey programme	2, 96, 127, 230
Ambiguities	31, 134f, 147f, 187, 197f, 200, 218, 234, 437, 446, 449, 457, 463
Ambiguity	23, 30f, 38, 67, 134f, 138, 169, 174, 178, 183, 188, 195, 197ff, 201, 215, 232, 234, 237, 242, 432ff, 436f, 445f
Anaphora resolution	17
Anaphoric control	26, 285, 368
Anaphoric trace	333f, 341
Apposition	25, 262, 288
ATB principle	301ff
Attachment preferences	21, 32, 148
Attribute grammars	7
Attribute-value pair	231, 455
Auxiliaries	125, 187, 200, 217f, 247, 354, 364
Auxiliary	18, 47, 106, 120ff, 187, 199, 218, 291, 298, 247f, 347, 364, 368, 412
Backtracking	132, 135, 140f, 147f, 423ff, 430
Belgian	19, 75, 82ff, 88
Binding component	23, 189ff, 193f
BMFT	1f, 15, 176
Boundaries	154, 361, 393
Boundary	38, 270, 297, 239, 332, 393f, 405
Bounded domination	151, 153, 358, 377, 385
C-structure	22, 140f, 153f, 156, 275ff, 282, 359f, 377, 382, 388f, 398, 401, 407, 448
C-structure path	389, 407
Cartesian product	31, 450
Categorial grammar	2, 23ff, 89, 202f, 211, 219f, 227ff, 232, 235, 253f, 455, 457

476   INDEX

CFG (= context free grammar)	11, 132, 134f, 140, 143ff, 148, 179
Chart parsing	108, 129, 132
Circular f-structure	26
Clitic pronouns	189, 191, 270
Coherence	11, 57, 141, 270, 361, 369, 377f, 382f, 386ff, 396, 402f, 405
Coherent infinitives	399
Combinatorial problems	19, 57
Compiled	21, 57f, 102
Compiler construction	21
Complementizer	79f, 193, 301, 304, 312ff, 321, 323, 371, 401f
Completeness	11, 16, 43, 45ff, 51, 141, 278, 361, 387f, 403
Complexity	20, 35, 52, 55, 65, 67f, 93f, 98f, 127, 135, 147, 199, 219, 263, 422
Compositional semantics	2, 31, 448, 457, 459
Computational grammar of English	20, 96, 125
Computational tractability	2, 98
Configurational language	9, 27
Constituent control (CC)	29f, 356ff, 360f, 374, 377, 382f, 388, 390, 393, 398, 405, 408f
Constituent coordination	26, 290ff, 296
Constituent structure	140, 282, 316ff, 325, 355, 410, 431, 446
Constraint	7, 11, 16, 43, 50f, 59, 73, 75, 84f, 89, 92f, 327, 334, 352, 371, 383, 398, 405, 407, 449
Constraint propagation	449
Context free grammar	11, 135, 140, 179
Context-free	7, 11, 14, 16, 19, 51, 57, 69ff, 94, 101, 131f, 134f, 140, 143, 146, 148, 155, 176, 179, 183, 201, 220, 229, 384, 412
Context-sensitive	11, 19, 70, 141
Control Agreement Principle (CAP)	14, 54ff, 60, 63f, 100, 110, 306
Control domain	359, 377, 382f, 388
Cooper	2, 30f, 432ff, 438f, 441, 444ff, 449, 457
Cooper's Storage Mechanism	2, 445
Coordination	15, 26f, 85, 94, 97, 229, 263, 289ff, 296, 298ff, 316, 248f, 368, 370, 468
Copying	31, 82, 112, 162, 169, 295, 330, 464, 469
Copying operation	31, 464
Cross-serial dependencies	12, 24, 93, 220, 224, 227f, 409
Definite Clause Grammars	17, 111, 129
Derivation	68, 94, 128, 147, 183, 224, 360, 374, 382, 394, 405, 456, 461
Descriptive adequacy	13, 409
Determinism	131, 147, 193, 238, 242
Deterministic parsing	132, 198, 201, 255

Diachronic process	25, 248, 254
Disjunction	12f, 17, 51, 66, 146, 218f, 386
Dutch infinitival groups	203, 219
Earley parser	22
Earley's algorithm	155
ECP	321, 338, 342, 344f, 348ff
Efficiency	16, 18, 22, 47, 61, 97f, 101, 131, 148f, 174, 196, 254
Efficient	16, 20, 22, 32, 50, 61, 67, 95f, 99, 108, 111, 131, 134f, 141, 148, 176, 179, 182, 201
Ellipsis	26, 290f, 295, 299, 310, 468
Empty category principle	28
Equi verb	374, 399
Ergativity hypothesis	311
EUROTRA-D-Begleitforschung	1, 15, 411
Existential constraints	11, 50, 141
Expressive power	24, 42, 45, 115, 202, 211, 219f, 235, 468
Extraposition	29, 181, 356f, 361ff, 369f, 374ff, 381, 383, 388, 390ff, 398, 407
F-structure	10ff, 16, 25f, 140ff, 145, 147, 149f, 154, 156, 163f, 166, 168, 170f, 176, 275f, 282, 284, 318, 359ff, 364, 366ff, 371, 374, 376f, 380, 383, 385ff, 397f, 401, 403, 405, 449, 453ff, 459f
F-structure path	385
Feature cooccurrence restrictions (FCRs)	14, 19, 53, 55, 58, 63, 65f, 101, 108, 115
Feature instantiation principles	13, 54
Feature propagation	20, 98f, 101ff, 105f, 110, 112ff, 126
Feature propagation rules	113ff
Feature specification defaults	14, 54f, 61, 102, 104, 112, 115
Feature system	95, 98, 100
Felicity	18, 42, 46f, 231
FIN fronting	301ff
Focus	27f, 30, 119, 151, 177, 181, 199, 327f, 341, 343ff, 351, 414ff, 423, 429, 431
Foot Feature Principle (FFP)	14, 54ff, 60f, 64, 99, 102, 104f, 108, 113
Formalisms	2, 4f, 7, 11, 15ff, 34ff, 39ff, 43, 45ff, 52, 58, 65ff, 89, 105, 202, 229f
French	25, 1o4, 188ff, 196ff, 201, 262f, 270, 277ff, 287f
FUG	18, 37, 47ff, 65ff
Functional control	26, 285ff, 368, 371
Functional structure	9, 29, 140, 282, 284, 356, 409, 466
Functional uncertainty	12, 29, 150, 176, 356, 360f, 384, 398, 402, 408ff
Gap threading	22
Gapping	26, 292ff, 310, 315
GB	2, 15f, 22f, 26ff, 43, 150, 152f, 177ff, 183ff, 197, 311, 329, 337, 346, 350f, 353

GB parser	22f, 183f, 197
Geach	203, 228, 455
Generalized Phrase Structure Grammar (GPSG)	1f, 7, 11, 13ff, 18ff, 23, 26, 30, 37, 43, 47, 52ff, 56ff, 64ff, 68, 95ff, 105ff, 112f, 115f, 123, 125f, 128f, 182, 228, 287, 290, 292, 304f, 316, 411ff, 420, 429f, 447
Generative (over)capacity	51, 70
Generative grammar	15, 22, 42, 124, 180, 317, 354
Generative power	11, 13, 24, 141, 177
German	2, 4, 6, 12f, 15, 23, 26ff, 82, 220, 289ff, 299f, 303f, 306ff, 311ff, 316ff, 330ff, 342f, 345ff, 350ff, 361f, 364, 368, 381f, 390ff, 399, 409, 411, 413ff, 418, 420, 422ff, 429, 431
Goto graph	133
Governable function	368, 390f, 398, 401
Government and Binding theory	2, 290, 300
GPSG 85	98, 110ff, 115f
Grammar	
compilation	101
development environment	99, 110, 112f, 118f, 122, 126, 128, 149
formalism	19, 35, 45, 57, 65, 97f, 100, 108, 110, 112f, 115f, 118, 122, 126ff, 178, 203
organisation	95
project	33, 97, 100, 102, 109, 124, 128
rules	20, 91, 100f, 111, 122, 131, 134, 144, 147, 154, 179, 183, 196
Grammatical functions	11, 16, 31, 65, 154, 176, 190, 197, 317f, 326, 350, 359, 389, 401, 408f, 450f, 453f, 460, 472, â
Graph unification	6f, 229, 237
Graph-structured stack	21, 135, 144
H-component	23, 186, 188, 190, 192ff
Head Feature Convention (HFC)	14, 47, 54ff, 60f, 63f, 99, 102f, 105, 107, 114, 120f, 307
Head features	27, 55f, 58f, 64, 290, 307
HPSG	15, 23, 56, 65, 218, 228, 255
ID (immediate dominance)	14, 53, 57, 99, 412
Immediate dominance (ID)	14ff, 32, 53ff, 58, 60, 63, 99ff, 106f, 109, 112ff, 127ff, 148, 305, 314f, 257, 412, 431, 467
Incremental construction	143, 145, 148f, 176
Indexed languages	19, 24, 92ff, 220
Individual constant	450
Individual variable	206, 450
Infinitival constructions	13, 29, 330ff, 356, 361ff, 368, 370
Intonation focus	30, 417, 419, 429
Island constraint	16

Japanese morpho-syntax	24, 230, 232
LALR(k)	132
Lambda-calculus	2, 31, 448ff, 472
Lattice	5, 63, 451
Left deletion	26, 292ff, 299, 310
Left-recursive	131, 374f, 377, 382
Lexical entry	11, 123f, 206, 208f, 275, 285, 236, 240
Lexical Functional Grammar (LFG)	1f, 5ff, 9, 11, 13ff, 18, 20ff, 25f, 29, 31f, 37f, 40, 43ff, 47, 51, 65f, 131f, 135, 140, 143ff, 148ff, 162, 176, 220, 228, 262f, 272, 275, 278, 282, 287, 318f, 350, 352, 356, 358ff, 365, 368ff, 378, 381, 384, 393, 409f, 448, 454, 457ff, 472
Lexical ID rules	116
Lexicon	8, 10, 20, 25, 95, 97f, 100, 108, 111, 115, 120, 122ff, 128, 149, 182, 205, 223, 231, 233, 236, 248f, 251, 254, 256, 318, 365, 378, 419, 459
LFG	
Linear precedence (LP)	14ff, 30, 32, 53, 56ff, 63, 99f, 113, 127ff, 148, 305, 308, 318, 411ff, 422f, 429, 431, 436, 448
Linguistic description	3, 230f, 254
Linguistic engineering	125
Linguistic theories	1ff, 14f, 18f, 33ff, 40f, 43, 47, 52, 66, 113, 129, 230
LISP	5, 21f, 67, 149, 165
List	20, 96, 99f, 103, 107, 120, 122f, 125, 127, 135, 138f, 144, 146, 155f, 161, 169, 175, 180, 203f, 206f, 219, 321, 459
Local tree	103, 105, 115, 306, 413f
Long distance dependencies	22, 149f, 154f, 157, 176, 178, 203, 458
Long-distance metavariables	13
Lookahead	133
LP (linear precedence)	53, 411f
LR (k)	21, 131ff, 147
LR parser	132ff
LR parsing algorithms	21
Machine ...	1, 10, 24, 30, 32, 48, 85, 111, 123, 149, 230, 232, 255, 411, 420, 422, 425f
Machine translation	1, 10, 24, 30, 32, 230, 232, 255, 411, 420, 422, 425f
Mapping from syntax to semantics	2
Merging algorithms	22, 162
Metarules	14, 19f, 53, 58, 100ff, 105f, 108ff, 113, 115ff, 119, 126, 128f, 182
Metarules (multiset variable in)	116
Metavariables	13, 151, 153, 358f, 377f, 385
Modal auxiliary	291
Modifiers	26, 122, 187, 217, 274, 287, 291, 233f, 236, 240, 242, 254, 437f

Modular principle-based parsers	23, 178
Montague	2, 30, 203, 209, 214, 228, 432f, 447, 452, 457
Montague grammar	203, 214, 452
Morphological analysis	123, 129
Move	16, 27f, 63, 108ff, 112, 138, 152, 161, 319, 328, 332, 336, 341f, 344, 350ff, 355
Move-alpha	27f, 152, 161, 319, 328, 342, 344, 350ff
Natural language processing	1, 3, 14, 32f, 41, 45, 67, 96, 122, 127, 134, 432, 434, 445
Negation	11ff, 17, 51, 214, 332
Nested Cooper Storage	30f, 432, 441, 445f
Non-local dependencies	29, 356ff, 363, 398f, 409
Non-modular rule-based parsers	23, 178
Norwedish	19, 75, 78ff, 83, 88
Object grammar	16, 21, 99f, 102, 112, 114, 116f
Order-free	9, 42f
Ordering of grammar rules	131
Parallel processing	135, 138, 147, 188
Parsing table	21, 132ff, 140, 144ff
Partial order	5
Partially free	413ff, 422
Path	10, 13, 58ff, 156, 201, 359, 385f, 389, 395, 401, 407, 410, 465
PATR	7, 9, 11, 13f, 18ff, 23, 37, 48ff, 56ff, 63, 65ff, 100, 105, 111, 203, 229
PATR II	7, 9, 20, 23, 67, 100, 105, 111, 203, 229
Phoneme	3, 96
Phonetics	3
Phonological rules	293
Phonology	3, 204ff, 209ff, 222, 231
Prague school of linguistics	30
Procedural	20, 65, 98, 105, 424, 429
Progressive or perfective aspect	24, 247
Quantifier scrambling	457, 463
Raising verb	459
Recognition	24, 43, 93, 129, 201, 232
Reduce-reduce conflict	136
Reduction	18, 35f, 48, 50ff, 65, 92, 133, 135, 137, 139, 143ff, 219, 451f, 471
Reentrancy	4, 17, 459
Regular expression	12f, 17, 360f, 388f, 395, 398, 402, 405
Restrictiveness	18f, 43ff
Right node raising	26
Right-recursive	374f, 382, 384
Rigor	18, 43, 45ff

Roles	150, 189f, 197, 233, 320, 329, 331, 333, 414, 423ff, 429, 441
Ross's "island constraint"	16, 177, 317, 356
Rule-to-rule hypothesis	245, 449
Scrambling	236, 254, 317, 333f, 336, 338ff, 342, 352, 354, 457, 463
Semantic component	10, 241
Semantic form	270, 362, 368, 371, 398
Semantic interpretation	100, 275, 433
Sentence disambiguation	21
Shift-reduce conflict	136, 138
Shift-reduce parser	133, 135
Slash feature	54, 61, 292, 304, 306f
SLR(k)	132
Source grammar	21, 101f, 106, 119
SOV-orderings	27, 328
Stack	19, 21, 70ff, 77, 80, 83ff, 89ff, 133, 135, 137f, 144ff, 156, 161, 163, 237f
Subcategorisation	100, 123f, 232f, 235f, 240, 252, 254f
Subject-verb agreement	4, 303
Substitution	471
Subsumption	5, 13
Syntactic parser	131, 182
Syntactic parsing	96, 131
Thematic	30, 179, 181, 188, 197, 200, 231, 233, 236, 318, 320, 326f, 329ff, 333, 341, 352, 368, 370, 414, 425ff
Thematic structuring	30, 425f, 428f
Topic	2, 26, 28, 31, 131f, 149, 291f, 296f, 299, 306, 311, 233, 242, 317, 322f, 336, 341f, 345, 351, 381, 402, 405ff, 419, 423, 429, 431
Topicalization	181, 301f, 305f, 314, 370, 398, 401, 424
Traces	29, 95, 156f, 161, 191, 300, 244, 331, 341, 349, 356
Transfer	10, 32, 325f, 420ff, 429
Translation	1, 10, 24, 30, 32, 148, 212f, 230, 232, 250, 255, 411, 420, 422, 425f, 428, 431, 433ff, 450ff, 460f, 463, 465ff, 472
Type raising	24f, 209, 214, 221, 227, 254, 454f, 468
Unbounded dependencies	13, 19, 70, 78ff, 85, 93, 116, 122, 228, 360
Unification	1ff, 9, 11, 13, 15ff, 23ff, 31f, 37, 51, 57f, 61, 63, 65, 68, 89, 97, 110ff, 114ff, 119, 129, 132, 140ff, 162, 202ff, 208ff, 215, 219, 227ff, 287, 230f, 237, 253ff, 349, 360, 387, 411, 448, 464f, 468f
Unification categorial grammar (UCG)	202ff, 219f
Unification grammar	1, 3, 7, 18, 25, 37, 68, 111f, 116, 203, 287, 229, 231, 360, 411

Unification in PROLOG	3, 6
Unification-based formalisms	2, 4f, 7, 11, 15, 17
Unification-based grammars	2
Uniqueness	141
Universals	15
Variable	23ff, 62, 70, 94, 103, 107, 110f, 114, 116, 144f, 153, 163ff, 168f, 171, 174f, 204, 206f, 210ff, 219, 224, 262, 277, 236f, 329ff, 333, 341, 345, 385, 395, 402, 435f, 440ff, 450, 454, 465f, 469
Variable categories	23, 214, 217, 219
Variable valued features	103, 110
Viable prefix	133
Walpiri version	26
Wh-movement	29, 152, 186, 191, 278, 323, 331, 333, 335f, 343, 354ff, 361, 398ff
Word order	1, 23, 25, 27f, 30, 178, 187, 195ff, 201, 262, 266, 272, 287, 300, 304, 316, 233f, 255, 317ff, 326ff, 336f, 342, 345f, 350ff, 360, 364, 411, 413ff, 420, 422f, 427ff, 431
X-component	23

STUDIES IN LINGUISTICS AND PHILOSOPHY

formerly *Synthese Language Library*

1. Henry Hiż (ed.), *Questions.* 1978.
2. William S. Cooper, *Foundations of Logico-Linguistics. A Unified Theory of Information, Language, and Logic.* 1978.
3. Avishai Margalit (ed.), *Meaning and Use.* 1979.
4. F. Guenthner and S. J. Schmidt (eds.), *Formal Semantics and Pragmatics for Natural Languages.* 1978.
5. Esa Saarinen (ed.), *Game-Theoretical Semantics.* 1978.
6. F. J. Pelletier (ed.), *Mass Terms: Some Philosophical Problems.* 1979.
7. David R. Dowty, *Word Meaning and Montague Grammar. The Semantics of Verbs and Times in Generative Semantics and in Montague's PTQ.* 1979.
9. James McCloskey, *Transformational Syntax and Model Theoretic Semantics: A Case Study in Modern Irish.* 1979.
10. John R. Searle, Ferenc Kiefer, and Manfred Bierwisch (ed.), *Speech Act Theory and Pragmatics.* 1980.
11. David R. Dowty, Robert E. Wall, and Stanley Peters, *Introduction to Montague Semantics.* 1981.
12. Frank Heny (ed.), *Ambiguities in Intensional Contexts.*
13. Wolfgang Klein and Willem Levelt (eds.), *Crossing the Boundaries in Linguistics: Studies Presented to Manfred Bierwisch.* 1981.
14. Zellig S. harris, *Papers on Syntax,* edited by Henry Hiż. 1981.
15. Pauline Jacobson and Geoffrey K. Pullum (eds.), *The Nature of Syntactic Representation.* 1982.
16. Stanley Peters and Esa Saarinen (eds.), *Processes, Beliefs, and Questions.* 1982.
17. Lauri Carlson, *Dialogue Games. An Approach to Discourse Analysis.* 1983.
18. Lucia Vaina and Jaakko Hintikka (eds.), *Cognitive Constraints on Communication.* 1983.
19. Frank Heny and Barry Richards (eds.), *Linguistic Categories: Auxiliaries and Related Puzzles. Volume One: Categories.*
20. Frank Heny and Barry Richards (eds.), *Linguistic Categories: Auxiliaries and Related Puzzles. Volume Two: The Scope, Order, and Distribution of English Auxiliary Verbs.* 1983.
21. Robin Cooper, *Quantification and Syntactic Theory.* 1983.
22. Jaakko Hintikka and Jack Kulas, *The Game of Language.* 1983.
23. Edward L. Keenan and Leonard M. Faltz, *Bolean Semantics for Natural Language.* 1985.
24. Victor Raskin, *Semantic Mechanics of Humor,* 1985.
25. Gregory T. Stump, *The Semantic Variability of Absolute Constructions.* 1985.
26. Jaakko Hintikka and Jack Kulas, *Anaphora and Definite Descriptions.* 1985.
27. Elisabet Engdahl, *Constituent Questions,* 1985.
28. M. J. Cresswell, *Adverbial Modification,* 1985.
29. Johan van Benthem, *Essays in Logical Semantics.*

30. Barbara Partee, Alice ter Meulen, and Robert Wall (eds.), *Mathematical Methods in Linguistics,* 1987.
31. Peter Gärdenfors (ed.), *Generalized Quantifiers,* 1987.
32. Richard T. Oehrle et al. (eds.), *Categorial Grammars and Natural Language Structures,* 1988.
33. Walter J. Savitch et al. (eds.), *The Formal Complexity of Natural Language,* 1987.
34. Jens Erik Fenstad et al., *Situations, Language and Logic,* 1987.
35. U. Reyle and C. Rohrer 9eds.), *Natural Language Parsing and Linguistic Theories,* 1988.